COMPARATIVE POLITICS

'What is distinctive about this authoritative and comprehensive book on comparative politics is the way in which it is underpinned throughout by a theoretical analysis centred on a new institutionalist approach.'
Professor Wyn Grant, University of Warwick

'*Comparative Politics* takes a fresh and original approach to the field ... it examines the role of structures, rules and norms in regulating the individual and collective behaviour of political actors. Each chapter provides a critical bibliography and key questions which will be particularly useful for students approaching Comparative Politics for the first time. Altogether this is a comprehensive and useful read which I warmly recommend.'
Ian Budge, Professor Emiritus Professor of Government, University of Essex

'This is a most useful book. Teachers of comparative politics often scramble around, with out-of-date textbooks and photocopies of more or less compatible articles. Here is a new book that gives an up-to-date, comprehensive and systematic introduction to the major strands of institutional thought and applies these to the major institutions, processes and policy areas. It will be a great help for many of us, academics and students alike.'
Peter Kurrild-Klitgaard, Professor of Comparative Politics, University of Copenhagen

COMPARATIVE POLITICS
Explaining Democratic Systems

EDITED BY JUDITH BARA
MARK PENNINGTON

With David S. Bell, Jocelyn A.J. Evans, Catherine Needham,
Brendan O'Duffy and David Robertson

Los Angeles | London | New Delhi
Singapore | Washington DC

SAGE Publications Ltd
1 Oliver's Yard
55 City Road
London EC1Y 1SP

SAGE Publications Inc.
2455 Teller Road
Thousand Oaks, California 91320

SAGE Publications India Pvt Ltd
B 1/I 1 Mohan Cooperative Industrial Area
Mathura Road
New Delhi 110 044

SAGE Publications Asia-Pacific Pte Ltd
33 Pekin Street #02-01
Far East Square
Singapore 048763

Library of Congress Control Number: 2008933628

British Library Cataloguing in Publication data

A catalogue record for this book is available from the
British Library

ISBN 978-0-7619-4372-3
ISBN 978-0-7619-4373-0

Typeset by C&M Digitals (P) Ltd, Chennai, India
Printed in Great Britain by TJ International, Padstow, Cornwall
Printed on paper from sustainable resources

Contents

Preface   vii
Contributors   ix

Introduction   1
Judith Bara

PART 1   THEORY AND METHOD IN COMPARATIVE POLITICS   11

1   Theory, Institutions and Comparative Politics   13
    Mark Pennington

2   Methodologies for Comparative Analysis   41
    Judith Bara

PART 2   INSTITUTIONS   67

3   The Nation-state and Nationalism   69
    Brendan O'Duffy

4   Electoral Systems   93
    Jocelyn A.J. Evans

5   Legislative–Executive Relations   120
    Catherine Needham

6   The Bureaucracy   145
    Mark Pennington

7   The Courts   174
    David Robertson

8   The Territorial Dimension   201
    Brendan O'Duffy

PART 3   ACTORS   227

9   Voters, Parties and Participation   229
    Judith Bara

10 Interest Groups   259
    Mark Pennington

11 Political Leadership: The Long Road to Theory   290
    David S. Bell

Afterword: Comparative Politics and the Three Approaches Revisited   308
Judith Bara

References   317
Index   331

Preface

The original proposal for this text evolved from the development of a new comparative politics course that the editors have convened in recent years at Queen Mary, University of London. Besides being designed to provide students with access to descriptive material with regard to political institutions and processes in a number of different countries, the course explicitly seeks to introduce three major theoretical paradigms that have sought to explain the operation of institutions in democratic states and to facilitate comparison across different political systems.

While we were able to recommend appropriate texts that have provided good descriptive material about a variety of different countries and introduction to methodologies used in comparative analysis, none were able to offer adequate discussion of competing theoretical perspectives at an appropriate level. We felt strongly that since a strategic objective was to enable *explanation* of political institutions, actors or behaviour within a comparative framework, we required an appropriate text to support this. Furthermore, we were keen to expose students to different general explanatory models in order to develop analytic and critical skills.

This book is thus primarily a text designed to introduce first-year undergraduate students to three major theoretical institutional frameworks and research paradigms in contemporary political science. As such, it is suitable both for first-year courses in comparative government and politics and introductory courses in concepts and methods of political science. Its core objectives are:

- To provide a readable introduction to modern comparative political analysis on the basis of 'new institutionalist' theoretical frameworks. The emphasis will be on different approaches to the task of explaining the similarities and differences in institutions and their effects on political and governmental practices in modern representative democracies. Thus it can be used as a basis for the examination and explanation of political institutions in one state or in several.

- To equip students with an appreciation of comparative research methods in political science.

- To outline key institutional features (electoral systems, territorial and functional divisions, and so forth) of government and politics in a selection of modern states.

- To examine the role of some of the major actors (voters, interest groups, leaders) in modern states.

Several authors have undertaken the development of the book, the majority of whom teach in the Department of Politics at Queen Mary. Those based elsewhere have had varying connections with the Department or have developed their own teaching and research along similar lines.

But this book is not simply based on cherry-picking appropriate elements of a particular course. It owes much to a number of other people who have provided invaluable input into the curriculum at different junctures, notably Adrian Blau, Pilar Domingo, John Meadowcroft and Wayne Parsons, whose contribution we appreciate. We are also grateful for the support of the Department and for the constructive suggestions and comments made by our seminar teachers and, of course, our students.

Finally, we would like to thank our publishers, Lucy Robinson and David Mainwaring and their team at SAGE Publications for their encouragement, assistance and professionalism – and above all for their patience – in guiding this project to completion.

Judith Bara and Mark Pennington
London, June 2008

Contributors

Judith Bara is Senior Lecturer in Politics at Queen Mary, University of London and Research Fellow in Government at the University of Essex.

David S. Bell is Professor of French Government and Politics and Head of Social Studies and Law at the University of Leeds.

Jocelyn A.J. Evans is Professor of Politics at the University of Salford.

Catherine Needham is Lecturer Politics at Queen Mary, University of London.

Brendan O'Duffy is Senior Lecturer in Politics at Queen Mary, University of London.

Mark Pennington is Senior Lecturer in Politics at Queen Mary, University of London.

David Robertson is Professor of Politics, University of Oxford and Vice Principal, St Hugh's College, Oxford.

Introduction

Judith Bara

About the Book

In this book we provide a new and distinctive introduction to the study of comparative politics. Most existing textbooks in this field tend to present either comparative descriptions of political processes and systems in a variety of different countries or focus on methodological issues involved in 'doing' comparative analysis. As such, these texts generally omit an adequate introduction to the major theoretical traditions in contemporary political science and thus to the development of skills in comparative explanation.

Our focus is on an explicitly theoretical analysis built around a variety of approaches that may usefully be grouped together under the label of the 'new institutionalism', which is one of the most important developments in contemporary political science. As this is so crucial to the raison d'être for our book it is worth spending some time in exploring its basis, before going on in Chapter 1 to discuss in detail the theoretical variants of institutionalism we regard as especially useful to an explanation of comparative politics, which are, broadly speaking structural, cultural and rational choice interpretations.

The 'New Institutionalism'

Steinmo, in his contribution to *The Encyclopedia of Democratic Thought* (Clark and Foweraker, 2007), suggests that institutions are the foundation of all types of political behaviour. In this analysis, institutions are seen essentially as sets of 'rules' which are either informal, as in the case of cultural norms, or formal, as in the case of legal or constitutional rules. If we did not have such guiding principles, Steinmo asserts, we would be in a situation tantamount to a Hobbesian state of nature.

Institutions are also fundamental to the organisation and practice of political life since without them, we would be unable to understand: who is able to participate in politics; what their particular rights and obligations might be; or how we can influence policy outcomes. In other words, institutions shape all types of political action. They thus *matter* but we also need to ask *how* and *why* they matter. In answering these questions and coming up with explanations, it is helpful to have a series of lenses through which we can provide frameworks to guide our research. We thus need theoretical models.

However, assertions that political institutions are important are hardly new. Institutions have been seen as the stuff of politics for many generations. The first, systematic approach to political science in general in the 20th century was institutional in nature. However, it became recognised quite early in the period following the Second World War that what passed for analysis was largely description or narrative, lacked theoretical perspective and was essentially unscientific. As we shall mention in the case of the development of comparative politics (see Chapter 2), changes brought about by behavioural approaches that focused on micro-levels of behaviour, enabled analysts to examine the behaviour of the mass public and facilitated the testing of theoretical models – or at least hypotheses. However, the use of such approaches in democratic states soon gave rise to criticism and unease among large sections of the political science community that suggested that the baby had surely been discarded along with the bathwater! Hence, the development of 'new' institutional approaches which sought to combine the more effective elements of both traditional institutionalism with beliefs in the essential role of theory and rigorous analysis propounded by behaviouralists. In other words, while *old* institutional approaches sought to *describe* political phenomena, *new* institutionalism seeks to *explain* them (Peters, 1996: 206).

March and Olsen (2006: 4–5), reflecting on their overall contribution to the debate on the role of institutions since 1984, suggest that institutions are 'collections of structures, rules and standard operating procedures that have a partly autonomous role in political life'. Furthermore, they are 'markers of a polity's character, history and visions. They provide the bonds that tie citizens together in spite of the many things that divide them' (2006: 4–5). Although some of this was evident in the thought of 'old' institutionalism, a further distinction among contemporary institutional approaches is that they accept the inevitability of change and development, which incorporates a willingness to take on board not only elements learned from other theoretical and methodological outlooks, but also to incorporate novel or difficult areas of policy which have not traditionally been associated with institutional analysis. Apter (1996) cites as examples immigration or the creation of an underclass resulting from a shrinking industrial base, which often exacerbate social conflict.

It is important to recognise some particular characteristics of the new institutionalism. First, it is not a monolithic movement. There are several variants which, as March and Olsen indeed suggest, although sharing a basic belief in the nature and importance of institutions, nevertheless 'focus attention on different aspects of political life, on different explanatory factors, and on different strategies for improving political systems' (2006: 4–5). These three essential 'perspectives' focus on institutional factors (or structures), cultural communities, governed by particular norms of behaviour and a belief that individuals are rational actors who operate according to their own self-interest. This indeed represents the basic stuff of our approach and will be examined in detail in Chapter 1.

In addition to this, we need to recognise that whereas 'old' institutional approaches focused simply on 'formal, structural aspects of institutions' (Peters, 1996: 206), the newer variants also take account of the actual behaviour of institutions. This is an aspect which has been developed from behavioural approaches and is exemplified by regarding the institution(s) under scrutiny as 'dependent' variables, explained by other factors, rather than as simply entities with particular characteristics.

Additionally, there is a deliberate attempt within the new institutionalism to give attention to outcomes of institutional behaviour. In other words, rather than concentrate on procedures operated by institutions, as older variants did, concern with what results from these procedures is seen as equally – if not more – important. Thus, rather than simply concentrate on 'how' legislation is enacted; there is recognition that outcomes, that is legislation, have consequences for society as a whole and its individual citizens. Policy outcomes can have definite effects in changing the political behaviour of citizens, as we can see from decisions by governments of certain countries, notably the USA and the UK, to go to war in Iraq in 2003, or to support the war effort. Many individual citizens disagreed with this and consequently changed their votes at ensuing elections, for example in the UK, Germany and Spain.

New institutionalists, irrespective of whether they favour a rational or structural approach, nevertheless accept that a political order is indeed far from static and that institutions change over time as a result of many factors or influences. However, as March and Olsen *inter alia* have pointed out, change is also a function of the specific nature of the institutions in question and cannot simply be brought about on the basis of a whim. They are dependent on changing rules that are entrenched and a reflection of local historical and cultural development. This often leads to inconsistency and even inefficiency in the behaviour of the institution and is usually carried out as a reaction to events rather than as part of an overall, strategic plan.

Overall therefore, following the parameters suggested by March and Olsen (2006), new institutionalists believe that:

- Rules and practices, which are socially constructed, govern the lives of all political actors.
- Such rules may constrain or enable action and hence affect the governing capacity of the political system.

- These rules are known and largely accepted. They provide for codes of appropriate behaviour and
- Political institutions, on the basis of these rules are able to set out the rights and duties of citizens and engage in the authoritative allocation of advantages and burdens for citizens. Political institutions can also act authoritatively to regulate in disputes and conflicts.
- Institutions provide for order and stability.

The main difference between the new institutionalism and other approaches, however, is that it takes as its basic unit of analysis, institutional rules, identities, norms and procedures rather than individuals or whole countries and seeks to be realistic in its assumptions. As such it takes on board satisfactory concepts derived from other approaches rather than rejecting them. In this way it enhances the knowledge pool and analytic viability of comparative politics, and indeed, of political science in general. This book will demonstrate how this works in relation to specific political institutions and actors. We will now look at the outline structure of the rest of the book and outline the nature of the content of the individual chapters.

Part 1: Theory and Method in Comparative Politics

Chapter 1: Theory, Institutions and Comparative Politics

The guiding chapter by Mark Pennington discusses how comparative politics as a discipline aims to provide explanations of the similarities and differences in decision-making practices that may be observed in different political regimes. Within this context considerable emphasis is placed on the notion of institutional analysis. Similarities and differences in the 'inputs' and 'outputs' of the political process are linked to the role that institutions play in structuring flows of power and resources in different political systems. The renewed emphasis on institutional analysis has been encapsulated by the growing interest in the so-called 'new institutionalism'. The 'new institutionalism' is, however, a far from united set of theoretical positions. While sharing a recognition that institutions are important, there are major differences between historical/structural analyses, cultural analyses and rational choice variants of institutional analysis. This first chapter will introduce the 'new institutionalism' and the competing modes of explanation covered by this umbrella term.

Questions to be addressed include: What is an institution? What is the significance of institutional analysis to comparative politics? What does it mean to think in terms of 'paradigms', 'approaches', 'frameworks' and schools of thought? What are the key differences between the structural/historical, cultural and rational choice variants of institutional analysis?

Chapter 2: Methodologies for Comparative Politics

Just as political scientists differ in their accounts of the role that institutions play in structuring political life, so too do differences emerge with regard to the methodological tools appropriate to comparative analysis. Some scholars prefer to make causal inferences through the use of large-scale statistical analysis, while others prefer the use of comparative case studies, and still others opt for the notion of 'thick description'. This chapter by Judith Bara introduces the major tools of comparative analysis using examples of published research to highlight differences between methodological approaches with which the different schools of comparative institutional analysis are or are not associated with a particular way of 'doing research'. On a more general level, the chapter considers broader questions pertaining to the rigour of research and the appropriate standards for drawing causal inferences in the social sciences.

Among the questions relating to this area are: How do political scientists go about the business of 'comparison'? What are the major differences between qualitative and quantitative traditions in comparative research? What are the rationales for the use of large-scale statistical analysis, focused case studies, and 'thick' descriptions? What problems might we encounter in undertaking comparative analysis?

Part 2: Institutions

Chapter 3: The Nation-state and Nationalism

The nation-state has long been a central concern of political scientists given the centrality of this unit of power to political life. The formation of the nation-state, however, and its functions continue to be highly contested topics within political science. Brendan O'Duffy examines the significance of the nation-state and the ways in which the different branches of institutional analysis conceptualise its role as a political institution. Attention will focus on disputes between those who view the state as an historical response to technological and economic change, those who associate the nation-state as a reflection of shared cultural traditions, and theorists who conceive of the nation-state as a mechanism for overcoming collective action problems.

Relevant questions include: What are the functions of the modern nation-state? To what extent are nation-states co-terminous with national identities? How does the experience of nationalism vary between states? To what extent is the character of nation-states being challenged by the growth of supranational entities such as the European Union? How do structural/historical, cultural and rational choice analyses differ in their accounts of nationalism and the role of the nation-state?

Chapter 4: Electoral Systems

The electoral system is considered to be the most easily manipulated part of a constitution. As Jocelyn Evans demonstrates, understanding how different electoral systems operate, therefore, and understanding how different electoral systems may affect other parts of the political process is an essential component of comparative institutional analysis. This chapter outlines some important questions associated with alternative electoral systems, including the effect on parties in the legislature, and the strength, stability and accountability of the governing party/coalition. These issues will be examined through an institutionalist lens, focusing on differing conceptions of the role and effects of electoral processes.

Questions pertinent to this topic include: How strong is the relationship between the electoral system and the number of parties? Are governments elected under single member district electoral systems stronger, more stable and more accountable than those under proportional representation systems? Is there a link between electoral systems and the character of legislative/executive relations? Do electoral systems affect the overall structure of decision-making in society? Are electoral systems a reflection of different cultural attributes or do they contribute to the shaping of such attributes? To what extent do different electoral systems affect incentives to vote?

Chapter 5: Legislative–Executive Relations

The division of power and responsibility between the legislature and the executive is one of the most important institutional variables that distinguishes between states. Catherine Needham explores the nature of legislatures and the executive, focusing especially on variations in the relationship between assemblies and the executive, particularly in terms of degrees of parliamentary autonomy in the legislative process and the significance of legislative executive power relations to the broader political process. The chapter will show how the structural, cultural and rational variants of institutional analysis conceptualise this relationship.

Questions to be addressed include: How does parliamentary autonomy differ between different states? What are the competing justifications for unicameral and bicameral systems? What roles do parliamentary committees play and how does their importance vary between states? What is the significance of legislative/executive relations from the different perspectives?

Chapter 6: The Bureaucracy

Bureaucrats and civil servants are key actors involved in the design and implementation of public policy in most contemporary states. These actors, therefore, have significant political power and influence.

As the extent of government intervention in the economy has grown over the last century, concerns have risen over the increasing degree of power that is concentrated in bureaucratic agencies. Such concerns have arguably been intensified with the rise of international bureaucratic agencies embodied in the European Union and organisations such as the World Trade Organization. Mark Pennington examines the role of the public bureaucracy from an institutionalist perspective focusing on the analysis of bureaucratic power from structural, cultural and rational choice perspectives.

Important questions to be dealt with include: How and why do the scope and functions of bureaucracies differ between states? How and why is the bureaucracy able to exercise power over legislators? How do rational/public choice accounts of bureaucratic power differ from structuralist and cultural interpretations? What are the mechanisms that can be used to check bureaucratic power?

Chapter 7: The Courts

In this chapter David Robertson introduces the theme of the rule of law and how it is institutionalised in the political system, in part through the judicial process. The focus of the analysis will be on the judiciary as interpreters of law and the political economy of judicial decisions. The chapter will consider the role of judicial politics in the governmental process, and address questions of judicial independence and judicial review.

Questions of relevance include: What are the links between constitutionalism and the rule of law and democracy? How independent are judiciaries from other branches of government? In what ways do judiciaries mediate the relationship between state and society? To what extent can judicial decisions be thought of as a process of structural domination, cultural evolution or rational choice?

Chapter 8: The Territorial Dimension

Although the nation-state is often the prime mover in the political affairs of modern societies, the character in which political power is exercised within nation-states varies considerably from country to country. As Brendan O'Duffy shows, in some states power is diffused quite widely to lower level government agencies at the local level (federalism) while in others the distribution of authority tends to be more centralised. This chapter will examine degrees of centralisation and decentralisation in selected states, theories that have sought to explain and/or to justify differing levels of centralisation/decentralisation in governance structures, and the significance of such debates to comparative institutional analysis.

Questions to be addressed encompass: What is meant by the term federalism? What are the primary differences between federal and unitary states? Why is the territorial division of power important from an institutionalist point of view? What are the implications for federalist theory of the rise of supranational bodies such as the European Union? How can debates about centralisation and decentralisation be analysed in structural, cultural and rational choice terms?

Part 3: Actors

Chapter 9: Voters, Parties and Participation

In recent years, many authors have pointed to trends, which suggest a shift away from electoral participation towards other forms of political activity – such as social movements and even direct action. It is important, therefore, to define precisely what affects the choices that people make in terms of how they express their political views. Judith Bara explores some of these themes and emphasises the institutional factors that may affect the extent to which people in different contexts do or do not vote and if they do, how they exercise their vote.

Among the many questions relating to this subject are: How does political participation differ from electoral participation? Why do people vote or not vote? What are the key debates in political science with regard to the significance of 'class-based' voting, 'pocket book' voting and 'cultural change' in voters' outlooks? Why has voting behaviour become more volatile in recent years?

Chapter 10: Interest Groups

Interest groups continue to be a major forum for political participation in many states. This chapter will explore what is meant by the term 'interest group' in political science and the factors that may affect the power wielded by such groups. Mark Pennington also considers how the different branches of new institutionalism analyse the role of political institutions in structuring the context in which groups mobilise and attempt to exert political power.

Questions to be addressed will include: What is meant by the term interest group? How, if at all, do interest groups differ from 'social movements'? What is meant by the term 'interest group power'? How do institutions affect the capacity of interest groups and social movements to exert power? How do structural, cultural and rational choice theories of institutions differ in their analysis of interest group politics?

Chapter 11: Political Leadership

It has become increasingly obvious that political leaders have become a major focus of attention for academic observers, the media and indeed the public at large. Indeed, leaders are often seen as the supreme representatives of their country, responsible for the shaping of policy and often institutions too. This chapter by David S. Bell will theorise whether or not significant variations in leadership exist in practice and how we can best develop tools to compare them. This chapter also demonstrates that it is not always possible to theorise specific elements in the political universe by using exactly the same theoretical models which may be appropriate to the analysis of roles played by other institutional actors.

Questions to be addressed will include: Is 'personality' a realistic variable to utilise in the process of explanation of political process or institutional arrangements? How can this be explained by different theoretical perspectives?

The discussion concludes with a short 'Afterword'. This draws together some of the themes introduced earlier and reprises how the three major paradigms operate in their different ways in aiding our understanding of the political universe.

Part 1

THEORY AND METHOD IN COMPARATIVE POLITICS

1 Theory, Institutions and Comparative Politics

Mark Pennington

CHAPTER OUTLINE

This chapter defines the nature of political institutions and discusses three theoretical frameworks for the comparative analysis and explanation of how institutions work in modern democratic states. These approaches, derived from the 'new institutionalism', are rational choice institutionalism, cultural institutionalism and structural institutionalism. In each case discussion focuses on three elements – ontology, explanation of why institutions matter and explanation of the origins of institutions and institutional change. The chapter concludes with a discussion of how elements of the three approaches might be synthesized in order to enhance explanation and analysis.

Introduction: Why Comparative Politics?

As its name suggests, comparative politics is concerned with the comparative study and analysis of political systems. It aims to overcome the shortcomings of approaches focused purely on case studies of individual countries and of those that build purely abstract theoretical models of decision-making. Comparing the similarities and differences between political phenomena across countries allows social scientists to judge if and how the experience of some states is similar to that of others and to assess whether theoretical models of how people make decisions are able to claim universal validity.

The primary focus of both theoretical and empirical work in comparative politics is on the comparison of institutional practices *between* states. It examines how institutions vary between states and the effect that different institutional practices have on the *outcomes* of the political process in different societies. More important, perhaps, it aims to develop an understanding of *how and why* different institutions have the effects on political outcomes that they do. Within this context, the role of institutions has assumed pride of place in contemporary comparative politics with the wider rise across the social sciences of what has become known as the 'new institutionalism'. Under the slogan 'institutions matter', a broad range of work has been conducted exploring the ways that institutions affect political outcomes. The term 'new institutionalism', however, conceals a considerable amount of disagreement between political scientists with regard to what exactly it is about institutions that affects the nature of the political process.

Three 'schools of thought'

Broadly speaking, it is possible to identify three distinct schools of thought within the new institutionalism (see, for example, Hall and Taylor, 1996). These are:

- Rational choice institutionalism
- Cultural institutionalism
- Structural institutionalism

Distinguishing the key characteristics of these different schools of thought within comparative politics will be the main task of this introductory chapter and is a unifying theme that runs throughout the course of this book. Familiarity with the *general* principles that define the different elements of new institutional analysis is crucial to developing the more *specific* aspects of comparative analysis (such as comparative electoral systems, or comparisons of the role of bureaucracy) that will be engaged in subsequent chapters. Before we explore the ways in which these different perspectives analyse and account for the role and significance of institutions, however, it is important to define exactly what is meant by the term *institution*.

What Is an Institution?

Lane and Ersson define an institution as, 'a rule that has been institutionalized'. Within this general definition, however, it is possible to distinguish two different ways in which 'rules may be institutionalized' (1999: 23).

'Hard' institutions

'Hard' institutions comprise those formal rules (the political equivalent of driving on the left rules) that characterise a political system such as the rules of the electoral process (first past the post voting rules versus proportional representation, or federalism versus a unitary state, for example). These 'hard' aspects of the political apparatus also include fundamental characteristics of the social system, such as laws pertaining to the existence or non-existence of private property, the existence or non-existence of monarchy and the absence or presence of the basic institutions of liberal democracy. Such 'hard' institutional practices are typically enforced by formal law, with infringements of the rules punished by way of legally recognised sanctions, such as fines and terms of imprisonment.

'Soft' institutions

'Soft' institutions, conversely, include those practices that are institutionalised via informal rules and practices rather than in the letter of the law. These may include the cultural traditions and linguistic modes that characterise forms of political address, such as the manner in which political demonstrations are conducted, or the social acceptability of discussing one's political beliefs in public. They may also include general belief systems and the sense of identity, which govern the expectations that people have about the way that others will or should behave. Soft institutional rules are not enforced by formal sanctions, but are usually maintained through force of habit and by the exercise of informal sanctions against those who 'break the rules'. These may include ostracism and a general unwillingness to engage with those who fail to conform to culturally accepted practice.

Institutional practice in reality

Societies may differ in terms of both their hard and soft institutional practices. It is important, therefore, to be aware that countries, which appear superficially similar in terms of hard institutions, may have dissimilar soft institutions and this may, or may not, be a significant factor in explaining the outcomes of the political process concerned. Likewise, societies exhibiting similar soft institutions may be characterized by different hard or formal rules.

Whether it is the hard institutional framework of formal law or the soft institutional norms embodied in habits, traditions and beliefs, the unifying theme of the new institutionalism is that *institutions matter*. Where the proponents of this view differ is in their account of precisely *how* institutions matter. Disagreements between political scientists on this question arise from fundamental differences in their world view, or ontology, concerning the nature of the relationship between the individual and society. The major purpose of this chapter is to examine the different ontological frameworks of the three branches of new institutional research in contemporary comparative politics.

Rational Choice Institutionalism

Ontology

Rational choice institutionalism in comparative politics represents an attempt to apply micro-economic models of rationality to the analysis of the collective choices that are made in the political process. Its central focus is the purposeful individual and her motivations and beliefs. As such rational choice theory adheres to the principle of *methodological individualism*. From a rational choice perspective individuals always make deliberate and conscious choices in pursuit of their personal goals. Even when action takes place in a collective setting such as an an interest group or the state, the individual actor must always be the focus of concern. As Buchanan and Tullock put it, 'collective action is nothing more than, the action of individuals when they choose to accomplish things collectively rather than individually. Institutions such as the state, therefore, are nothing more than the set of processes, the machine, which allows such collective action to take place' (1962:13).

Centrality of the individual

If individual action forms the core of rational choice institutionalism then the following primary assumptions about the nature of individual choice are central to rational choice ontology:

- Individuals are predominantly self-interested – they choose how to act on the basis of achieving their personal goals, whether these are of a material or non-material nature.
- In pursuit of these goals, individuals act as 'maximisers' who seek the biggest possible benefits and the least costs in their decisions.
- The chosen course of individual action will be affected by changes in the structure of costs and benefits at 'the margin'. The marginal principle implies that other things being equal, any increase in the cost of an action will decrease the likelihood of that action taking place.

Why institutions matter

Building on these primary assumptions, rational choice institutionalism analyses how different institutions affect the pattern of costs and benefits – the *incentive structures* – that face individual political actors. Individual action always takes place in context of institutional practices whether 'hard' or 'soft', and the different incentive structures which people face under different regimes may fundamentally affect the outcomes of the political process. According to this view, individuals always make their choices in the same way, that is, they act as maximisers of benefits over costs, but the *outcomes* of these choices will be affected by the institutions that are present.

The major concern of rational choice institutionalism is on the propensity for different institutions to channel the self-interested choices of political actors towards outcomes, which are positive or negative from a collective point of view. The origin of this approach derives from micro-economics and Adam Smith's notion of the invisible hand. In *The Wealth of Nations* Smith sought to demonstrate how, if institutions are properly structured, the pursuit of self-interest by actors within society can lead to beneficial social results, even if those results are *not* the specific intent of the actors concerned. Smith did not, as is sometimes implied by critics, maintain that the pursuit of self-interest *always* produces the best results, but focused on the crucial role of the institutional context and in particular the existence of private property and competitive markets as the key factor in determining whether this is so. Following in the wake of Smith, contemporary neo-classical economics has developed a sophisticated framework to explain how self-interested behaviour in the economic marketplace is able to generate outcomes beneficial for society as a whole, and those contexts where 'market failures' are likely to be prevalent (Sandler, 2000).

Lessons from economics

In economic theory 'market failures' are usually thought to derive from the existence of free-rider or collective action problems and/or from principal versus agent problems. The former occur when individuals are able to derive benefits from a particular good without paying their full personal share of the costs. Collective goods include such things as the maintenance of clean air. The benefits of a clean atmosphere may accrue to all individuals within a given area, *irrespective* of whether they make a personal contribution to the reduction of pollution. In this situation, the rational choice for the individual is to 'free-ride', consuming clean air without making a contribution to its provision, while hoping that others will be willing to foot the bill. If all individuals reason in this way, however, then no one will contribute, the air will remain polluted and choices, which are rational from the viewpoint of the individual, will turn out to be collectively *irrational*.

Principals and agents

Principal versus agent problems refer to the difficulties that occur in monitoring relationships between individual actors both within and between organisations. If individuals are predominantly self-interested it cannot be taken for granted that they will fulfil their responsibilities to those with whom they have economic or political relations. Other things being equal, the propensity for actors to shirk their responsibilities will be dependent on the ease with which 'principals' may monitor the performance of their 'agents'. In economic theory, principal versus agent problems often refer to the difficulties for the shareholders (the principals) of companies to exert effective control over the managers (their agents) who are contractually responsible for increasing the value of the company stock. Shareholders need to know that managers are not paying themselves salaries and other benefits unwarranted by company performance. Such problems may also occur within companies in terms of the relationship between managers and workers. Managers need to ensure that workers are meeting the terms of their contracts by, for example, arriving at work on time, meeting production targets and so on. The capacity of managers to discourage workers from shirking on the job will be affected by the relative ease or difficulty of monitoring their performance. The costs involved in the monitoring of others behaviour in this context are usually referred to as transaction costs.

Collective goods

Rational choice institutionalism is primarily concerned with the existence of collective action and principal versus agent problems in the political process and the extent to which different institutions in different societies exacerbate or help to overcome such dilemmas. Following the work of Mancur Olson (1965, 1982), collective action problems in politics have been a particular concern for rational choice theorists. According to this perspective, many of the outcomes of the political process have the character of collective goods – they are provided to everybody, irrespective of the contribution that actors make and hence are subject to the free-rider problem. Olson uses this analysis to explain a variety of political phenomena. In *The Logic of Collective Action* (1965), he explains that the existence of a shared interest between members of a particular group or social class does *not* guarantee that groups or classes will be able to act politically owing to the prevalence of the free-rider problem. Group or class interests have the character of a collective good where what is individually rational for members of the group or class concerned may not accord with the interests of the group as a whole.

In the *Rise and Decline of Nations* (1982), Olson furthers this analysis to account for the greater propensity of producer interests in industrial democracies to overcome the collective action problem than consumer interests. The former, having a smaller potential membership may find it easier to identify potential free-riders and to enforce sanctions against them, whereas the latter being so numerous find it difficult to distinguish free-riders from the population at large.

Dealing with 'free-riders'

Both 'hard' and 'soft' institutions are analysed by rational choice theorists in terms of their contribution to raising or lowering the costs of collective action and the likelihood of overcoming free-riding behaviour. Hard institutions may increase the severity of collective action problems if they operate to raise the costs of organisation. Thus, the existence of laws restricting the right to assemble and to engage in public demonstrations may intensify the free-rider problem by adding to the costs of collective action in terms of the risks of fines and potential imprisonment facing potential participants (Chong, 2002). Tullock's (1974) account of the incentives or lack of incentives to engage in revolutionary politics provides a useful example of this approach. According to Tullock revolutions in politics are relatively rare phenomena precisely because they constitute the ultimate form of the collective action problem. For many forms of political revolution to be successful, the participation of large numbers of people is required. The scale of the numbers required, however, provides considerable opportunities for free-riding, an incentive that is reinforced by the considerable costs afflicting participants should the revolution fail. The latter may be especially pronounced in totalitarian regimes where the punishment for failure may be death. Soft institutions may be equally significant in this regard. If cultural conventions in a particular society discourage 'taking to the streets' then this will constitute an additional barrier that may reinforce the problem of free-riding.

Principal versus agent problems in the political process typically focus on the relationships between voters (the principals) and politicians (their agents). Voters in democracies elect politicians, but the capacity for voters to ensure that politicians keep their promises in the period between elections is seen as a function of the relative difficulty of monitoring politicians' behaviour and in the final analysis the costs of voting itself. Complex procedures for the registering of voters may, for example, raise the costs of monitoring politicians, discouraging people from exercising their vote, relative to societies where voting is a much simpler exercise.

Similar problems are also analysed in the relationship between politicians and bureaucrats or civil servants. From a rational choice perspective, different institutional arrangements will affect the capacity for politicians to ensure that the public bureaucracy is delivering services in a properly efficient manner (see, for example, Tullock et al., 2002).

The origin of institutions and explaining institutional change

Recognising that institutional factors operate to condition the incentives that individuals face is to leave open the question of how the institutional arrangements concerned were arrived at in the first place. It is at this point that the rational choice paradigm splits into what might best be described as 'strong' and 'weak' versions.

'Strong' versus 'weak' rational choice

Strong rational choice maintains that the prevailing set of political institutions at any given time is itself the product of the interaction between individual agents pursuing their personal interests. Those who see such processes resulting in positive social outcomes include members of the Chicago School of political economy such as Becker (1985) and Wittman (1995). They maintain that institutions are chosen rationally by self-interested agents and constitute an efficient response to the solution of collective action and monitoring problems. Seen in this light, inefficiencies owing to the existence of 'market failures' prompt policy responses from the state to ensure that an efficient societal equilibrium is achieved.

'Weak' versions of rational choice theory allow greater scope for the role of ideas in the process of institutional choice. According to this view, ideas that are *not* reducible to self-interest can play an independent role in building institutions. Ideas are seen to influence the institutional context of decision-making and owing to errors in institutional design may lead to the creation of deficient incentive structures. Adherents of the Virginia School of public choice theory such as James Buchanan (1991) subscribe to this view. They argue that the process of institutional choice is subject to human error, in part owing to imperfect information and in part because of collective action and principal versus agent problems involved in the process of institutional design. As a consequence, the decision structures that emerge from such processes will often be sub-optimal from a societal point of view. Thus, 'market failure' will often be replaced or even worsened by 'government failure' (Tullock et al., 2002).

Ideas and interests

With regard to the interrelationship between ideas and interests, consider the Russian Revolution of 1917. Whereas 'strong' rational choice may interpret this event as a rational response by self-interested agents to replace an inefficient set of social structures, a weaker variant would point to the significance of ideas in shaping what people *think* is an efficient response to their interests, that is, *the idea of socialism*, as a key factor influencing the character of events. The latter would nonetheless emphasise that ideas have ultimate consequences for the incentives that individuals face. Thus, the idea of socialism helped to create socialist institutions, which resulted in a set of incentives that many would argue, was responsible for the inefficiency of the Soviet economy and the chronic difficulties of reforming the system from within (see, for example, Kornai, 1992). Working in this vein, the most sophisticated versions of 'weak' rational choice emphasise the dynamic interplay between ideas and the interests they help to create as the driving forces of institutional and political change (North, 1990).

Cultural Institutionalism

Ontology

The role of ideas and beliefs as recognised by the 'weaker' variants of rational choice theory plays a still larger role in the ontology of cultural institutionalism. From the perspective of cultural theory individuals always make decisions in a manner that reflects the prevailing ideas and beliefs widely shared by members of the communities of which they are a part. This does not require that actors necessarily agree with all the ideas and beliefs concerned, but that action is informed by reference to a set of common practices and norms.

Group processes

Seen in this light, individual perceptions are largely a product of the social environment and hence it is the belief structures that constitute the latter that form the focus of political analysis. In contrast to the methodological individualism of rational choice theory, the focus on group level processes by cultural theorists is often described as a form of methodological holism or collectivism. Thus:

- People define their interests according to conceptions of meaning, symbols and traditional practices derived from the cultural environment.
- In order to act within society, people internalise cultural norms and practices without subjecting these to rational scrutiny.
- The manner in which people make their decisions will be affected by the context of cultural norms in which they are operating.

Why institutions matter

Institutions matter to cultural theorists because institutional practices, whether of the hard or soft variety, are the embodiment of cultural values and beliefs. Hard institutions, such as parliaments and courts, and soft institutions, such as dress codes and modes of speech, are a reflection of historically shared legacies and experiences, which people define as part of their 'way of life' and 'who they are'. Thus, what it means to call oneself 'British', 'German', 'French', 'working class', 'middle class', 'rural' or 'urban', is a reflection of shared experiences and meanings that have been forged through a particular set of historical events.

Values, beliefs and symbols

It is cultural values and beliefs that help individual agents to make sense of the world around them. Owing to the complexity of the social world people cannot always think through in a strictly rational manner what their interests are and how best to pursue them. Just as one often relies on brand names when choosing between products in a supermarket rather than checking the prices and quality of each potential purchase, so cultural identifications and symbols act as a sort of 'short cut' allowing actors to operate more effectively and to situate themselves in the political world. Individuals act in ways that advance their image of cultural identity and affiliation, which is transmitted via the process of socialisation in families, schools, political parties, and religious or ethnic groups.

For cultural theorists such as Almond and Verba (1963), social symbols and traditions help people to define the boundaries of what constitutes reasonable behaviour. Issues such as the attitude to public demonstrations and the use of political violence will be reflective of historical traditions, which have evolved in response to shared memories and interpretations of political events. Similarly, the manner in which political debate and argument is carried out and even attitudes towards the electoral process itself will be shaped by a shared sense of historical experience. In societies that have lived under periods of authoritarian or totalitarian rule, for example, and where democratic reforms have been bought at a considerable sacrifice, voting rights may be reified in the cultural imagination to a far greater extent than in societies where open elections have long since been the established norm.

For cultural institutionalists the meanings associated with particular traditions and practices also form the stuff of political conflict. While cultural symbols provide a shared set of historical reference points within a society, these meanings are fundamentally *contested* (Scott, 1985). Cultural practices help to define those groups that are powerful from those which are less so. The status granted to particular occupations and professions may, for example, vary across societies depending on the prevailing stereotypes and historical associations in the countries concerned. From a cultural perspective, people mobilise and act politically in accordance with symbols either in opposition or support of cultural norms and traditions that operate to include some groups to the exclusion of others. Symbols such as the use of language and mode of dress are fundamental aspects of political communication. Thus, national flags, anthems, legal practices and modes of speech and dress will tend to occupy symbolic status in the political imagination either as representative of success and inclusion or as symptomatic of exclusion or historical oppression.

Reflecting norms and practices

It is the sheer variety of cultural experience throughout the world that is, for cultural institutionalists, central to the enterprise of comparative politics. Rational choice theorists assume that most people make their decisions in a similar manner, that is, a calculation of benefits over costs, with institutions providing constraints which affect the margins of the costs and benefits concerned. Cultural theorists, in contrast, see institutions as decisive in determining *how* people make their decisions, that is, whether or not they act rationally at all. Thus, from a cultural perspective, political action motivated by institutions that symbolise nationalism, patriotism, religion or the struggle against some form of oppression is seldom driven by rational choice, but is more likely to reflect an emotional response to a shared set of meanings that define one's identity. Issues such as the distribution of power or the ability to overcome collective action problems cannot be predicted according to the existence of formal structures, but require a deeper attempt to understand the meanings attributed to such practices and how the relevant meanings differ between one society and the next.

Notwithstanding its focus on the sheer variety of political phenomena, there are divisions within the cultural perspective in terms of the capacity of political scientists to generalise from their results. For many proponents of cultural institutionalism, and especially those associated with a 'postmodern' world view, cultural research is primarily concerned with the meanings and values that exist in *unique* cases, meanings which may not be interpreted in the same manner outside of the very *specific* context concerned. It is therefore difficult, if not impossible, to generate universal theories about the likely nature of political behaviour on the basis of culture, let alone any other phenomena.

For survey researchers such as Almond and Verba, however, while culture should be the primary focus of political behaviour, rather than individual rationality or some form of structural determinism, the identification of cultural variables *does* enable the analyst to engage in precisely the sort of generalisation that postsmodernists reject. Thus, the same cultural traits exhibited in different societies would be expected to produce similar political outcomes across the countries concerned.

The origin of institutions and explaining institutional change

Just as there are disagreements within the cultural camp about the capacity to generalise from individual studies, so too there are disputes about the appropriate manner in which to account for the origin of different institutional practices. This tension within cultural theory is evident in the changing emphases to be found within the work of the French social theorist Michel Foucault, who is often considered to be the primary influence on the emergence of 'postmodern' cultural and political analysis.

Foucault's contribution

In works such as *Madness and Civilization* (1965) and *Discipline and Punish* (1979), Foucault documented the manner in which language or discourse had been used to 'normalise' certain types of behaviour and to label previously unproblematic, though minority forms of life, as 'deviant'. At the core of Foucault's social theory is an anti-essentialist or 'de-centred' conception of the human self. In stark contrast to the insistence of rational choice theorists on the primacy of the rational individual who is seen to have a stable set of preferences which accord with an underlying essence, Foucault sees individual identity as a fluid property that emerges from the conflict between competing discourses or representations of reality. The sense of self, therefore, does not accord with an objective individual essence, but is 'imprinted' on the human body by the various modes of thought to which it is exposed. It is the combination of historical events and their discursive interpretation that shapes the self and that creates the sense of identity by, for example, the labelling of certain types of behaviour as 'normal' or 'deviant'.

Closely related to this view of the human self is Foucault's conception of the manner in which discourse operates as the primary source of social power. For Foucault it is the socio-cultural process of labelling via discourse and in particular the effect of dominant discourses, which operate to privilege certain practices and modes of thought and to marginalize others.

The power of language and discourse

In works such as *Discipline and Punish*, Foucault adopts an approach to the formation of institutions and cultural practices, not dissimilar to the structuralist or functionalist approach of Marxist theorists such as Gramsci discussed below. In this view, specific discourses and cultural modes are adopted by ruling groups in society precisely because they benefit from the forms of social control concerned. Power in this sense is seen in thoroughly negative terms with dominant interests acting to repress other sections of society via the imposition of exclusionary discourses. Towards the end of his life, however, Foucault increasingly rejected this functionalist account. While its potentially repressive character is not ignored, power is seen as a potentially positive force, which can create actors of particular kinds and enable them to do things that they could not otherwise have accomplished. According to this view, power in the sense of rules that facilitate certain forms of behaviour to the exclusion of others is an essential component of *any* functioning society (Foucault, 1991).

In his work on 'governmentality' and the 'care of the self', Foucault (1988, 1991) no longer views power as being 'imposed' on individuals by dominant social actors. While the origins of power can sometimes be traced to the deliberate intent of actors seeking to establish particular discursive norms, powerful discourses are just as likely to owe their existence to historical accidents and to have emerged as the unintended consequence of responses to particular historical events. In adopting this tack in his later works, Foucault follows a long line of cultural theorists who maintain that in order to operate in society individuals *must* to a large extent operate within institutions and practices that they have *not* sought consciously to create or invent. Individuals must accept certain rules, such as those of language, without consciously thinking about them. Rather than being the result of deliberate invention by a particular individual or group cultural rules and practices are better seen as a product of complex evolutionary processes. In the case of language, for example, new words and phrases are often spread by a process of imitation and adaptation in which their initiators are not consciously aware of how they will be used and adapted by others. Similarly, the users of words and phrases are typically unaware of the multiple different actors that have initiated such symbols and the 'reasons' for their adoption. What matters is that by following certain rules and traditions individuals are able to communicate and understand other actors on the social stage to a much greater extent than if they sought somehow to 'invent' a new language for themselves. From a cultural institutionalist perspective, many political practices and institutions evolve in a similar way and are, to a significant degree, the legacy of historical accidents.

Structural Institutionalism

Ontology

The structural variant of institutional theory differs from both the rational choice and cultural modes of analysis in fundamental ways. It differs from rational choice in denying that it is individuals who are the principal actors on the social stage. While adopting a form of methodological holism, it differs from cultural theory by rejecting the view that the significance of institutions can only be understood with reference to the cultural meanings that individuals and groups ascribe to them. For structuralist theorists, institutions and social structures exercise power *in their own right* with both individual interests and the meanings that actors attribute to institutions being largely the product of their place in the overriding institutional structure of the society concerned. Institutions actually create the beliefs that individuals and groups have. Thus, for structural institutionalists:

- Institutional structures determine the content of people's interests and beliefs.
- Action on the social stage is primarily a reflection of the relationships between the functional parts of institutional structures.
- Different institutional structures are governed by different 'laws of motion'.

Why institutions matter

Institutions matter to the proponents of structural institutionalism, because it is institutions that determine the interests and beliefs of different social actors. Macro-structures matter because it is the internal logic of institutional systems that determines the nature of the political process and the outcomes it produces. Actors in this sense are seen as the bearers of functional roles and a correspondent set of political beliefs in an overall structure that operates according to a logic of its own. Both 'hard' and 'soft' institutional practices are seen to reflect the overall logic of larger-scale structures such as 'capitalism', the 'nation-state' and more recently 'globalisation'. Seen in this light, the task of the political scientist is to identify the underlying dynamics or laws that govern social systems *as a whole*.

In functionalist accounts it is 'the system' itself (whatever the particular 'system') that is the primary actor on the political stage. Social structures and institutions are conceived as having a purposive function of their own, *independent* of the beliefs that actors hold about the nature of these structures. Individual agents and even collectives such as interest groups, social classes or states do not, according to this view, choose the social arrangements within which they operate, and neither are such arrangements the product of historical accidents. Rather, institutions have a purpose 'of their own' and it is these 'system requirements' that determine the course of political events. Structuralist theorists, therefore, pay relatively little attention to the 'micro-details' of the political process and concern themselves with comparison between larger groups of countries governed by similar systems or with the comparative role played by different countries in larger macro-structures such as the international economy. Differences in electoral rules, between federal systems and unitary states and between presidential and cabinet forms of government, for example, are thought to constitute minor variations in political practice relative to the fundamental similarities between *all* societies characterized by macro-structures – such as capitalism and the nation-state – of which they are a part.

Marxist structuralism

Marxist and neo-Marxist theories have traditionally formed the mainstream of structuralist political science. In Marxist theories institutional practices reflect the underlying nature of the prevailing 'mode of production', such as 'capitalism', or 'feudalism'. The interests of social actors are defined in terms of their functional relationships to the structures concerned. Thus, the interests of capitalists as owners of the means of production are functionally separate and in conflict with those of the proletariat whose interests are defined by their lack of access to industrial capital. From a Marxist perspective the interests of proletarians and capitalists are not defined by the subjective views of individual members of these particular groups, but with regard to their objective relationship to the means of production and the functional requirements of the economy in its particular stage of development.

Marxist accounts of liberal democracy are predicated on a very specific account of how capitalism operates as a social order and of its 'system requirements'. Central to this perspective is the labour theory of value and the 'falling rate of profit' thesis. For Marx and his followers, the value of commodities is determined by the number of labour hours taken to produce them, or more specifically, the number of labour hours deemed to be 'socially necessary' for their production (Marx, 1906). 'Living' labour power, according to Marx, is the *only* source of economic value, with the profits that capitalists make from the employment of labour constituting a form of 'exploitation'.

Capitalists as a class are, owing to their control of the means of production, able to extract 'surplus value' from the proletariat without making any addition to the social product. According to Marx, since the value of commodities is a product of labour alone the capacity for capitalists to extract a surplus from the proletariat declines as the component of capital used for the employment of machinery increases. Individual capitalists are impelled by the forces of market competition to invest in labour-saving technology, for fear of being driven out of business by their rivals. As they do so, however, their capacity to extract a surplus declines since machinery constitutes a form of 'dead' labour which cannot add anything to the social product on its own. The latter constitutes an 'internal contradiction' within the logic of the capitalist system and it is the functional role of the capitalist state to ameliorate this contradiction via the introduction of policies designed to boost the rate of profit.

Critiquing Marxist structuralism

Most contemporary analysts, even socialists, consider Marx's labour theory of value and the notion of 'surplus value' entirely discredited by the subjective or marginalist theory of value (see, for example, Dunleavy and O'Leary, 1987; Elster, 1985) developed by writers such as Wicksteed (1933) and Bohm-Bawerk (1959). The latter contends that the relative scarcity of commodities (that is, how much of a particular commodity there is, in relation to how much people want it) and the availability of substitutes, is the major determinant of their value rather than the amount of 'labour' used in their production. According to this view, *all* factors of production – labour, land *and* capital, contribute to the value of commodities.

Under competitive market conditions, each factor of production tends to be paid its 'marginal product', that is according to the increase in yields induced by the addition of an extra unit of the factor concerned, up to the point where yields cease to increase (an outline of this theory can be found in any basic textbook on microeconomics). Marginalist economics calls into question the entire Marxian analysis of the structural properties attributed to capitalism. According to this view, since labour power is *not* the only source of value there is no inherent tendency for the rate of profit to fall and hence the functional role of the capitalist state in responding to this supposed 'contradiction' is redundant.

Rejecting Marx's theory in the above vein does not, however, discredit a structuralist account of capitalist institutions or other social systems per se. The defining feature of structuralism is not the commitment displayed to any *particular* account of how social structures operate, but an insistence that structures have some sort of logic or purpose of their own, independent of the actors that populate the systems under study. The task of the political analyst is to identify what the structural dynamics are – though there is clearly considerable room for disagreement between theorists when it comes to identifying the structural properties concerned.

Non-Marxist structuralism

Non-Marxist versions of structural theory focus less on 'capitalism' as the primary force and more on other systems such as the nation-state. The primary theme of this work is the manner in which macro-structural parameters such as class structure, demography, technology or geographical conditions interact to produce particular political outcomes. In the more thoroughgoing versions of this perspective individual actors have little if any significance to the course of political events. One example of a structural approach which is highly deterministic, but does not develop an explicitly Marxist analysis is Skocpol's (1979) account of the factors that led to large-scale political upheavals in France, Russia and China. According to Skocpol, the revolutions that occurred in these societies were essentially revolutions 'without revolutionaries'. Background structural conditions, such as external stress upon the state, a breakdown in the ability to maintain internal order and the existence of strong community structures among peasants constituted *sufficient* structural factors to *cause* revolutionary action, irrespective of the subjective beliefs about the appropriate response to such conditions held by individual agents.

Until recently, many structuralist writers conceived of institutions operating in accordance with 'historical laws'. Marxists, in particular, saw society progressing through a series of historical epochs, each with its own mode of production, which would eventually collapse under the strain of structural tensions, giving way to a more progressive social form. The culmination of this process would see the replacement of market capitalism (itself seen as a progressive advance on the feudal era) with a socialist mode of production. The 'purpose' of capitalism as an historical structure, therefore, was to bring about the conditions under which socialism could arise.

The experience of state socialism in the 20th century and the fact that many societies appear to have moved *away* from socialism towards the adoption of a more or less market-oriented economy has undermined the faith of many structuralist theorists in the validity of Marx's 'laws of history'. Nonetheless, the defining characteristic of structuralist thought continues to be the view that it is structures that determine the course of social events. Non-Marxist structuralists continue to search for the particular macro-parameters that drive the process of social evolution. Goldstone (1991), for example, attempts to explain the breakdown of state structures in terms of deteriorating demographic conditions.

According to this view when financial emergencies, divisions within the ruling elite and the mobilisation of protest movements coincide with a worsening of the ratio of resources to population, then the structures of the state will crack. The overriding implication of this analysis is that *any* state faced with a similar array of macro-forces would succumb to the same fate. It is, therefore, structural variables such as population to resources ratios which are responsible for the pattern of political development and not the 'choices' exercised by individuals or cultural groups.

The origin of institutions and explaining institutional change

From a structuralist perspective, institutions themselves are not the product of individual rational choice, or of cultural and historical accidents, but owe their existence to underlying economic and technological conditions. According to this view societies do not choose the institutions they have. Rather, institutions are in a sense 'chosen for them' by historical and technological factors largely outside of their control. Particular economic and technological conditions give rise to particular institutional forms. Marx's theory of historical materialism, for example, maintains that the 'superstructure' of society, that is, both the 'hard' institutions of formal law and the 'soft' institutions embodied in cultural symbols and meanings, are determined by the economic and technological 'base' of the society concerned. In the strongest versions of this thesis, there is little if any independent role for ideas in the process of institutional development. The prevailing climate of opinion is seen as subordinate to the underlying structural/technological conditions that determine the content of ideas.

Neo-Marxist explanations of Thatcherism

A typical example of this approach is found in neo-Marxist accounts of the rise of Thatcherism and the 'neo-liberal' policies, introduced in its name. According to writers such as Aglietta (1979) and Jessop (1990), the shift towards a policy agenda based on deregulation and the creation of flexible labour markets reflected an underlying shift in the technological base of the capitalist economy. As the dominance of so-called 'Fordist' mass-production techniques, which had required a large state bureaucracy, and Keynesian demand management policies to maintain consumer demand gave way to more flexible 'post-Fordist' production processes in the 1970s, Thatcherism represented a functional response to the 'system requirement' for administrative structures correspondent with these technological developments. Taking this view, the market liberal philosophy of the Thatcher administration had relatively little role in shaping the policy agenda in the 1980s, with the clear implication that even a nominally socialist administration would have been 'forced' to implement policies of a similar type.

Marxist theories of politics are invariably of a structuralist nature. Again, however, it is important to recognise that not all structuralist theories are, or need necessarily be, Marxist. It is possible to support the view that changes in political systems are driven by changes in technology, such as the effect exercised by the invention of the printing press on political communication, without subscribing to an ideology that sees society progressing on a structurally determined path towards socialism.

Non-Marxist accounts of nationalism

Gellner's (1983) non-Marxist account of nationalism as a largely modern phenomenon falls into this category of analysis. In contrast to cultural accounts, which emphasise the deep historical roots of nationalism in shared customs and traditions, Gellner contends that the nation-state is a relatively recent phenomenon that was made possible by a very particular set of technological and economic circumstances. These included industrialisation, capitalism, the spread of the mass media and systems of public education, all of which facilitated the development of shared cultural consciousness on a scale that had not previously been possible. Gellner's account is structuralist (though not Marxist), because it implies that it is the coincidence of structural variables such as capitalism and the mass media that 'caused' the nation-state to develop, rather than the subjective beliefs about the virtue or otherwise of the nation-state held by individuals and groups.

Synthesising Theories of Institutions in Comparative Politics

The analysis thus far has treated the variants of institutionalist thought as distinct approaches to comparative political analysis, each with their own particular view on the nature of the relationship between the individual and society and of precisely how it is that 'institutions matter'. While there are some irreconcilable differences between the various theoretical paradigms, there are, nonetheless, important areas where there is room for compromise and where some analysts have sought to combine and synthesise elements of the different traditions. Arguably some of the most important work in the 'new institutionalism' has been engaged in precisely this sort of theoretical synthesis and it is to this potential that attention now turns.

Ontology

One of the most fruitful areas for a synthesis between different ontological viewpoints is that between rational choice and cultural theory. 'Hard core' proponents of rational choice theory typically assume that individual actors possess certain interests and pref-erences that exist *independently* of the social context in which they are situated, and have been attacked for neglecting the manner in which cultural norms condition peo-ple's perceptions of what their interests are. A less rigid version of rational choice the-ory, however, may be accommodated with a cultural perspective in this regard. More nuanced versions of rational theory, exemplified in the work of Chong (2002), recog-nise the role played by socialisation in shaping an individual actor's sense of identity, so long as it is not suggested that people are constituted *wholly* by their cultural sur-roundings. What matters for rational choice theory is that individuals have the capac-ity to challenge elements of the prevailing cultural norms 'at the margin' and via such agency can contribute to the evolution of *new* cultural forms.

Synthesising culture and rationality

Institutions such as the traditions and practices that constitute a sense of cultural iden-tity can be explained partly in terms of the instrumental benefits they provide to those who adhere to the relevant rules. According to this view, people subscribe to common norms and values in order to gain access to the material and social benefits associated with membership of an identifiable reference group (Hardin, 1995). These may be fol-lowed out of habit, but equally may result from deliberate choice. In the latter case, individuals may consciously shift their cultural practices and subscribe to new values in order to access benefits that would otherwise be unavailable, as for example when immigrants from rural areas adopt urban mores in order to access employment and other social benefits (Chong, 2002).

Consider in the above light the cases of language and fashion. The majority of the words that people speak and the style of clothes that people wear are not, for the most part, the product of rational reflection but stem from the unconscious adoption of social rules and traditions derived from the cultural environment. Nonetheless, such cultural norms are constantly undergoing a process of incremental adaptation as actors introduce new words or phrases, or adapt styles of dress – modifications, which may subsequently be spread via a process of emulation and imitation. Actors, there-fore, are affected by the whole of which they are a part, but are simultaneously involved in shaping and *changing* the content of that whole.

For rational choice theory *accounting for social change* is the interesting part of social analysis. The incentives facing individual actors when considering a challenge to established norms are what matter. Are there incentives to challenge particular norms and what sort of people and situations are likely to produce a challenge to social and political phenomena? These are the sorts of questions that a culturally informed version of rational choice theory seeks to address.

Chong (2002) presents such an account in his analysis of changing attitudes to racism in the American Deep South. Northern whites engaged in business frequently adopted racist attitudes having moved to the South in order to maintain good relations with local suppliers and buyers. Southern whites who challenged racist norms in contrast, tended to be those who were independently wealthy and who could afford to isolate themselves from the community of which they were a part. Working in a similar vein, Posner (1992) accounts for the concentration of groups such as gays and ethnic minorities in metropolitan centres as a reflection of differential incentives to challenge norms.

According to this view, minority groups are unlikely to challenge established practices in rural areas or small towns that are characterised by relative cultural homogeneity, owing to the capacity of close-knit communities to monitor their neighbours' behaviour and to enforce the power of ostracism. In large number metropolitan contexts, by contrast, cultural minorities are better able to escape the effect of social pressure, owing to a combination of high monitoring costs (the greater the number of people, the greater are the difficulties involved in 'checking up' on one's neighbours) and the greater capacity of minorities to 'exit' from economic relations with individuals and groups who disapprove of their behaviour and to 'enter' into relations with alternative social groups.

Synthesising culture and structure

Another possible area for theoretical synthesis occurs between cultural analysis and the less rigid forms of structural institutionalism. The Italian neo-Marxist theorist Antonio Gramsci is held by some to have enriched Marxian analysis in his attempt to reassert the role of individual agency and of cultural ideas in understanding the process of social change. Gramsci (1971) sought to move Marxism away from the crude form of economic determinism, which views the role of ideas as epiphenomenal to the determining role of the economic base. For Gramsci, orthodox Marxism was incapable of explaining the support for Fascism from the working class in Italy and, more generally, the apparent diversity of political responses to be found across capitalist states with similar levels of technological and economic development.

Gramsci's contribution

According to Gramsci, while the economic structure of capitalist society is based on the structural conflict of interest between the proletariat and the bourgeoisie, the specific manifestation of this conflict will be dependent on the *particular* cultural circumstances of the country concerned. Economic forces affect the interests that particular classes in a given structure possess but *do not* determine how actors will subjectively perceive these interests. On the contrary, for Gramsci the Marxian notion of class struggle is one that is frequently conducted in the realm of culture and ideas. Politics is seen primarily as a struggle for cultural hegemony in which subordinate classes are subject to competing interpretations of their structural position and where power is exercised when the dominant class is able to convince the proletariat that its interests are coterminous with those of the ruling elite.

Seen in this context, there is no inevitability that the proletariat will acquire the appropriate ideological consciousness necessary to bring about the transformation from capitalism to socialism – they may come to be convinced by cultural appeals to alternate arrangements such as fascism or social democracy. Gramsci, therefore, while maintaining a broadly structural Marxist account of class conflict under capitalism, allows greater room for the role of ideas in shaping the future direction in which the character of that conflict may be expressed.

Bringing the three approaches closer together ...

Recognising the role of institutional rules provides some overlap between a culturally informed rational choice theory and elements of a more structural analysis. Put simply, different institutional structures provide different incentives and opportunities for actors to challenge prevailing cultural norms. Structures are simply the set of rules that govern the relations between actors. These rules affect the interests held by actors and also their access to resources. Crucially, however, different rule structures affect the capacity for actors to *transform* the rules *from within*. What this implies is the need for a comparative account of the extent to which different rule structures allow or prevent scope for the exercise of individual agency and both the intended and unintended consequences that follow from it. Arguably, this sort of 'structuration' analysis (see Giddens, 1984) is what informs the 'weaker' variant of institutional rational choice with its comparison of incentives facing actors under monopolistic as opposed to more competitive rule structures (see, for example, North, 1990).

... But not completely

At the ontological level, the residual difference between the major variants of institutionalist thought that prevents a complete synthesis between the perspectives centres on the significance of individual action to the understanding of social phenomena. For rational choice theorists, while culture and institutional structures may condition individual action, in the final analysis it is still the incentives and beliefs of *individual* actors that drive the explanation of how social structures are to be understood and how they are maintained or changed. Rational choice theory is incompatible with any account that posits the existence of cultural groups or structures as independent actors on the social stage. According to this view people may share common interests with other actors derived from cultural allegiance or from a structural position in society, but this does not mean that the relevant groups are actors in any meaningful sense. Group-based action or inaction may for rational choice theorists only be understood in terms of the incentives that individuals face to participate in such action and the beliefs they hold about it. However for many cultural and structural theorists albeit in different ways, groups and social institutions *can* exercise a form of agency within the political process.

Why institutions matter

The potential theoretical affinities between a weaker variant of rational choice theory and a cultural perspective again become evident when attempting to understand why it is that 'institutions matter'. At issue here is the significance of cultural institutions and the manner in which they enable actors to cope with conditions of complexity and what Herbert Simon (1957) has termed 'bounded rationality'. According to Simon, individuals cannot always base their decisions on a cool computation of benefits over costs. The human brain is fundamentally limited in its capacity to process information and to make computations and must therefore resort to habits, traditions and rules of thumb. Making use of traditions provides regularity in peoples' lives and while rarely leading to optimal or 'perfectly efficient' results, provides for 'adequate' outcomes and enables 'effective' behaviour by reducing the amount of information that must be processed. Seen in this light, the cultural conventions and belief systems that form the core of cultural analysis are compatible with a weaker strain of rational choice. While habitual behaviour cannot be considered as fully rational, neither does such action represent evidence of an irrational or purely emotional basis to human decisions.

On the contrary, traditional rules can act as important *aides-memoire*, which make it easier for those who follow them to achieve their objectives under conditions of complexity. Rule-guided or habitual action is still *purposeful* action and is thus compatible with a rational choice approach which recognises the problem of imperfect information and the need for actors to adopt 'satisficing' strategies to deal with such conditions. Many political institutions can be analysed in these terms. Constitutional traditions such as monarchy, for example, may be maintained owing to the risk that in trying to design a more efficient set of arrangements, imperfect information may lead to a choice of still less effective procedures.

Making choices about behaviour

To recognise that people adopt rule-following strategies does not, it should be emphasised, necessarily undermine the principle of methodological individualism. It is a mistake common to adherents of both 'hard core' rational choice theory and of some cultural theorists to suggest that methodological individualism implies that all actors make their decisions in precisely the same way – that is, according to the rational calculation of advantage. For strict rational choice theorists on the one hand, a focus on habits and traditions ignores people's *universal* responsiveness to incentives and relative prices and is to be rejected precisely because of the focus on *group level* factors such as culture. For some cultural theorists on the other hand, recognition that actors make decisions in ways other than the cool calculation of benefits over costs is to concede the case for some form of methodological holism – and is to be welcomed as such (March and Olsen, 1989).

A commitment to methodological individualism, however, need not specify *how* people make choices. Individuals may be perfectly rational, boundedly rational, habitual rule followers, or even automatons. All that matters for the methodological individualist is that it is *individuals* who makes decisions – *in whatever way* – and not 'cultures' or 'structures' (Agassi, 1960, 1975; Whittman, 2004).

The latter may only be understood in terms of the individual agents that make them up. In the case of culture, for example, the adherence of people to traditions may be explained in terms of the propensity of *individuals* to be 'rule-following' actors who imitate the behaviour of their fellows and of the relationships between individuals who are seen as leaders, entrepreneurs or trendsetters, and those actors who are the led. It is therefore possible to have a form of cultural analysis that *does not* subscribe to methodological holism. Recognition that individuals make their decisions in a variety of different, though interconnecting ways, may thus result in a culturally informed variant of institutional rational choice.

Cultural-rational approaches using path dependency

A further area where the concerns of rational choice and cultural analysis overlap is the focus on the manner in which institutional rules may operate to block certain forms of social change. The concept of 'path dependency' is of particular relevance in this context (Alston et al., 1996; Steinmo et al., 1992). This suggests that societies may become 'locked in' to institutional arrangements owing to random historical accidents and what economists describe as 'network externalities'. The latter occur where the benefits of consuming a good depend positively on the number of other individuals who do so. The value of learning a particular language, for example, often depends on how many speakers there already are. Likewise, products or services, such as membership of a telephone network, may be chosen on the basis of the number of actors already consuming the good concerned.

What matters, is that, beyond a critical threshold, people may opt for a product on the basis of the number of other consumers using the good, rather than on the superiority of the product itself. As a consequence, the choices that people make will often be affected by random contingencies resulting from the previous choices of other actors. In this sense, random cultural and historical events might account for the existence of particular institutional rules, but individual rational choice may help to explain whether or not adherence to these rules is likely to be stable. At issue here would be the extent to which actors have sufficient incentives to opt for an alternative set of arrangements.

The concept of path dependency might, in a similar vein, be combined with a more structural analysis (Granovetter, 1985). Thus, in situations where institutions and traditions have persisted for long periods of time and have become deeply entrenched, to speak of people having a 'choice' of how to behave in such situations may be to stretch the meaning of the word to breaking point. Much of the work described as 'historical institutionalism' falls into this pattern of analysis.

Synthesis but not integration

Notwithstanding the room that exists for synthesis between the various approaches, it is again important to highlight the central points which preclude the existence of a fully integrated approach. The fundamental issue in this context is whether the nature of how people make their decisions is the product of particular cultural and structural institutional forms. Following the works of Karl Polanyi, it has long been the claim of theorists in both the cultural and structuralist camps that the model of economising behaviour depicted by rational choice theorists is limited to the cultural and structural context of the modern market economy. According to this view, responsiveness to prices and incentives, and questions of scarcity is not a universal characteristic of human action but the product of a very specific set of cultural and institutional practices that have existed since the late 18th and early 19th centuries (Polanyi, 1944). The implication of this stance is that under a different set of cultural or structural conditions individuals would *not* behave in the manner depicted by the rational choice approach. For rational choice theorists, however, scarcity is a fundamental aspect of human existence and hence people will respond to incentives *irrespective* of the institutional context in which they are embedded. Different institutional structures simply alter the incentives that people face. The cultural values that form the basis of those incentives may vary across societies – in some societies actors may strive for material wealth, whilst in others the pursuit of leisure may be their primary objective. Either way, individuals must make trade-offs and be responsive to incentives in pursuit of the goals concerned. Culture and institutions condition the parameters of rational choice, but they do not, in this view, determine the existence or non-existence of rational self-interested action.

The origin of institutions and explaining institutional change

Rational-structural approaches

Turning finally to the question of how and why particular institutions exist, some surprising theoretical overlaps are discernible. At first glance, perhaps the most improbable of these occurs between the 'strong' version of rational choice theory and structural Marxism. Notwithstanding the individualistic base of the former and the holistic structuralism of the latter, there are remarkable similarities between the way that these approaches analyse the origin of institutions and the process of institutional change. For the 'hard core' rational choice theorist, institutions arise and are chosen owing to their efficiency-enhancing properties. According to this perspective, assuming that individuals are rational utility maximisers then they will opt for those institutional forms that maximise both individual and social utility. Institutions, therefore, are always efficient – because if for some reason they are not, then utility-maximising actors would change them accordingly. Viewed through this lens, the process of institutional change is driven by shifts in technology and relative prices. Individual actors will respond to changing technologies and shifts in the relative scarcity of goods by adapting political institutions to the new conditions concerned in order to maintain efficiency (see, for example North and Thomas, 1973).

While this account focuses on the responsiveness of utility-maximising agents, the parallels with structural Marxism are nonetheless clear. In classical Marxist accounts it is the underlying nature of the economic base that determines the institutions of society at any given time and which drives the process of institutional change. According to this view, developments in technology, in the 'forces of production' to use Marxist terminology, will bring about changes in the institutional rules of society, that is, changes to the 'relations of production'. If there are structural tensions between a given set of forces of production and the prevailing relations of production, then some form of societal revolution will be necessary to bring social structures back into line.

The implication of strong rational choice and structural Marxism is that social institutions have a tendency to approach optimality; either they represent an efficient response to the utility-maximising behaviour of individuals (rational choice), or they are seen to fulfil a necessary role commensurate with a particular historical stage in societal development (Marxism). As such, both these schools allow little, if any, room for the role of ideas and the possibility of human error in understanding the process of institutional development. The assumption is that people or 'structural forces' know what the optimal set of social arrangements actually is. Weaker variants of rational choice theory and the culturalist perspective would reject this view, arguing that the process of institutional change is affected by the ideas held by individuals and groups about desirable institutional forms. These ideas may turn out to be erroneous but this does not undermine the independent role of ideas in the process of institutional development. On the contrary, 'incorrect' ideas about appropriate institutional changes are just as likely to prevail as are 'correct' ideas. There is as a consequence no inexorable tendency for social systems to approach optimal or efficient forms.

Rational-cultural approaches

Seen in the above light, there is again considerable scope for theoretical synthesis between the weaker version of rational choice theory and a cultural perspective. This approach may in turn find some affinity with a non-Marxian form of structural institutionalism. Such an approach would focus on the relationship between ideas, the structural rules that these ideas help to create or set up and the incentives or lack of incentives to change the relevant institutional structures should they turn out to contain errors and inefficiencies. North (1990) adopts precisely this kind of framework in an attempt to explain the persistence of inefficient institutional forms.

According to North, prevailing institutional practices may owe their origins to a combination of historical accidents and misguided attempts at deliberate institutional design. Inefficient institutions may persist according to the incentive structure that they create. Even inefficient rules may operate to the benefit of some groups in society who will seek to maintain the status quo, preventing moves towards a more efficient set of practices. What matters to the prospects for efficiency enhancing improvements is the extent to which those who would benefit from institutional change have sufficient incentives to bring about the necessary modifications. According to North inefficient institutions may often survive precisely because the relevant incentives are skewed in favour of inertia. On the one hand, those with ruling interests who benefit substantially from the status quo will use all of their powers to resist institutional change. On the other hand, if the gains from institutional reform are likely to be widely spread across a large number of dispersed agents, then agents are unlikely to mobilise in favour of new rules owing to the prevalence of collective action problems. In this situation even though the total gains to society at large may exceed the benefits currently flowing to ruling interests, efficiency-enhancing reforms are unlikely to be enacted (North, 1990).

SUMMARY

This chapter has outlined the basic principles underlying three theoretical approaches derived from the 'new institutionalism' in political science and their relevance to comparative political studies. Understanding these basic analytical principles is crucial to an appreciation of the more specific aspects of comparative political analysis explored in the chapters that follow:

- The ontology of each approach has been examined, together with their defence of why institutions matter and their explanation of the origins of institutions and institutional change.

- The discussion has focused in abstract terms on the general principles that distinguish between different branches of institutionalist theory

- Potential areas where theoretical synthesis may be possible have been considered.

FURTHER READING

Alston, L., Eggertsson, T. and North, D. (1996) *Empirical Studies in Institutional Change*. Cambridge: Cambridge University Press.

A useful series of case studies exploring the dynamics of political and institutional change from a 'soft' rational choice perspective.

Chong, D. (2002) *Rational Lives: Norms and Values in Politics and Society*. Chicago, IL: Chicago University Press.

This is a theoretical work which explores the interaction between individual incentives and socio-cultural norms – it attempts to bridge the gap between rational choice analysis and more cultural theories that emphasise the role of socialisation in shaping political behaviour.

Lichbach, M. (2003) *Is Rational Choice Theory All of Social Science?* Ann Arbor, MI: University of Michigan Press.

Primarily a defence of rational choice theory, but also contains useful discussions of both cultural and structural explanations in political science.

March, J.G. and Olsen, J.P. (1989) *Rediscovering Institutions*. New York: Free Press.

A key text widely credited with having revived interest in exploring how cultural norms act as 'institutions' and the effect of cultural norms on political outcomes.

Skocpol, T. (1989) *States and Social Revolutions: A Comparative Analysis of France, Russia and China*. New York: Cambridge University Press.

An empirical work conducted from a broadly structuralist perspective which explains the dynamics of revolutionary political change in terms of macro-structural forces.

QUESTIONS FOR DISCUSSION

(1) What is the likely impact on a political system when the 'hard' or formal rules of political interaction conflict with the 'soft' cultural norms in the society concerned? Historically, in what situations do we observe conflicts between hard and soft social norms?

(2) Does support for the principle of 'methodological individualism' equate with support for rational choice accounts of individual behaviour?

(3) How does rational choice theory account for the way in which people pursue 'non-material' goals in politics?

(4) Are cultural theories in comparative politics purely descriptive?

(5) With reference to examples, how might technological change affect the development of political institutions?

Key Words for Chapter 1

cultural norms / free-rider / individual / institution / new institutionalism / principal-agent / rational choice / structuralism / structuration theory

2 Methodologies for Comparative Analysis

Judith Bara

CHAPTER OUTLINE

This chapter considers how and why comparative political analysis developed and identifies the main methods employed to account for similarities and differences between political phenomena.

Introduction

Before progressing to discussions of specific institutions and actors, it is necessary to appreciate the research methods that are appropriate to the relevant theories and their application in a comparative context. It is these issues that this chapter will now address.

As we have already noted from Chapter 1, political scientists are not in agreement with regard to which theoretical approach provides the most effective explanation of why political institutions have developed in particular ways, and of how people behave politically. On the one hand, much the same can be said with regard to the analytic methods used in comparative politics in order to test theories and hypotheses and to identify differences and similarities in how the political process works in different countries. Indeed, we might suggest that the actual process of 'comparing' represents a method in itself (Hopkin, 2002) – after all, comparisons are made in many disciplines, especially in social sciences. On the other hand, 'comparative politics' suggests that there is something specific about looking at institutions and other political phenomena in different countries, time periods or levels of political activity and explaining why it is, for example, that decision making is carried out differently in presidential or parliamentary systems (see Chapter 5).

In Chapter 1, Mark Pennington suggested that comparison tries 'to overcome the short-comings of approaches focused purely on case studies of individual countries and of those that build purely abstract theoretical models of decision-making'. In reality it seeks to go much further than this. Its purpose is to provide frameworks that will be rigorous and enable the results of analysis to be regarded as credible. In other words, comparative political analysis aims at providing a more *scientific* basis to the study of political institutions and behaviour, and to avoid unsubstantiated generalisation which will prevent results of such investigations from being regarded as reliable. It must be stressed that the three explanatory approaches introduced in Chapter 1 do not have their own dedicated methods. Methods used in studies that are comparative in nature are similar to those used in political science in general. The choice of method will often be dictated by the nature of the topic under consideration. Studies that focus on policy making would be more likely to use in-depth interviews, often involving only a few key individuals, whereas if we want to analyse public opinion or voting behaviour, we would tend to use large-scale surveys.

Scientific Method

The development of modern scientific method and with it, the advent of modern social science, occurred in the 19th century. This was mainly as a result of the influence of philosophy and social enquiry, pioneered by the first modern political sociologists, Marx, Durkheim, Weber, and the elite theorists, Mosca, Pareto and Michels. What was so different about these thinkers was that unlike many of their predecessors they engaged in:

- systematic, scientific, logical approaches;
- explanation guided by theoretical perspectives;
- and were related to the 'real world' in that empirical evidence sought to 'prove' theories.

However, there is disagreement about whether or not methods used in political analysis should be regarded as scientific. Scientific method is generally associated with activity undertaken in natural sciences, such as physics, chemistry or biology. Clearly political activity is very different from the behaviour of atoms in a test tube or how different substances may be combined to provide medicines, but this need not mean that it is less rigorous. The idea that the study of politics is unscientific is reinforced by common images of those undertaking political analysis, which are very diffferent from our common images of natural scientists. Whereas political scientists are imagined carrying on their work through activities such as reading in libraries, undertaking surveys or talking to politicicians, natural scientists are seen as working in laboratories (usually in white coats) where they engage in experimentation. However, this really tells us little about what actually constitutes scientific method.

The essential characteristics of scientific method are summarised in the box opposite, although these may not necessarily be carried out in exactly the same sequence.

Box 2.1   Scientific method: characteristic activities

Creation of a statement of a problem or issue to be investigated, for example why do many younger people choose not to participate in elections.

Identification of a theoretical explanation to be used in guiding the investigation, for example, a rational choice explanation.

Translation of abstract ideas in this theoretical explanation into concrete factors, identifiable in the real world, which are capable of being investigated, for example, selecting relevant voters.

The development of measures of the important explanatory factors (or variables) in the theoretical explanation. How do we 'measure' levels of electoral participation? Do we take one or more elections? Do we focus on general elections only or include local or other types of election?

The development of a research design to guide the inquiry so that information gathered truly tests the validity of the explanation to the fullest extent possible. Where do we find our data, materials, participants?

The selection of a set of methods that implement this design, for example, a survey, in-depth interviews, large-scale statistical analysis. Would we use results of previous analysyis, especially survey work or public opinion polls, or would we undertake a new survey?

How do we analyse the material we collect?

Source: Blalock, H. and Blalock, A. (1970) *Introduction to Social Research*. Englewood Cliffs, NJ: Prentice Hall, reproduced with permission of Pearson.

The precise analytic methods selected in political research, irrespective of the theoretical perspective used, will obviously vary according to the nature of the topic under investigation. Sometimes we need to concentrate on narrative accounts, such as official papers, diaries or memoirs. We might also use material resulting from studies carried out by someone else or on the results of interviews or surveys, especially if they are seen as credible. At other times, availability of material is regarded as a more effective since to carry out a large survey is costly, so we might use official statistics or aggregate data such as that provided in a census. If we are working on a smaller scale, we may need to conduct primary interviews ourselves, possibly to test someone else's assertions or theories and of course we may well want to compare or contrast examples (or cases) drawn from different regions, countries or time periods. It is in this area that we are back within the territory of comparative politics.

Concepts, Variables and Measurement

Concepts

The basic building blocks in comparative political analysis are *concepts*. These serve three main scientific functions by helping to organise, describe and compare political phenomena in order to assist in the creation of categories. Since the aim of scientific inquiry is to provide understanding and explanation, concepts help by establishing criteria which distinguish unambiguously between categories. For example, to differentiate clearly between parliamentary and presidential types of executive.

With regard to comparison in particular, concepts enable distinctions to be made *between* themselves and others, which might share certain characteristics or bring about similar outcomes. For example, political parties can be distinguished from interest groups, social movements and other agencies that purport to *represent* peoples' views. But concepts, through establishment of categories, can also distinguish *among* themselves. Take the concept of liberal democracy, a standard category in many classification systems dealing with regimes, we can identify different forms of practice and even draw up a continuum between strong and weak liberal democracies. This enables us to work on the basis of variation.

Variables

In a practical sense, the power of concepts in scientific research is based on their capacity to vary, which in effect transforms them into *variables*. Regimes can vary in terms of *type* on the basis of being characterised as liberal democracies as opposed to autocracies or transitional or communist regimes on the basis of criteria. But at the same time liberal democracies can also vary on the basis of *degree* – between strong and weak liberal democracies as suggested above. We will also see later in Chapter 9 how voters might consider themselves to be strong or weak partisans – identifying to a greater or lesser degree with a given political party. A given set of variables, designated as independent variables, are also employed to explain variation in another variable, designated as the dependent variable. So *voting for a left of centre party* might be a dependent variable capable of explanation by reference to a series of independent variables such as the social class, ethnic origin or religion of the voter.

Operationalising concepts

The way in which concepts are *operationalised*, or made suitable for use, is to define them in such a way so as to ensure that they are capable of 'travelling' across time, space (that is, between countries) and cultures (Lijphart, 1971). This may involve a certain amount of 'stretching', for example, to focus on essential, general characteristics rather than those associated with specific contexts. For example, Pennings et al. (1999) explain how the concept of consociational democracy, orginally used to describe the accomodation reached between opposing parties in The Netherlands to mitigate the effects of fragmentation, was recast by Lijphart (1977) to allow comparison with other fragmented cultures, such as Cyprus or Sri Lanka.

Measurement

In order to apply concepts and variables to the real world and enable the identification of similarities and differences, we need to be able to *measure* them. In many cases the basis of measurement is clear. If we are comparing economic performance among governments, we might look at a standard measure such as gross domestic product or income per capita, on the basis of a common value system, such as US dollars or euros. Sometimes, however, we would need to construct measures, such as what constitutes levels of participation. One of the factors would undoubtedly be voting regularly in general elections, but decisions about other forms of participation are more contested, such as participation in interest group activity, taking part in a protest march or simply contacting a member of parliament. This can be solved to some extent by reference to the three levels of measurement employed in political investigation – the nominal, ordinal and interval levels.

By *nominal* we mean that variables are distinguished on the basis of name, a form of description. So we can distinguish between parties on the basis of their names or middle-class or working-class electors. *Ordinal* variables distinguish between different levels, such as strong, medium or weak partisanship or left, centre or right parties. *Interval* variables are essentially based on scales, which are divided numerically on the basis of equal intervals between categories, such as income categories. It is this type of category which enables quantification.

Validity

Of course we also have to take care that the concepts we use are valid. Pennings et al. show that concepts need to demonstrate both internal and external validity. Internal validity is directly related to comparative analysis and is demonstrated when the concept is 'truly comparative, that is yield the *same* result for all cases under review'. External validity means that concepts apply to all cases of a similar nature – in other words the technique can be replicated in exactly the same way and be expected to produce more or less the same results. It is this aspect of comparative politics which gives rise to the idea that it can be used as an instrument to predict political outcomes.

Why Comparative Politics Is Important

The process of comparison lies at the very heart of analysis. One cannot easily make assertions about the particular characteristics of an event, institution or form of behaviour without making comparisons with another. If we are trying to be as scientific as possible, we need to examine situations where the phenomena we are investigating occur and compare these with other situations in which they do not occur. In natural sciences, such experimentation generally take place under what we commonly describe as *laboratory conditions* – that is, situations that are tightly controlled by regulating the environment and which can be recreated in order to test and re-test through experimentation. In a discipline such as political science, we cannot manufacture artificial conditions in this way, so political scientists use comparison as a means of analysing similarities and differences. Comparative politics also allows us to contextualise our analysis.

In general, most work in comparative politics compares between countries, although of course there is no reason why we should not compare between levels of political activity, such as how decisions are made at national (or macropolitical), local or regional levels of political organisation within one country, or indeed, how different political parties undertake specific activities. Comparison between how political activities are carried out in the present with how they operated in the past, often to assess efficiency or impact of a particular change or reform, also represent legitimate foci for comparative study.

Reasons for Comparing between Countries

Gaining knowledge

There are a number of particular reasons why analysts compare at a macropolitical level, such as the desire to find out more about politics in different countries, which has obvious practical applications in terms of aiding appreciation of how different practices operate. This is also believed to help in understanding our own country (Hague and Harrop, 2007: 84). We may also wish to verify whether there is evidence of behavioural trends or patterns, for example to see how far member states of the European Union have established similar types of practice in carrying out directives.

Evaluating good practice

A particular focus in recent years has been for the purpose of seeing whether institutions, policies or processes have been chosen because politicians wish to learn from successes or failures of institutions in other countries, and to emulate practice which has worked well. This is often found within studies of what has been labelled as 'policy transfer' which examine how governments have adopted particular policies, and accompanying advice, from countries where they have been hailed as innovative and successful, such as the Blair governments in the UK adopting social policies pioneered during the Clinton presidency in the USA (Daguerre, 2004; Dolowitz et al., 2000).

Objectivity

Another increasingly popular reason for comparing between countries is in order to avoid limited perspectives or ethnocentrism, and to boost objective approaches; indeed the two traditions underpinning political science, normative analysis and institutional empiricism, are themselves open to the criticism that they are based on Western values and hence biased. Behaviouralist techniques too have experienced difficulties when analysing countries with radically different cleavages and values. (Marsh and Stoker, 2002). To label this as ethnocentrism may perhaps give the criticism a rather value–laden label, but it does suggest that in order to make general statements about political processes, we need to compare data from a variety of situations.

Of course there may also be occasions when, conversely, it is desirable to substantiate claims of institutional 'uniqueness'. After all, how do we know something is 'unique' if we do not look at other situations?

One of the goals of political science is to produce testable hypotheses especially to establish that universal assertions can be substantiated and comparative techniques provide an excellent opportunity to assess how general hypotheses can be applied.

This also relates to the desire to establish a systematic, 'scientific' approach to analysis, especially in areas where experimental conditions are unable to be used and contexts cannot be replicated exactly. In part, this also helps to ensure reliability and credibility of the results of analysis and to validate new methods. So, is comparative politics an attempt to make political analysis more 'scientific'? In order to consider this question, we need to examine briefly how it developed.

Development of Comparative Politics

Classification

It is difficult to be precise about exactly when comparative politics was first discussed in the literature of political science, or indeed, political theory. In practice, however, it is quite easy to recognise the use of a comparative approach among several well-known theorists, one of the most quoted being Aristotle. His work also introduces us to one of the most widely-practised techniques employed by comparative analysts: the establishment and application of classification systems or typologies. Those operating at a macropolitical level attempt to classify forms of regime or political system on the basis of differential criteria, such as competitiveness of elections or respect for human rights, thus enabling us to differentiate between, for example, democratic, totalitarian or autocratic systems (Finer, 1970). Of course we also encounter classification systems for distinct institutional arrangements within the macro-polity, such as party systems. Who has not encountered discussion of the comparative advantages and limitations of single, two-party and multi-party systems? Or proportional and plurality electoral systems? But for the present let us concentrate on the macropolitical level and Aristotle's contribution.

Early Comparative Classification: Aristotle

Aristotle, writing around 350 BCE, was fascinated by the question of why different types of political regime had emerged in the ancient world. He was also a proponent of 'good' government and as such set about devising a classification system which would serve both as an explanation of difference and as a model to follow in building 'good' government systems. Aristotle's scheme is thus astonishingly clear and easy to follow as he bases his 'types' on two criteria – how many people rule and in whose interest do they rule? The resulting classification identifies six *types*, although there are only three basic *forms*, as demonstrated in Table 2.1. These three forms are based only on the number of 'rulers' – one, the few or the many. If we consider whether they rule in their own interests only, or in the interests of all citizens, we arrive at the six types, three of which are seen as operating on the basis of narrow interests, and hence are 'bad' – tyranny, oligarchy and mob rule, and the other three operate on the basis of the 'common good' and are thus perceived as 'good' – monarchy, aristocracy and democracy.

Table 2.1   Aristotle's classification of governments

	Type based on ruling interests	
Form	**Ruling in interests of ruler/s alone**	**Ruling in interests of all citizens**
Rule by single ruler	Tyranny	Monarchy
Rule by the few	Oligarchy	Aristocracy
Rule by the many	Mob rule	Democracy

Of course, with the benefit of hindsight, there are several flaws with this classification. First it is imbued with Aristotle's own preferences – for 'good' government and is thus favourable to monarchy, aristocracy or democracy, rather than being an objective system. Second, if we consider the conception of citizenship appropriate to Greece in the 4th century BCE, this is highly restrictive and discriminatory (see Chapter 9).

Much of this type of knowledge became submerged until the Renaissance in the 15th century and especially the Enlightenment in the 18th century. Renewed interest was largely due to the advent of modern theoretical ideas about the state (Hobbes, Locke, Montesquieu) and the growing importance of scientific method (Newton, Darwin).

Early modern comparative classification: Weber

A major figure to take up the notion of classification in the early 20th century was Max Weber. His three-type scheme was based on three authority structures, linked to cultural conventions and focused on the notion of stability (Lane and Errson, 1994: 11–12). First, Weber identifies traditional authority, which is based on custom and practice and associated with non-differentiated, non-modern societies in which rulers often combine roles and functions of political, military and religious leadership.

The second type, legal-rational authority, the epitome of modernity, is based on rationalist interpretation of office, which is divorced from religion, custom and practice, and is underpinned by the rule of law. Hence, leadership is contingent on the office-holder obeying the rules which circumscribe his/her functions and, at a political level, is based on gaining and holding office through legally constituted elections or other accepted procedures (Weber, 1922, 1978). All aspects of the modern state, according to Weber, are constituted and constrained in this manner, as we can see in the case of bureaucracy (see Chapter 6).

Weber's third type, charismatic authority, is characteristic of a society in a state of crisis or transition, brought about as a result of rapid change or dislocation. These situations require a leader, tantamount to a Biblical prophet, who will be able to command authority and obedience as a result of his/her personal qualities (or charisma) and enables the situation to be transformed and stabilised. By definition, this form of authority is temporary and eventually authority patterns will take on characteristics of one of the other types.

Modern comparative classification

The 'systems' approach

One of the most important influences on the development of modern comparative politics is the 'political systems' approach developed by Gabriel Almond and his colleagues in the 1960s (see especially Almond and Powell, 1966). Essentially, this adopts the view that all political systems, irrespective of regime, are based on the notion that there are seven universal functions to be fulfilled, albeit by different institutions and in different ways. Thus we have four input functions: political socialisation and recruitment, interest articulation, interest aggregation, political communication; and three output functions: rule making, rule application and rule adjudication. These last three are clearly derived from notions of the separation of the powers of government derived from 18th-century ideas that are most closely associated with Rousseau and Montesquieu. Hence we can compare both among and between regime types to see how these functions are carried out.

However, such an approach is also somewhat problematic since, although it purports to be objective, it is based, like Aristotle's, on the notion that a certain form of regime, liberal democracy, is a goal which other regimes should strive to emulate.

Regime types

Such broad schemes are also bound to be susceptible to criticism for failing to account for every possible example, or to distinguish adequately between variations within types, or to be 'timed-out' by new developments within the political arena. Finer's scheme, mentioned above, although commendable in its efforts to incorporate for subcategories to allow for maximum inclusion of all political regimes, is a good example of having been 'timed-out', and has been modified by several scholars, such as Crick (1973). In another example Ball and Peters (2005: 51–8) show how the threefold classification may no longer be relevant. Instead of the three liberal democratic, totalitarian and autocratic types discussed by Finer, they suggest four broad types, with the possibility of devising subcategories. This demonstrates how such typologies are constantly evolving.

Ball and Peters' typology

Ball and Peters retain the *liberal democratic* type that is based on a series of characteristics comprising open competition for power through elections on a universal franchise, held at regular intervals between several political parties. There is also relatively open recruitment to political office, separation of the powers of government, pressure groups able to operate and support for civil liberties and so forth. Indeed, this type covers most of the countries our three institutional approaches are set to deal with.

Communist systems are those which maintain an ideological basis derived from the work of Marx, have a legally dominant party, central planning of the economy, lack of separation of the powers of government and very limited support for pressure groups or civil liberties. Obvious examples here are Cuba or North Korea.

Transitional systems are those which are in the process of democratising, notably most of the former soviet republics and the countries of central Europe. However, there is considerable variation in the extent to which the process has become embedded and some of these countries, such as the Czech Republic, are more advanced along this route than others such as Albania.

Autocratic systems that are depicted as more difficult to classify, are seen as consisting either of conservative regimes or military dictatorships. Conservative regimes comprise traditional monarchies with weak political infrastructures, such as Morocco, conservative dictatorships, such as are prevalent among a number of former colonial states in Africa or theocracies such as Iran. Military dictatorships are either 'direct', such as the Democratic Republic of Congo or 'civilian-military' regimes, such as Peru under Fujimori. There are also, according to Ball and Peters, radical military regimes, although the overlap between all these sub-types is considerable and demonstrates the difficulties of categorisation.

Development of Comparative Method

There are a number of books that discuss different aspects of comparative politics, including how it developed, and many of them take different approaches and are often quite critical of each other. They do, however, tend to acknowledge that the development of comparative politics both as a sub-discipline of political science and in terms of making progress with genuinely comparative research, owes much to the efforts of one scholar – Jean Blondel. He has made a life's work of studying, applying, developing and promoting comparative method on an international basis, for purposes of both teaching and research. His depiction as to how the method has developed is instructive.

Blondel's contribution

Blondel (1995) asserts that there are three phases in the development of comparative (political) method in the 20th century.

Constitutionalist – legalistic phase

This comprised the first half of the 20th century. Since constitutions had proliferated in Europe, the Americas and other regions of the world, they were seen as 'modern' and used as subjects for comparison. It became clear that this was unsatisfactory since many examples of constitutions were not only distorted but, like the constitution of the former Soviet Union, were contradictory and misleading. The approach was useful in providing a basis for detailed examination of political institutions, but these were essentially descriptive rather than systematic or scientific. (See also Lowndes, 2002: 90–2.)

Behaviouralist phase

This developed mainly from the 1940s through the 1960s and was heavily influenced by American scholarship. Behavioural theory had begun to be applied as an explanatory tool to the national arena in the USA. It is based on an approach predicated on the belief that what should be studied is what actually happens in reality rather than what is stated in formal terms. So, scholars went out and asked people questions, analysed their responses and produced conclusions as to the behaviour of both people and institutions in the 'real world'.

This was soon extended to other countries and pointed out discrepancies in terms of the 'constitution' problem in many states. The growth in behavioural studies was made possible because new analytic frameworks, based on a 'systems' approach were being introduced, which highlighted not institutional structures but universal functions and modes of behaviour.

At a general level we could say that we have a 'political system', an 'economic system', a 'legal system' and so on. This goes beyond different terminology; it signifies a new way of looking at things. Sociological concepts were very influential in explaining differences in behaviour patterns between groups, for example, the relationship between class and voting behaviour. (See also Sanders, 2002.)

Neo-institutionalist phase

It soon became apparent, during the 1970s, that although behaviouralism was a more scientific approach to examining political structure, behaviour and events, and allowed for genuine comparison, it was an insufficient method for explaining all relevant phenomena.

In a sense, abandoning constitutionalism with its emphasis on institutions had resulted in 'throwing out the baby with the bathwater'. Institutions had been discarded more or less completely, with an over-emphasis on process or culture. So a movement based mainly on rationalist approaches started to re-examine institutions in a more eclectic manner, building on the earlier approaches rather than discarding them. Since then studies, although they may *focus* on one element, combine institutions, behaviour, practices and even constitutions. As Blondel says, 'this renders comparative (method) better able to account for the considerable variations which exist in the contemporary world' (1995: 9; see also Lowndes, 2002: 92–108).

The 'New Eclecticism' phase?

In order to demonstrate that comparative politics is constantly developing beyond Blondel, Landman (2003: 241–53) suggests a fourth phase – the New Eclecticism – which developed in the 1990s and tries to combine individual, institutional and cultural aspects of politics. This clearly takes account of developments in cultural explanations, especially post-materialist values, globalisation and alternative forms of political involvement and participation (see Landman, 2003: chapters 9 and 10).

To Qualify or to Quantify?

There are two methodological traditions in political science, indeed in the social sciences generally, qualitative methods and quantitative methods, with practitioners of each tradition tending to be critical of the other. Even today, as Peter John puts it '[t]he divide between quantitative and qualitative research remains highly pronounced' (2002: 216), although it also has to be said that this antagonism is now far less marked.

Qualitative Methods

There are a number of forms of qualitative method and some material may even take a numerical form, for example numbers of parliamentary bills passed under arrangements for private members' legislation when comparing success rates of such bills between different assemblies, or examining demographic and cultural characteristics in relation to territorial dispersion of different minority groups when trying to establish why federalism is more suitable as a means of resolving conflict in some multicultural states but not in others. This use of *numbers*, however, is in order to provide material for comparative purposes within studies which are clearly determined by qualitative methodology.

The key distinguishing features of qualitative methodology are that the research undertaken is interpretive, often descriptive, usually unstructured and lacking in objectivity. Indeed:

> [o]ne form consists of open-ended questions embedded in a structured interview or questionnaire ... We call this qualitative with a small *q* ... other forms, variously called fieldwork, participant observation and ethnography, are what we call qualitative with a big *Q*; they rely almost entirely on open-ended explorations of people's words, thoughts, actions and intentions. (Judd et al., 1991: 299)

Devine points out, however, that '[q]ualitative methods, therefore, are good at capturing meaning, process and content' (2002: 199). Examples of different forms of qualitative methods used in comparative political research are in-depth interviews, focus groups and participant observation.

In-depth interviews

In-depth interviews are widely used in a variety of studies that seek to establish what roles specific political actors play in policy-making, decision-making, campaigning, and so on. Such interviews do not use highly structured 'yes–no' type questions which form the basis of most large-scale survey research but ask open-ended, unstructured questions such as 'how did you go about establishing a campaign to change the party's strategy on Europe?' Or, 'as a minister at the time of this major trade union reform, how significant was the role played by your senior civil servants?' The conduct of the interview is based on a general 'interview guide', which pinpoints the main areas the interviewer wishes to investigate and allows for particularly interesting or pertinent remarks to be identified and elaborated (Devine, 2002: 198–9). Devine shows how such methods can gain useful, additional insight into areas that have long been regarded as the domain of qualitative analysts, such as why people switched votes (White et al., 1999). Comparative studies using this technique would be either primary studies which compare and contrast practice between different tiers of government or specific roles, such as ministerial input into certain types of decision in different countries.

Focus groups

A development of in-depth interviewing that has been used more extensively in recent years is the focus group interview technique where interviewers bring together a small group of people and have a simple list of topics that respondents are asked to talk about. There are no set formats for questions and interviewers may join in the conversation and give their own views. The technique has been used widely in market research since the 1940s and was taken up by social scientists as offering an insight into 'the dynamic effects of interaction on expressed opinion' (Fielding, 1993: 137).

In political science it has been used either as a major methodological tool underpinning a study, such as Gamson's (1992) analysis of political opinion formation in the USA or as one of several techniques employed, such as in Needham's (2007) investigation of the use of consumerism in public service reform in different levels of government in the UK. The method has, however, been treated with a certain amount of disdain due to its use by political parties in, allegedly, tailoring policies to suit public demands. Focus groups are also useful in the initial stages of more formal, structured interview situations in order to acquire appropriate background information and build up a context or to get acquainted with phraseology and jargon used by a target population.

Participant observation

Participant observation (also designated as ethnography) is a technique developed primarily by anthropologists in order to build an in-depth appreciation of indigenous cultures. It is also heavily influenced by the Chicago School of sociology exemplified by the work of Erving Goffman in the 1960s, which focused on the behaviour of people in everyday situations in a variety of institutions, such as prisons or asylums (Goffman, 1961). Basically a researcher enters an institution or organisation 'undercover' and participates in its activities without the knowledge of the regular participants. As such he/she has the opportunity to experience both what it is like to operate in the particular environment and to observe the behaviour of others. It is not a widely used method in political investigation although there have been notable examples. One of these is Fielding's (1981) controversial study of the National Front as the embodiment of the neo-fascist right in Britain in the 1970s, where he explains his methods as a combination of participant observation (the most controversial aspect), content analysis of documents and interviews with both participants in the movement and critics. Other studies using similar techniques have dealt with interest groups and protest movement in the UK (Roseneil, 1995) and the USA (Eliasoph, 2000). In comparative terms, results of studies based on participant observation undertaken in different countries can be compared and it is especially suited to projects which use a cultural framework.

Limitations of qualitative approaches

Criticisms of qualitative methodology – traditionally levelled by quantitative analysts – are that it is prone to subjectivity, prejudice, idiosyncrasy and ethnocentrism. Hence it cannot be used as a basis for generalisation. Essentially it is not scientific and is thus an inappropriate basis for comparative projects. This is because the results of each example of qualitative analysis are closely associated with the specific analyst(s) involved in the individual studies and hence cannot be treated as sufficiently similar to any other. However, these sorts of criticisms are rather harsh as there is often significant effort at objectivity and avoidance of ethnocentrism. Since the overriding aim of most qualitative analysis is to explain and understand the *meaning* attached to actions, events or argument, there is no reason why different meanings cannot be compared. Furthermore, if we take good design, clarity of definition and rigour of investigation and analysis as being significant elements of scientific inquiry, qualitative projects can obviously aspire to be scientific (Devine, 2002).

Quantitative Methods

Quantitative social science methodology developed mainly from positivist philosophy and seeks to be objective and scientific. One of the main concerns of quantitative scholars is accurate and objective conceptual definition whereby such theoretically derived concepts can be operationalised and measured (Sanders, 2002). The work of quantitative analysts is susceptible to statistical analysis in order to estimate inference, contingency or causality in terms of making statements about relationships between variables. Essentially this refers to scholarship that is based on measurement; answering questions such as 'how much?', 'how many?' or 'how often?' as well as 'why?'

Advantages and limitations of quantitative approaches

Despite John's (2002) assertion that one of the great strengths of quantitative analysis is that it produces enormous amounts of data that can be utilised by other analysts, there are nonetheless limitations to such quantitative studies. It is most important that the process of collection and treatment of this material is managed effectively and ethically, and there should be a realisation that quantitative analysis cannot give a full picture; at best it will generate close estimates. After all, political behaviour is a complex set of activities, informed by context and ideas. It is thus essential that the measures used in the production of these estimates are as appropriate (valid) and independent (reliable) as possible as this will mean that results will be more credible. This means that the measuring device must be completely unrelated to the material under investigation. Choice of precise data to be used, especially when using samples, is of crucial importance for quantitative projects.

It is essential that measuring devices in quantitative analysis are reliable as this means that whoever uses a device to replicate an experiment, the results will be the same. Bouma and Atkinson (1995: 104) give the example of 10 students each weighing the same baby on the same set of scales getting the same result – or a very close approximation – being a measure of the *reliability* of the scale, that is of the measuring device.

Social scientific methods of observation represent measuring devices and need to be proved to be reliable but may differ quite widely in type. Among the best known are questions used in surveys, for example, those that seek to determine partisan identification. However, many of the questions common to surveys of voting behaviour actually measure something else, such as voter preferences (John, 2002: 219). To simply ask 'how strongly do you support the (named) party?' is also problematic and it may be more beneficial to construct a 'scale' of strength of support, ranging from very weakly to very strongly. Bouma and Atkinson (1995) outline five types of quantitative investigation.

Types of quantitative investigation

Simple case study

This type of study answers the question 'What is going on?' by examining a single case for a period of time and recording results. This may involve an individual, a small group, an institution or indeed a country. No comparison is made with similar entity. This is not particularly useful for comparative purposes, although it may be useful for purposes of deciding whether a larger project might be viable, or for initial testing of hypotheses.

Comparative studies

These studies obviously involve comparison of the same measurements for more than one individual, group, institution or country. The basic question is 'Are groups A, B and C different and if so, how do they differ and why?' This is a common approach adopted in comparative politics and such studies require selection of relevant variables which are meaningful to all cases chosen, as well as selection of appropriate measurement devices. The concepts involved here clearly need to be able to 'travel' across time and space, in other words, to have the same meaning in all situations covered. There are many examples of this type of study in comparative politics whereby groups of scholars adopt a common analytic framework and each individual applied this to a different country. This is especially useful for studies of political parties, such as the study reported in Broughton and Donovan (1999).

Longitudinal studies

Studies such as these involve more than one case study of the same group. Such studies are undertaken with similar time intervals between them. The basic question is 'Has change occurred over time, and if so, how much change?' A variant of this is to measure a situation, such as support for a particular party, then introduce a stimulus or catalyst, such as suggesting that certain policy changes would occur and measure levels of potential support again afterwards to measure any change which could have occurred as a result of this.

Longitudinal comparison

This approach is a combination of the above two mentioned – comparative and longitudinal. Unlike the practice in comparative studies, the observations would be carried out at regular intervals because change(s) over time are being looked at.

Experimental studies

If the aim of a study is to examine how change in *one* variable has an effect on *another*, then a form of experimental study may be appropriate. As Bouma and Atkinson

(1995: 126) assert, the researcher has to have some control over variation in the stimuli. In brief, such designs will often involve an experimental group and a control group, which will be as similar as possible. One group will be given a stimulus, the other will not, and their reactions will be compared.

More and more data generated by quantitative research studies is being made available for secondary use on a wider scale. Some of this is 'official' material published by governments or international institutions, such as that produced by *Eurobarometer*, the regular reports of research commissioned by the European Union to assess a variety of opinion and practice within the member states. In 2007, for example, *Eurobarometer* reported on discrimination across the European Union. This enables material to be utilised for a variety of related studies. Other material is produced as a result of academic studies, such as the Comparative Manifestos Project which has produced two extensive data sets covering estimates of postwar manifesto content and other numerical material in over 50 countries (Budge et al., 2001; Klingemann et al., 2006). Obviously it is very important to ensure that such secondary quantitative material is reliable and there have been a number of concerns expressed about the veracity of official statistics (May, 1997).

Whether to choose a qualitative or quantitative approach to comparative analysis is often determined by variables such as the nature of the data concerned or whether the researcher adopts a structured or unstructured strategy. Such differences between the approaches are summarised in Table 2.2.

Table 2.2   Comparing qualitative and quantitative research

Aspect of research	Quantitative	Qualitative
Relationship between subject and researcher	Distant	Close
Research strategy	Structured	Unstructured
Nature of data	Hard, reliable	Rich, deep
Relationship between theory and research	Confirmation	Emergent

Source: Adapted from Bouma and Atkinson (1995: 208).

Orginal source Bryman, A. (1994) *Quantity and Quality in Social Research*. London: Unwin Hyman.

Qualitative–Quantitative Synthesis?

There are obviously clear distinctions between the qualitative and quantitative traditions but this does not mean that each set of methods is inaccessible to the other. Indeed, there is every reason to use both qualitative and quantitative methods to examine particular phenomena in order to maximise authenticity of outcomes – a practice often referred to as methodological triangulation (Denzin, 1970). Reference was made earlier to qualitative efforts to understand voter volatility (White et al., 1999) which complements the work undertaken by the British Election Studies (see Clarke et al., 2004). Studies which use content analysis techniques, such as those by the Comparative Manifestos Project cited above also represent efforts to synthesise best practice of both traditions.

In recent years there has been greater willingness by both qualitative and quantitative practitioners to listen to each other more effectively and discuss ways of combining best practice in both traditions; referred to as methodological pluralism (Read and Marsh, 2002). In many ways, the distinction between the two traditions is false and in part derives from the practice of differential focus on specific questions. For example, quantitative practitioners have prioritised the quest for causal, objective explanation whereas those using qualitative methods have concentrated on subjective meaning because their subjects are human beings.

What is important is that the research project is well-designed and that the specific methodologies employed are appropriate and reliable. This has also been facilitated by technological advance in terms of the development of computer-assisted research techniques which can help minimize human error. Much of the 'stand-off' between quantitative and qualitative practitioners was a function of their insistence that their differences were not only a function of methodology but also related to differences in epistemology (see Chapter 1).

The challenge of postmodernism?

Some commentators now believe that the epistemological foundations of the social sciences have indeed been undermined by the emergence of postmodernism (Devine, 2002). Citing Williams and May (1996), Devine suggests that indeed the epistemological roots of modern thought which have developed since the Enlightenment are under severe pressure from the critique offered by postmodernism; methodologies too, to the extent that their ability to present a *true* picture of reality has been severely criticised. What they represent, according to a postmodern perspective, may be simply a reflection of the researcher's prejudice, so that efforts to engage with consolidating credibility of results are meaningless (Devine, 2002; Denzin, 1997). However, as Devine further points out, the postmodern focus is 'caught in a hall of mirrors' (2002: 203) since it is far too preoccupied with *researchers* rather than *research topics*, and, as an approach, postmodernism as yet has been little involved in empirical political science despite the fact that there is growing theoretical interest in its ontology and epistemology.

One such area is discourse theory which, to date, has not really 'engaged with mainstream political science' (Rhodes, 2006: 100) but which offers considerable scope for analysis of cultural factors and power relationships. Discourse analysts focus specifically on the nature of language, as set within specific contexts. As such, much of the analysis undertaken by discourse theorists focuses on textual or documentary materials, such as speeches or transcripts of exchanges among individuals, for example debates in parliaments (Fairclough, 2003). Much of the theoretical basis of such a methodology is derived from linguistics theory.

How to Compare?

So, how (and what) should we compare?

Should we compare phenomena *in general*, for example, should we compare constitutions, parliaments, bureaucracies, across as many as possible of the range of representative democracies?

Or should we compare these phenomena *between states*, for example compare the American constitution with the French constitution or the German Basic Law?

Should we engage in *historical comparison*, which involves making comparisons between one period and an earlier or later one? For example, is it useful to compare electoral reforms which took place in the early stages of democratisation in established democracies with those undertaken in recent years in recently democratised countries? This form of analysis allows us to compare whether procedures, policies, practices and so forth have changed over time. However, if long time periods are examined, it may be difficult to isolate causal factors.

Should we focus on *large-scale comparisons*, using many examples or cases, possibly based on secondary aggregate data, such as United Nations indicators like GDP per capita or attitudinal studies such as the World Values Survey or *Eurobarometer*?

Or should we make systematic comparisons between small numbers of cases, for example, to test propositions, for example, that human rights legislation is more likely to be enacted and supported in established democratic states than in those recently emerged from dictatorship? We then of course need to determine how many countries would be appropriate.

Alternatively, we might favour individual case studies, possibly in conjunction with other investigators. This would be either because we wish to engage in more interpretive analysis, or because we want to test theoretical propositions and show 'deviant' behaviour (Landman, 2003: 34–5).

'Most similar' or 'most different'?

A key question, as with all comparative studies to an extent, is should we seek to compare countries which are *very similar* or which are *very different*. This was indeed a central debating point in comparative politics until fairly recently and is an argument which dates back to the 19th century and especially to the work of J.S. Mill

(Dogan and Kazancigil, 1994; Hopkin, 2002: 252–5; Peters, 1998; Przeworski and Teune, 1970).

The rationale for using *very similar* countries is that meaningful comparison and theory testing can only take place where countries are as similar as possible in the area being tested, for example, if we are looking at aspects of coalition government, we would only look at countries which regularly experience coalition governments. In this way we should be able to identify the factors which explain differences. Conversely, if we compare *very different* countries and the theory still holds, it is arguable that this strengthens the applicability of the theory.

The choice, yet again, will depend in part on the purpose of the project being undertaken and the availability of appropriate data.

Problems with Comparative Political Analysis

Numbers of cases

If we are comparing across nations, there is likely to be a problem with limited numbers of cases or countries. Comparative analysis is always constrained by the number of cases with reliable available data, which means that such analysis should always acknowledge the limitations of what it can achieve. This is especially problematic in quantitative analysis where few cases mean that we can only employ a small number of variables. In order to overcome this we may be tempted to compare 'like with unlike', for example, individual behaviour with an organization's behaviour, which would lead to completely unreliable outcomes.

If we only have only a few cases this might lead to problems of over-generalisation or scaling up results that might apply to small groups of country of institution and infer that they apply in the generality of cases, a situation termed the 'individualistic fallacy'. The most common examples of this sort arise when generalising from individual responses in surveys to whole districts or even countries. The opposite situation, inferring behaviour of individuals from aggregate data like censuses is equally problematic and is known as the 'ecological fallacy' (Landman, 2003: 53–5).

Following a common framework

Comparative analysis often relies upon similar analysis being undertaken in several countries; analysis that is often carried out by different analysts, possibly not at the same time. This also encompasses differential definition of concepts by researchers (over and above problems of cultural consistency), especially in terms of consistency and specificity. How do we know that each analyst is working in exactly the same way?

Problems of cultural relevance

This implies that terms of reference will be constant, but in different cultures, different terms may not be constant, for example, 'liberal' means something different in the UK and the USA, and these are countries which purport to use the same language (see Landman, 2003: 436).

Interdependence

Cases, even nation-states, may not be independent of each other. Practices in one country can become the norm in another due to interdependent links, which have been heightened as a result of globalisation. This can limit our scope for comparison, though by the same token.

Inappropriate indicators

Comparing nations using criteria that may only be applicable to one type of nation can be problematical. Thus, indicators of economic or political development may be easily applicable in Western Europe, but not so applicable in other parts of the world where economies and society may be structured very differently. Comparative cultural studies are particularly vulnerable to this problem.

Selection bias

This is a particular problem for comparative analysts as we are usually unable to select our sample cases for analysis on a random basis. Hence we cannot be certain that the objects of our studies are representative. In order to overcome this we need to ensure that all the examples we choose are subject to intervention by the same variables – unless we are engaging in specific experimental studies that require application of stimuli to one group but not another.

Value judgement

Finally, there is the problem of maintaining objectivity. At the very least, we should avoid introducing our own personal prejudices, based on approval or disapproval of behaviour and practice. This may possibly be related to cultural or ideological positions and has been seen as a particular problem in qualitative analysis. However, there is recognition by quantitative analysts that even the most empirically oriented approach is not devoid of some degree bias which may be embedded within the analytic perspective itself, and this should be minimised by good and transparent research design and practice (King et al., 1994).

What all this suggests is that in comparative analysis there are a number of inherent problems. Despite these we can minimise their potential impact by adopting a very clear and systematic approach. It is most important to have a clear rationale and to be explicit about the purpose for engaging in comparative analysis in terms of what it is meant to achieve, how it relates to answering a specific question or testing an hypothesis and ensuring that there is an analytic framework that enables selection of appropriate methods and data. If we are able to meet these challenges successfully we are well on the way to producing effective comparative analysis and explanation.

SUMMARY

- Comparative method attempts to make the study of politics more systematic, analytical and scientific, using scientific concepts and variables which are able to be 'measured' effectively.

- It has developed through a series of phases since the mid-twentieth century. Each has sought to build on and improve techniques.

- Comparative analysis may be carried out using qualitative or quantitative methods or a combination of the two.

- There are a series of comparative approaches from large-scale comparisons, using many countries and based mainly on aggregate international indices, such as GNP or surveys to small numbers of country-based cases or single country-based case studies, often following a common framework.

- There are a number of problems associated with comparative analysis but the effects of these can be minimised by having a clearly defined purpose with a rationale, a theoretical model, appropriate methods, transparent data collection techniques and clear, evidence-based research. Such an approach lends itself to qualitative, quantitative or any other form of methodology.

FURTHER READING

Ball, A. and Peters, B.G. (2005) *Modern Politics and Government*, 7th edn. Basingstoke: Palgrave Macmillan.

A straightforward, concise introduction to the study of politics which facilitates better understanding of the basis of comparative politics, mainly through classification systems.

Caramani, D. (ed.) (2008) *Comparative Politics*. Oxford: Oxford University Press.

A new publication which offers a wide range of examples as well as further discussion on theories and methods.

Hague, M. and Harrop, M. (2007) *Comparative Politics: An Introduction*, 7th edn. Basingstoke: Palgrave Macmillan.

A clear and easily accessible introduction to comparative politics with useful examples and case studies.

Landman, T. (2003) *Issues and Methods in Comparative Politics: An Introduction*, 2nd edn. London: Routledge.

A substantial introduction to the nature and methods of comparative political analysis, which draws on contemporary material and includes a useful discussion on institution building.

Landman, T. (2008) *Issues and Methods in Comparative Politics: An Introduction*, 3rd edn. London and New York: Routledge.

For those who would like to pursue a more quantitative approach.

Marsh, D. and Stoker, G. (eds) (2002) *Theory and Methods in Political Science*, 2nd edn. Basingstoke: Palgrave Macmillan.

The rich variety of chapter topics in this book provides an appreciation of how a comparative approach can utilise different methods and frameworks.

QUESTIONS FOR DISCUSSION

(1) How has the field of comparative politics developed and what are the main contemporary trends in comparative politics today?

(2) Is a 'science' of comparative politics possible?

(3) Does it matter whether we use large numbers of cases or very few when we undertake comparative analysis?

(4) How would you design a project to test a proposition that 'human rights' are more likely to be supported in liberal democracies than in autocratic systems?

Key Words for Chapter 2

classification systems / comparative method / concepts / measurement / most different / most similar / qualitative methods / quantitative methods / scientific method / typologies / variables

Part 2

INSTITUTIONS

3 **The Nation-state and Nationalism**

Brendan O'Duffy

CHAPTER OUTLINE

This chapter considers two central building blocks for comparative political analysis – the nation-state and nationalism. After explaining how these developments came about, different theoretical approaches are applied to exemplify contrasts and similarities in terms of how nationalism and the nation-state deal with problems associated with fostering national unity and dealing with minority groups.

Introduction

The nation-state is the central unit of comparative politics. While comparative political scientists might be interested in the specifics of political institutions such as the legislature, executive, bureaucracy and the judiciary, they tend to compare the institutions of one nation-state against those of another nation-state. The main reason for the focus on the nation-state is that since the 19th century the nation-state has evolved to become the legal entity maintaining ultimate authority (sovereignty) in international law. Thus both the internal aspects of sovereignty such as those that determine individual citizenship, as well as external aspects of sovereignty such as those determining borders and the legality of war, are predicated on the assumption that the nation-state is the primary unit of authority and, by extension, political legitimacy.

But why do we refer to the 'nation-state' rather than either 'nation' or 'state'? The reason, as developed in this chapter, is that the two concepts are co-dependent: neither makes sufficient sense or describes reality without the other. Nations, by definition, seek statehood (though they may settle for internal autonomy within states, such as contemporary Scotland within the UK or Catalonia within Spain) and states, in practice, try to enhance their stability and legitimacy by constructing or enhancing a national identity among its population.

Defining Terms and Concepts

Like the hyphenated concept of 'liberal-democracy', the nation-state represents a relationship between two (usually) compatible and interdependent phenomena. For our purposes, the *nation* will be defined, following Anthony Smith (1998), as a human collectivity that shares a common culture (including historical memories of a shared past, language, religion or other aspects of ethnicity), is aware of its collective identity and expects to be governed by and live with members of that collectivity. A nation differs from an *ethnic group* in that an ethnic group, such as the Berbers of Morocco, Coptic Christians in Egypt, indigenous communities in Latin America or immigrants to European countries, do not normally aspire to separate statehood but instead are usually willing to settle for recognition and protection of minority rights within existing nation-states.

However, when, an ethnic group develops political aspirations for statehood or substantial autonomy within an existing state, we can refer to such movements as *ethno-national* in the sense that they seek to achieve institutionalised power over a defined territory for the benefit of a particular ethnic group. Thus, among the Tamil minority in Sri Lanka there evolved after independence in 1948, movements among the minority seeking linguistic and educational rights protections as a minority. Their limited success led to the emergence from the early 1970s of an explicitly ethno-national separatist movement seeking independence for a new state – Tamil Eelam – which they hoped to carve out of the island-state of Sri Lanka.

The *state* will be defined, following Max Weber, as the legally recognised institutions and territorial boundaries, within which the recognised authority monopolises the legitimate use of force. *Nationalism*, as an ideology, will be defined, following Ernest Gellner, who treats ethnic boundaries as equivalent to Smith's nation, as a 'theory of political legitimacy, which requires that ethnic [or national] boundaries should not cut across political ones, and in particular, that ethnic [or national] boundaries within a given state ... should not separate power-holders from the rest' (1983: 1).

Thus defined, a nation-state is an ideal-type that is not meant to describe reality but instead as a concept that describes a *variable* relationship between 'peoples' and the institutions of government within a specific territory. This relationship is highly variable because only about 10 per cent of states can be considered 'pure' nation-states, where the population is predominantly ethnically homogenous (with more than 90 per cent of the population from a single ethnic group [Connor, 1994]). Examples of pure nation-states include Norway, Japan, Iceland, Germany, Austria and post-Second World War Poland. In about 25 per cent of states, the largest national group accounts for between 50 per cent and 74 per cent of the population. Examples include Switzerland where German speakers represent 64 per cent of the population, Belgium where Flemish speakers form about 60 per cent of the population. Finally, in about 30 per cent of states, the largest national group accounts for less than half of the total population. Examples of this last group include Nigeria where the Yoruba people represent just over 20 per cent, Ethiopia where the Amhara represent about 38 per cent and India, where Hindi speakers represent about 40 per cent of the population (O'Leary, 2001: Table 1). Not surprisingly, nationalist challenges to state legitimacy are common in multi-national states, and often violent since nationalist challenges to existing states tend to deny the state the monopoly of legitimate force.

The variability of the nation-state relationship can be explained by the political force of nationalism, particularly its ability to justify statehood according to ethnic and/or national identities. The following section presents an overview of the dominant types of nationalist movement to emerge in the modern era, especially since the early 19th century.

Nationalism as a Political Ideology: Liberal and Illiberal Forms

Most scholars of nationalism agree that it emerges as an ideology in Europe from the end of the 18th century, initially associated with the liberal principle of popular sovereignty, as a secular replacement for traditional forms of authority. Nationalism is therefore closely associated with democratisation and anti-imperial (including anti-colonial) political developments. The *sacral monarchies* of the middle ages, which based their justification of authority on the divine (godly ordained) right of kings, were increasingly challenged by the secular humanist ideas and beliefs produced by the Enlightenment in the early modern period in Europe. Rationalist principles of scientific discovery, the chronicles of explorers in describing civilisations of other gods, the spread of literacy, all challenged divine justifications of political power by groups attempting to establish the supremacy of parliamentary forms of government. Sacral monarchies, such as the Holy Roman Empire, gave way to hereditary monarchies in most of Europe from the 15th to 17th centuries.

Resting power on a hereditary lineage was no longer secure in the face of challenges from emerging bourgeoisie as pressure for participation in representative institutions increased. The French Revolution of 1789 famously justified the overthrow of not just the corrupt monarchy of Louis XVI but also the principle of monarchic rule by stating in the Declaration of the Rights of Man, 'The principle of all sovereignty resides in the

Nation'. Earlier, in 1776, Britain's American colonies had similarly declared their sovereign independence '*by Authority of the good People of these Colonies*, solemnly publish and declare, that these United Colonies are, and of Right ought to be Free and Independent States'. Earlier still, in 1642, the English parliamentarian Ludlow justified the revolutionary seizure of the powers of ordinance (to raise and fund an army or militia) by asking 'whether the King (Charles I) should govern as a god by his will, and *the nation* be governed by a force like beasts; or whether *the people* should be governed by laws made by themselves, and live under a government derived from their own consent' (quoted in Tanner, 1966: 118).

The advantages of cultivating national consent for governance were exposed most substantially by the early modern state's challenge to maintain larger standing armies and military power. From 1700 to 1870 military costs increase state 'absorption' of five five per cent to 25–35 per cent, and conscription of five per cent of national populations (see Figure 3.1). As taxes and conscription rose, demands from the public for participation in governance rose, forcing states to justify sacrifices on national grounds.

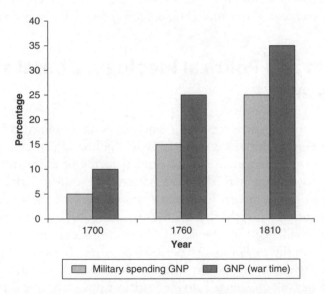

Figure 3.1   European military spending as percentage of GNP (peacetime and wartime)
Source: Mann, M. (1995) 'A political theory of nationalism and its excesses', in S. Periwal (ed.) *Notions of Nationalism*. Budapest: Central European University Press.

The need to cultivate national loyalty to the state was exemplified by English parliamentary debate in 1776, on the use of foreign mercenaries (professional soldiers) in the war against the rebellious American colonies. A member of parliament quoted from Sir Walter Raleigh's (1552–1618) *History of the World*:

They [foreign professional soldiers] are seditious, unfaithful, disobedient, devourers, and destroyers of all places and countries, whither they are drawn, being held by no other bond than their own commodity. Yea, that which is most fearful among such hirelings is, that they have often, and in time of greatest extremity, not only refused to fight in defence of those who have entertained them, but revolted to the contrary part, to the utter ruin of those princes and states who have trusted them. (Adolphus, 1802: 355)

That Raleigh could, already in the 16th century, argue that foreigners were untrustworthy exemplifies the direct relationship between nationalism and state legitimacy, at least within the English/British context. More generally, these assumptions about loyalty and constitutional independence (for the American colonists) assumed the existence of distinct nations as the holders of state sovereignty and the equally important liberal condition of consent, which remains the distinguishing criteria between liberal and illiberal forms of nationalism.

These early and successful justifications for nation-state consolidation and/or liberation from autocratic, monarchic rule were exemplary movements that were adopted and adapted by a swathe of 19th-century European nationalist movements, both on the continent and among European colonies in the Americas and eventually by anti-colonial nationalist movements in Asia and Africa in the 20th century. Peter Alter describes three main types of nationalist movement which nicely demonstrate the liberal and illiberal forms that nationalism can take, often within the same countries.

Risorgimento nationalism

This term is derived from the Italian word for 'resurrection'. This form of nationalism emerged in the early 19th century as 'national awakenings' led mainly by bourgeois professionals and intellectuals who demanded emancipation from the rule of absolutist imperial rulers. Thus the Greek nationalist movement against Ottoman (mainly Turkish) rule, the German nationalist movements against the princely states of the Prussian-dominated Confederation and Italian Risorgimento against Austrian rule of the Hapsburg Empire, all justified the territorial unification of culture communities. The ideas of the 'German Romantics' such as Johann Gottfried Herder were influential in justifying statehood to enhance and promote meritocratic governance to defend and promote the unique genius of the German linguistic culture. For Herder, the self-determination of individual will could only be achieved within ones 'mother tongue' because of the unique meaning revealed through a 'native' language. These nationalist ideas were also consistent with liberalism in the sense that they celebrated the unique genius of all natural nations. The Italian Giuseppe Mazzini believed that '[e]very people has its special mission which will co-operate towards the general mission of humanity. That mission is its nationality. Nationality is sacred' (quoted in Cowie and Wolfson, 1985: 383).

Because of their initial compatibility with liberalism, nationalist movements in absolutist states tended to be initiated by educated middle classes, writers, academics and lawyers who resented their blocked upward mobility within the bureaucracies, armies and economies of such states. Their arguments against the corruption and weakness of the imperial state then appealed to a cross-class alliance including commercial and industrial classes seeking expansion of markets, but also to the urban petty bourgeoisie, civil servants, artisans, peasants who sought to reform or abolish the links between large landowners and the imperial state. These kinds of alliances were characteristic, with important variations, of the nationalist movements that united Germany in 1871, Italy in 1862 and the unsuccessful Irish Home Rule movement from around 1882 (Alter, 1985: 69–76).

Integral nationalism

This is classified by Alter (1985) as a 'counter-type' to Risorgimento nationalism because it subsumes the individual into serving the nation-state. The proponents of integral nationalist projects portrayed the nation as a secular equivalent of religion, but one that was influenced by the Darwinian principles of natural selection and survival of the fittest. The result, as exemplified by the ultra-nationalisms of the National Socialism movement in Germany from the 1930s, in fascist Italy and in Japan, were forms of nationalism based on a creed of absolute devotion to the state and its rulers, a demonisation of enemies within and without and territorial expansion to integrate ethnic kin and/or conquer lesser peoples (Mann, 1995).

What is remarkable about this type of nationalism is that it was supported by some of the same classes that championed liberal Risorgimento nationalism in previous generations, not just in Germany and Italy, but also in popular forms of expansionist national imperialism in Victorian Britain (for example during the Boer War), in France after their defeat by the Germans in the 1870–1871 Franco-German War, as well as in the 1930s in Spain, Belgium, Austria, France and Ireland. The old and new middle classes, facing threats from industry and international capital above and the unionising proletariat below, supported these movements. Having liberated themselves from absolutist monarchies, the same classes of artisans, civil servants, shopkeepers and middle and large farmers supported fascist nationalism to protect their interests and pride from the extreme insecurity of the depressed 1930s. In states such as Germany, where bureaucratic authoritarianism survived in alliance with large landowning *rentier* classes, the transitions to democratic governance from the last quarter of the 19th century produced strains that overwhelmed state institutions and led to strident demands for re-integration of the national state and by extension, the expulsion of ethnic minorities, who became 'enemies of the Reich' in Nazi Germany.

Reform nationalism

This contrasts with both Risorgimento and integral nationalism in that it is generally a product of state elites, bureaucrats, military leaders and members of the nobility who develop a top-down programme to reform an existing nation-state from within. This type of nationalism usually emerges when non-western countries face competition and cultural influences from western nation-states, as exemplified by the nationalist reforms undertaken by Japan in the second half of the 19th century, in response to American military and commercial domination of Japan's island territory. Under the Meiji dynasty, from 1868 to 1912, Japanese elites adopted western-style nationalist institutional reforms to professionalise the state and transform the feudal economy into a thriving industrial economy able to develop regional military dominance by the turn of the century (Alter, 1985: 35–6).

Similar state-led reform projects characterise the style of nationalism that developed in Turkey after the break-up of the Ottoman Empire after the First World War. The movement led by the army officer Mustafa Kemal (after 1934 he became known as Kemal Atatürk) was sparked by the Greek occupation of Izmir in 1919. It sought to reform the Turkish nation away from the multi-national ethos and diffuse territoriality of the Ottoman Empire into a composite, republican form of nationalism based on vernacular Turkish (rather than Arabic) language within a more finite (though with contested borders) and defensible territory. Atatürk believed it was necessary to adopt the western republican principle of secularism (separation of religion and state) in order to cultivate loyalty to the Turkish Republic rather than to transnational Islam. Reforms included the abolition of the caliphate in 1924, followed by the banning of the fez and the veil, the adoption of Latin and Greek into the school curriculum to replace Arabic and Farsi, and the creation of a latinised Turkish alphabet. Under Atatürk's secular Republic, ethnic minorities such as Kurds, refugees from the Caucasus (Circassians) and Bosnians were not recognised as distinct groups but merely as members of the Turkish republic who were suffering from false consciousness.

This overview of the dominant forms of nationalism is meant to demonstrate that nationalism can take many forms and evolve from liberal to illiberal within the same culture, depending on the internal and external pressures on the state caused by processes of modernisation. We should not treat nationalism as a static ideology associated with particular nation-states but instead as one that can change and adapt to political, economic and social circumstances. In the contemporary UK for example, we can see undercurrents of all three types of nationalism. The quest by Scottish and Welsh nationalists for devolution and by Irish nationalists in Northern Ireland for Irish reunification could all be interpreted as forms of Risorgimento nationalism in which these historic ethno-nations are resurrecting national ambitions for autonomy and potential statehood. Similarly, the response of some far-right groups to large-scale immigration has led groups like the British National Party to call for integral forms of national policies to limit immigration and promote Englishness. Finally, the Labour Government led by Gordon Brown has responded to these pressures by calling for state-led reforms of education, citizenship and immigration policies to promote Britishness, based on tolerance, liberty and a sense of fair play (Brown, 2008). These British examples also reveal the potential for the state to regulate the politics of nationalism in ways that avoid the excesses of previous phases of national challenges to the state system, of which more will be said in the concluding section of this chapter.

In order to develop a better understanding of the conditions under which these different types of nationalism emerge and flourish we need to compare and contrast competing theories of nationalism, according to the analytical framework developed by Mark Pennington in Chapter 1.

Theories of Nationalism

Modernist theories

There are two main strands in the academic study of nationalism and the evolution of nation-states. On one side are 'modernists' who, while disagreeing on economic, political and military aspects of modernity, agree that nations and nationalism are by-products of the modern era, (that is from the beginning of the 19th century). Peter Alter's classification as previously mentioned exemplifies a modernist perspective in treating nations and nationalism as by-products of forces of modernity. Different modernist theorists emphasise different aspects of modernisation but they tend to agree that nationalism as a belief system grounded on the primacy of the nation-state as the highest level of political authority is only possible in the modern era.

By modernity, these scholars generally recognise the transformative *structural* effects of developments such as the:

- mechanisation and commercialisation of agriculture from the late 16th century in north-west Euope;
- expansion of national reading publics allowed for by the standardisation of vernacular languages;
- expansion of trade enabled by surplus agricultural production;
- development of mercantile capital and naval power;
- industrialisation and urbanisation;
- shift from traditional to rational/legal bases of authority;
- bureaucratisation of government administration;
- expansion of taxation and conscription into standing armies to pay for and execute large-scale warfare;
- growth of democratisation from the early 19th century.

Rational choice theories

A second strand of modernist thinking follows a *rational choice* approach by emphasising that the structural changes associated with modernisation still leave room for individual autonomy in deciding whether to exit from, voice reformist opposition to or remain loyal to a nationalising state.

Primordialists, perennialists and ethno-symbolists

Both structuralist and rational choice variants of modernist interpretations of nationalism are challenged by a range of scholars, including *primordialists, perennialists* and *ethno-symbolists* who generally accept the transformative impact of modernisation on ethnic and national identities and their political implications for statehood. However, they tend to put more emphasis on the continuous political and social effects of pre-modern ethnicity, including real or perceived kinship, collective myths, symbols, legends and conceptions of territoriality that remain relatively constant and politically significant, despite the transformation from pre-modern to modern forms of statehood.

Structuralist Accounts

Structuralist explanations of nationalism emphasise the economic and political forces that create demand for the construction of national identity and the use of nationalism by economic classes, the political and intellectual elites, to achieve or perpetuate their economic or political interests. In this way they share the rationalists' assumptions that leaders of such movements are using nationalism instrumentally, as a tool to achieve individual or collective interests. But structuralists differ from rationalists by arguing that structural changes associated with modernism – ideological, economic, political and social – constrain choices made by rational individuals.

Hobsbawm's 'invented tradition'

Eric Hobsbawm (1990) identifies two phases of nationalism that have shaped states in the western system. The first *pre-democratic* stage is consistent with liberal-bourgeois Risorgimento nationalism, described previously. Hobsbawm and Ranger (1983) emphasise the invention of tradition by the nationalising states of Europe, whose governments were dominated by representatives of commercial and industrial bourgeois classes. In order to preserve social order under the strains produced by industrialisation, trade union mobilisation, urbanisation, the state and/or capitalist elites invented traditions to integrate the lower classes and preserve and enhance the capitalist system by expanding markets internally and externally. Thus, Hobsbawm emphasises the late 19th century 'invention' of traditions such as the British coronation ceremony, the French celebration of the storming of the Bastille (90 years after its occurrence), annual May Days, national military parades, national sporting associations (such as the Football Association in England and Wales).

In the pre-democratic phase, from the turn of the 18th century to about 1870 when government was based on limited representation, the state only needed to achieve a limited amount of active popular consent to its policies, so a diffuse patriotism, reflecting limited connection between the society and the state, was enough to sustain the capitalist order. Such patriotism was developed through national education systems (in a single, national language) and the state-led invention of symbols (such as monuments), traditions, ceremonies to bind society into loyalty to the nation and its state.

Hobsbawm identifies a second phase of nationalism, characterised by ethnic and linguistic exclusivity, which flourished in Europe from about 1870 to 1914. This phase is caused by the widening demands of participation by the lower classes in the democratic politics of surviving multi-national empires. Hobsbawm identifies the petty bourgeoisie as the 'lesser examination-passing classes' who advocated separatist nationalism in order to improve their own economic and political prospects relative to the proletariat below and the dominant capitalist classes above. These class-based movements explain for Hobsbawm the emergence of ethno-nationalism in the east among Armenians, Georgians, Lithuanians, Macedonians, Albanians, Ruthenians and Croats and in the west among Basques, Catalans, the Flemish, the Welsh, the Scottish and the Irish (Hobsbawm, 1990: 102–33).

Anderson's 'imagined communities'

A second prominent Marxist interpretation of nationalism tries to move beyond Hobsbawm's class-specific and Euro-centric explanation to provide a broader psychic and cultural understanding of the forces that produce nationalism. Benedict Anderson's *Imagined Communities,* published in 1983, shares the modernist emphasis on secular humanism and the shift from godly to temporal forms of governmental authority. Anderson emphasises the role of a specific mode of production – 'print-capitalism' – from the early 16th century in creating stable national languages of state administration and commercial publication. The invention of the printing press, which led to a tenfold increase in printed volumes between 1500 and 1600, created incentives for publishers to expand their markets for such literature by publishing in standardised vernacular languages rather than the elite languages of administration such as Latin, Qur'anic Arabic and Examination (Mandarin) Chinese. The result was a standardisation of vernacular languages such as (King's) English, Parisian French, and (High) German as languages of state administration and, later in the 19th century, as national languages that allow people in disparate regions of a state to imagine themselves as members of a national community.

For Anderson, the transition from national identity produced by print-capitalism to actual nationalist political movement is explained in the first instance by the experience of colonial administrators in the Spanish and Portuguese Americas, who resented the discriminatory practices of their imperial masters. Like their North American colonial counterparts, they resented what they considered unfair taxation and trade restrictions. They also suffered from blocked upward mobility within the colonial state administration because of the suspicion that those born in the colonies would have been degraded by their contact with 'native' culture. Of the 170 viceroys appointed by the Spanish empire up to 1813, only four were 'Creole' (that is, those of Spanish descent but born in the colonies). Faced with limited prospects within the imperial state, these administrative classes, supported by publishers of 'national' newspapers, advocated national separation from the Spanish and Portuguese Empires and supported liberation movements such as those led by Simón Bolivar that liberated Venezuela, Ecuador, Columbia, Panama, Peru and what became 'Bolivia' from Spanish Imperial control between 1814 and 1825. In Anderson's view, the South American nationalisms set precedents that influenced subsequent European nationalist movements against Empire later in the 19th century (1983: chapter 5).

Gellner's 'cultural homogeneity'

A third structural theory, developed by Ernest Gellner in *Nations and Nationalism* (1983) rejects the capitalist determinism of both Hobsbawm and Anderson but shares their view that modern structural change *caused* both nations and nationalism. Gellner's theory is structuralist in that it emphasises the social and political changes produced by the modern development of industrialisation. It is also *functionalist* because Gellner believes that industrialisation creates a need for the state to establish and maintain a common culture, especially a dominant national language. In the pre-modern Agrarian Age members of one localised cultural community (such as the Cornish in England) did not need to share a common language with other communities within the same dynastic realm because their mode of production was localised. Industrialisation produced a demand for cultural homogeneity because higher skill-levels, particularly literacy and numeracy, were required to create a work force that was mobile and capable of being trained and re-trained to fill the specialised requirements of industrial production and the administration of complex public and private organisations. Since the industrial state became politically dependent on economic growth, the state had to create a national culture through a standardised national educational system. For Gellner, 'the monopoly of legitimate education [becomes] more important than the monopoly of legitimate violence' (1983: 34) and this imperative for the state to create cultural homogeneity is not reducible to any specific class interests.

Gellner's emphasis on culture, education and state power leads to the development of a typology of nationalisms that attempts to predict what kind (liberal versus illiberal, ethnic versus civic) of nationalism emerges in a particular modern context (1983: 94, Figure 2). Where an ethnic minority community has access to education in the national tongue and access to power (through representation or access to administration), a more liberal form of nationalism is likely to emerge that unites multiple ethnic minorities into a shared 'civic' national identity. This trajectory is characteristic of 'classical liberal Western nationalism' such as that which integrated the Scots and the Welsh (but not most of the Irish) into a British civic nationalism or integration of a variety of Europeans into a civic American identity in the USA.

By contrast, where ethnic groups are not provided with either access to education in the national tongue or access to political power, they are more likely to turn inward and seek liberation from the state. Gellner labels this second trajectory as 'Habsburg' nationalism because it describes the pattern of ethnic-nationalist movements by Hungarians, Romanians, Serbs, Croats and Slovenians who were denied upward mobility within the Austrian-dominated Habsburg Empire and logically turned inward to attempt to carve out more culturally homogeneous states. This pattern has characterised the type of ethno-national conflict that has occurred between Britain and the Republic of Ireland (over Northern Ireland), Basque separatism in Spain, in the Balkans and Central Asia after the break-up of the Soviet Union, across the Indian sub-continent, and across sub-Saharan Africa where colonial borders were particularly insensitive to ethnicity.

Paramount role of 'modernisation'

The structuralist emphasis on the economic and political structures associated with modernisation is a significant challenge to theories that emphasise the ideological or ethnic forces that produce nationalism. Their emphasis on blocked upward mobility and/or protection of class status as catalysts for nationalist mobilisation are important parts of the explanation of the timing and extent of many challenges to empires or states.

Like other structuralist accounts of comparative politics, those applied to the study of nationalism can be criticised for underestimating both individual agency and cultural resonance. Hobsbawm's class theory, for example, can account for general tendencies such as the petit-bourgeois dominance of ethno-nationalist movements but has a harder time explaining, for example, the limits of international class solidarity during the First World War or the cross-class nature of many 20th century nationalist movements. We turn now to rationalist accounts, which attempt to explain more precisely why individuals choose to support collective nationalist movements.

Rational Choice Accounts

Rational choice accounts of nationalism share some core assumptions with structuralist accounts. Both argue that nations and nationalism are by-products of modernity. Both emphasise that elites use nationalism *instrumentally*, as a means to an end, to achieve or preserve economic, political and social status, privilege and power. The rationalist ontology, with its methodological bias towards quantification of costs and benefits, tends to place, like many structuralist accounts, an emphasis on economic influences rather than less easily measurable factors like ideology, culture and psyche, although it is important to emphasise in this section that there are important developments within rational choice that do broaden conceptions of costs and benefits to attempt to include broader interests such as status and cultural identity. Compared to structuralists, rationalists place more emphasis on individual choices to be nationalist, whether as parents choosing a language of education for their children, citizens supporting a nationalist movement or as politicians seeking office or exerting state power in their own interests.

For rationalists, the nation is one of several layers of aggregation (along with family, clan, tribe, community, region, continent, globe, cosmos) within which individuals attempt to coordinate with other individuals to pursue individual interests such as physical security, economic opportunity, political power and so on. The nation-state and the institutionalisation of national culture are recognised by rationalists as being particularly important because of (1) the state's monopoly of the legitimate use of force and (2) the state's imposition and/or regulation of national culture or cultures that affect individuals directly through their opportunities to access citizenship, education, economic and political opportunities.

Notions of 'variable' assimilation

Rationalists attempt to improve on structuralist accounts by explaining the timing and extent of nationalist challenge to other national groups and/or the state. David Laitin, for example, reminds us that neither economic factors nor cultural factors on their own explain which multi-national or multi-ethnic states experience political violence (2007: 9–22). After the collapse of the Soviet Union, Russian speakers in Estonia faced as much discrimination as Russian speakers in Transneister, Moldova, but only in the latter did significant violent separatism emerge. Therefore, national cultural differences or enmity based on Russian dominance in the Soviet Union cannot explain the differences in the decisions taken by Russians in these two countries. Similarly, Laitin and other rational choice proponents want to explain the significant variation in rates of assimilation of members of minority linguistic groups into dominant national languages.

For rational choice theorists, both collective nationalist violence and collective support for a particular linguistic regime can be explained by the aggregation of individual strategic choices. Thus, Laitin explains the revival of the Catalan language within Spain as the result of a coordination game in which individuals supported the Catalan revival, despite the costs of isolation from the rest of Spain, because of rational calculation that others within the Catalan region would support it (including the regional government who subsidised publication in the language) and, by contrast, penalise those who prioritised Castilian (Spanish) (2007: 42–5). A similar process of rational strategic calculation explains why the Russian minority (30 per cent) in Estonia are apparently choosing to learn Estonian to gain full citizenship, entry into universities, and public- and private-sector jobs rather than attempting secession or cultural autonomy within Estonia (Laitin, 2007: 47–9; though Laitin does not consider the impact of the fears of Russian speakers regarding Moldovan-Romanian re-integration, fears which sparked Russian-speakers' quest for separation). However, in situations where an individual calculates the cost of assimilation into another linguistic culture is too high, they are inclined to reject assimilation and remain in the margins of society.

Thus, according to Laitin, Jews in early modern Europe chose to remain isolated from their wider societies because the costs of losing their economic niche in banking were greater than the benefits of assimilation. Similar calculations are made by Harijan (untouchables) in India who faced high costs by transiting from street cleaning, and by Roma (Gypsies) who rationally choose to maintain their advantages as seasonal labourers rather than enter more competitive industries through assimilation (Laitin, 2007: 49–53).

Laitin and other rational choice proponents like Russell Hardin (1996) have made important contributions to rational choice theories of nationalism. By focusing on the interests of national (or ethnic) entrepreneurs as well as the cost–benefit calculations of citizens and subjects, they enable us to explain more variation in the timing and extent of nationalist mobilisation. However, in their quest to rationalise decision-making they increasingly rely on considerations of cost and benefit that are neither easily quantifiable, nor reducible to individual 'interests'. For example, Laitin cites three main variables that predict nationalist mobilisation: economic consequences (to the individual or family) of national status, the probability of in-group status and out-group status. Economic consequences are clearly amenable to rationalist analysis but the latter two are more complicated. By in-group acceptance, Laitin means 'the levels of social support and *stigma* given by members of a community for the identity choices made by their peers' (2007: 55). Both status and stigma are qualitative evaluations that involve rational calculation but also feelings, emotions, based on contemporary experience *and* historical memory, myths and their reinterpretation over historical periods of interaction.

If, as Laitin suggests, members of an ethnic, national or racial group resent their fellow group members for adopting a 'foreign' culture, the basis of resentment is likely to be caused by more than just rational economic or political criteria, but also by notions of pride and fears for the collective loss or denigration of culture or loss of sovereignty over a perceived homeland. Similarly, out-group status (the degree of acceptance of the assimilating minority by the majority community) is not easily reducible to rational criteria but also involves subjective value judgements about the influence of new members based on historical memory, racial or ethnic stereotype. These issues cannot simply be reduced to rationalists' residual error category – imperfect information – but are also influenced by subjective national memory, myths and symbols that influence feelings about ethnic and nationalist 'others'. Do parents in Catalonia, Estonia, Sri Lanka and countless other challenged national states mainly think about maximising their children's opportunities for upward mobility or do they also consider the importance of perpetuating a pre-modern political and social culture for their children *and* for the wider members of a national community?

To understand why ethnicity and nationalism are such perennially important resources in the marketplace of ideas, we need to consider explanations of nations and nationalism that emphasise the subjective, non-rational accounts. The following discussion of pre-modern accounts of nations and nationalism presents a set of explanations that place more emphasis on the independent effects of culture, as well as psychological explanations of behaviour that propose non-rational, emotional behaviours.

A final query on the rationalist approach neatly introduces us to the culturalist framework. Is it merely coincidence that the most individualist political culture – the (US) American – produces the most forceful proponents of rational choice theories of nations and nationalism (for example, Brubaker, 1996; Hardin, 1996; Roeder, 2005)? It could be argued that academics from cultures that have been shaped by a melting-pot ethos (however mythical) of hybrid (mainly European) culture, frontier settlement, and Protestant individualism apply these values to their analysis of individual behaviour. To make a controlled comparison, many Canadian academics in the field, apparently influenced by the national experience of cultural and national pluralism (particularly with regard to the Quebec/French language question), but also lately in terms of collective rights of indigenous communities – 'first nations' – and others, emphasise the empirical and normative importance of ethnicity and 'plural nationalism' (for example, Kymlicka, 2001; Taylor, 1992; Tully, 1995).

The next section presents theories of nations and nationalism that emphasise the durability of pre-modern institutional cultures and then considers the implications of durable ethnic and nationalist cultures for contemporary politics.

Pre-modernist Accounts: Cultured Beliefs and Institutions

The Frenchman Claude Seyssal wrote in the early 16th century that '[a]ll nations and reasonable men prefer to be governed by men of their own country and nation – who know their habits, laws and customs and share the same language and life-style as them – rather than by strangers' (quoted in Hastings, 1997: 114). Well before the modern influences of industrialisation or advanced military state development, there were strong assumptions that a nation should have a government that corresponds to its particular culture. For Adrian Hastings, institutionalised national cultures such as those of 'Germans, French, English, Spaniards Italians, Danes, Dutch ... are all firmly in place well before 1500' (1997: 114).

Ethno-symbolists and cultural institutionalists

Anthony Smith and his 'ethno-symbolist' school, as well as cultural institutionalists such as John Armstrong and Adrian Hastings, have developed the most comprehensive analyses of the ideational forces that bond solidary groups in pursuit of social, economic and political power and authority. For these opponents of the modernist (or constructivist) explanations, nation- and state-building are profoundly shaped by pre-modern solidary alignments based on perceived, extended kinship groups or *ethnie*: a named unit of human population which shares myths and memories of collective historical experiences, a shared culture (including religion, language and customs) with a sense of solidarity and subjectively-felt entitlement to a specific territory or homeland.

These approaches are careful to distinguish their theories from those of either biological or cultural 'primordialists' who assert that *ethnies* and nations are extended kinship groups linked to some pre-existing biological or cultural community. Instead, ethno-symbolists and perennialists argue that pre-modern ethnic and proto-nationalist identities and interests shape modernisation as much as they are shaped by modernisation. There is little doubt, for example, that Gaelic culture in Ireland was an important obstacle to Anglicisation of language, religion and politics. A 'Celtic-Christian' synthesis was responsible for standardising the language by transforming it from oral to written form. These processes were 'ethnogenic' in that important myths based on the Ulster and Fenian cycles were chronicled, along with the *Brehon* legal code, poetry, genealogies of Irish kingdoms – including that of Irish high king Brian Boru – and literary productions such as the eighth century *Book of Kells* that represented Ireland's status as a bastion of Christianity (Hutchinson, 2005: 27). However mythical, these oral and literary cultures limited the prospects for Anglicisation and religious reformation. Though English marginalised Gaelic language under the pressure of partial conquest, the resulting nationalism that contested the British state was distinctively Irish, if not exclusively Gaelic, in both its constitutional and violent forms.

Myths and symbols

Ethno-symbolists emphasise the independent role of myths, memories and symbols as the sinews of solidary bonds linking different classes, interests and status groups. The most enduring and successful ethnic and national groups institutionalise their culture in two main ways: through a well-developed written vernacular language, usually codified as a scriptural language (Latin-based languages of Europe, Arabic in the Muslim Empire stretching from the steppes of Asia to the Iberian peninsula (and north Africa); and a demotic ethnie (usually also defined in part by religion, such as the Catholic Irish ethos of 'Faith and Fatherland' from the late 16th century, Catholic Franks, Calvinist Protestant New English in North America and Ireland, Calvinist Dutch Afrikaners in southern Africa (contemporary South Africa), Jewish Zionists in Palestine (and contemporary Israel) and so forth.

Centrality of religion

For both Smith and Hastings, religion plays a particularly important role in sanctifying national origin myths (for example, Clovis in France, Sava in Serbia, St Patrick in Ireland) as well as in interpreting military victories and defeats as divinely pre-destined. For Hastings, the modern nation was cast in the mould of Judeo-Christian national belief, starting with the biblical model of Israel as a distinct sovereign (in the eyes of God) territorial entity comprised of and for a people with a particular language and religion (Hastings, 1997: 18; Smith, 1998: 171–2). Accordingly, the institutionalisation of religion and language with the state occurred much earlier than most modernist scholars assume. The key development was the solidification of vernacular languages as languages of both worship and state administration. If print-capitalism solidified national languages, it was specifically the translation and dissemination of Protestant Christian literature in English that was the subject of mechanised printing: the Bible itself, but also hymnals and prayer books. By contrast, the decision by Elizabeth I not to translate the Bible into Gaelic during the late 15th century attempted conquest of Ireland is alleged by Steven Ellis and others to be an important explanation of the persistence of an alternative Catholic-Irish 'Faith and Fatherland' nationalism that limited Ireland's integration into the British state because it limited the exposure of the Gaelic Irish population to Protestant reformist theology (Ellis, 1999).

The centrality of religion to pre-modernist accounts is clearly illustrated in the comparison with nations and nationalism in Islam. Both Gellner and Hastings recognise that the pattern of nation-state formation in the Islamic world followed a different pattern than within Christendom. Whereas in the latter, the process of modernisation instituted vernacular languages as the languages of state (King's English, Parisian French, modern Greek and so forth), in the Islamic world the language of the Qur'an – Arabic – remained universal across the empires and modern states of the Middle East and North Africa. Arabic and Islamic faith remained transnational language and belief systems for several reasons. First, the main strands of Islamic thought expressly resists any subordination of Allah's sovereignty to temporal (including territorial) authority. Second, according to John Armstrong, the historical impact of nomadic lifestyles in these core Islamic areas also increased the influence of local tribal hierarchies rather than wider territorial forms in western states, where soil conditions encouraged more sedentary (territory-specific) forms of social organisation (Armstrong, 1982: chapter. 2, cited in Smith, 1998: 183–4).

Synthesising Cultural Universalism and Structural Localism

This combination of cultural universalism and structural localism helps explain some of the significant developments in contemporary post-colonial states. Many of the states of the Middle East and North Africa, constructed by western powers after the collapse of the Ottoman Empire, have experienced a deep tension between the secular state and the transnationalism of Islamic faith. A pattern emerged from the end of the Second World War when secular nationalist movements gained independence from European colonial rule and established, western-style secular nation- and state-building policies. Examples include Kemalism in Turkey after the First World War, Nasser's secular nationalist revolution in Egypt, the Front de Libération National in Algeria, Baathist socialist nationalism in Syria and Iraq, and the Palestinian Liberation Organisation. Eventually, all of these secular nationalist states were challenged to varying degrees by Islamic revivalist parties and movements, who offered those disgruntled with the authoritarian secular state the alternative of government and social organisation based on Islamic values. The survival of an alternative ideology based on a pre-modern belief system is, therefore, further testament to the limits of a purely modernist and constructivist explanation of nations and nationalism.

Miroslav Hroch adds a third pre-condition for predicting durable nationalist movements: institutions or traditions of ancient statehood. These were important in explaining the strength of national movements among Poles, Magyars, Norwegians, Czechs and Croatians during the 19th century, but were also important in Ireland from at least the 14th century (Hroch, 1995: 78–9). In sum, the opponents of modernist explanations argue that pre-modern ethnicity *institutionalised* practices, including government and religious organisation that create vertical bonds between elites and the gradually politicised masses. Thus the promoters of 'imagined communities' or 'invented traditions' have limited palettes from which to 'paint' national identities or institutions. Likewise, the scope for individual agency is significantly constrained by pre-modern cultural institutions such as language, customs, mores, conceptions of justice and territoriality.

In their attention to the institutionalisation of national culture within explicit territorial boundaries, ethno-symbolists are explicitly attempting to synthesise cultural and behavioural theories with the structural and rationalist factors emphasised by modernists. Smith, for example, argues that the 'triple-revolution' of modernity – global expansion of trade and commerce, the state administrative revolution resulting from expanded warfare and the development of mass culture in the age of industrialisation – did produce the first nationalisms, as ideologies integrating society and state. But these were almost invariably centred on a core or dominant ethnic community or *ethnie* such as the Frankish core at the heart of the medieval French state, the Anglo-Saxon core of the British empire state, the white Anglo-Saxon Protestant (WASP) core of the emergent USA, the Hindu core of the modern Indian state, the Han dominance of modern China, the Russian core of the Soviet Union and so on. Despite the scale and extent of subsequent cultural assimilation and integration of non-core cultures in all of these cases, the legacy of ethnic origins of modern states are still relevant politically, as exemplified by challenges by pre-modern non-core nations or cultural minorities in all of the examples just listed. The final section will show how theories of nations and nationalism influence the comparative theory and practice of national conflict and conflict regulation.

Implications for Comparative Politics of Nation-state Relations

The debates among the three main strands of theory of nations and nationalism are not merely academic debates but have practical political and policy consequences. They affect the statecraft and nation-building policies of western governments involved in 'regime-change' in Iraq and Afghanistan, for example, as well as the approach to minority rights and national self-determination claims in post-Soviet Baltic states, central Asia and Eastern Europe, and the promotion of democracy in multi-national states throughout the developed and developing world.

Structural and rationalist remedies for internal conflict

Structural and rationalist modernist perspectives are used to support nationalities policies and conflict resolution strategies centred on civic-national 'power-dividing'. They emphasise how the treatment of underlying structural causes (such as economic inequality) tries to promote constitutions and institutions that maximize individual autonomy and liberty. If modernists are right and nations and nationalisms are 'constructions' then it follows that the problems of 'nations without states' or contested ethno-national territorial claims can be solved through the promotion of civic forms of nationalism. In this form the state is meant to be ethnically neutral, citizenship is primarily determined by residence rather than blood lineage, and internal territorial boundaries do not correspond to ethnic 'homelands'.

In this model, government is composed of representatives of *individual* people, based on the separation of powers of the executive, legislature and judiciary. Constitutional rights protections are for the *individual* rather than ethnic or national minority. Meritocracy and education are seen in this perspective as the best way to overcome structural causes of ethnic and national conflict because they provide upward mobility within the state and economy and reduce the rational incentives of 'ethnic entrepreneurs' to challenge or control the state. If a Scot, Gordon Brown, can become Prime Minister of the UK, then Scots should, so the argument goes, recognise that their interests in upward mobility and status recognition can be accommodated within the British state, rather than in a separate Scottish nation-state.

Cultural approaches to conflict regulation

By contrast, those who adopt a pre-modernist or non-modernist perspective, who believe with the ethno-symbolists that ethnic origins matter because of their impact on institutional practices of communication, territoriality, justice and status relations, advocate forms of conflict regulation that promote or at least recognise the salience of old and new ethnic and national communities and promote constitutions and institutions predicated on the durability and political importance of such ethno-national bonds. Ultimately, states should correspond with ethnic or national boundaries, meaning that state jurisdictions can be adjusted through processes of national self-determination. If not, governance should be, if necessary, based on principles of power sharing between or among ethnic or national blocs in a parliamentary system, elected by proportional representation to max-imise minority ethnic or national representation. In this view, the ethnical neutrality of the state should not be assumed but questioned and, if necessary, modified to promote rights and opportunities for both individual citizens *and* ethnic and national groups. In this view, a Scottish Prime Minister does not necessarily satisfy the interests and identity needs of Scottish people. Instead, substantial autonomy (through devolution) and the option of national self-determination are also required.

Similarities and differences

Both variants recognise empirically and promote normatively the principle of consent for constitutional government. But they differ over what unit of population (the individual or the group) that should be accorded the right of consent.

Empirically, it is not clear whether civic-national power dividing is better than ethno-national power sharing. On the one hand, power sharing in ethnically and nationally challenged states is notably unstable outside of the developed West. Power sharing combined with multi-nationalism has been successful in maintaining the stability of Switzerland, Belgium and Canada. But in less prosperous regions, without long-standing traditions of elite cooperation, such as Cyprus, the Lebanon, and Rwanda, power-sharing experiments have failed and been followed by intensified violence. Philip Roeder reports that power-sharing systems that include territorial autonomy for ethno-national groups are six times more likely to escalate to violent conflict and 10 times more likely than power-dividing systems to lead to demands for national self-determination (Roeder, 2005: 76–7).

On the other hand, civic-nation building and power dividing appear to work better only in cases where ethnic or national minorities are not territorially concentrated, such as in new settler societies such as the USA and Australia. In such cases the relatively open frontiers and lack of rooted connection between a people and a place make exit solutions more viable. People in these states had more opportunities and incentives to move to new areas if suffering from discrimination and the act of movement itself further mixed up the cultural pool, making assimilation into an overarching American or Australian identity easier. By contrast, there are less opportunities and incentives for assimilation to a dominant culture in states where ethnic or national minorities have long-standing association or attachment to a perceived homeland – such as Tamils in Sri Lanka and India, Chechens in Russia, Basques and Catalans in Spain – where divisions have been re-enforced by myths and memories of competition with a dominant nation as well as contemporary opportunities to use territorial control to protect interests. Roeder recognises the difficulties of civic-national power dividing in such cases and advocates partition into more ethnically homogeneous states if the components of existing states do not share loyalty to an existing state (Roeder, 2005: 81).

Recent Developments in Practice

Recent developments suggest potential for a synthesis of modernist, civic-national approaches and pre-modernist 'ethno-national' approaches. The British–Irish approach to the Northern Ireland conflict, for example, has been successful in combining both ethno-national power sharing and a form of British–Irish, civic-national power dividing. The peace process was built on the acceptance that the conflict in Northern Ireland was essentially about opposing self-determination claims of the Irish nationalist minority (approximately 40 per cent of the population) who seek reunification with the Irish Republic and British unionist majority seeking to maintain Northern Ireland's place in the UK. The British–Irish approach has been to balance the power-sharing approach with power dividing. So 'ethno-national' power sharing was designed for Northern Ireland's devolved Assembly but power was also divided by devolution within the UK, by the creation of a North–South Ministerial Council linking Northern Ireland with the Irish Republic and continued British–Irish intergovernmental institutions to manage the complex set of relations (O'Duffy, 2007). Similar hybrid formulae have been developed in post-Apartheid South Africa where elements of ethno-national power sharing, collective rights protections and autonomy benefiting ethno-national groups have been carefully combined with civic national power dividing through federalism, and individual rights protections (Sisk and Stefes, 2005).

The challenge for comparative political analysis is to understand under what conditions it is possible to combine the modernist and pre-modernist approaches to achieve structural change conducive to individual mobility and forms of rights protections and governance acceptable to meet the needs – both material and non-material – and interests of individuals and ethnic and national minorities.

SUMMARY

- This chapter has defined, discussed and explained the concepts of nation-state, nationalism and ethnic groups.

- This led us to examine nationalism as an ideology and explore its various forms.

- Theoretical explanations have been provided in order to provide explanations for the development of nationalism and nation-states. These are based on structural, cultural and rational choice institutionalist approaches.

- We have also considered how different theoretical perspectives can assist both comparative political analysis and the resolution of real world problems associated with fostering national unity whilst respecting minority rights.

FURTHER READING

The transcript of a historic debate between a prominent modernist, Ernest Gellner and his former student and now critic of modernist explanations, Anthony D. Smith, offers students a good introduction to the primary schools of thought in the study of nations and nationalism. The Smith-Gellner Debate (1996) was published as 'Do nations have navels?', in the journal *Nations and Nationalism*, vol. 2.3.

For a critical survey of the most prominent modernist accounts, and the introduction of his own, more culturally-centred alternative 'ethno-symbolist' approach, see Anthony, D. Smith (1998) *Nationalism and Modernism*. London: Routledge, or, for students new to the study of nationalism, see his *Nationalism: Theory, Ideology, History*. Cambridge: Polity, 2001.

Three notable structuralist accounts of nationalism were published in 1983. Two were sophisticated Marxist analyses emphasising capitalism as a driver of nationalism:

Benedict Anderson's (1983) *Imagined Communities: Reflections on the Origin and Spread of Nationalism*. London: Verso. Eric Hobsbawm's and Terence Ranger's (eds), *The Invention of Tradition*. Cambridge: Cambridge University Press, 1983. A third structuralist account that explicitly refuted the Marxist assumptions of class and capital was Ernest Gellner's ([1983], 2006) *Nations and Nationalism*. Oxford: Blackwell, commendable for its elegant typology of nationalisms.

Three modernists who combine structuralist and rationalist assumptions in overtly 'political' interpretations of nationalism are Jack Snyder (2000) *From Voting to Violence: Democratization and Nationalist Conflict*. New York: Norton. John Breuilly (1993) *Nationalism and the State*, 2nd edn. Manchester: Manchester University Press, and Michael Hechter (2001) *Containing Nationalism*. Oxford: Oxford University Press.

A recent rational choice approach that also considers the independent effects of culture as key elements of cost-benefit calculation is David Laitin's, (2007) *Nations, States and Violence*. Oxford: Oxford University Press.

Finally, a stimulating introduction to the study of nationalism, which is written from a primordialist perspective, is Steven Grosby's (2005) *Nationalism: A Very Short Introduction*. Oxford: Oxford University Press.

QUESTIONS FOR DISCUSSION

(1) Why does it matter for comparative politics whether nations and nationalism have modern or pre-modern origins?

(2) What are the strengths and weaknesses of the structuralist, rationalist and culturalist perspectives on nationalism? Can you think of ways of synthesising these perspectives to strengthen our understanding of nation-state relations?

(3) If nations and nationalism are merely 'invented' or 'imagined' modern 'constructs', why are nations and nationalism so difficult to deconstruct or replace with new forms of political legitimacy? Discuss with reference to the challenge of ethno-nationalism to contemporary states.

(4) Consider the centrality of 'blocked upward mobility' to the structuralist and rationalist explanations of nationalist challenges to states.

(5) In what ways do theories of nationalism contribute to the theory and practice of ethno-national conflict regulation?

Key Words for Chapter 3

civic-nationalism / ethnic group / ethno-nationalism / modern versus pre-modern nations / nation / nationalism

4 Electoral Systems

Jocelyn A.J. Evans

CHAPTER OUTLINE

Using the three theoretical perspectives introduced earlier, this chapter will now consider the nature of electoral systems and their relationships with the broader political arena, paying special attention to effects for party systems and government formation.

Introduction

Despite being one of the cornerstones of liberal democratic legitimacy, elections are increasingly treated with something little short of contempt in precisely those nations where their presence has acted as a model to other developing democracies. In the recent past, it has been a rare election in any Western democracy at which declining turnout, voter apathy, political disengagement or some other form of negative perception of the ballot box and those who use it to run for power has not arisen as an issue. The politicised, engaged few raise this as a matter of concern and urgency which devalues and threatens democratic life and freedoms in these nations. The depoliticised but equally engaged few counter that a withdrawal from politics is a sign of a healthy society with few explosive issues, and generalised consensus. An increasingly apathetic remainder believe that voting 'doesn't achieve anything', 'doesn't change anything' and that parties 'are all alike'.

An adjunct to this argument from the politically mobilised is that elections are not just a matter of how many people vote for which party, and by extension who wins: the very nature of the electoral system itself affects the type of government which is formed, and by extension what policies are created. In this respect, the number of people who turn out to vote is to some extent immaterial – the electoral system itself will have an effect; no matter what the abstention rate. Moreover, the type of electoral system can even play a role in who turns out to vote – and who they vote for. Lastly, electoral systems can be used to manipulate both politics and the society that it governs: they are a product of the initial democratisation – and indeed sometimes later re-democratisation – process, reflecting both the shape of social status quo as well as the political elite's desires in shaping the future status quo.

A framework for discussion: three institutional approaches

This chapter will look at precisely these issues and frame them within the three schools of institutionalism expounded in Chapter 1. First, it will consider the different types of electoral system which exist, both in terms of their formula – that is, how they use the aggregate of individual votes to work out the winners, the losers and their respective share of the spoils – the structure of constituencies and the logic of representation between voter and member of the legislature.

Second, from the rational institutionalist perspective, it will focus more specifically on the output of electoral systems. If politicians can use electoral systems to change how the political system more broadly works, in a highly rational manner, then we should expect to see certain outcomes from one type of electoral system over another, just as we would expect to see different characteristics of the parties and candidates competing in one type of system over another. Is it possible to generalise as to the common or 'ideal-type' characteristics of what each system produces?

Or is the structural institutionalism explanation correct – that what counts are macro-institutions such as the economy and territorial sovereignty, rather than electoral laws? Alternatively, are electoral systems simply by-products of cultural and social norms, reflecting historical traditions which require fundamental structural changes within society to depart from the immutable?

Grounding theory in reality

Using a number of historical and contemporary cases, we go on to look at the reasons for and effects of imposing change. For example, why did France undergo change from a proportional representation to a two-ballot majoritarian system in 1959, and what were the effects? As we shall see, the reasons for the change are context-specific, but how elites have used the manipulation of the system to try to achieve certain goals tells us far more about the role of elections and electoral systems than any steady-state environment, such as the UK. From the theoretical perspective, were such changes at one end indeed manipulation by elites, or at the other the result of macro-structural context beyond rational or indeed cultural 'control'? Often these goals have related to the nature of the party actors in the system, how the share of the spoils is divided up, and which parties prosper or fail as a result. But equally, in deciding who governs – in number and in profile – the electoral system has crucial implications for what emerges in the longer term from the election outcome.

Do electoral systems impact on voters?

Turning the perspective around from electoral output to electoral input, we will turn to the 'consumers' whom the electoral system is meant to serve – the voters. The policies which the winning parties and candidates enact are partly a reflection of the perceived desires of the electorate. Given the democratic criterion of the mandate – that is, that any elected official or group will submit to a future election after a specified length of time – the output of the system in terms of policies, for example, should influence how the voters behave next time round – who they vote for, and indeed whether they vote at all.

To what extent is this affected by the electoral system itself? Will unsuccessful governments be punished more or less severely in a plurality system than in a proportional system? Are voters more or less likely to turn out at all, according to which electoral system is in place, whether through a rational perception of the marginal return of their vote under the electoral law in place? Or does the cultural institutionalist theory hold, with turnout largely determined by social norms and mores?

Are electoral systems 'major' or 'minor' institutions?

Overall, we will try to tease out the admittedly complex relationship between electoral input and output to examine the extent to which the electoral framework has an effect on politics more generally. From an institutionalist perspective, we should expect the large variation in electoral systems to have visible effects on, amongst other things, party competition, government composition, the 'style' of politics within a nation and even what considerations voters give to their vote before marking their ballot paper, but the three schools will differ in ascribing the causality of this. Are the outcomes the product of aggregating rational preferences, or more a socio-cultural given? Or can all of this be relegated to the micro-state of irrelevant minutiae when weighed up against economic and geopolitical context, as structural institutionalism would suggest? Indeed, at this point we may put the structural institutionalist perspective to one side for the moment, along the lines already suggested for this model by Mark Pennington in Chapter 1, which suggests that elections and electoral systems are regarded as minor institutions and can thus largely be discounted as strong explanatory factors. However, we will return to it when we switch elections from independent to dependent variable, and look at the process of electoral system change, as opposed to the effects electoral systems themselves have.

As we shall see from the two remaining perspectives, however, both the effects and institutionalist explanations are not always as clear-cut as might be expected, not least because electoral systems do not exist in a vacuum – they are products of the very political culture which we might expect them to shape. However, whatever the direction of causality, there are nevertheless strong associations between electoral systems and other political variables of this type which help explain and predict how the electoral process interacts with and influences the political landscape in a country.

Measuring Electoral Systems

The literature on different types of electoral system is large and comprehensive, and so we do not intend to go into the finer intricacies of the different election formulae, district magnitudes, electoral thresholds and the like. For this information we would refer the reader to the gems in this literature (for example, Farrell, 2001; Lijphart, 1994; Rae, 1967). Instead, we will explain the basic tenets of these concepts, presenting the elements to electoral system type that have a direct bearing on political life and structures within a country. At first glance, there are many potential aspects to electoral systems which might have an effect on parties, on voter choice and on policy-making. However, as Lijphart in particular has shown, only a small number have clear effects in this respect (1994: 10ff). For many others, the evidence of an effect is remarkably absent.

From votes to seats

The most oft-cited variant in electoral systems is the formula by which votes are converted into seats. From the rational perspective of the role of elections – to arrive at a decision which aggregates individual wishes and ensures a varying level of representation of those wishes – it can never hope to provide the optimal outcome for everyone who takes part. There will never be as many outcomes as there are voters – there must always be some level of 'discounting' individuals' desires, unless all individuals are in complete agreement on what their preferred outcome is. The cultural institutionalist explanation would largely see the outcome as optimal – a mirroring of patterns of social structure and beliefs within the electorate via the electoral law.

Issues of proportionality

In concrete electoral terms, this means that the way that individual choices are related to outcomes – most commonly, how votes are converted to seats – will depend on the formula used, and the *proportionality* of this formula. At the aggregate level, how closely does the proportion of seats won by a party match the proportion of votes cast for that party? To be of any use to us methodologically, proportionality needs to be quantifiable and hence measurable (see Chapter 2). The most common measure used for proportionality is Rae's index, which takes the difference between each party's vote and seat share, sums the differences and takes an average.[1] More proportional systems will see less distance between the vote and seat shares for parties, and the proportion of smaller parties with no seats at all will be lower than majoritarian or plurality systems.

In real-world terms, proportionality indicates the style of governance and representation which occurs in a country. Generally, two ideal-types of representative politics are cited in the literature (Farrell, 2001: 11–12; McLean, 1991) – the 'microcosm' and 'principal–agent' models.

Microcosm Model

The microcosm model, corresponding to the cultural institutionalist perspective, argues that legislatures should be miniature versions of the society they represent. As far as possible, they should mirror the different social divisions in the society, with representatives of those divisions weighted according to the size of the various sub-populations. At the extreme, this would mean that the representatives would have the same social traits – gender, social class, religion, ethnicity and so forth – as their constituents and, extrapolating from a social psychological perspective, the same views and attitudes. More realistically, however, this proportionality has come to mean the composition of parties in the legislatures, given that not all socialist or Labour Party candidates will necessarily be working class, and not all Agrarian Party candidates will be farmers (though they will probably come from rural communities).

Principal–agent model

This 'reality' of microcosm representation has been extended to its logical extreme by the rational institutionalist principal–agent model, which argues that the make-up of the legislature is immaterial – what matters is the effectiveness of the decision-making and the representation of the electorate's wishes. Effective government, with clear and rapid policy-making, appropriate checks and balances (but not overbearing corporate or minority veto) and a legislature made up of capable politicians rather than a sample of the electorate, are the main precepts of this model. According to the principal–agent model, there is no need for there to be any sociological similarity between the representatives and the electorate, as long as the views and wishes of each representative's electorate are put forward efficiently and productively.

Between these two ideal-types, a differentiation is seen between the notion of representation as emanating from a self-aware and defined group – the working class, a trades union, an ethnic group, an issue-group – and representation as closer to a business transaction whereby constituents 'employ' a representative for a limited period, namely the period of incumbency, to act on their behalf. In principal–agent theory, the aim is to find a representative or group of representatives whom the majority support, so that these can act to form an effective government. A microcosmic model cannot achieve this, nor does it aim to. Instead, it aims to provide a composite, cooperative set of divergent views to negotiate a consensus.

The electoral 'formula'

Returning then to the vote-seat conversion, there is a generalised – although somewhat simplistic – assumption that electoral formulae are what matter in determining the proportionality of a system. In fact, there are a number of determinants of, and distortions to, proportionality. In particular, district magnitude (which we consider below) is another key variable in this respect. Farrell (2001: 13ff.) mentions four others:

- Malapportionment – whereby changes in constituency profile and size over time mean that unchanged electoral boundaries and constituency sizes result in unequal representation (see Reeve and Ware, 1992: 49–50).
- Gerrymandering – where politicians deliberately redraw boundaries, often in bizarre ways, in order to maximise concentrations of supporters and consequently win more seats.
- Electoral thresholds – where parties need to win a certain proportion of the vote to qualify for seats, and which we will discuss in more detail later.
- Party laws – which impose certain criteria on the kinds of party which are allowed to run in a race.

Lijphart (1994) mentions a number of other variables, including ballot structure, presidentialism and apparentement (the implicit cartelisation of separate party lists) as potential factors affecting proportionality. However, the direction of their effects is far less consistent and predictable than electoral formula and district magnitude to which we now turn.

Electoral formula I – majoritarian and plurality systems

'Elections which require the victorious candidate to hold at least 50 per cent + 1 of votes cast' is the simplest definition of what constitutes true majoritarianism. In this 'pure' form, the system must ensure that a candidate will emerge with such a condition fulfilled. Ensuring that such a result is always obtained might imply undemocratically limiting the number of candidates eligible to stand to two, for example, but in practice, laws such as all candidates satisfying the eligibility criteria standing at the first round, but only the top two candidates standing in a second, run-off ballot, as in the French presidential elections, ensures that the winner has the support of over 50 per cent of the voters.[2] The necessity of winning the absolute majority is seen by its proponents as a condition of legitimation: under this conception of democracy, the majority will is absolute in determining the victorious candidate, and places them above other institutions and actors who do not similarly have the 'will of the people'.

'Lesser' forms of majoritarianism whereby 50 per cent + 1 is not a *sine qua non* also exist. For instance, in French legislative elections which also include two ballots, and in which an absolute majority at the first round also ensures victory, any candidate with more than 12.5 per cent of the vote is entitled to progress to the second round, where only a plurality of votes, that is, a relative majority, is required to win. Indeed, the plurality system – or 'first-past-the-post' as it is often labelled – is the more common of the majority-oriented systems, characterising British general elections, for instance.

Alternative vote, which operates in Australia and some Polynesian states, adopts a more nuanced system of pure majoritarianism which relies upon a series of ranked preferences on the ballot paper to ensure 50 per cent + 1. If the first-placed candidate only has a plurality of votes, then the last-placed candidate is eliminated and their candidate's second preferences reallocated to the remaining candidates; elimination occurs until one candidate has at least 50 per cent + 1. Consequently, it is possible for a candidate who came second or, in closely run races lower, on first preferences to win the seat eventually. One of the most well-known examples of this was the Australian election of 1998, where the extreme right party One Nation candidate, Pauline Hanson, who had the greatest number of first-preference votes, lost the Blair constituency to the third-placed Liberal Party candidate, who received more second-preferences from other candidates, including those of the originally second-placed Labor Party candidate.

Electoral formula II – proportional representation systems

The most common systems are those referred to as proportional representation (PR) systems. Here, the electoral formula is designed to ensure that, as far as is possible, the proportion of votes received by a party will be reflected in the proportion of seats held in the legislature. As we noted above, this is not entirely possible in practice, due to the limited number of seats available. Also, as we will see in the following section, there may be other obstacles to close proportionality which impede a straight vote-seat ratio, however 'fair' the electoral formula is. But certainly, such systems will explicitly search to provide a more proportional allocation than a plurality or majoritarian system which, even if its vote–seat ratio is close, will only be so coincidentally.

Because a single-member constituency can never be guaranteed to produce a proportional result, a more complex formula generally needs to be employed to produce this outcome. More simply, however, the focus of the election and the ballot structure shifts, from a candidate-based vote to a party-based vote. In the majoritarian and plurality systems, a single candidate was elected to the constituency on the basis of their vote being higher than everyone else's (although what constituted 'higher' depended on the system in place). In the proportional systems, the number of seats which a party wins is based upon the size of the vote – just because party x's vote is smaller than party y does not mean that party x will not get a share of the seats. Instead, it will precisely get the share which corresponds to its share of the vote. Consequently, there will generally be multiple seats across constituencies – so-called 'district magnitude'. One of the key determinants of proportionality in an electoral system, if not the most important one, is indeed the number of seats within each voting district, or 'district magnitude'.

District magnitude

District magnitude (M) can range from one to potentially hundreds, and there is no direct relationship between M and whether a majoritarian, plurality or proportional representation electoral formula is employed, although typically plurality and majoritarian systems will have a district magnitude of one, and PR systems will have multi-member districts.[3] Proportional representation systems, however, will always be greater than one, up to the largest M, namely nation-wide constituencies where an entire legislature is elected using a list vote. The two most well-known examples of this are the Netherlands and Israel, where 150 members of the *Tweede Kamer* and 120 members of the *Knesset* are elected by a single national party list. In terms of proportionality, this district magnitude will result in as close to an entirely proportional system as possible.[4] Each party will receive the proportion of votes which it receives in seats, allowing for rounding and parties receiving too few votes to win a single seat. Therefore, except for those individuals voting for a tiny party with insufficient votes for a single seat, no vote is wasted – they all contribute to increasing a party's share of seats.

As M grows, greater proportionality appears.[5] Conversely, of course, if there are only four seats, say, in a constituency, then if five relevant parties contest this constituency, there will be an inevitable drop in proportionality, given that the fifth party cannot hope to win a seat. This explains the finding that while PR systems exhibit higher levels of proportionality than plurality systems, it is in fact the higher M which is responsible for this proportionality – but among PR systems, electoral formulae holding M constant will explain variation in proportionality (Lijphart, 1994; Taagepera and Shugart, 1989).[6]

To allow for multiple candidates from each party contesting a set of seats, a party list is provided. One common list system which has been described as characterising in particular the 'newer democracies' (Farrell, 2001: 82–3) is the 'closed list' whereby the party chooses its set of candidates and puts them in ranking order. Voters have no choice in which of these candidates to vote for, but vote simply for the party. According to how many votes this party wins, the upper corresponding proportion of the list will be elected. In the older democracies, the list systems tend to have varying degrees of 'openness'.[7] In these cases, there is the possibility of not only voting for a party list, but of also expressing some preference amongst candidates, either by ticking a box next to this candidate's name or by writing their name in a space on the ballot paper. How these personal votes are used varies according to system, and allows voters more or less individuation amongst candidates, something which is entirely absent in the closed list. Some systems, such as in Belgium, use the personal vote as little more than a potential bonus for candidates if they receive a large number of personal votes; other systems such as the Swiss case allow voters to distribute votes amongst candidates on different lists, a practice known as *panachage*.

The formula by which seats are allocated, however, is the key complexity to proportional systems. Generally, these formulae can be divided into two types – those which use quotas and those which use divisors (Taagepera and Shugart, 1989: 29–35). Explanations of the exact mathematical workings of these formulae, such as the Hare and Imperiali quotas, and the modified Saint-Laguë and d'Hondt systems which use divisors, are beyond the scope of this chapter, and can be found in any of the key texts on electoral systems.

Electoral formula III – mixed systems and single transferable vote

Mixed systems

Two types of electoral system remain. The first is the 'mixed' system usually exemplified by Germany, although variations on this exist in countries such as Japan, Mexico and Hungary. This system contains both candidate-based and party-based votes, thus corresponding to both microcosm and principal-agent models. The first vote is cast for a constituency candidate and, as with a plurality system, the candidate with a simple majority of votes wins the seat. Fifty per cent of the *Bundestag* seats are allocated on this basis. The second vote is a closed party list vote, and the voter casts an independent vote, either for the party list of their chosen candidate on the first vote, or a split-ticket vote, that is, for one of the other party lists. Any party which wins at least 5 per cent of the second votes cast is then entitled to a share of the remaining 50 per cent of the seats, based upon what share it has won of the list vote. The list seats are allocated to 'remedy' any disproportionality produced in the constituency seats.

In representative terms, this allows the voter the possibility of looking for constituency representation (pragmatic vote), whilst at the same time supporting smaller parties whose programmes they support, but with no chance of winning a constituency (ideological vote). In terms of the electoral system, the allocation of the list votes allows for high proportionality while retaining the constituency link. The proportionality may be limited, however, by a threshold condition whereby a party must win a certain proportion of the list vote to be entitled to a share of the list seats.

In terms of the three institutionalist schools, this example provides a good example of their contradictory perspectives. The imposition of a threshold can be seen as a rational act to determine outcomes – to exclude smaller extremist parties, for instance. The cultural institutionalist argument would be that such measures may inhibit smaller movements, but that a growth of such movements at a social level may well render such artificial measures ineffective. Lastly, the structuralist argument would simply emphasise that the rise of extremist parties is rather a function of geopolitical and economic factors, in which the electoral system played a small or entirely insignificant role. In reality, a combination of all three pertains – rational manipulation can hinder the development of political actors, but social support for such movements can mobilise via other outlets if not the electoral one, particularly if the macro-structural context is conducive to this.

Single transferable vote

A similar notion of candidate linkage with increased proportionality is present in the single transferable vote (STV). It is only used in three countries – Australia, for its Senate elections, the Republic of Ireland and Malta. In this system, the election is held across a number of constituencies, each containing multiple seats. Unlike the PR list system, there is freedom of choice of candidates – party affiliations can be entirely ignored. Voters list their preferences by numbering each candidate. A quota is established beyond which candidates will be elected, up until the allocation of all constituency seats. If any seats are filled by first preference votes, the 'excess' votes beyond the quota of all elected candidates are reallocated to the remaining candidates according to their own share of first preferences. If there are still seats vacant after this, or indeed no candidate is elected on first preferences alone, then in similar fashion to the alternative vote system, candidates are eliminated in reverse order and their second preference votes distributed. This elimination occurs until there are equal numbers of candidates with quota surpluses to seats to be filled.

This complex formula, despite being based upon candidates and consequently retaining the notion of constituency linkage, attains a high degree of proportionality. In addition, where there is a level of political diversity in a constituency and candidates from a number of parties or political affiliations are elected, constituents can be more confident of finding a representative close to their own political view than in a single-member plurality system.

Political Effects of Electoral Systems

Voter–representative relationship

The first political effect that an electoral system imposes, which we have already considered, is the relationship between the voter and their representative. In closed list systems with a low number of constituencies or high district magnitude, the link between the voter and an individual representative is all but absent. They may well have a number of representatives from a party representing a social group, but there is only a direct link to a party, not to a person. In the first-past-the-post environment, the relationship is the inverse: the voter has a single representative of their constituency, whether or not they voted for that person in the election. In these systems, the emphasis of accountability is put strongly upon the constituency representative as an intermediary between government and the electorate.

In highly proportional systems, individuals will need to rely upon a far less clear representative channel of their party, or at best the elected representatives who have no necessary link with a locale beyond the nation itself. Because of this less clearly defined channel, these representatives will in all likelihood have far more confounding pressures and priorities than a constituency representative. However, they will at least be more likely to have a party representative for whom they voted, as opposed to the 'winner-takes-all' logic of plurality and majoritarian systems.

Government formation

With regard to proportional representation systems, it is far more unlikely that a party will win an absolute majority of seats. A winning candidate can consequently quite easily hold a minority of seats in a single constituency, and hold less than an absolute majority of seats in the legislature. Consequently, one of the key traits of PR systems is the presence of coalition governments. Coalition formation may take place before or after the election, as determined by the electoral law of the country or as developed by custom and practice.

Whenever this negotiation takes place, however, it is clear that parties need to consider their coalition options prior to an election, in order to plan their campaign strategy, as well as modify where necessary their programmes to allow cooperation with other parties.[8] Here we can see the advantage of synthesising the pure rational and cultural institutionalist models. As we have noted, PR corresponds more closely to the cultural perspective and the microcosm model. The parties and their resultant vote shares will result in an array of actors who engage in coalition-bargaining and formation. Whilst their ideal positions may be indeed seen as a result of beliefs and attitudes derived from their social context, a measure of rationality must be introduced to account for ideological shifts to allow cooperation with parties holding diverse beliefs.

Traditionally, the view of electoral system effects on government formation has been that proportional representation, by providing this balanced representation from the microcosm perspective, also provides unstable and immobilist government. This view was based upon observation of coalition governments in the presence of proportional representation systems such as the French Fourth Republic, Weimar Germany and post-war Italy. In these cases, it is true that governments were weak, often being brought down by rebellions amongst small numbers of their supporters in the legislature, and that as a result, clear policies were often sunk, leaving only weak legislation which offended no-one but solved nothing. Respectively, the fall of the Fourth Republic, the rise to power of the Nazi Party and the collapse of Christian Democracy have been seen as to a greater or lesser extent the by-product of a proportional electoral system which granted too much representation, and hence heterogeneity, to make a workable government or legislative system.

A similar, though more involved line, has been forwarded by economic voting theorists (for example, Bingham Powell and Whitten, 1993) who argue that, in the case of coalition governments, generally voters often find it very difficult to identify responsibility amongst multiple coalition partners for economic performance, for instance, but equally for other policy matters. For instance, if the economy fails, was it the finance minister's fault or the prime minister's? What if they belong to two different parties? If a voter is to penalise them next time, who does he or she vote for instead? Given that the line of accountability is thus unclear, the responsiveness of coalition governments is lessened, and hence they feel less pressured to act as the electoral sanctions are lower. From the rational institutionalist perspective, the lack of monitoring effectiveness amongst the electoral principals allows a shirking of responsibilities by governing agents.

Is single-party government more responsive to voters?

This has been the basis upon which proponents of majoritarian and plurality electoral systems have based many of their claims – that a single-party government with a clear possibility of alternation is more accountable and thus will be more responsive. Yet, despite the above evidence of PR atrophy, it is not true that all coalition governments are weak, unstable or unresponsive. For instance, many of the smaller European democracies such as the Netherlands and Belgium, as well as post-war Germany and the Scandinavian countries, have been governed very successfully and effectively by coalitions. Conversely, many of the majoritarian systems have produced periods of less than responsive single-party government – political market failure in rational terms – and, in the French case, unresponsive coalitions. However, it is true that these have generally been held accountable more frequently – for instance, the failing Conservative and Labour governments of the 1970s in the UK were both thrown out by a dissatisfied electorate, and there has not been a re-elected incumbent French government from 1978 to 2007.

However, Lijphart is unequivocal upon this point '[t]here is no evidence that coalition cabinets in multi-party systems are less responsive than one-party majority cabinets; on the contrary, coalition cabinets are usually closer to the centre of the political spectrum – and hence closer in their policy outlook to the average citizen ...' (1994: 144). I shall return to the party–voter distance in due course. To summarise briefly on this aspect, however, it is evident that the responsiveness of governments depends as much upon exogenous factors limiting their room for manoeuvre and policy alternatives as upon their institutional definition and composition.

Rational institutionalist accounts in this respect place too much emphasis on principals' scrutiny determining agents' responses. Cultural strictures in the shape of historical institutions may predetermine both sets of actors' behaviour. But, more radically, the structural institutionalist account presents the alternative of macro-determinism – it is far from clear that single-party governments would have survived the contextual issues which caused the collapse of the French Fourth Republic (the Algerian crisis), Weimar Germany (economic collapse) and 'First' Republic Italy (the *Tangentopoli* corruption scandals). We will look at these examples more closely in terms of electoral change later.

Party system format

Given that more proportional electoral systems are meant to give a more reflective and nuanced model of society in terms of who is elected, and who is returned to government on that basis, we might expect the party system, as a key intervening variable between voters and legislature/government, to co-vary. Most obviously, perhaps, from the cultural institutionalist perspective we should expect party systems to correspond with the electoral system inasmuch as the number of parties vying for power should reflect the number of social groupings competing within the political system; the rational institutionalist model would see this covariance as a reflection of market demand being met by party supply. More instrumentally, the number of parties in a system should in all likelihood be affected by the electoral laws which partially determine the framework of competition.

Is the party system a consequence of the electoral system?

This is one of the most discussed relationships in the literature on electoral systems, and is generally referred to as 'Duverger's Law' and/or 'Duverger's Hypothesis'. In his own words, the former states that 'the single-ballot plurality system tends towards the two-party system [*le dualisme*]' (1951: 306, author's translation), the latter that 'both the two-ballot plurality system and proportional representation tend towards multi-party systems [*le multipartisme*]' (1951: 331, author's translation). Both have convincing, although ultimately simplistic, explanations. In a simple majority system, the need to secure a majority of the vote, and thereby an absolute majority of seats, means that there will be an aggregating tendency both by parties and voters towards a dualistic competitive system. From a rational perspective, multiple parties split the vote, which does not favour a party winning an absolute majority of seats. From the voters' perspective, support for a major party able to garner this level of votes, or its nearest rival, is the most sensible way of ensuring a useful vote (see below). The culturalist account would see such aggregation as an institutionalist imperative that 'overthrows' social multiplicity.

In the PR/two-ballot plurality case, the dynamic is different. For a two-ballot plurality system, there is less pressure on both parties and voters to aggregate in the first instance. Victory at the first ballot, although desirable, may not be feasible, given the need for an immediate absolute majority, and consequently parties may focus more on the possibility of cooperation and coalition, mutual desistment pacts (whereby parties stand down at the second ballot) and other competitive strategies to ensure victory at the second ballot. Consequently, a number of political parties may persist within blocs, rather than two parties dominating and eventually eradicating smaller third parties. The same institutionalist arguments as above would apply in their inverse.

This logic is more pronounced in the case of the PR systems. These are designed precisely to allow representation of third, fourth and further parties. Consequently, as many parties as share the vote according to the PR electoral formula will be represented, with no notion of having to choose between two front-runners. However, as we have already noted in relation to the PR system and its 'microcosm' underpinnings, parties are representatives of social groupings and issues. If those social groupings and issues do not exist within a political system, then why should PR encourage new parties to emerge?

Or is the electoral system a product of the party system?

It is precisely this question which has stimulated a debate between 'sociologists' and 'institutionalists' (Cox, 1997: 13–27). Sociologists maintain that it is not that party systems are a consequence of the electoral system, but precisely the inverse – the PR electoral system is a product of the party system, itself a reflection of divisions within society. The strongest proponent of this line has been Stein Rokkan, whose social structural explanations of political competition have defined this view (see Rokkan, 1970; also Lipset and Rokkan, 1967). Where PR was adopted as an electoral system, this was an elite response to enfranchisement of new sections of the electorate (in particular, the working class) to dampen the effect of a large number of new voters potentially voting for socialist parties, or equally to ensure the representation of potentially disruptive minorities often on the geographical or cultural fringes of the nascent nation-states. Once again, a synthesis of the rational and cultural institutionalist models provides the best foundation for this explanation. However, in this respect, there are cases of effective representation of regionally based minorities under plurality systems, most notably French Canadians in Quebec.

Overall, where interest-groups are present with a potentially solid electoral base, a plurality system will tend to suppress their representation, and consequently the expansion of their vote, more than a proportional representation system. However, a PR system cannot be relied upon either to generate new political parties by itself, or necessarily to increase significantly a party's share of the vote, beyond incentivising the vote more. As we shall see later, where the suppression of representation is excessive, electoral reform may result, such as in New Zealand. However, whether this is an example of cultural institutionalism reaching a 'tipping-point', or a rational response of actors to perceived market demand is a moot point.

Ideological effects

Ideology at the level of parties cannot be separated from party systems, but for the sake of clarity we have separated it in this chapter. Following Sartori's perspective that the number of parties, whilst important, is only part of party system dynamics, but that the competitive dynamics engendered by the system format are equally important, the role of electoral systems in producing such dynamics is another political effect. From the rational perspective, other things being equal, two-party competition across time tends to engender convergence of parties ideologically towards a centrist median point (Sartori, 1976; see also Downs, 1957). Parties wishing to maximise their vote will tend to converge on the centre ground in order to appeal to as wide an electoral audience as possible, and consequently moderate their appeal.[9] To the extent that parties function as opinion-leaders, we can expect this to have an additional feedback effect, moderating voters' opinions as well.

In proportional representation systems with more numerous parties, the situation is more complex, depending upon the ideological distribution of the electorate of each party. There is no incentive to converge upon the centre, necessarily, but rather to maximise the vote of the cluster of voters near to a party's relative ideological position. As Sartori (1976) has noted, there may be either centripetal or centrifugal pulls in a multi-party system, depending on the distribution of parties and voters, and thus to this extent the presence of proportional representation does not tell us about the ideological distribution of the vote. However, to the extent that in a proportional system, (actual or potential) government coalition formation is a likely necessity for winning power, parties need to be aware of their ideological neighbours, both in terms of ensuring small enough ideological distance to make a coalition viable, and in terms of not wasting vital resources in competing with these neighbours too aggressively, at the expense of competing against members of opposing coalitions. Cultural institutionalism largely removes the calculation in the above processes – parties are located in political space due to their socio-attitudinal baggage. Rational calculation can then be synthesised into but equally limited to shorter-term tactical considerations in competitive terms.

The electoral systems which illustrate this most starkly are the preference voting systems such as alternative vote and STV. Here, the logic of coalition formation is mirrored at the constituency level. Candidates need to be aware not only of the first preferences which they receive, but also of the second and third preferences which accrue from other candidates. Such a process can only be supported by the rational account, given the information-processing which must be carried out. Cultural institutionalism could account for an awareness of competing candidates, but not their relative appeal to each voter. A candidate proximate to others is more likely to accrue potentially vital second preference votes than one with a distinct stance which wins a strong set of first preferences, but far fewer second preferences among other candidates. The Australian example of the extreme right candidate winning many first preferences, but very little support from the mainstream party supporters demonstrates this admirably.

Again, however, we need to be conscious of the fact that ideology is not simply a position which can be chosen at will. Parties compete with ideological baggage and are not able to simply jump to a winning position. Thus, the extent to which they can shed this baggage to adopt a position which seems likely to benefit them under a certain electoral system may well do as much damage as good, portraying them as fickle, short-termist and at the extreme unfit to govern. Rational considerations cannot entirely eradicate the cultural 'imperative', and indeed underline the importance of being guided by this.

Institutional Effects of Electoral Change: Some Examples

One of the key means of identifying cause and effect in social sciences, and indeed in any empirically-based discipline, is to look at change in variables of interest and ascertain whether there is associated change in outcomes. So far, we have talked very much in terms of how electoral rules are associated with differing levels of proportionality, party supply, ideological distribution and so on across different countries. However, the acid test of causality for electoral systems would be to see how a change in electoral system in a single country affects political outcomes. Of course, it is very difficult to identify cases where only the electoral system has changed. Usually a change in electoral system is symptomatic of broader change in political institutions. In some cases, it may be that all other institutions have developed, and the electoral system, now anachronistic, needs to be 'brought into line' – an argument strongly supported by structural institutionalism. However, it is excessive to claim that this contextual change is the whole story – precisely the contextual importance of these changes gives insight into the actual role that electoral systems play.

France

An archetype of electoral and institutional change was the move in France from the Fourth to the Fifth Republic. The Fourth Republic (1946–1958) incorporated a highly proportional system which allowed a large number of smaller parties to compete in a polarised multi-party system, and to win representation in the legislature. These parties were in many cases federations of regional parties, particularly the Socialist Party (SFIO), or small political 'clubs'. Consequently, governments were highly heterogeneous, centre-anchored coalitions very much in the sway of their members, and therefore highly unstable and ineffective. In 1959, the Fifth Republic switched to the two-ballot plurality system for legislative elections and, from 1965 onwards, a two-ballot majoritarian system for presidential elections. The new majoritarian logic saw a reduction in the number of parties, a disappearance of the smaller parties from the National Assembly, with some small centre-right parties coalescing in the UDF, for example, as well as a nationalisation of the Socialist Party into a single party, rather than a regional federation. The mid-1970s saw two main parties on the left (communists and socialists) and on the right (UDF and Gaullists) and a switch in 1981 to one of the key characteristics of a moderate pluralist system – alternation of power with the left winning an absolute majority of seats.

To what extent was the electoral system fundamental to this change? The new competitive logic undoubtedly played a role in the dissipation of the centre-based governments and parties, and the appearance of left and right blocs (Bartolini, 1984). The centripetal logic of this electoral system – cooperating with one's political neighbours to ensure sufficient support to defeat one's enemies – also brought many of the anti-system forces of the Fourth Republic, such as communists, the extreme right and Gaullists themselves, into the more moderate fold. However, we cannot ignore other equally important elements in the changes.

First, as well as electoral change, political parties underwent institutional change – the National Assembly, which had been very powerful, particularly in its committee structures, became weakened by the proactive (rational) instigation of a strong executive President.[10]

Second, parties and the legislative electoral system received almost no mention in the Constitution, and thus were institutionally weakened as well as reformatted. Third, the charismatic presence of Charles De Gaulle in the position of the presidency drew enormous popular support to the Gaullists, forcing other parties to regroup and mobilise in order to counter this presence. Last, it was only François Mitterrand, the Socialist President of 1981, who managed to force the French Left into this reorganisation, and over a period of almost a decade: electoral dynamics were not sufficient in that respect.

Equally, although the electoral system at the national level remains identical, very different dynamics have emerged today. The extreme right *Front National* succeeds in spite of the bipolar logic of the system; Presidential candidates in 2002 proliferated to 16, from the six in 1965, with a similar increase in the number of parties at the legislative elections; the ideological spread of these parties has re-opened, from Trotskyite left to extreme right. Many of these shifts have been attributed to globalisation, the growing dominance of the EU as a decision-making arena and a new political issue, and a redundancy of the old political divides upon which the traditional party system based itself. Consequently, in France, current debate is over constitutional and institutional reform – proof that electoral systems and electoral system change can be as reactive as proactive, as structuralists would claim.

Germany

A similar desire to avoid the effects of excessive proportionality motivated the reform of the German electoral system after the Second World War. The five per cent threshold designed to prevent small parties from winning seats on the basis of the list vote initially limited the system to the Socialists, the Christian Democrats, and the minority Liberals. To the extent that these parties were moderate and limited in number, this institutional reform worked. However, in more recent years, the number of parties grew to include the Greens and, post-reunification, the former East German Communist Party, the PDS. In addition, though not represented at the national level, three extreme-right parties have experienced some renaissance, winning representation in some *Landestag* regional legislatures. In the 2005 German elections, the system provided the Christian Democrats with only a four-seat majority over the Socialists, despite the unpopularity of the Schröder government and no absolute majority, forcing a very drawn-out negotiation to form a Grand Coalition.

Italy

Similar electoral outcomes have contributed to electoral reforms in other countries, such as Italy. In this case, the proportional system had since 1946 seen the domination of the Christian Democrat (DC) party with support from various left and right coalition partners such as the Socialists, Social Democrats, Liberals and Republicans (the *pentapartito* in the cases where all parties belonged simultaneously). The increasing atrophy of the DC-led governments, and growing dissatisfaction with high levels of political corruption and clientelism[11], led to electoral reform in 1993 based upon the desire to elect a clear and accountable majority. By the 1996 election, the centrist DC had disintegrated, leaving two main coalitions, *Ulivo* on the left and *Casa delle Libertà* on the right. Again, the collapse of the DC cannot be ascribed purely to the electoral system – popular dissatisfaction with the party led to massive electoral losses in the first post-reform elections in 1994 – but the split of the party in both directions illustrates a perceived need to abandon the previously hegemonic centre.[12]

New Zealand

Conversely, the New Zealand case saw a call for a change in electoral system following a number of elections, held under the plurality system, that had returned National Party governments with fewer votes but more seats than the opposition Labour Party. Additionally, failure to enact promised policies during their incumbency and a perception that smaller parties were being excessively penalised by the plurality scheme led to the 1992 referendum landslides in favour of adopting the German list system. Since 1996, there has been a massive increase in the representation of smaller parties in the system. Again, it is important to recognise that these parties were already in existence prior to the adoption of PR. Thus, PR should not be seen as producing a multi-party system from nowhere, but rather enabling other parties who may perish under a plurality system to thrive.

Electoral System Influences on Voting

When we consider electoral system effects, it is often easy to overlook the effects that the system will have upon the very participants who legitimise democratic elections, namely voters. One reason for this is that we look at elections as a black box with multiple inputs (votes) being processed into the range of outputs which we have considered above – distribution of seats, winning parties/coalitions and by extension formation of government or executive. That the mechanics of the black box should have an effect on the output is a given. But that it will also influence the input is perhaps only becomes clear on further reflection.

Indeed, this black-box version of events is in some ways not very helpful. It works if one thinks of representation in terms of the rational institutionalist account – the process takes an incredibly complex set of desires and views, and converts them into a workable and hopefully effective means of representation. But if one thinks of representation in terms of the culturalist 'microcosm' model, then the electoral system, beyond its necessity for the sake of selection, can be seen as much as a dysfunctional black box in pursuing that aim as an aid to the process. As we have seen, all electoral systems, no matter how egalitarian and oriented towards proportionality, produce distortions in terms of vote–seat ratios; voters know this. Consequently, if we apply this metaphor to how voters view electoral systems, it gives us a clue as to the kinds of institutional effect that it has upon them: voters see electoral systems as more or less likely to provide them with what they do *not* want, and consequently they adjust their actions accordingly.

Might electoral systems discourage voting?

Perhaps the most extreme effect of an electoral system is to put people off voting at all. Electoral laws (rather than systems) are most commonly seen as discouraging voting, either actively or as a by-product of their rules. Most notoriously, literacy rules and other hurdles to voter registration have been employed in a number of countries, including the USA, to exclude certain groups from voting. Even where individuals have been theoretically enfranchised, biased application of such laws have effectively disenfranchised them, even to the extent that discriminated groups have been discouraged from trying to register (Milbrath, 1965). Similarly, even when there is no will to disenfranchise certain sections of society, the requirements of the system may do this anyway. The time and effort required to register, if this is an active duty for a citizen, or even to find the time to attend a polling station, may for some individuals be too high a price to pay, given competing responsibilities, such as work or childcare, geographic distance from a polling station, or the physical ability to get to a polling station no matter how close it is.

Does my vote matter?

Once a voter reaches the polling station, however, one might expect all systems to be equal. Not so. First, voters are aware of the effects of the electoral system under which they will be voting from previous elections. While they may not be conversant with the intricacies of the d'Hondt formula or mathematical measures of proportionality, they do understand that a 15,000 vote majority for an incumbent candidate in a plurality system would require a constituency sea-change which would be startlingly evident if it were likely to happen. In a more proportional system, however, that same majority – if it exists – may be irrelevant given the presence of an STV system such as Ireland (Eire), or matter only for the constituency seat but much less for the proportional vote, in a mixed system like Germany.[13] Incentives not to turn out may be twofold in the plurality or majoritarian case. For supporters of the incumbent, the view that the candidate's majority is big enough to allow the voter to stay home rather than vote and still get the desired result may increase abstention. For supporters of the opposition candidates, such a majority may be seen as an insuperable obstacle, rendering their time, effort and vote all wasted.

Why people do still vote under such circumstances is one of the key arguments in the psephological literature – rational accounts have to include such additional variables as civic duty, calculations of lost utility in the case of the favoured candidate being defeated, imperfect information as to the likelihood of affecting the outcome of the election, etc (Green and Shapiro, 1994). Perhaps more convincing is the culturalist take, that individuals are socialised to vote as a habit, and that other things being equal, will turn out. What is empirically certain is that, *ceteris paribus*, proportional systems enjoy higher turnout than plurality and majoritarian systems (Blais and Carty, 1990).

Can I make a difference by voting tactically?

Of course, the worry of 'wasting' one's vote may not be enough to discourage voting altogether. Instead, some voters may engage in tactical voting. In a constituency whose less lucky incumbent cannot be sure of a 15,000 vote majority, opposition supporters can contribute to his or her defeat even when their own favoured candidate is likely to trail in third or fourth place. In this case, a plurality system might encourage these supporters precisely not to vote for their preferred candidate, but instead support the second-placed candidate on the logic that rather than see their favourite win, they would prefer to ensure the loss of the incumbent.

Tactical voting, as a predominantly rational activity,[14] is generally a phenomenon of plurality and majoritarian systems, however. In a list system, the proportion of votes a party list receives will contribute to their overall seat allocation, and so to vote for a list other than the favourite is non-rational, as it can only reduce the party's proportion of the vote, no matter how infinitesimally in the case of a single voter. In a STV system, and indeed any multi-member constituency system, the ranking of preferences, quotas and allocation of surpluses renders such logic redundant. Put simply, candidates do not need to win the first seat in a multi-member constituency, only one of the seats, so aggregate preference order matters. Paradoxically perhaps, tactical voting received most attention in the USA in 2000 when the presence of a third-party candidate, Ralph Nader, saw a *lack* of tactical voting partially responsible for the loss of the Democrat candidate, Al Gore, in the key states of Florida and New Hampshire in the Presidential race.[15]

Or by 'splitting my ticket'?

In mixed systems, and any system which has multiple institutions as part of its vote, a form of strategic vote called 'ticket-splitting' offers voters the calculated possibility of expressing more than simply the expression of their favoured candidate. In the Italian and German systems, voters cast a vote for the constituency candidate and for a list, and there is no need to vote for the candidate's party on the list – quite the opposite. Sophisticated voting, casting the constituency vote according to a majoritarian logic (that is, picking a mainstream party with a chance of winning) and the list vote according to a proportional logic (that is, voting for a smaller favoured party to increase their vote share) allows both pragmatic and ideological styles of voting.

Do voters appreciate their potential effect?

However, such considerations require of voters a level of political involvement and political knowledge (see Chapter 9). Such voters need to be aware of the possibility of voting for different parties (a fairly low threshold to attain), the existence and relative strengths of parties (a threshold that is higher than one might imagine) and the political awareness of positioning vis-a-vis political parties which allows one to judge the value of voting pragmatically in one ballot, while retaining ideological allegiance in another (a high threshold). Generally, elections and in particular ballot structures which give voters more nuanced options – open lists where candidates can be ranked, or STV systems where lower preference-votes matter – are also ones which require greater input from the voter. There is evidence that, from the perspective of turnout, those ballots which require more of voters, may disincentivise voting for individuals with lower 'cognitive mobilisation', that is those who are less educated, less engaged with the political system, socially dislocated or otherwise less likely to have the desire or capacity to engage with a complex and nuanced electoral system.

Empirically, the evidence appears to be that such systems turn off many voters with low levels of cognitive mobilisation (Anduiza Perea, 2002: 663–4) and conversely that educated, politically engaged and socially implanted voters will be more likely to vote in such systems than with more basic 'black-and-white' electoral systems – closed lists and single-member plurality systems. Those who believe that preference expression is necessarily a good which will reinvigorate participatory democracy are only correct for the section of society which is most likely to turn out anyway. Budding electoral engineers may not be able to construct the outcome which they desire.[16] Turnout is as much a cultural given as a rational outcome (see Chapter 9).

Of course, as we noted in relation to changes in the electoral systems, it is always dangerous to assume that cross-sectional synchronic comparisons make good models for single nation diachronic comparisons. Given that this is only a statistical association, rather than an immutable law, an electoral engineer who changed from a preference-ranking list to a closed list might not see a rise in turnout among less mobilised voters and a fall in turnout amongst the cognitively mobilised. Turnout is a function of many interrelated and confounding factors. The change in ballot structure by itself might raise the profile of the election, engender renewed interest and raise turnout among all groups; or it might be seen as a cynical ploy, which 'cheapened' the election by making it simpler and depress turnout. Similarly, changing the ballot structure might incentivise differing competitive strategies among parties, which itself could well affect turnout.

Voters do matter

Despite the popular apathy alluded to in the introduction, electoral systems and their effects continue to fascinate scholars, because of the unique role they continue to play in linking mass publics with the political sphere. In an era when the possibilities of direct democracy, alternative representative forums and the trans-nationalisation of communities are becoming increasingly viable from the point of view of technology and infrastructures, elections still represent for the vast majority of people the principal political event of any given period, whether they choose to take part or not. The cultural institutionalist account of voting as a socialised habit still accounts well for those who vote, although the decline in turnout in recent years suggests that this behavioural trait is declining, although this does not necessarily strengthen the rational accounts – both models may simply not apply.

It is certainly true that mass movements have enjoyed a renaissance in recent years, with virtually-linked global movements meeting simultaneously in multiple nations providing an additional channel of representation and voice. But, to date their effects remain somewhat peripheral and unclear, despite their high profile, and their context is as much socio-cultural as it is political – a new pattern of cultural tradition may well be developing. However, in these respects, there are strong similarities with the traditional electoral process. It may seem somewhat tenuous to link the lack of clarity of effect of, say, the 'Make Poverty History' movement and electoral formulae on government formation.

Yet, this complexity is in both cases precisely due to their both being products of the social, cultural and political context of the time. From the competing institutionalist perspectives, the rational and cultural schools are far more adept, particularly in their synthetic format, at accounting for the effects of electoral systems on the micro-activity of actors. But in looking at the format, and particularly the *changes* in format of the electoral system, the structural school provides a clear warning to those who place too much emphasis on any rational attempt to manipulate institutions – context cannot be escaped.

As many of the authors cited above note in their own conclusions, electoral engineering can be a very unpredictable and dangerous activity. For newly democratised countries, selecting which electoral system to implement is crucial in terms of ensuring effective government where possible in a period when a nation absolutely requires clear direction; representation of minorities who, in the democratisation process, need to be included as a *sine qua non* of liberal democratic progress, whatever the cultural traditions and national stability; and political engagement by a newly enfranchised mass public. In older democracies, many of the discussions around 'government responsiveness' or 'proportionality' often see these essentially abstract notions as ends in themselves – they are not. The end should be to ensure that concrete weaknesses in an electoral system or its outcomes which need to be addressed are the basis for electoral change. The quest for proportionality, as an end in itself, and a consequent attempt to change the system, may not result in the expected or desired result.

A system with relatively homogeneous and territorially dispersed social groups is unlikely to see an explosion of representation among new parties if PR is introduced. Similarly, a regionally defined minority may find representation within a majoritarian electoral system so long as a degree of institutional autonomy and well-apportioned constituency boundaries accompany this, as in Canada or post-devolution Scotland. Equally, the pursuit of proportionality may just as easily provide support and representation for groups not originally identified as desirable in this respect. The British electoral system may undervalue the Liberal Democrats as a party, but it also contributes very strongly to the exclusion of less salutary movements such as the British National Party.

SUMMARY

- In this chapter, we have highlighted associations and causal relationships between elections and political life, in order to break down some of this complexity.

- Electoral systems, then, should not be seen as tools for elites to manipulate political outcomes and impose social and political frames.

- Instead, electoral systems should be filters to channel aggregate views, desires and attitudes into mutually acceptable outcomes and enable elites to enact policy which is both reactive (to electoral input) and proactive in the lead it takes.

- Different formulae and systems strike different balances of these two aspects, but in both cases they should principally be an endeavour to adapt to and facilitate, rather than shape, their social and political context.

Notes

1. Other measures include the Loosemore-Hanby and the Gallagher indices, which use different operationalisations of the same principle of average vote/seat difference (Lijphart, 1994: 58–62; Norris, 2004: 88–93).
2. But not necessarily of the electorate – abstention and spoiled ballots, neither of which is factored into the vote tally in France, can reduce the winner's support to less than 50 per cent of the registered electorate.
3. However, under the single non-transferable vote system, which has been used in Puerto Rico, Japan and Taiwan, among others, multiple members will be elected according to their plurality ranking.
4. According to Farrell, South Africa, which also operates a nationwide list, has the highest level of proportionality (2001: 157).
5. For an empirical demonstration of this, see Laakso and Taagepera (1989: 31–4).
6. For an alternative view, Farrell (2001) cites Katz (1997) who suggests that electoral formulae matter more in differentiating between proportional and non-proportional systems, and that district magnitude only matters in intra-PR differentiation.
7. For a study of ballot structure as a means of classifying electoral systems, see Blais (1988).
8. For a detailed analysis of the formation of coalition governments, see Laver and Schofield (1990).
9. For an alternative view, which sees parties with more distinct programmes as being more appealing to voters, see Merrill and Grofman (1999).
10. Many accounts of the shift from parliamentarism to presidentialism in France talk of them as two competing political traditions which have alternated from the Revolution until the contemporary Fifth Republic. While this is a valid culturalist account at the elite level, this tradition is more difficult to identify at the mass level, and moreover the decision to change from one to the other, and how that would be implemented, was a highly rational one. For instance, the retention of a weakened elected Assembly was a bargained outcome between Guy Mollet, Michel Debré and Charles de Gaulle.
11. The electoral system contributed to clientelism with the open list system encouraging a *voto di scambio* (exchange vote), voters winning preferential treatment for voting for named candidates.
12. Whether this dynamic continues is a moot point – the 2006 elections were held once more under the old proportional representation rules.
13. It can even potentially be an undesirable trait for the candidate, as under the Italian *scorporo* system which removes the surplus votes of winning candidates in plurality constituencies from their associated list vote.
14. A culturalist account of tactical voting would see it as a practice to which voters have become accustomed through the historical pattern of their electoral system. Indeed, the notion that an habitually lower-placed party is an institutional 'loser' may well be

a hurdle that requires a critical mass of support – or rejection of the traditional 'winners' – to be overcome. The synthetic rational-cultural account would then see a decision made to precisely vote for the 'loser' to allow it to win.

15. This of course assumes that Nader voters would have preferred a Democrat victory to a Republican one.

16. Similar cognitive mobilisation effects exist for electoral thresholds and compulsory voting, although in these cases, the lower group do not react in the expected way to 'fairer' proportional systems and obligatory turnout – it is the higher group who vote more often under low thresholds and when voting is compulsory (Anduiza Perea, 2002: 657ff.)

FURTHER READING

Duverger, M. (1963) *Political Parties: Their Organization and Activity in the Modern State*. New York: Wiley.

'Duverger's Law' linking electoral system to party system is still debated today, and this English translation of the seminal book in French provides the broader context for his consideration of parties and elections.

Farrell, D. (2001) *Electoral Systems. A Comparative Introduction*. Basingstoke: Palgrave.

This is undoubtedly the most accessible and most complete of all explanations of how electoral systems and electoral laws work.

Lipset, S. and Rokkan, S. (eds) (1967) *Party Systems and Voter Alignments: Cross-National Perspectives*. New York: The Free Press.

The introduction to this book is still one of the most widely cited – and criticised – works on the origins and structure of voting and elections. Its value comes from the social and historical context which it provides for the development of electoral behaviour, and the choice of electoral systems, across democracies.

Norris, Pippa (2004) *Electoral Engineering. Voting Rules and Political Behaviour*. Cambridge: Cambridge University Press.

This book considers the impact of electoral reforms on political behaviour, and how socio-cultural norms and social structure of representation can be affected by changes to electoral laws.

Taagepera, R. and Shugart M. (1989) *Seats and Votes. The Effects and Determinants of Electoral Systems*. New Haven, CT: Yale University Press.

This classic older text examines the effects of electoral laws in rigorous fashion, but makes the maths behind its empirical analyses accessible.

QUESTIONS FOR DISCUSSION

(1)   How far does the 'disaffection' theory go towards explaining decline in voting, and political participation more generally? How strong is the case for changing the electoral system as a way of invigorating democracy in this respect?

(2)   As the size of district magnitude increases, so greater proportionality appears. For proponents of the microcosm view of representation, how should they decide at what point to stop increasing district magnitude? At what point does the microcosm approach become unmanageable?

(3)   Explore the extent to which nations are adopting different electoral laws for different types of election (for example, general and local elections, mayoral elections, regional assemblies, and so forth). Has this historically always been the case, or is there now more differentiation between laws? If so, why is this?

(4)   Look for examples of elections in which parties and/or candidates have made strategic choices in the campaign that have significantly affected the outcome. Particularly where parties have failed – failed to secure election or won fewer seats than expected in the legislature – explore whether alternative strategies would have produced better results, and the extent to which the electoral system played any role in this.

Key Words for Chapter 4

electoral system / list systems / party system / plurality systems / proportionality / proportional representation / single transferable vote

5 Legislative–Executive Relations

Catherine Needham

CHAPTER OUTLINE

This chapter explores the role of legislatures and executives, focusing especially on the relationship between the two at a national level. In particular it looks at degrees of parliamentary autonomy in the legislative process and the significance of legislative–executive power relations to decision-making in the broader political arena, as well as discussing the value of different explanatory paradigms in the explanation of these processes.

Introduction

The division of power and responsibility between the legislature and the executive is one of the most important institutional variables in distinguishing between states. By understanding the relationship between legislative and executive institutions it is possible to trace the contours of the macro-political environment in a given state. Crucial variables such as presidentialism versus parliamentarianism cannot fully explain different political outcomes between states but they represent one of the most overt and important differences between political systems.

The chapter begins by defining legislatures and executives, and then gives an overview of the roles performed by these institutions. It goes on to look at the differences between parliamentary, presidential and semi-presidential systems. It considers how far different political outcomes between states can best be explained by differences in their macro-political structures (parliamentary/presidential/semi-presidential) or whether other institutional and non-institutional variables have more explanatory power. Rational choice, structural and cultural perspectives on legislative-executive relations are also explored within the chapter.

Defining Legislatures and Executives

The structure of legislative and executive institutions in a state is one of the key variables in the political system, helping to explain how the system operates and why different states have different political outcomes. Such outcomes include whether or not a state has established a stable democracy, how far divergent interests in a state are represented in government and whether a state is able to deliver a strong economy and successful policy programmes. Weaver and Rockman (1993) describe legislative and executive arrangements as a 'first tier' variable in explaining political outcomes, whereas other features such as federalism, the party system and the bureaucracy are second or third tier variables.

Roles of legislatures and executives

The roles of the legislature and executive are understood most easily in Montesquieu's (1748) division of administrative powers into legislative, executive and judicial functions. All these powers were to be separate from and dependent on each other. Legislatures would debate and make laws, executives would implement and enforce them and judiciaries would interpret and apply the laws. This tripartite distinction is a starting point for understanding legislative and executive roles, although it only begins to hint at the functions of these multi-purpose institutions, and can give a somewhat misleading idea of the division of labour between them. In defining legislatures and executives it helps to start by outlining their roles, although we should recognise the limitations of talking about legislatures and executives in abstract terms. As King puts it, 'Legislatures are not monolithic entities any more than executives or interest groups are; they are made up of parties and factions, of ideological tendencies, of interest-group representatives, and of individuals with all kinds of axes to grind and career considerations to keep in mind' (1981: 78). Thus while discussing common features in the roles of legislatures and executives we must remain alert to the complexity of their design and political practice.

It is also important to remember that the three theoretical perspectives – the structural, cultural and rational choice approaches – offer distinctive understandings of how legislatures and executives operate and interact.

In understanding legislative and executive roles it is also important to keep in mind the key distinction between presidential and parliamentary systems. In presidential systems the executive is separately elected and holds office independent of the political composition of the legislature. In parliamentary systems, the executive is appointed on the basis of gaining support from a majority of the legislature and holds office only so long as that support continues. The political significance of such arrangements – and the status of the hybrid semi-presidential system – will be returned to later in the chapter, having first considered some definitional issues.

Legislatures

Norton defines legislatures as 'constitutionally designated organisations for giving assent to binding measures of public policy' (1990a: 1). In democratic systems, legislatures are comprised (in large part at least) of elected members and embody the democratic principle of representation of the people. They are the most transparent institution of government, offering more media and public access than the relatively closed institutions of the executive and judiciary. Members of the legislature may be elected on the basis of proportional or majoritarian electoral systems. In majoritarian systems (such as the UK), each constituency will have its own single member of parliament, elected by a simple majority. In proportional systems, constituencies may have multiple members (as for example under the single transferable vote system used in Ireland) or some members may be elected on a regional basis, as in Germany's alternative member system. Legislators in both systems will normally belong to a political party and be elected on a party label, although states vary in the extent to which parties have clearly defined manifestos (as in the UK) or rather more vague policy platforms (as in the USA).

Most legislatures, particularly at the national level, are bicameral. In other words they have two chambers where one house will usually be elected on the basis of the popular vote, while the second may be elected on a regional basis or appointed in whole or in part. Examples of countries with regionally determined second chambers are the federal systems of Germany and the USA. Appointed second chambers are a feature of the national parliaments of the UK and Canada. The balance of powers and functions between the two chambers varies between political systems, although in most democracies the chamber elected on the basis of the popular vote will be the dominant chamber (despite often being called the lower house). Generally, appointed second chambers are weaker than those that are elected, because the former lack democratic legitimacy.

Although assenting to public policy is a feature common to legislatures, the legislative function itself is sometimes described as only one of multiple purposes, and not necessarily the most significant. As Packenham puts it 'The principal function of most of the world's legislatures is not a decisional function. Other functions – that is legitimation and recruitment and socialisation to other political roles – seem to be more important' (1970: 521). Certainly the policy-making role of legislatures is shared with executives, although systems vary in the extent to which legislators can take the lead on policy. In some states, the executive will have initiated almost all legislation passed; in other states, legislators may have more scope to place initiatives onto the agenda.

Types of Legislature

'Transformative' or 'arena' institutions?

A number of authors have sought to develop typologies, or categories, of legislatures in order to capture these differences between systems. Polsby's (1975) distinction between transformative and arena legislatures is one of the most widely used. He argues that differences between legislatures depend in large part on the extent to which they are independent from outside influences (particularly the executive). Transformative legislatures have a capacity, independent of the executive, to shape and transform policy proposals into law. They can therefore be seen as strong legislative bodies. Arenas, by contrast, provide a setting in which political actors interact, but have little or no scope to modify legislation presented by the executive, and can therefore be seen as relatively weak bodies. Arenas may be best understood as forms of political theatre, which dramatise and simplify policy issues for public and media consumption, whereas transformative legislatures directly influence the content of public policy. Transformative and arena-type legislatures are of course ideal types: most real world institutions will fall somewhere on a continuum between these extremes. Polsby gives the example of the United States Congress as coming close to the transformative model of a legislature with the UK Parliament falling towards the arena end of the continuum.

Degrees of influence on policy

Other authors have developed alternative ways to distinguish between types of legislature, although still focusing on the crucial variable of legislative independence from the executive. Mezey (1979) argues that the key difference between legislatures is the extent to which they can modify and reject executive policy. Norton (1990b) adds a third criterion: can the legislature substitute its own policy for that of the executive? For example, although the UK Parliament in occasional rebellious periods has modified or rejected government legislation, it has no mechanism to substitute its own legislation. The US Congress does have such a substitution power. Control over budgetary issues is also an important measure of legislative influence. In most systems the executive will present the budget to the legislature, but there is variance in the extent to which legislators can modify and add to the draft bill. Circumstances, such as those in the USA when a deadlock between President Clinton and Congress over the budget caused government to temporarily shut down in 1995, are unusual.

In measuring how far legislatures have the ability to modify and reject executive policy, Mezey calls attention to the extent to which such powers must be real and not merely constitutional – in other words they must be embodied in 'soft' institutions (political norms) as well as 'hard' constitutional arrangements. He argues that legislators must be able to impose constraints on executive policy without risking legislative dissolution; otherwise the constitutional power to modify or reject will remain a largely hypothetical one, unused by legislators who do not wish to risk their jobs in new elections. We must also be sensitive to points of executive influence during the legislative process. Even if legislative committees impose hundreds of amendments to a draft bill, we must observe how many of these amendments were initiated by the executive rather than by legislators acting independently.

Degrees of public support

Mezey adds a further dimension when considering the power of legislatures: how far the institution has public support. Embedded institutions, those with strong public support, will be able to resist challenges to their legitimacy from outside interests (including the executive) and are therefore likely to endure. Legislatures that lack public support are vulnerable to dissolution or closure, and therefore are weak institutions, even if their formal powers could be classed as 'transformative'. He gives the example of the Philippines after the Second World War, in which the legislature had expansive powers but little elite support, and was dissolved by President Marcos in a 1972 coup. The extent of public support will be a feature of how far the legislature fulfils the expectations of elites and mass interests in society, with particular emphasis on meeting the needs of elite groups (Mezey, 1979).

Representing voters

Much attention has therefore been placed on the extent to which legislatures make law and their relationship with the executive in doing so. However, as multi-functional institutions, legislatures play a number of important roles beyond that of passing legislation. As the representatives of local populations, legislators bring the interests and concerns of voters into political debate. This may range from supporting the case of an individual voter who is a victim of maladministration by the bureaucracy, to articulating the interests of the local economic needs of their constituency, to more broadly representing the public interest in relation to issues such as food safety, education and foreign affairs. Through the defence of these interests, legislators publicise and debate policy issues, providing a forum in which the media and the public can be made aware of and educated about political controversies. Thus legislatures are seen to fulfil an important educative function.

The role of representing voters comes with its own tensions, however, since legislators must balance the interests of their own constituents and the wider public, for example in the closure of an under-utilised hospital or the siting of a waste incinerator. Legislators must also balance representation of constituent interests with loyalty to their party's policy agenda: parties that promise low taxation, for example, provide reduced opportunities for legislators to bring extra government spending into the constituency. King also points out that legislators have to balance the need for policy expertise, essential to the educative function, with their claim to represent the interests of ordinary voters – to remain one of 'us' rather than 'them', as King puts it (1981: 84). Rational choice theorists have examined how legislators balance all these different loyalties and the incentives that shape their voting patterns. In a classic study of the US Congress, for example, Mayhew found that members of the US Congress were motivated primarily by the desire to secure re-election, driving their policy priorities and voting behaviour.

Socialisation and recruitment

The roles of recruitment and socialisation to other political roles, highlighted by Packenham above, are also important. In many states, particularly those with parliamentary rather than presidential systems, politicians begin their national political careers in the legislature before progressing to leadership positions in the executive. Legislatures are thus recruitment grounds for political leaders, and environments within which politicians learn about the 'soft' institutional norms that shape political life as well as the hard constitutional parameters of the system. The political party will play a key socialisation function, providing social and in some cases economic resources for incoming members. Cohesive legislative parties will be able to offer promotion opportunities – into government office or onto prestigious committees – for their members, usually in return for member loyalty to the party line. Thus party loyalty may be a function either of strategic calculation by ambitious members (the rational choice explanation) or may be rooted in the socialisation of members into party norms (the cultural explanation). In either case, institutional rules (voting arrangements, committee allocations, bill timetabling), shape the context within which loyalty is expressed and faithfulness to the party line rewarded.

Balancing the various roles

Even in arena-style legislatures, legislators may perform these educative and socialisation roles robustly. Indeed, with less time devoted to the development or modification of policy, members of the legislature may have more time to give to other roles. Representing the interests of voters is likely to be a concern for all legislators, particularly those with small electoral majorities who must prove to constituents that they are delivering for the local area. However, those legislators who lack the power to modify, reject or substitute executive-inspired policy will be much more constrained in what they can offer local constituents. Compare for example the 'pork barrel' politics of the US Congress, in which members can add items to the presidential budget with an eye to the needs of their constituents, with the UK Parliament, which must accept the government budget without amendment. The expectations which voters place on their representatives will also vary between states. For example, in the USA and Italy there is a well-established tradition of legislators delivering for their local electorate, whereas the British approach (at least traditionally) emphasised the independence of the parliamentarian from constituent demands.

Holding governments to account

Once laws are passed, legislators play a role in ensuring that the executive is acting within the law and implementing policy effectively. This may include approving budgetary requests, overseeing spending, evaluating policy implementation and investigating claims of maladministration or impropriety. In most legislatures, committees will be the focal point for executive scrutiny, with each committee shadowing a particular executive department. The ability of legislators to evaluate and investigate executive actions varies widely, linked in part to the design, culture and resources of the committee system. US Congressional committees are well served with staff and resources to conduct hearings, and can command time on the floor of the chamber to discuss reports. Similarly, committees in the German Bundestag have a large degree of autonomy, using party, civil service and interest group advisors to contribute to the legislative and scrutiny process. In other states, such as the UK and France, legislative committees must perform the scrutiny function with few resources and little confidence that their reports will receive attention in a government-dominated parliamentary timetable. Here it is clear that institutional rules on timetabling and resources play a key role alongside committee cultures and the incentive structures facing members in explaining the influence of legislative committees.

Committees often develop cultures of cross-partisanship to increase the effectiveness of executive scrutiny. However, even the best-resourced legislative committees will struggle to give thorough attention to a bureaucracy employing hundreds of thousands of staff with a billion dollar budget. Coverage of the bureaucracy will therefore be patchy and may reflect the political interests of committee members rather than the areas of public policy that require investigation. Oversight is often at its most effective when legislators are able to interest the media in their inquiry – much more likely if a salacious sexual or financial angle is involved than if an inquiry deals with technical aspects of policy implementation.

Limitations to parliamentary scrutiny

The vigour with which legislators perform the scrutiny role is limited by a number of factors. In parliamentary systems, where the executive holds office on the grounds of commanding a majority in (one house of) the legislature, legislators from the government's party play an additional and conflicting role: that of sustaining the executive in office. The impetus to ensure that the executive is acting properly will be weakened to avoid bringing down the government or attracting censure to cabinet ministers. Tensions between supporting and scrutinising the executive are most pronounced in parliamentary systems, since the executive in presidential systems is separately elected and is not dependent on majority support from the legislature. However even in presidential systems legislative scrutiny may be offset by a desire of legislators to show support to an executive from their own political party. Indeed in all systems, a common bond of party is likely to place a limit on public rows between the legislature and executive. Internal party channels, to which the media and public have little access, are likely to be an important arena for the resolution of disputes (King, 1976). Thus we must be wary of reading too much from an absence of observable conflict between legislatures and executives. Each of the three theories – rational choice, structural and cultural explanations – alerts us to the ways in which actors can accept apparently suboptimal outcomes due respectively to reciprocal deals, cultural norms or economic conditions.

Executives

This discussion of legislatures highlights the extent to which executive roles cannot neatly be bounded by the notion of implementing and enforcing the law. Executives provide leadership within the political system, which is likely to go beyond the implementation of legislation to include the initiation of policy, oversight of the bureaucracy, party management and the arbitration of conflicts within the political system. Executives represent the country in international affairs as well as performing ceremonial functions at the domestic and international level. For that reason they are often seen to symbolise the nation, although the formal role of head of state may be played by a monarch in a constitutional monarchy such as the UK or Holland.

Presidential or cabinet systems?

Whereas the legislature is a multi-member body with many hundreds of legislators, executive power is exercised by a single person, in the case of a president, or by a small number of people in a cabinet system. The political executive is usually the head of a large bureaucracy, employing hundreds of thousands of staff and spending a substantial proportion of state GDP. However, formal executive power will be embodied not in the bureaucracy as a whole but in its political masters – be it a president (in presidential systems) or a cabinet (in parliamentary systems). Thus executive power is concentrated whereas legislative power is diffuse. There is an important distinction though between single person (presidential) executives and collective (cabinet) executives. Although presidents will usually have a cabinet of advisers, presidential systems place executive authority solely in the hands of the president. Even in parliamentary systems that are dominated by a strong prime minister, executive power is formally exercised collectively rather than individually.

Unlike legislatures, executives are relatively opaque institutions, with much of their work shielded from direct public scrutiny. Whereas the role of the legislature is to debate and publicise policy issues, inviting the public and the media to observe the policy process, decision-making within the executive is usually hidden from view. Thus the process of understanding the balance of power within the executive and between the executive and other institutions in the political systems can be more difficult than studying the legislature. Sources such as off-the-record media briefings, leaked reports and the memoirs of former cabinet members can be vital tools to understand executive politics.

Controlling the policy agenda

A striking feature of executives across democratic states is the extent to which they control policy initiation and agenda setting. This is true even in relation to 'transformative' legislatures such as the US Congress. The ability of the executive to take the initiative in the political system is built on the advantage of holding concentrated power, based on an electoral mandate, and is exacerbated by party discipline and media expectations. Legislatures experience serious obstacles even in terms of clarifying policy preferences for themselves, let alone insisting that these should take precedence over those of their chief executive – especially if such assertions are in opposition to the ideas of the government leadership. With a small team of decision-makers dominating executive policy-making, it is much easier for presidents and cabinets to develop and coordinate policy than it is for hundreds of legislators.

Fulfilling an electoral mandate

Most executives will have been elected on a platform of policies – either directly in a presidential system, or indirectly in a parliamentary system – and can therefore claim a democratic mandate to pursue their ideas. Indeed, voters are likely to expect the president or prime minister to implement their manifesto promises, and may base their future voting behaviour in part on the extent to which promises are fulfilled. The media tends to find it easier to report policy in terms of what the president or prime minister has done or not done, rather than to report on the diffused lines of accountability offered by legislative politics.

Where the party or parties of the executive have a majority in the legislature, the two institutions have a common interest in promoting a coherent and successful policy agenda, limiting legislative resistance to executive influence. Here cultural influences and individual incentives are likely to run in tandem, promoting a common agenda. Even in systems where the executive must govern alongside an opposition-dominated legislature, members will usually respond to an agenda set by the president. It is rare for example, even in a transformative legislature such as the US Congress, for members to develop their own policy agenda in opposition to that of the president. Newt Gingrich's 1994 *Contract with America*, a policy platform for Republicans who took control of Congress during the presidency of Democrat Bill Clinton, was a rare and ultimately unsuccessful effort to do just that.

Implementing policy

In addition to initiating legislation, a key role of the executive is to implement policy once it has been approved by the legislature. Usually laws will set out the broad parameters of policy, leaving the political executive and bureaucracy to work out the detail and identify the best mechanisms for implementation. On the technical detail of policy, political executives may be heavily reliant on bureaucratic expertise. Given the vast size of the state in most advanced democracies and the complexity of its organisation, presidents, prime ministers and cabinets will struggle to remain informed about all but the most high-profile policy areas. Political leaders must prioritise, giving attention only to those areas which seem to be the most troublesome, or which offer electoral rewards or sanctions. High-profile areas such as the economy, foreign affairs and security will demand more attention from the political executive than some of the more technical and regulatory activities of the bureaucracy. Given the widely-shared hypothesis that bureaucracies are resistant to policy change (see Chapter 6), political leaders may struggle to steer the state machine in a particular direction. In some systems, bureaucrats may be able to utilise links to legislative committees, interest groups and political parties as a counterweight to executive leadership.

Collective responsibility

A prime minister is assisted in the job of bureaucratic management by the cabinet, which will be drawn from the same party and coalition of parties, and should therefore promote the will of the executive within government departments. Collective responsibility of the cabinet protects individual members from censure, whereas a president, whose cabinet is no more than a collection of appointed advisors, is left more exposed. However, prime ministers must struggle to a greater degree than most presidents with the challenges of managing a collective executive. Cabinet members are high-profile politicians, often with their own support in the legislature, and their views cannot easily be sidelined. This management role is particularly difficult when the cabinet is drawn from a coalition of parties, each with a different set of political requirements. The delicate job of negotiating and trading off policies between different wings of the cabinet, necessary in all political systems, will be intensified as coalition members demand support for their policy interests in return for supporting those of others. Here the job of the prime minister can become one of negotiation and compromise, on the Dutch model, rather than the strong political leadership usually associated with prime ministers in single-party executives such as in the UK.

Balancing party and government leadership

Aside from developing and implementing policy, most executive leaders will also hold the real or *de facto* leadership of their political parties. As the most high-profile representative of that party, the president or prime minister will be presented by the media as the party leader, even if – as in the USA and Germany – the executive leader does not formally hold that role. Executive leaders will therefore play a role in managing the party bureaucracy, which is likely to involve candidate selection, fund-raising and communication with grass-roots members. The tensions between this role and that of executive leader have been vividly demonstrated across political systems in corruption scandals involving the misuse of office for party political gain. Few countries in recent years have been free of scandals linking senior politicians to the improper distribution of government contracts or patronage powers in order to raise money for party campaigning.

Personality in politics

The range of roles fulfilled by the head of the political executive – from leader to negotiator, from head of state to party fund-raiser, from policy visionary to technical expert – highlights the diversity of skills needed by the incumbent(s). The success of a political leader will depend in part on his or her ability to marshall the resources at his or her disposal – both personal and institutional – and to make the most of political circumstances such as legislative majorities and positive public-opinion ratings.

Analysis of the executive has therefore often focused on the personality of the president or the prime minister and their presentational flair. However, others have argued that the personal leadership style of one incumbent versus another is too narrow and atheoretical a prism through which to consider the executive. Rhodes and Dunleavy (1995) draw attention to the role of the 'core executive' as a whole, encompassing a range of institutions involved in the operation of central government, which will change from issue to issue and often involve political leaders in negotiation rather than direction. As Smith puts it, 'Power depends on relationships between actors and not command. Frequently outcomes can be positive-sum rather than zero-sum games. In order to achieve goals actors have to negotiate, compromise and bargain' (1998: 67–8).

Legislative–Executive Relations

Analyses of legislative–executive relations have tended to see the powers of legislatures as declining in relation to those of executives over the last hundred years. Although such claims have been made for decades (for example, by Bryce in the 1920s), and to some extent rest on an overemphasis on the legislative role of legislatures, it is possible to point to a number of trends which have assisted executive dominance of the system. These trends have made it more difficult for legislatures to fulfil not only their law-making role, but also some of their other roles, including executive scrutiny, education and socialisation. The growth in the scope and complexity of the state, including the size of the bureaucracy and its monopoly of policy expertise, for example, makes it increasingly difficult for legislators to scrutinise executive actions.

Diminishing the role of legislatures?

Civil service reforms in many countries since the 1980s have exacerbated these trends through pushing more powers out to arms-length agencies and the private sector, over which legislatures have limited oversight. New institutions at the intergovernmental or supranational level, especially the European Union, but also the World Trade Organization and the G8, have created new arenas within which executives can operate relatively independent of legislative oversight. In this environment of institutional proliferation, it is judicial bodies that have acquired new relevance, determining the balance of power between institutions and their scope to interfere in the lives of citizens. Public policy issues, such as police powers, health provision and environmental protection, become matters for the courts as much as for legislatures (see Chapter 7).

Media Influence

At the same time, the emergence and influence of new forms of media (cable and satellite television, the Internet) have ensured that legislators no longer play a key role in educating public opinion. The media itself has become a source of policy information for those that want it, while at the same time downgrading its coverage of legislative debates. Media outlets, which aim to simplify and personify political debates, have looked to the executive leader for their sound bites and photo opportunities, eschewing the complexity of the legislative process. Presidents and prime ministers have responded to this attention by reshaping their own presentational style and policy priorities to maximise positive coverage: vague policy pronouncements from telegenic political leaders replace detailed political programmes. Political leaders appear on daytime television shows and in glossy magazines to offer unspecific policy sentiments, rather than facing legislative interrogation or the tricky questions posed by political reporters.

Plebiscitary democracy

The rise of plebiscitary forms of democracy has further weakened the claim of legislatures to represent public opinion, particularly given declining turnout in legislative elections across advanced democracies. Executives can now go directly to the people through a range of techniques such as referenda, opinion polls, focus groups, citizens' juries, town-hall meetings and so on. Such techniques can offer a more accurate and informed account of public attitudes than that claimed by legislators, given declining turnout in legislative elections (see Chapter 9).

Are strong legislatures really necessary?

Thus legislatures struggle to maintain their importance in the face of economic, social and technological changes that have been to the advantage of the executive. The extent to which legislatures have been able to retain relevance in the political system has varied between countries. However, King (1981) points out that we should not necessarily assume that such a strong legislature is a desirable feature of the political system: independent legislatures in the French Fourth Republic and Weimar Germany are not associated with effective policy-making, nor did the American Congress deal effectively in the 1970s with the challenges facing the US economy and welfare state.

Similarly, we should not assume that legislative–executive relations must be a zero-sum – in other words that the more power is held by one institution; the less is held by another. If both institutions enjoy high levels of public support, and are perceived as democratically legitimate, it is likely that the legislature and the executive will be important institutional players. In systems where public trust in the political system is declining, electoral turnout is low and a military power waits in the shadows to dissolve democratic institutions, both executive and legislature power may be weak. Thus the overall stability of the regime is an independent variable shaping the power of both executive and legislative institutions. The relationship between regime stability and legislative–executive relations is returned to later in the chapter.

Parliamentary and Presidential Systems

One of the key variables in explaining the relationship between executives and legislatures is the distinction between parliamentary and presidential systems, and it is to that institutional difference that attention now turns. Whereas the soft institutions of politics – the political norms and practices – can be hard to observe and measure, constitutional distinctions between parliamentary and presidential systems should be easy to draw. Some of the implications of the parliamentary/presidential divide can be less obvious, however, and the existence of hybrid systems, that include a president and a prime minister, confuses the picture further. It is important to clarify the key features of these systems before going on to look in more detail at their impact.

Parliamentary systems

In parliamentary systems, the executive is drawn from the party or coalition of parties that hold a majority of seats in (one of the houses of) the legislature. The executive is collective (a cabinet) and holds office on the basis of its ability to command continued support in the legislature. Thus the personnel of the legislature and executive overlap, and there are no separate elections for executive office. The government's authority is entirely dependent upon parliamentary confidence. If the government loses that confidence, a new executive must be formed, either from existing parties within the legislature or from a new configuration of parties following a general election. The timing of elections is normally flexible within parliamentary systems, and called by the leader of the majority party or coalition of parties. A prime minister leads the executive and appoints members of the cabinet, although cabinet members are his/her colleagues (rather than merely advisors) with their own power base in the party. The prime minister will be head of government but the position of head of state will normally be held by a monarch or a titular president.

Presidential systems

Presidential systems, in contrast, provide for the direct election of an executive leader who will normally be both head of state and head of government. This single person executive is elected by universal suffrage (sometimes indirectly through an electoral college) to execute the laws mandated by the legislature. Thus such systems are characterised by a strict separation of powers and personnel between the legislature and executive, and shared democratic legitimacy since both hold a mandate from the electorate. Presidents are usually elected for a fixed term and have security of tenure during that term, outside of the exceptional circumstances that might warrant impeachment.

The president appoints members of the cabinet, who act as his agents rather than shared holders of executive authority. Most analyses of presidential executives tend to focus on the USA, either because other presidential regimes are hybrid systems (discussed in more detail below) or because, like Rose (1991), we might argue that large numbers of presidential systems are essentially authoritarian and therefore of little interest in cross-national comparisons of democratic regimes. However, this essentially US-centric approach can be criticised in turn by arguing that too much attention has been paid to one, albeit influential, case, which in many ways is quite 'deviant'.

Semi-presidential systems

Semi-presidential systems are the hybrid system, with an elected president governing alongside a prime minister who is accountable to parliament. However, the criteria that systems need to meet to be classed as semi-presidential are contentious. The classic definition is given by Duverger (1980) who argued that such systems have a directly elected president, with significant *de jure* and *de facto* powers, along with a prime minister who has to enjoy the confidence of a directly elected parliament. However, as Siaroff (2003) points out, this definition is problematic because it depends heavily on subjective judgement about what are considered to be significant *de facto* presidential powers. Thus it is not always clear which states should be counted as being semi-presidential. France is usually included as a classic case, as is Finland, although systemic reforms since 2000 have weakened the power of the Finnish President. Austria, Ireland and Iceland have directly elected presidents, although their *de facto* powers are weak, leading Stepan and Skach (1993) to exclude them from their list of semi-presidential states. Conversely, others such as Elgie (2004), call for them to be included, since they are neither pure presidential or pure parliamentary systems. Many post-communist states also classify as semi-presidential, including Poland, Bulgaria, Ukraine and Moldova.

The potential for intra-executive conflict in the semi-presidential model is well-developed, as the prime minister is expected to act as both the agent of the president and of parliament. It can also be shown that variance may exist in the balance of power between the president and the prime minister within the semi-presidential category, depending in part on whether the president controls the appointment and dismissal of the prime minister or whether such power is held by parliament. Perhaps, like Siaroff, we should consider paying more attention to a broader range of variables in presidential power, such as whether the president chairs formal cabinet meetings, has broad emergency powers and plays a central role in foreign policy. Several writers indeed emphasise the importance of institutional rules, developing subcategories of regimes to encompass different patterns of presidential dominance with hybrid systems.

Such categorisation is, however, further complicated by the variance within states over time. The semi-presidentialism of France looked different in the president-dominated years of de Gaulle (1962–1969) than it has in the years of *cohabitation* (1986–1988, 1993–1995, 1997–2002) when a president has had to govern alongside a prime minister from an opposition party. The power of the president will clearly be greatest when his or her party has a majority in the legislature, ensuring that the prime minister operates largely on the president's instruction. In periods where the executive and legislature are controlled by different parties, the president must deploy skill to avoid the political initiative being taken by a prime minister from a rival party. In such a situation jurisdiction may be informally shared, with the president monopolising 'high politics' such as defence, foreign affairs and the economy, and the prime minister taking control of more detailed aspects of policy.

Theorising Executives and Legislatures

If we want to know why a country adopted a particular set of institutions – parliamentary, presidential, semi-presidential – we can utilise different theoretical positions to try to find the answer. The rational choice approach understands institutions as the outcome of strategic bargaining between self-interested actors. Rational choice theorists often employ game theory – explaining political outcomes by exploring how actors take strategic decisions and anticipate the decisions of others – and understand institutional selection as the choice of the rules of the game. Thus political actors seek to adopt the institutional configuration that will best meet their interests and will support that configuration for as long as those interests are met. For example, the choice of electoral system will be shaped by the preferences and strength of existing political parties, which will seek to integrate new actors without losing their dominant position.

Cultural theorists consider how existing cleavage structures, for example along ethnic, linguistic or class lines, influence the choice of a given set of institutions, as we will see in Chapter 9. The winner-takes-all presidential system, for example, may be seen as unsuitable for countries where communities are divided along ethno-linguistic lines. Historical factors may be relevant here, with a focus on how past institutions shape present institutional design, exploring how institutions are 'path-dependent'. Historical experience of strong or weak political leadership is likely to shape regime choice, and play a role in explaining the relative powers of legislatures and executives. In the UK, parliament emerged not as a legislative body but as an institution to assert certain rights against the sovereign. The US system was designed to limit executive control, as were some of the constitutions adopted in Western Europe after 1945, influenced by recent memories of fascism. The French Fifth Republic, established in 1958, was an attempt to reassert executive power into a legislative-dominated system, creating a dual-executive structure.

These theories can also offer explanations as to why institutions persist in their given form rather than breaking down. Why, for example, do opposition parties continue to sit in legislatures in which they are effectively excluded from policy influence? Rational choice theorists would argue that institutions endure because the risks of change are too great: there is uncertainty of outcome and collective action problems inhibit agreement on alternatives. Cultural theorists argue that people follow societally-defined rules even when not in their own interests. Institutions like political parties socialise new members into the values that define the institution, creating the 'club'-like environment which is seen as characteristic of many legislatures. Structural theories identify the broader economic purposes served by institutions – such as securing fiscal stability and reassuring financial markets – which may act as a brake on institutional reform.

As well as seeking to provide explanatory theories (why institutions exist in the form that they do), comparative theorists have also sought to explore normative questions such as which type of regime – parliamentary, presidential or semi-presidential – performs best. Clearly this depends in large part on what a regime is required to do. If the goal of the political process is to ensure high levels of legislative input into policy-making, a presidential system is likely to do so more effectively than a parliamentary system. Parliamentary systems offer no career ladder for politically ambitious people other than serving in the executive, thus giving them an incentive to prefer a weak assembly and strong executive, whereas presidential systems provide powerful legislative committee posts, giving such individuals an incentive to strengthen legislative power (King, 1981: 80). However, to assess which regime type performs better overall, it is important to develop some criteria of effectiveness. Two approaches have dominated the literature: first, measures of the *stability* of the system; and, second, measures of the *performance* of the system.

Regime Survival

There has been a robust debate among political scientists about whether presidential and parliamentary systems are better at delivering stable democratic regimes. One of the best known contributions is that of Juan Linz (1990), whose assessment of regime breakdown in Latin American presidencies led him to conclude that parliamentary systems offer greater scope for resolving political tensions, particularly in polarised societies. The divided legitimacy in presidential systems, in which both legislature and executive can claim a mandate from the people, can paralyse decision-making, offering no democratic basis on which to resolve conflict. Accountability becomes blurred as both institutions claim credit for policy successes and offload the blame for policy failures. Rigidity is also introduced into presidential systems by fixed-term elections, and the winner-takes-all nature of single-person executive elections that preclude power sharing. Whereas parties might help to link the interests of the executive and the legislature, the increased personalisation of presidential politics means that parties are sidelined in plebiscitary elections. Linz is deeply sceptical about the potential of presidential systems to ensure democratic stability, particularly in states with deep political cleavages and multiple parties. As he suggests, it is perhaps no accident that in situations such as these, the military is likely to intervene.

Linz argues that Latin American cases offer more insight into presidential regimes than the 'deviant' case of the USA. However his findings have been challenged by a number of authors. Shugart and Carey (1992), looking at a broader range of cases, highlight the increased accountability and transparency of presidential systems over parliamentary regimes, and do not find presidencies any more likely to break down. Horowitz argues that Linz is too focused on the experience of Latin America, failing to give adequate attention to the ways that parliamentary systems have failed to establish stable democracies in parts of Asia and Africa, particularly where majority ethnic groups can shut other groups out of power (1990: 74). Horowitz argues that it is not the presidential/parliamentary split *per se* that matters, but rather the difference between majoritarian and proportional electoral systems. The winner-takes-all nature of majoritarian electoral systems – in which one party is likely to secure control of legislative and executive power – weakens both presidential and parliamentary systems. Proportional electoral systems, on the other hand, encourage multipartism and enable minorities to gain meaningful representation. Thus, Horowitz argues that they are more stable than winner-takes-all majoritarian systems, regardless of whether the system is presidential or parliamentary.

Mainwaring (1993) similarly looks to variables beyond simply the presidential/ parliamentary divide, although he reaches a different conclusion to Horowitz. Mainwaring argues that, despite proportional systems being more inclusive, they tend to disperse power and make it difficult for governments to be effective. In particular, he finds that 'the combination of a multiparty system and presidentialism is especially inimical to democracy' (1993: 198). This is because the tendency towards conflict between the executive and legislature in a presidential system is exacerbated by multipartism, leading to institutional immobilism, compounded by ideological polarisation and difficulties of inter-party coalition building. Multipartism is less problematic in parliamentary regime, since they 'have more coalition-building mechanisms that facilitate multiparty democracy' (Mainwaring, 1993: 223). Thus there is a range of perspectives on regime stability, with much of the variance appearing to come from case selection, alongside uncertainty about which set of institutional outcomes (inclusivity and power sharing versus accountability and strong leadership) are most closely correlated with regime endurance.

Regime Performance

Setting aside the issue of regime stability, it is also important to consider how different types of executive–legislative arrangements vary in their performance once in office. Although this is a vital measure in determining the appeal of different political arrangements, it is by no means clear how performance should be measured. Following Elgie (2004: 321), we might ask whether 'studies should focus on economic issues like GDP', economic growth or inflation? Or on quantifiable or pseudo-quantifiable political issues such as cabinet stability, Freedom House scores for human rights or the presence of divided government? Or rather, should they focus on more qualitative political matters, such as political leadership, policy effectiveness or the quality of political life?

Weaver and Rockman (1993) have conducted one of the best-known assessments of the performance of different types of political system. They measure the performance of government on a range of criteria such as its ability to set and maintain priorities, to implement policy, to coordinate conflicting objectives and to represent diffuse interests. However, like many of the writers on regime stability, Weaver and Rockman look beyond the presidential/parliamentary distinction to explain most of the variance in regime performance. They conclude that, 'The distinction between parliamentary systems and American checks and balances captures only a small part of the potential institutional influences on governmental capacity' (1993: 446). In understanding the differences between political systems it is important to explore the significance of 'second' and 'third tier' variables (Weaver and Rockman, 1993), as well as some of the soft institutions such as political norms.

What role does party play?

The role of party – one of Weaver and Rockman's second-tier variables – can be crucial in understanding the relative powers of legislatures and executives. Parties connect the executive and legislature, directly in parliamentary systems and more informally in presidential ones. A number of authors have argued that executive–legislative relations are better understood by focusing on political parties and the party system, rather than on whether the system is presidential or parliamentary. Two features of the party system are particularly significant: the number of parties represented in parliament and the internal cohesiveness of those parties. Both of these features will themselves be shaped by a range of factors, some of them institutional such as the electoral system, and some of them cultural such as the cleavage structures within society.

In his classic study, Polsby (1975) argued that it may be the internal characteristics of political parties that make the legislature transformative or arena in nature. In particular he focuses attention on three criteria: the extent to which parties are broad coalitions versus narrow groups of interests; how far parties are highly centralised and hierarchical versus decentralised and non-hierarchical; and how far the composition of voting blocs on successive issues is fixed or shifting. Thus according to these criteria it is possible to draw clear distinctions between US political parties – coalitional, decentralised and flexible – and UK parties, which are less coalitional, more hierarchical and fixed. However the impact of these variables is an ambiguous one. Legislatures with a small number of cohesive and hierarchical parties may provide a mandate and majority support for a powerful single-party executive, leaving the legislature with little scope for policy initiative. In contrast, legislatures with decentralised parties and shifting coalitions may struggle to coordinate their activities sufficiently to substitute their own policy agenda for that of the executive.

Federal or unitary systems

Other important 'third tier' variables include the federal or unitary nature of the state. Federalism decentralises power, taking many issues out of the arena of national politics, but it also increases the significance of the second chamber of the national legislature if that chamber is representative of provincial interests. The German Bundesrat, for example, controlled by the German *Lander* (or regions) is one of the most powerful second chambers in Western Europe.

Bureaucracy

Characteristics of the bureaucracy may also be important in understanding executive–legislative relations. For example, do highly centralised and 'closed' bureaucracies, such as those of the UK and Canada, limit legislative oversight, whereas more decentralised open systems, such as the USA and Switzerland allow greater legislative input?

Macroeconomic factors

It may be, as structural theorists argue, that government effectiveness is hampered not by institutional design, but rather by macroeconomic factors. Padgett argues that a growth in executive workload 'combined with the increased internationalisation of the economic and political order has reduced the capacity of chief executives in almost all advanced states for exercising their constitutional prerogatives' (1994: 15). Similarly Weaver and Rockman point out that it is possible to argue that, '[M]ost shortcomings in governmental effectiveness are inherent in governing complex societies with a high level of demands on government, rather than the consequences of any particular set of institutions' (1993: 16) In systems where decisions over economic policy have been transferred out of the state – as, for example, in the case of eurozone countries – there is a limited extent to which government economic performance is a feature of anything internal to the political regime.

'Veto' players

Thus there is a multiplicity of variables that explain regime performance. Tsebelis' (1995, 2002) work on 'veto players' is one of the most important contributions to understanding the interaction between these variables. Veto players for Tsebelis are individual or collective actors whose agreement is required for a policy decision. Focusing on the capacity of political systems to produce policy change, Tsebelis argues, that systems with fewer, more congruent and more cohesive groupings of veto players will find it easier to bring about change than those with multiple players. He lists Westminster systems, dominant party systems (such as Japan) and single-party minority governments as having only one veto player, whereas coalitions in parliamentary systems, presidential and/or federal systems have multiple veto players. Along with Weaver and Rockman, he concludes that presidential regimes and coalition governments in parliamentary systems have more in common with each other (given their high number of veto points/players) than either does with single party parliamentary regimes.

With its emphasis on the way that individuals or groups use political institutions to advance their preferences, Tsebelis' approach is consistent with rational choice explanations of political change. However his work cannot tell us who should count as a veto player in a given political system, for which it is necessary to rely on an understanding of the hard and soft political institutions that shape the power distribution in a political system, as well as key cultural factors. The strength of Tsebelis' approach is that it provides a parsimonious (in other words fairly simple) theory, with multiple empirical illustrations, and gets us out of generalisations about legislative–executive relations that rest too heavily on a parliamentary versus presidential distinction.

Multi-tasking and Interconnection

To understand legislatures and executives, we have to recognise their multiple roles and interconnectedness. Legislatures' assent to public policy, although in most systems policy will be initiated by the executive, and legislative influence will extend no further than the scope to modify or reject the legislation. Thus legislatures will often be significant actors as a result of other roles – education, recruitment, socialisation, scrutiny – rather than as law-makers. Alongside agenda setting, executive leaders must implement policy, manage the bureaucracy, and provide political and partisan leadership. The size and complexity of the modern state has tended to give the executive more freedom to undertake policy implementation free from legislative oversight, although it has also weakened the ability of political leaders to manage the bureaucratic machine.

Legislatures and executives can be divided into presidential, parliamentary or semi-presidential regime types, and something of the balance of power in the political system can be deduced from this categorisation. In parliamentary systems, the executive is collective and dependent on majority support in the legislature, creating incentives for majority parties (or coalitions) to work together across institutional lines to keep the government in office. In presidential systems, executives and legislatures have separate mandates tending to produce greater legislative independence and weakening the bonds of party. Semi-presidential systems exhibit so much diversity that the category itself is open to question, although they all feature a popularly-elected president and a prime minister who is responsible to parliament. Thus executive authority is shared, although the implications of this for policy-making will vary according to factors such as the formal powers of the president and prime minister, their party affiliation, and the stage of the electoral cycle.

The three theoretical approaches use different methodologies to understand legislative–executive relations. For example, rational choice approaches have often focused on trying to understand the incentive structures facing individual legislators and executive members, consistent with its preference for methodological individualism. Such researchers may use survey data and interviews to understand why members vote in particular ways. They may look at the impacts of different sets of rules – committee systems, voting arrangements, electoral cycles, cabinet decision-making – on incentive structures, strategies and political outcomes. Cultural explanations may focus on how the internal behaviour of legislatures and executives is shaped by informal cultural assumptions, or may look at how these institutions are influenced by broader social factors. Prevailing notions of leadership, for example, may shape the balance of power between the executive and legislature. Structural theories explore how legislative and executive arrangements are functions of prevailing 'macro' variables, such as relations between states and the class structure within or between countries. Such theories can highlight similarities of political outcome between political systems with superficially different executive-legislative arrangements.

Comparativists have struggled to explain which type of executive–legislative relationship is more stable and which leads to stronger governmental performance. Such questions are of more than abstract interest – they are key debates for constitutional designers seeking to establish new political systems as part of a transition to democracy. Theorists from the structural, cultural and rational choice approaches all have something to offer constitutional designers, yet it is clear that institution choice itself will be a key variable in shaping the way that economic forces, cultural cleavages or individual preferences play out once a system is established. 'First tier' factors such as presidentialism versus parliamentarism will be important institutional variables, but their impact will be heavily conditioned by the powers of other institutions – the judiciary, bureaucracy, party system – as well as by the configuration of soft institutions which lie outside the constitution.

SUMMARY

- This chapter has examined the roles played by legislatures and executives in modern democratic systems, as well as the relationship between them.

- The focus has been mainly on influencing the political agenda and implementing public policy, including the degrees of influence enjoyed by executives and how legislatures can call governments to account.

- Comparisons have been made between the way in which these institutions operate in presidential, parliamentary and semi-presidential systems.

- The three theoretical paradigms have been discussed in relation to legislatures and executives, and we have also considered the need to look to broader national and geopolitical institutions as factors in providing for a thorough explanation of how legislatures and executives operate.

FURTHER READING

Norton, P. (ed.) (1990a) *Legislatures*. Oxford: Oxford University Press.

This book provides a collection of classic texts on legislative powers. It is complemented by Norton (1990b)

Linz, J.J. (1990) 'The perils of presidentialism', *Journal of Democracy*, 1(1): 51–69, and Linz, J.J. and Horowitz, D. (1990) 'Comparing democratic systems', *Journal of Democracy*, 1(4): 73–9.

These two articles offer a discussion of the impact of legislative–executive design on regime stability

Weaver, R.K. and Rockman, B.A. (1993) 'When and how do institutions matter?', in R.K. Weaver and B.A. Rockman (eds), *Do Institutions Matter?* Washington, DC: The Brookings Institute, together with Tsebelis, G. (2002) *Veto Players: How Political Institutions Work*. Princeton: Princeton University Press.

These contributions give us two different perspectives on regime performance as it relates to legislative–executive relations. Other useful material can be found in the following sources:

King, A. (1981) 'How to strengthen legislatures: assuming that we want to', in N.J. Ornstein (ed.), *The Role of the Legislature in Western Democracies*. Washington, DC: American Enterprise Institute. pp. 77–89.

Mezey, M. (1979) *Comparative Legislatures*. Durham, NC: Duke University Press.

Rhodes, R. and Dunleavy, P. (eds) (1995) *Prime Minister, Cabinet and Core Executive*. London: Macmillan.

Smith, M.J. (1998) 'Reconceptualising the British state: theoretical and empirical challenges to central government', *Public Administration*, 76(1): 45–72.

QUESTIONS FOR DISCUSSION

(1) Imagine that you are a constitutional expert helping a newly democratising country to design a political system. What would you want to know about the country before recommending that it opt for presidential or parliamentary institutions?

(2) Through what mechanisms can executive institutions be held accountable for their actions?

(3) How would rational choice theory explain the behaviour of individual members of a legislature when voting on adoption of legislation?

(4) Is it the case that the powers of legislatures are in decline relative to those of executives?

Key Words for Chapter 5

cabinet / committees / executive / legislature / parliament / performance/ president / prime minister / semi-presidential / stability

6 The Bureaucracy

Mark Pennington

CHAPTER OUTLINE

This chapter sets out the basis for a comparative account of bureaucratic processes and the analysis of bureaucratic power, firstly by considering some important definitional issues surrounding the concept of bureaucracy and then by examining how the various branches of the 'new institutionalism' have examined the role of bureaucratic organisations. Particular questions we consider are:

- Why are bureaucracies able to wield the power that they do?
- In whose interests is this power wielded?
- How does the extent and nature of bureaucratic power vary between states?

Introduction

Understanding the nature of bureaucratic power is particularly important given that in recent years many states have adopted a range of reforms, which have been designed to control the perceived excesses of public bureaucracies. To judge from most media coverage, the legislature and executive and the various struggles between these particular branches of the state constitute the very stuff of politics – this would appear to be where the real source of power lies – the realm where laws are formulated and legislation passed.

Examining the relationship between the legislature and the executive can tell us a good deal about the distribution of power within the structures of different states. To what extent is power decentralised to individual legislators – to what extent is legislative power subject to a series of checks and balances from competing legislatures – and, to what extent do legislative checks and balances themselves act as controls on the power of the executive and in particular that of the president or prime minister? As is often the case, however, appearances can be deceptive. Most political scientists recognise that while the role of prime ministers, parliaments and political parties is crucial to an understanding of the macropolitical environment, when it comes to the day-to-day processes of decision-making and especially the implementation of public policy, attention should turn to the critical role played by the public bureaucracy.

Defining Bureaucracy: The Contribution of Max Weber

By far the most influential definition of bureaucracy derives from the German sociologist Max Weber (1968, 1978). Weber defined the concept of bureaucracy in terms of an *ideal type*. It is rare to find an example of an ideal type in real world politics. Ideal types are useful nonetheless in that they help analysts to identify real phenomena *in relation* to the pure model. Comparison of real world actors, organisations and events with the theoretical ideal allows the analyst to label the phenomena in question according to its proximity to the ideal typical model.

Organisational forms

For Weber, an ideal typical bureaucracy has a very definite organisational form which is adopted owing to its efficiency-enhancing properties. The increasing spread of bureaucracies in political and economic life throughout the 19th century was, Weber believed, a manifestation of the advance of enlightenment notions of scientific rationality against more traditional and informal social modes. More specifically, Weber and his followers distinguish between charismatic, traditional and rational/legal forms of organisation – the latter of which corresponds with the spread of bureaucratic forms (Gerth and Mills, 1948). Rationality defined in this sense is a technical notion. The adoption of bureaucracy, whether by a private firm or a government agency, is a neutral, administrative tool that aids the efficient implementation of the organisation's goals. The following list sets out the characteristics of a Weberian ideal type bureaucracy:

1 The official's post is his/her sole or major occupation.
2 There is a clear career structure with promotion by seniority or merit according to the judgement of superiors.

3 The official may not appropriate for his or her personal use the post or its resources.
4 The official is under a unified code and disciplinary system.
5 Individual officials are personally free, but constrained by their employment when performing the impersonal duties of their offices.
6 There is a clear hierarchy of officials.
7 The function of each official in the hierarchy is clearly specified.
8 Each official has a contract of employment.
9 Officials are selected by professional qualification, ideally through competitive examination.
10 Officials have a money salary, usually with pension rights and reflecting their position in the hierarchy.

Consider in this context, points 6 and 7. Having a clear hierarchy of officials within an organisation, each with their own specified role, might be considered to aid efficiency in two significant ways. First, the rank-structured nature of the organisation reduces the need for negotiations regarding the performance of tasks. Knowing who has authority to make decisions, and whose job requires that the orders of superiors in the hierarchy are carried out, saves time that would otherwise be wasted in debates over who should be 'in charge'. The efficiency of military organisations in achieving their goals (winning battles), for example, might be seriously compromised if 'rank and file' soldiers are at liberty to negotiate which orders they are willing to follow. Second, the clear assignment of specific tasks to specific individuals, may improve the output of an organisation owing to the productivity-enhancing effects of the division of labour. Breaking down tasks into small, discrete units and employing specialists to perform these tasks, is likely to boost output relative to an organisation in which the same people perform multiple different roles. Assembly line techniques in factories, for example, have considerable advantages in productivity terms, relative to processes where individual craftsmen make and assemble the components of industrial products themselves.

Weber's model provides a basis for comparison between states in terms of their proximity to the bureaucratic ideal type. Within this context, much has been made of the tendency for continental European countries, in particular Germany and France, to resemble more closely the Weberian model than predominantly 'Anglo Saxon' societies such as the UK and USA, where the style of public administration is relatively less concerned with adherence to formal rules. Such differences are, however, relatively minor when compared to those between developed industrial nations and many countries in the developing world. In general the non-Western world is less accepting of bureaucratic methods and procedures than are the countries of Western Europe, North America and Australia.

Even in societies where formal administrative bureaucracies exist – and this is so in virtually all developing countries – the norms governing the operation of such organisations are frequently of an informal or traditional nature. Recruitment, for example, is often based on family ties and clan loyalties rather than on the formal examinations or similar 'meritocratic' criteria. Similarly, in contrast to point 3 of the ideal typical model, it is common for individual bureaucrats to take bribes and to appropriate state funds for their own personal use. In a comprehensive study of African political economies, van de Walle (2001) describes bureaucracies here as conforming to a 'patrimonial' organisational type and attributes the failure of most 'development aid' in the African continent, to the widespread appropriation of aid monies by state officials for their own private use.

Bureaucratic rationality

For Weber the elements of the ideal typical bureaucracy are the defining character traits of a perfectly rational and hence efficient bureaucratic form. What though is the precise meaning and significance of the term rationality when used in this particular context? Superficially, the notion of technical rationality sounds very similar to that put forward in the rational choice variant of new institutional theory that has been discussed at various points throughout this book. There are indeed some important similarities between the Weberian model of rationality and that of rational choice theory. The key similarity is that both refer to what is often known as *instrumental rationality* – the choice of the best means appropriate to achieve a given set of ends. In rational choice theory, individuals are considered to act on the basis of what will maximise their utility. For Weber, meanwhile, the adoption of the bureaucratic form of administration represents the most efficient way to achieve public policy objectives.

The major difference between these two senses of rationality concerns the level of analysis at which rational action is thought to be operative. Recall that for rational choice theory – collectives, whether they are states, interest groups, or in this case bureaucracies – can only be analysed in terms of the individuals that make them up. For rational choice theory it is individuals who are the rational choosing agents –organisations as such do not choose. According to this perspective, at the societal/public policy level there is no maximising agent, with a clear set of ends and means, which chooses to adopt policies. What we call public policy emerges as the result of bargaining between a multiplicity of actors each advancing their own individual interests. Both the choice of the bureaucratic form, therefore, and still more important, the internal operation of bureaucratic organisations should always be analysed in terms of a dynamic of interaction between predominantly self-interested actors.

A tool of rational administration

The Weberian conception of bureaucracy as a tool of rational administration, by contrast, conceives of individuals as cogs in a machine, with no personality and interests of their own. In the classical Weberian model, civil servants are assumed to be impartial administrators of public policy, whose primary motivation is to implement through bureaucratic means what their political masters and ultimately the electorate have willed. It is this notion of bureaucracy as a neutral administrative tool that rational choice theory questions. Seen in this light, individual bureaucrats are not neutral agents pursuing the aims of the public bureaucracy, but pursue interests of their own – interests which may diverge from some larger organisational or social purpose.

Educating the public?

A public-education bureaucracy, for example, may have the stated aim of improving the educational status of the public, but individual employees of the bureaucracy may have other motivations, such as the maximisation of on-the-job leisure. This is but one example of the collective irrationalities and inefficiencies that rational choice theory suggests may emerge from the interaction of self-interested behaviour, in the absence of institutional incentives that can channel such behaviour in the appropriate direction. In the specific case of bureaucracy the key issue for rational choice institutionalism is the existence or non-existence of low cost mechanisms which enable the effective monitoring of bureaucratic performance.

Reality rather than an 'ideal type'

The discussion will return to some of the organisational issues raised by the rational choice account of bureaucratic action at a later point. It is worth noting at this juncture, however, that Weber himself did not think that actually existing bureaucracies operated in accordance with the model of perfect rationality that he describes. For Weber the 'rational bureaucracy' was itself an 'ideal type'. In the real world, Weber was well aware that bureaucrats might pursue interests of their own or those of a particular class or group. Although he thought it an invaluable tool to promote organisational efficiency, Weber was mindful of the possibility of a bureaucratic takeover of society. He was particularly concerned that the spread of rule-bound organisations based on rigid hierarchies, especially in the public sector, would stifle individual initiative and entrepreneurial creativity in favour of a bureaucratic personality type. Weber, therefore, was aware that the growth of bureaucratic organisations was in part at least connected to the growth of the state.

Comparative Bureaucracy and the Comparative Role of the State

One of the most important ways that the role of bureaucracies across a range of societies can be compared is to look at the extent of bureaucratic organisation in a given society relative to that found in others. Probably the most influential determinant of bureaucratic influence is the extent of the state itself – what role is it that the state plays in a society relative to private individuals and organisations?

Notwithstanding the much touted efforts of politicians in some liberal democracies to engage in acts of 'privatisation' and to restrain the growth of the public sector, a defining feature of all such democracies over the longer term, has been the continual growth of government. This trend is manifested most clearly in the increasing share of national income absorbed by the state. From a position at the end of the 19th century when government spending in countries such as the UK was little more than 10 per cent of GDP, in the 20th century and especially after the Second World War – all the major democracies saw a substantial expansion of government. Even in societies known for their alleged adherence to a *laissez-faire* market economy, such as the USA, there has been a notable expansion in the size of the government sector such that it now accounts for well over a third of national income. In some countries the rate of government growth has been prodigious. In Sweden, for example, the size of government in relation to GDP has almost doubled since the 1960s.

Different variants

As indicated by Table 6.1 there are notable cross-country differences between developed liberal democracies in both the historical and contemporary scope of the state sector. In general, the size of government in the so called Anglo-Saxon world (including the UK, USA, Canada, Australia), has tended to be smaller than in continental Europe and in Scandinavia, although this has not always been so – as recently as 1960, for example, the Norwegian and Swedish states were smaller than that of the UK. Developing countries (not shown in Table 6.1) in general tend to have smaller government sectors than those found across the developed industrial democracies.

As Peters (2001: 7) points out one of the reasons why the state sector is smaller in the developing world relates to the substantial role played by agriculture and, in particular, subsistence production. Where people are consuming their own produce or are engaged in informal, barter-centred forms of trade rather than in monetary transactions, there are fewer 'free-floating' resources which can easily be taxed. Significantly, however, the role of the state in most contemporary developing countries is considerably greater than was the case when the now industrialised world was at a comparable level of economic development.

Table 6.1   General government expenditure as a percentage of GDP

Country	1913	1937	1960	1980	1996
Australia	16.5	14.8	21.2	34.1	35.9
Austria	17.0	20.6	35.7	48.1	51.6
Canada	–	25.0	28.6	38.8	44.7
France	17.0	29.0	34.6	46.1	55.0
Germany	14.8	34.1	32.4	47.9	49.1
Italy	17.1	31.1	30.1	42.1	52.7
Ireland	–	25.5	28.0	48.9	42.0
Japan	8.3	25.4	17.5	32.0	35.9
Norway	9.3	11.8	29.9	43.8	49.2
Sweden	10.4	16.5	31.0	60.1	64.2
Switzerland	14.0	24.1	17.2	32.8	39.4
UK	12.7	30.0	32.2	43.0	43.0
USA	7.5	19.7	27.0	31.4	32.4
Mean	13.1	23.8	28.0	41.9	45.0

Source: Tanzi, V. and Schunecht, L. (2000) *Public Spending in the 20th Century: A Global Perspective*. Cambridge: Cambridge University Press.

What is clear is that all countries, irrespective of the starting point, have witnessed an increase in the relative size of government. It is also evident, that contrary to much of the rhetoric about the 'rolling back of the state' and the alleged disempowerment of the public sector over the last 25 years, in most cases what has occurred is simply a reduction in the *rate of public sector growth* and not a decline in the relative size of the public sector per se. In the UK, for example, government spending as a proportion of GDP is as high today as it was in the mid-1980s, and in countries such as France and Germany the size of the public sector has actually increased in relative terms. The only clear-cut case in Western Europe where there has been a reduction in the relative size of the state in recent years is that of Ireland.

Estimating the size of the state sector

The proportion of GDP absorbed by government expenditure provides an indication of the relative size of the state sector and hence of the extent to which public bureaucracies play a determining role in the allocation of resources and the delivery of services. Other things being equal, the higher the level of government spending, the greater the role played by bureaucratic methods of resource allocation. Other things rarely are equal, however, and as a consequence the overall share of government spending provides only a rough indication of the scope of public bureaucracy. In order to gain a more nuanced appreciation of the extent of bureaucratic organisation it is necessary to distinguish the various ways in which the state intervenes in social and economic life. Broadly speaking, we can identify three key types of intervention that have an important bearing on the extent of public bureaucracy in a given society.

These are as follows:

- Direct production.
- Regulation.
- Transfer payments.

Direct production

As the phrase suggests, direct production involves the state in the actual delivery of goods and services where key sectors of the economy are nationalised – they are owned and operated by the government. When large portions of the economy are held in direct government ownership, as was the case in the formerly socialist countries of Eastern Europe or as was until the 1980s the case with utilities such as telephones and electricity supply in the UK, the scope of public bureaucracy is likely to be extensive. The people employed within these industries will effectively be part of the public bureaucracy, and since direct production activities are labour intensive, the state will constitute a very significant employer. The UK National Health Service is, for example, one of the largest single employers in the world. Even in situations where lower-level employees (such as nurses and doctors) are not classified as bureaucrats, when the state undertakes direct production activities, a large administrative bureaucracy will be required to manage the activities performed by such lower-level staff.

Regulation

In cases of regulatory intervention the state does not engage in the direct ownership and operation of industries per se, but seeks by way of rules and mandates to affect how private actors and the market economy operate. Health and safety rules, employment law and various forms of environmental planning all fall under this category of intervention. As with direct production, this particular form of government activity can also mean a substantial role for public bureaucracies. The more the government seeks to regulate the behaviour of private individuals and organisations, then the greater the number of personnel who must be employed by bureaucratic agencies charged with enforcement of the relevant regulatory rules.

Transfer payments

The third and final form of intervention to be distinguished is transfer intervention. This involves the state in the transfer or redistribution of income from one section of the population to another. The provision of unemployment benefit, social security and public pensions for the elderly, are all examples of transfer interventions which are usually introduced in an attempt to even out what might otherwise be thought of as excessive social inequalities. Although primarily focussed on the provision of a welfare safety net and/or the reduction of income inequality, such intervention may also involve the targeted provision of subsidies to particular industries or sectors of the economy deemed by the government to be worthy of protection or promotion. The European Union Common Agricultural Policy (CAP), which seeks to guarantee the incomes of European farmers, constitutes a significant example of such intervention.

Unlike direct production and regulation, increases in the level of transfer intervention, though reflected in terms of higher taxes for the populace at large, need *not* necessarily imply an increase in the size of the public bureaucracy itself. The distribution of transfer payments is *not* a particularly labour-intensive activity. Whereas increases in the level of production by the state or the number of rules and regulations that government issues require increases the number of people directly employed by the public sector, this is not the case in terms of increasing transfer payments. Suppose for example, that the government decides to increase public expenditure on old-age pensions. While the additional expenditure will require higher taxes, inscribing higher values on pension cheques does not necessarily require any additional staff relative to a position in which lower levels of benefits are to be distributed.

Dunleavy's model

Based on the classification of intervention forms discussed above, it is possible to devise a typology of bureaucratic agency types. The work of Patrick Dunleavy (1991) is particularly useful in this regard. For Dunleavy, the distinguishing characteristic of a bureaucracy is the character of its budget – the nature of the money that it spends. Dunleavy identifies three broad types of agency budget and then classifies four basic agency types depending on the type of budgets that are present.

Budgetary spending categories

- Core element – staff and administration.
- Bureau element – transfers to private sector, for example, public pensions, farm subsidies and contracts with private firms.
- Programme element – transfers to public sector, for example, supervision of grants to local authorities and individual schools.

Bureaucratic agency types

- Delivery bureaucracies – for example, defence, nationalised industries.
- Regulatory bureaucracies – for example, environmental planning, health and safety directorates.
- Transfer bureaucracies – for example, social security, agriculture departments.
- Control bureaucracies – for example, education.

In Dunleavy's model, the core element of a bureau's budget represents that part of the budget spent directly within the agency on staff, administration and general running costs. The bureau element, by contrast, refers to that part of the agency budget which flows out as transfer payments to private individuals and organisations or as contracts to private firms. The programme element, meanwhile, constitutes expenditure which is transferred to other public sector bodies. In general, agencies involved in direct production (delivery agencies) and regulatory functions tend to have a high proportion of core spending – most of the money spent by these agencies goes on staff and administration. Transfer agencies on the other hand, such as social security departments, have a relatively large bureau element, with a high proportion of the expenditure recirculated in the private economy. In the case of control agencies the bulk of expenditure is transferred to other public agencies and circulates throughout the public sector.

It should be apparent from these distinctions between intervention forms and agency types that the scope of public bureaucracy may not simply be inferred from the level of government expenditure and of taxation rates. It is, for example, possible to identify societies with high levels of government spending, but *without* these societies necessarily having the highest levels of public bureaucratisation, because most of the spending concerned consists of transfer payments (bureau budgets) which are recirculated within the private economy. Likewise, it is possible to identify societies with lower government expenditures, but with relatively higher levels of bureaucratic organisation because a high proportion of the public expenditure that does take place is concentrated on direct production and regulation (core budgets).

For example, in the 1970s government spending as a proportion of GDP was lower in the UK than in Sweden, but the UK may well have had a larger public bureaucracy at the time. Although Sweden had (and still has) a substantial transfer-based welfare state, unlike the UK it has never had a large nationalised industrial sector. In the UK, although transfer payments were (and still are) less generous than in Sweden, substantial sections of industry were held in state ownership during the post-war period – many of which were of course subsequently privatised in the 1980s and 1990s. In a more extreme form, a similar pattern is evident in much of Latin America and Africa, where government expenditures on transfer-based welfare payments are trivial by the standards of the USA and Western Europe, giving the impression of a relatively small state sector, but where actual levels of public bureaucracy are quite high, given that most government spending in these societies is concentrated on direct production and regulation (Yeager, 1999).

In order to ascertain the role of the bureaucracy within a society, therefore, it is important to make comparisons in terms of the mix of intervention forms present. Such comparisons are of particular importance in the context of recent reforms to the public sector that have occurred in a number of states. Where the funding of services continues to be provided by the state out of general taxation, but the actual delivery of services is contracted out to private for profit firms or charitable, not for profit organisations it is now increasingly difficult to delimit clear boundaries between the public bureaucracy and the private sector.

The New Institutionalism and Public Bureaucracy

Whatever the function that bureaucracies perform, most political scientists recognise that when it comes to day-to-day decision-making and even to the process of law-making itself, it is within bureaucratic institutions that an important source of political power resides. This raises three important questions: first, in whose interests is this power exercised? Second, how is bureaucratic power exercised? And third, what mechanisms are available to politicians and to society more generally, in order to keep bureaucratic power under control? Each of these questions can be analysed in comparative terms with regard to the 'new institutional' theories that are the focus of this book.

There is fairly broad agreement between political scientists across the different strands of new institutional thought about some of the basic sources of bureaucratic power. At the most general level, four key factors are thought to enable the bureaucracy to wield political clout.

Expertise

Government ministers need to rely on the specialist expertise that members of the bureaucracy possess. In cases such as environmental protection or some aspects of health policy, for example, a high level of technical expertise may be required which is not available to politicians. Owing to time constraints, politicians may not be able to acquaint themselves with the necessary levels of knowledge. While there are some mechanisms that may facilitate a degree of information gathering by politicians, such as scrutiny committees, for example, this is not usually equivalent to the knowledge held by professionalised bureaucrats, especially in the more technical policy fields.

Permanence

Bureaucrats also tend to have greater job security than politicians who are frequently moved between jobs, for example during cabinet reshuffles, and who may even lose their place in the legislature following a subsequent election. As a consequence, ministers can never acquaint themselves with the detailed running of an organisation or of the relevant policy issues and must rely on advice from bureaucratic representatives. The extent of bureaucratic power in this regard may be lessened when the same government is in power for a longer period of time. The long tenure of the Thatcher/Major Conservative Government in the UK, for example, is widely held to have resulted in an unprecedented degree of party political control over bureaucratic agencies. Even in these cases, however, individual ministers rarely stay in the same job for more than a few years and are likely to remain significantly dependent on bureaucratic support.

Bureaucratic procedures

In the course of their work bureaucratic agencies develop administrative routines and institutional practices that are not readily understood by outsiders. Politicians frequently lack familiarity with the details of legal and bureaucratic operating procedures and this increases their dependence on bureaucratic support mechanisms, especially during the drafting of new legislation.

Control of implementation

Although they are officially responsible for the delivery of public policy, politicians are dependent on the support of the bureaucracy for the implementation of their legislative programmes. Teachers and health service workers, for example, are responsible for delivering improvements in education and healthcare and, owing to the information and time constraints facing politicians, have considerable discretion to adapt the policies concerned to their own objectives.

There is fairly broad agreement that some or all of the above factors contribute to the existence of bureaucratic power. It is when we turn to the question of in whose interests this power is exercised and the more specific institutional processes through which power arises and how it may be contained that differences emerge between rational choice, cultural and structuralist accounts.

Rational Choice Institutionalism and Bureaucratic Politics

Bureaucratic interests and bureaucratic power

As ever, for rational choice theory the starting point of analysis is the rational, self-interested individual. The most frequent assumption made by rational choice analysts is that bureaucrats are much like people operating in the private market economy, where workers are assumed to want higher wages and entrepreneurs are assumed to prefer higher profits. More specifically, bureaucrats are expected to seek benefits such as higher salaries, greater social status, greater job security and better working conditions. Unlike private entrepreneurs, however, bureaucrats are not able to pursue profits in order to achieve such objectives because they are employed within the public sector and do not officially own productive assets. Instead bureaucrats rely for their income on grants, which are given to them by the legislature in the form of a budget.

Within the above context, institutional rational choice points to two utility enhancing strategies that might be adopted. According to William Niskanen (1995) and his followers, bureaucrats will seek to maximise the size of the budget that they obtain from the legislature. Other things being equal, bureaucratic pay, job security and status are assumed to be positively related to the size of the agency budget. According to Dunleavy (1991), however, the extent to which bureaucrats are likely to pursue a strategy of budgetary growth varies according to the type of agency concerned. Bureaucrats working in delivery or regulatory agencies, which are labour intensive, have strong incentives to increase budgets because any spending increases and associated benefits are retained within the agency concerned. In transfer type agencies, however, unless spending flows to organised interest groups such as farmers or large industrial contractors who are able to supply benefits to bureaucrats in exchange for increased spending, there are relatively fewer incentives to push for expenditure increases, because most of the benefits flow outside the relevant agencies, either to disorganised private actors or to other public bodies. Incentives in such organisations may point instead towards a 'bureau-shaping' strategy, wherein civil servants attempt to mould the form of their organisation in such a way as to increase the role of bureaucrats in high-status policy work rather than more mundane routine roles.

It is, of course, one thing to suggest that bureaucrats want to maximise their budget, or to shape their organisation into a more favourable form but quite another to maintain that they will actually be able to achieve such objectives. From a rational choice perspective, however, bureaucrats often find themselves in a particularly powerful bargaining position with respect to their political masters and to the electorate at large and it is this bargaining power that enables them in large measure to secure their goals.

The key issue for rational choice theory is that more often than not bureaucrats are monopoly suppliers of goods and services within the public sector. The agencies that they work in are often the sole supplier of a particular service and even where this is not the case entry into the relevant market is not usually fully open to outside competition. As a consequence of such limited competitive forces politicians cannot easily judge whether public agencies are performing efficiently, that is, that they are producing a given quantity and quality of service for the lowest possible price. It is this relative absence of competition that enables bureaucrats to obtain higher budgets than are necessary or to adopt inefficient organisational forms. Bureaucrats are also aided by the relative lack of incentives for politicians to put a downward check on expenditure pressures. Politicians are unlikely to see efficiency savings as a major source of electoral gain, because these will be spread thinly across a largely unorganised electorate. Those who gain from inefficient spending increases (public sector workers and organised recipients of subsidies such as farmers for example), by contrast, tend to be those who rely on government spending for a significant proportion of their income and are usually better organised. The electorate, meanwhile, also finds itself at an informational disadvantage relative to both bureaucrats and politicians. Owing to the fact that many public services are provided 'free at the point of delivery', voters do not have ready access to information about the costs of service provision. In the absence of price information and the ability to choose between competing service suppliers on value for money terms, it is even more difficult for the electorate to judge the efficiency of the public bureaucracy than it is for politicians (see Tullock et al., 2002).

From a rational choice, or as it is often known in this context, a public choice perspective, the structure of incentives set out above leads to an inefficient supply of public services, which departs considerably from the model of perfect efficiency implied by the classical Weberian model. The resultant inefficiency will take the form either of excessive government spending – where budget maximisation incentives are prevalent or an inefficient organisation of public service delivery mechanisms – where bureau-shaping incentives are more significant, or a combination of these institutional failures.

Applied in a comparative context, institutional rational choice is concerned to examine the nature of bureaucratic incentive structures and the way in which these vary across states. The approach implies that incentive structures which enhance or constrain the extent of bureaucratic power in a given society will be dependent on the relative size of the public sector, the organisational form of public bodies and the degree of monopoly power within the structures of the state itself.

In general terms, the rational choice approach suggests that states with relatively higher levels of government spending will be most susceptible to the bureaucratic inefficiencies discussed above. Thus, the USA, Ireland and Hong Kong, which have below average levels of public spending as a percentage of GDP, may be considered less prone to the exercise of bureaucratic power and inefficiency than societies such as France and Germany where public spending is notably higher. The extent to which budget-maximising behaviour is the dominant bureaucratic strategy will, however, also vary depending on the organisational form of the public sector in the country concerned. In countries such as Sweden, for example, although government spending is very high relative to GDP, a high proportion of this activity is of the transfer type, where according to the Dunleavy model, budget-maximising strategies are less likely to occur. In these circumstances, a large percentage of the spending concerned may be recirculated in the private market economy and will thus be subject to price competition. Bureaucratic inefficiencies in such a context may be less severe than in societies where the state is heavily involved in direct production activities.

The latter point is of further relevance in terms of a third factor that may affect the comparative reach of bureaucratic power – the extent to which state institutions are organised on a centralised or monopolistic basis. From a rational choice perspective centralist institutional structures are likely to enhance bureaucratic power over the electorate and its political representatives. The absence of choice in such systems increases the costs for both politicians and the electorate of monitoring bureaucratic performance because there are no or few alternative service providers with which to make value for money comparisons. In more politically decentralised states and in particular under federal institutions (such as Switzerland, for example), by contrast, bureaucratic power may be constrained by the existence of competing political units, which enable both the electorate and politicians to compare the relative efficiency of different political jurisdictions (Olson, 2000; Yeager, 1999).

It should be evident from this account that any empirical predictions derived from the rational choice approach need to be sensitive to the diversity of institutional practices across states. A state with a high level of government spending may, for example, turn out to be less prone to bureaucratic inefficiency than might initially be thought, if the structures of the state concerned are relatively decentralised (as in Sweden, for example). Likewise a state with relatively lower levels of government spending may be subject to bureaucratic power if those state organisations that do exist are organised in a more centralist and monopolistic fashion (health care in the UK, for example). Clear-cut comparative predictions may still be derived from the rational choice framework – a society with low levels of government spending and with a decentralised, federal political structure (Switzerland, for example) would be expected to be the least susceptible to bureaucratic power and inefficiency, whereas a high-spending centralist state would be thought especially prone to such ills. Before such comparative analyses can be made, however, it is crucial that the political scientist has an adequate understanding of the variations in institutional practices across states and the likely effect of these variations on the incentive structures concerned.

Rational choice theory and bureaucratic reform

From the perspective of its adherents one of the great strengths of institutional rational choice theory is its capacity to generate proposals for institutional reform. If public policy failures are attributable to a deficient set of incentive structures, then it follows that policy outcomes may be improved by redesigning the relevant institutional incentives. It is in this context that rational choice has been particularly influential in the recent past with a number of key public sector reforms across liberal democracies drawing their inspiration from the rational choice account of bureaucratic behaviour.

For many rational choice theorists if the source of bureaucratic power is monopoly within the structures of the state itself, then the solution to these problems is to open up public bureaucracies to greater competition. According to this view, monitoring the behaviour of bureaucratic providers is easier both for politicians and voters in situations where relatively easy cost and quality comparisons can be made between alternative service providers. Based on this analysis, institutional rational choice points to a set of reforms ranging from the radical, such as proposals for the outright privatisation and marketisation of service provision, to more modest attempts to introduce market-like incentives within the structures of the public sector itself (Tullock et al., 2002).

In the case of outright privatisation, the supply of services is transferred directly into the private sector, with the relevant organisations being auctioned off to individuals and companies. The privatisation of the steel industry, telecommunications, electricity, gas and water services in the UK were examples of this particular policy. In such circumstances, former state enterprises are subject to open competition in the private market and must secure sufficient customers in order to stay in business. Where companies have been privatised as monopolies or semi-monopolies, regulatory frameworks have been designed in order to limit monopoly power (via price caps in the case of water, for example) and to facilitate future competition from new market entrants. British Telecom was, for example, privatised as a monopoly concern, but now faces a range of new telecommunications operators.

A somewhat less radical measure which has often been proposed in the areas of education and health care services is the introduction of voucher mechanisms. In this case the delivery of services is opened up to competition, with state schools and hospitals required to compete for funding with private providers. Funding of such services continues to be provided by the state and raised out of general taxation, but decisions over the allocation of funds between providers are decentralised to individual consumers. The more radical of such schemes, as with the Swedish system of education vouchers, decentralise funding directly to service consumers who choose directly where to spend the money concerned. In less radical variants, state agencies continue to allocate funding but are supposed to follow a formula where, 'the money follows the parent or patient', that is, to shift resources away from less popular organisations, towards more successful ones in order to enable the latter to expand. Such proposals were evident in the Blair administration's plans for education and health care reform in the UK. The introduction of voucher schemes is often combined with greater use of the price mechanism in the delivery and allocation of services. Rather than providing services 'free' at the point of use, charges are introduced to enable consumers to make efficiency comparisons between providers and to encourage them to do so. Providers, it is argued, will thus face competitive incentives to improve the efficiency of service delivery.

A still less radical set of rational choice inspired reforms focus on the 'contracting out' of public services. In these cases allocation of resources and services remains within the state sector rather than being decentralised to individual consumers. Rather than have the production of services retained completely within the state sector, however, private companies are able to compete for the relevant contracts in terms of price and/or quality. Such reforms are less radical than privatisation or voucher schemes because they retain a role for the bureaucracy in choosing service providers rather than have this function decentralised to individual consumers.

Problems for the rational choice theory of bureaucracy

Notwithstanding the influence it has had over recent policy trends, rational choice accounts of bureaucratic politics are not without significant weaknesses. By far the most important of these is the apparent difficulty that the approach has in explaining the process of institutional change and the dynamics of institutional reform. In the former case, it is not readily apparent from the rational choice framework how public sector incentive structures are actually created in the first place or how they can be changed over time. When accounting for the growth of government, for example, it is not clear whether the growth in expenditure can be accounted for purely by bureaucratic empire building and monopolistic inefficiency, or whether other factors outside of direct bureaucratic influence have inadvertently created an environment in which public bureaucracy has been able to thrive. It seems implausible to suggest that all, or even most, of the relative growth in government throughout the 20th century can be put down to the monopoly power of civil servants alone.

In a similar vein, it is not apparent how the rational choice approach can account for the recent movement towards privatisation and more competitive bureau structures. If their institutional power is as great as rational choice accounts suggest then one might expect that bureaucrats would be able to use this power to thwart a programme of reforms which are designed to undermine their interests. If politicians have as few self-interested reasons to secure the efficiency of bureaucratic organisations as rational choice accounts maintain, then why have they suddenly acquired an interest in public sector reform? Some of the movements towards a more consumerist approach to service delivery might be accounted for by technological developments that have made it easier for services to be provided in a more decentralised manner. In telecommunications, for example, the advent of satellite and digital technology has meant that telephone companies, which were long considered 'natural' monopolies, can be opened up to competition. It seems implausible, however, to account for economy-wide privatisations, such as those of the Thatcher administration, solely in these terms.

The problem for rational choice theory, therefore, is that in order to break out of a given societal equilibrium, there needs to be an external shock to the system which breaks up prevailing incentive structures and may pave the way for the creation of alternative arrangements – as is the case with the advent of wars or economic crises.

As such there is a need to combine the approach with at least some elements of a more structural institutionalism. Similarly, in order for institutional change to occur there needs to be a change by at least some segments of the society concerned in the ideas that shape underlying conceptions of where their self-interest lies. The development of such ideas may be prompted by inefficiencies in the prevailing social order which provide an incentive to consider alternatives, but the content of the relevant ideas cannot be reduced to individual self-interest – a variety of different paths to reform may be pursued. As a consequence, there is a need for rational choice accounts to be combined with more ideas-based theories, such as those offered by the cultural variant of institutional theory.

Cultural Institutionalism and Bureaucratic Politics

Bureaucratic interests and bureaucratic power

The role of ideas and shared values which is sometimes underemphasised in rational choice theory assumes centre stage in the cultural institutional approach to bureaucratic behaviour. According to this perspective, both the nature of bureaucratic interests and the extent of bureaucratic power will be determined in large part by aspects of the cultural environment from which they derive. Such processes of value socialisation may occur at different levels ranging from variations at the societal level, with different attitudes to the nature and role of bureaucratic organisations varying across countries, to those found at the administrative level, where there may be differences in the cultural traits of different bureaucratic organisations *within* a particular society.

With regard to interests, bureaucrats are considered to identify these with reference to the organisational cultures of which they are a part.

Such cultures will be a subset of attitudes and norms operating at the wider societal level. Building on the work of Mary Douglas (1982, 1987), many cultural theorists categorise societal attitudes towards the role of bureaucracy in terms of four key cultural types: hierarchical; egalitarian; individualist; and fatalist (Hood, 2000; Thompson et al., 1990).

Hierarchical cultural norms are reflected in a respect for rank-structured social relationships and the authority of social elites to enforce binding decisions without the need for negotiation, consultation or the participation of those who may be affected by the decisions concerned. One may note in this context that any society which comes close to the ideal typical Weberian model is, almost by definition, likely to exhibit a hierarchical set of cultural norms, with a 'top-down' style of management predominating.

Cultures governed by more egalitarian norms, by contrast, place greater emphasis on the participation of front-line workers and service users. Rather than granting authority to bureaucratic experts, participatory procedures attempt to draw on the knowledge of those delivering and using services 'on the ground'. The mode of decision-making in such cultures is likely to be more consensual, with a much greater place for consultation, negotiation and majority-based decisions arrived at via committee-style procedures, rather than on the vertical enforcement of organisational rules.

Individualist cultures fall mid-way between the hierarchical and egalitarian types. They place less emphasis on the importance of organisational rules than the hierarchical tradition, in favour of a more personalised process which gives considerable scope for autonomous individual action. Unlike the egalitarian cultural type, however, they place less emphasis on consensus and majoritarian decision-making relying instead on a more competitive decision mode. Inequalities of status between individuals are an accepted part of this style of decision-making. These inequalities are not, however, the product of a fixed hierarchy which assigns status on the basis of qualifications or other rule-based procedures, but are more fluid, emerging spontaneously from an entrepreneurial process, as those exhibiting greater foresight and skill in negotiating their own individual 'deals' accumulate resources accordingly.

Fatalist cultural types have little faith in either hierarchical organisational rules or in processes which rely on participation or the striking of deals between individuals to generate positive social outcomes. According to this frame of understanding, in so far as social progress is possible at all, this is largely due to random events and historical accidents which lie outside of individual or collective control. Societies influenced by fatalist norms are often held to exhibit distrust towards formal organisations and to subscribe to the belief that most individuals are fundamentally corrupt. As a consequence the prevailing mood in fatalist societies is one of public apathy, with little faith in the capacity of *any* process to generate appropriate 'solutions'.

The cultural categories set out above are of course ideal types and are rarely, if ever found in their pristine form. Most societies would be expected to contain elements of each of the different cultural traits, with the precise 'mix' a product of the peculiar history of the society concerned. For cultural theorists, the categories set out by Douglas are useful, in that they enable political scientists to label societies according to the particular character of the mix and according to the dominant cultural forms that are present.

From the perspective of cultural institutionalism, different cultural attitudes towards the role of bureaucracy will be reflected in the relative social status of bureaucrats themselves. In a society more inclined towards hierarchical norms, for example, the status of bureaucratic interests may be that of an elite. In more individualist or egalitarian cultures, by contrast, both the structure of bureaucratic organisations and the manner in which bureaucratic roles are carried out may depart substantially from the Weberian ideal. In such societies bureaucratic organisations, far from being the repositories of public trust and respect, may be regarded with a high degree of suspicion.

The extent of bureaucratic power in a given society is also from a cultural perspective a product of prevailing norms and attitudes. Although, for reasons such as their superior expertise and control of implementation, bureaucracies in *all* societies have considerable scope for discretionary action, the extent of that power and the ability of bureaucracies to pursue their objectives unhindered by other social actors will also be a function of prevailing cultural attitudes. Other things being equal, societies exhibiting more hierarchical cultural traits will be more likely to acquiesce to bureaucratic procedures than those where egalitarian or individualist norms are more widespread.

Within the above context, political commentators have frequently contrasted the bureaucratic culture in continental European states, especially Germany and France, with the 'Anglo-Saxon' attitude usually found within the UK and the USA (Peters, 2001). In Germany, and to a lesser extent in France, bureaucratic structures are held in relatively high regard by the general population and tend to be based on rank-structured relationships of authority and status, with an emphasis on the enforcement of formal organisational rules. In the UK and the USA, however, a combination of participatory and entrepreneurial/individualist styles of decision-making are reflected in a more informal set of operating procedures. Owing to the cultural distaste for rule-bound hierarchies in such societies, bureaucratic structures allow much greater scope for bargaining and negotiation both within bureaucracies and between bureaucratic agencies and their clients. This is not to suggest that bureaucratic forms of organisation are unimportant in countries such as the UK and USA, but that insofar as they are, their mode of operation does not conform as closely to the Weberian ideal as those found in continental Europe.

The norms prevalent in individual bureaucracies may themselves be situated in terms of their proximity to the wider cultural norms in the relevant society. The very nature of work in military bureaucracies or the police force – the need for rank structure and strict enforcement of discipline for example – may mean that the culture of these agencies falls closer to a hierarchical pattern than in the society at large. Other agencies, such as higher education bureaucracies, for example, may be less rigid in terms of their operating norms than the wider culture owing to the inquiry based nature of educational work. Even here, however, cross country differences in cultural attitudes towards the nature of education will remain a key determinant of bureaucratic norms. In a hierarchical culture where education is seen in terms of the transmission of knowledge and traditions from one generation to the next, such bureaucracies may come closer to the norms of a rank-structured organisation than those found in a society where education is viewed in terms of developing the critical competences necessary to challenge established modes of thought.

The meanings associated with bureaucratic norms provide shared understandings of bureaucratic roles in society but such meanings are fundamentally contested. Both at the societal level and at the level of individual agencies, a cultural perspective suggests that those groups situated in a subordinate position by a given bureaucratic culture may seek to challenge the prevailing norms while those granted a more privileged status will use their political power to defend their own institutional 'world view'. Bureaucrats may, for example, use their discretionary power to limit consultation with actors exhibiting different norms and values and may seek to resist the introduction of working practices that contradict long-established operating procedures.

In the UK, for example, the Department of Transport, has frequently been criticised by environmental groups for its supposed commitment to a 'culture of road-building' and for its unwillingness to consult with groups seeking an alternative transport policy less reliant on the expertise of road-building engineers. In a similar vein, the UK Treasury has often been noted for its tendency to scupper the plans of politicians from 'spending departments' such as health and education ministries owing to a widespread belief among Treasury officials that their primary role is to protect the integrity of public finances and to ensure value for money for taxpayers.

Cultural institutionalism and bureaucratic reform

If shared norms and organisational practices form the core of cultural approaches to understanding patterns of bureaucratic behaviour, then cultural-inspired strategies for bureaucratic reform focus on attempts to change the prevailing cultural norms both at the societal level and at the level of individual agencies.

As noted earlier, one of Weber's concerns about the growth of bureaucracy was his belief that employment in hierarchical and rule-bound organisations might encourage the effective takeover of society by a bureaucratic personality type. For Weber, while bureaucracies have undoubted efficiency advantages over less formal administrative structures, they also lead to countervailing disadvantages. By far the most important of these is a stifling effect on creativity, innovation and enterprise. Concerns of this nature have been at the heart of many recent attempts to reform the nature of bureaucracies, especially in Western liberal democracies. Politicians have been of the view that bureaucratic procedures have become too cumbersome and have been responsible for slowing down the rate of economic progress owing to the bureaucratic obsession with the enforcement of regulatory rules. Such concerns have been particularly pronounced with the rise of so called 'knowledge-based' economies, which it has been claimed, require a more informal entrepreneurial style of decision-making.

In response to such concerns, attempts have been made in a number of countries to change the management style of government organisations, moving them away from the traditional Weberian style bureaucracy to one which emphasises 'business-like' practices mimicking the more entrepreneurial style of decision-making found in the private sector. Many of the reforms described as the 'new public management' fall under this category and overlap with the rational choice inspired reforms discussed above (see Osborne and Gaebler, 1992). However, whereas rational choice emphasises a change in institutional structures and in particular the adoption of markets or market-like incentives, reforms drawing on cultural theory focus less on changing the formal rules within which bureaucracies operate and more on changing the internal culture and personnel of bureaucratic agencies. Changes in recruitment practices have been particularly significant in this regard with moves to 'fast-track' people with private sector experience into 'failing' public bureaucracies in an attempt to introduce a more dynamic management culture. Thus, in the UK the Blair administration's policy of encouraging private sector actors to take over the management of schools and hospitals seems in part at least to have been inspired by a belief in the importance of changing the organisational culture of public agencies.

Reform strategies drawing on cultural theory are also influential at the level of individual bureaucracies as well as at the societal level. The central thrust of cultural institutionalism is that the cultural norms of an individual bureaucracy must be compatible with the goals of the organisation. If, for example, an agency is responsible for achieving egalitarian policy objectives, which aim to empower currently disadvantaged social actors as might be the case in a welfare or social security ministry, but the agency concerned is driven by a hierarchical administrative culture, then the relevant policy goals may be undermined.

Thus, policy failures are interpreted as a mismatch between the culture of individual agencies and the nature of the policies they are supposed to implement.

Consider in this light the charges of 'institutional racism' levelled against metropolitan police forces in the UK. Concerns were raised in the Macpherson Report that an internal culture of discrimination against members of ethnic minorities was responsible for the failure of police services to attract personnel from black and Asian backgrounds. This cultural bias was in turn responsible for the failure of the police to prosecute crimes against ethnic groups and subsequently for the frequent breakdown of relations between the police and members of ethnic minority communities. In this particular case, the internal culture of the police was deemed incompatible with the policy objective of maintaining public order – the police cannot perform this primary task effectively if their internal working norms operate in such a way as to alienate large sections of the population. Subsequent attempts to reform the police service have, as a consequence, focused on attempts to break up the dominant culture by encouraging members of ethnic minorities to join the force.

Just as cultural theory may suggest certain paths of institutional reform, so it points to the likely sources of opposition to reform. Other things being equal, one would expect societies or individual agencies which have traditionally approximated hierarchical cultural traits to be those most resistant to the introduction of more egalitarian or individualist working practices. This appears to have been precisely the case in terms of the 'New Public Management' style reforms discussed above. Opposition to such reforms has been strongest in those societies such as Germany and France, where public attitudes to Weberian-style bureaucracy are more favourable and where there is suspicion of private sector involvement in public management. In Anglo-Saxon societies such as the UK and New Zealand, by contrast, where individualist norms are an established part of the wider culture, there has been relatively less resistance to new management practices in the public sector.

Problems for cultural theories of bureaucracy

The contribution of cultural institutionalism to understanding strategies of bureaucratic reform and the likely resistance to such reforms also draws attention to the primary weaknesses of cultural theory as a whole. The central problem in this regard is the chronic difficulty that the approach faces when accounting for the process of cultural evolution. If the influence on individuals of prevailing cultural norms is as all pervasive as cultural theories seem to imply, then it is far from obvious how changes in cultural values and in subsequent policy practice can be accounted for without stepping outside the confines and assumptions of the cultural model. In the specific case of bureaucratic reform, for example, it is difficult to see why a society governed by hierarchical operating norms should ever get to the point of considering egalitarian or individualist reforms, let alone that it should be able to overcome any resistance to such reforms. To simply assert that cultures can and do evolve and to account for policy changes in such a manner would be to avoid the fundamental questions of why and how the evolution of cultural attitudes takes place. In short, it is doubtful whether the process of cultural change can itself be explained with reference to cultural concepts.

The central difficulty for the cultural approach is that in order to explain the process of cultural evolution it must draw on concepts that are external to the cultural model. Either, it must account for cultural change in terms of the incentives that face *individual* actors to challenge prevailing cultural norms and thence to bring about incremental cultural change – which would be to adopt elements of the rational choice approach. Or, it must incorporate macro notions of technological/economic change, or those based on external shocks such as wars and natural disasters, that break up existing cultural patterns – which would be to adopt a more structural institutional approach. The strengths and weaknesses of rational choice theory have been considered above, so it is to the structural perspective that attention now turns.

Structural Institutionalism and Bureaucratic Politics

Bureaucratic interests and bureaucratic power

From a structural institutionalist perspective, bureaucratic power is likely to be exercised in accordance with the structural requirements of the overall system, of which the bureaucracy is a part. More specifically, the bureaucracy is an important part of the state and the purpose of the state in any social order is to maintain in the long run the stability of whatever the system happens to be. These structural requirements are the product of a given level of economic and societal development and the manner in which these forces interact with one another. Structuralist perspectives can loosely be divided into those drawing on elements of Marxist or neo-Marxist theory which focus on the system requirements of capitalist liberal democracy, and non-Marxist perspectives which focus more on the state itself as the primary structural force within societies.

For Marxist-inspired variants of structural institutionalism, in modern liberal democracies the overarching system is capitalism and the market economy. The purpose of the state, therefore, and of the bureaucratic element within it, is to use whatever power it possesses to maintain the capitalist system. According to this view, the extent of the public bureaucracy will be a product of macro-structural forces in the historical development of capitalist institutions commensurate with underlying levels of technology and the particular class relationships that these developments foster and sustain. Seen in this light, the adoption of the modern rationalistic Weberian form of bureaucratic organisation was, and still is, a system requirement of a particular phase in the history of capitalist development. Bureaucrats will, in turn, seek to adopt those policies which are commensurate with a given level of technological progress, while thwarting the implementation of those policies that might threaten the structural integrity of the liberal democratic order.

One frequently cited example of the Marxist approach is that of Bowles and Gintis (1976) in their account of educational policies in the USA. Bowles and Gintis argue that rather than seeking to reduce social inequalities, state officials prefer policies that perpetuate social hierarchies and prepare people for the differential roles they will play in capitalist industry. Similar processes are held to be operative in other policy fields, for example, environmental planning and social security such that even seemingly radical measures are watered down or manipulated by the bureaucracy in such a way as to be compatible with business interests.

Marxist accounts of bureaucratic behaviour can be divided into two distinct schools: functionalist and non-functionalist/instrumental. In the functionalist variant of Marxist bureaucratic theory, bureaucrats as such do not have specified interests of their own – they are simply a part of the state structure – the cogs in a machine which is pre-programmed to serve the long-run interests of capitalism and its ruling class – bureaucrats as such therefore, have no distinct motivations– but are propelled by the logic of social and technological conditions to act in the way that they do (Poulantzas, 1978).

The non-functionalist or instrumental version of Marxist bureaucratic theory (Miliband, 1969) suggests that bureaucrats have personal interests within the policy process and that these interests are intimately linked with the fortunes of the capitalist class. The argument here is that bureaucrats are to a greater extent drawn from the ranks of the capitalist class – and if not actually business people themselves are likely to have close contacts with capitalist interests through various social networks, which lead them to identify their own interests with those of capitalism. In this sense, bureaucrats pursue their own interests as a distinctive class within the political system – a class whose interests happen to coincide with the interests of capital owners.

The division between functionalist and non-functionalist strands in Marxism is also evident in non-Marxist variants of structural institutionalism. For this tradition of thought the primary structural force operating in society is not necessarily capitalism but that of the modern bureaucratic nation-state. Following Skocpol (1979) these theorists focus on the relative *autonomy* of states from social pressures derived from the electorate, interest groups or the members of a particular class – and as a consequence on the capacity of states to implement policies over and above the preferences and interests of the society they rule. In this view, policies including nationalisation of industries and the expropriation of property may be carried out even in the face of opposition from powerful groups such as those representing business or organised labour.

In its functionalist variant, the logic of bureaucratic employment propels civil servants to use their influence to implement policies that will maintain the integrity of state structures – notably the monopoly of the use of violence, and the capacity to steer the trajectory of economic development. According to this perspective, state officials do not have specific interests, but are led by structural forces to perform such a functional role. In its non-functionalist version, the interests of state officials lie directly in the maintenance of their managerial position at the apex of the political economy – a position that they use to defend against any interests and policies that might threaten such a role.

With their focus on system requirements, structural institutional perspectives tend not to focus on the micro-level variations that distinguish the bureaucratic regimes of different states. Rather, the emphasis is on the fundamental similarities that characterise states operative within the context of macro-social processes such as capitalism, or the development of the nation state. Comparative analysis of bureaucratic processes is conducted at the macro-scale with differences between the bureaucratic capacities of states, varying according to the particular stage of historical or technological development in the societies concerned. States confronting similar background circumstances such as geographical conditions, access to natural resources, information technology, and shifts in the balance between industrial and agricultural sectors and interest group or class processes are expected to respond to such structural parameters in a fundamentally similar way (Wilensky, 1975).

A somewhat less determinist style of analysis is evident in those non-Marxian theories that emphasise the relative autonomy of the state. The emphasis here is placed on the *unique* structures that characterise individual states and the particular imperatives that these internal structures generate. In this more pluralist style of account, states contain an array of bureaucratic elements with contradictory interests (states within states). Certain bureaucracies may, for example, have strong links with particular economic sectors such as agriculture or minerals extraction and these may diverge from the interests of officials operating in different sectoral fields. Policy development is thought be a function of the constellation of macroeconomic forces prevalent at a particular time and the manner in which these structural forces affect the balance of the internal power struggles between competing elements of the bureaucratic elite.

Structural institutionalism and bureaucratic reform

Of the three variants of institutional theory, the structural approach has the least to say when it comes to policy proposals aimed specifically at reforming the bureaucracy. The reasons for this lie in the nature of the structuralist analysis itself. Since the political system is seen to operate according to structural laws, which have to play themselves out – it is difficult to see how specific interventions can change systems fundamentally. Indeed, it is difficult to conceive of policy interventions, which can be separated from the prevailing structural logic of the system under study.

Insofar as structural institutionalists have sought to discuss patterns of bureaucratic reform this has usually been as part of an attempt to explain the playing out of underlying structural dynamics rather than the normative advocacy of specific institutional arrangements. One such example has sought to explain the recent shift in liberal democracies away from traditional models of centralised, Weberian-style bureaucracy towards a focus on the emergence of more 'governance' based modes and the 'new public management'. Service delivery in this context is decentralised to networks of actors consisting of private sector firms, non-governmental organisations and public sector agents engaged in various 'partnerships'. Drawing on the Marxist influenced 'regulation theory' a number of analysts have claimed that these processes are part of a structural requirement mandated by the underlying shift in capitalist dynamics from 'Fordist' production techniques to so-called 'post-Fordist' models. According to this view, the predominance of Fordist mass production techniques in the post-war era required a centralised state bureaucracy to enforce uniform regulatory rules, but the shift towards more flexible, diversified modes of production stimulated by developments in information technology has since required that the structure of the welfare state mirrors this more decentralised mode of implementation (Jessop, 1990).

Problems for structuralist theories of bureaucracy

Just as the rational choice and cultural approaches to comparative politics face problems in accounting for the dynamics of institutional change so too do structural approaches encounter theoretical and empirical problems in this regard. The primary difficulties for structural analyses follow from their tendency towards deterministic modes of explanation. To recognise that factors such as technological change can create opportunities for the creation of new institutional forms, whether in the public bureaucracy or anywhere else is one thing, but to imply that technology or other 'structural forces' in some sense determine the policies adopted is quite another. The implication of such accounts is that state officials can simply 'read off' from a given set of technological and social circumstances what the appropriate policy response should be. There is, as a consequence, little sense that bureaucrats and other policy makers may face a range of different options from which they must choose.

That agency and choice have a role to play in the development of state structures is readily evidenced in the very different bureaucratic institutions that have existed and still exist in societies exhibiting similar levels of technological and social development. As van de Walle (2001) has noted, the states of Africa and East Asia entered the post-colonial era with predominantly rural/agricultural communities and similar levels of technological and economic development, yet contrary to structural logic bureaucratic institutions the capacity of state officials to enforce formal rules was much greater in the latter countries than in the former. In a similar vein, the impact of globalisation and the arrival of post-Fordist production methods across liberal democracies appears not to have produced a uniform shift towards new public management methods. While some countries, notably the UK and New Zealand, have moved towards a more contract-based form of public administration, others such as France and Italy have made little, if any, movement in this direction at all.

That there is an element of choice involved in the evolution of state institutions suggests that such processes cannot be considered in terms of macro-structural developments alone. At some point, the focus on structural dynamics needs to be replaced by, or at least complimented by, an account which emphasises the role of ideas and/or individual incentives. A focus on ideas and cultural traditions would suggest that when deciding how to respond to changes in the macro-environment state officials may face a range of policy alternatives – the choice of which will be conditioned by norms and values that may vary between states. Recognising the role of incentives, conversely, suggests that individual bureaucrats may have more to gain from adopting certain types of institutional reforms than from others and hence that it is the variation in incentives across different bureaucracies that should be the focus of concern.

SUMMARY

- The study of bureaucratic institutions continues to be one of the most important elements in comparative politics owing to the almost universal growth in the number and scope of bureaucratic organisations in the last century.

(Continued)

(Continued)

- The precise character and nature of this bureaucratic growth, however, varies considerably between states and it is in seeking to explain and account for these institutional differences that comparative politics has an important role to play.

- Political scientists have sought to account for these differences in different ways and in light of the strengths and weaknesses of the new institutional accounts of bureaucratic politics which we have considered in this chapter, it seems likely that the most successful attempts to explain these differences will be those that appreciate the interaction between macro-structures, ideas and individual incentives.

FURTHER READING

Hood, C. (2000) *The Art of the State*. Oxford: Oxford University Press.

This is a clear and well-structured application of cultural theory to analyse the politics of bureaucratic reform. The book contains chapters on each of the major cultural 'types' – hierarchical, egalitarian, individualist and fatalist.

Milliband, R. (1969) *The State in Capitalist Society*. London: Wiedenfield and Nicholson.

This is a rather old text, but one that still contains perhaps the best Marxist-inspired analyses of public bureaucracy.

Niskanen, W. (1995) *Bureaucracy and Public Economics*. Cheltenham: Edward Elgar.

This book contains a series of essays which explore elements of the rational/public choice theory of bureaucracy. Some of these are presented by way of formal mathematics, but there are sufficient chapters presented in a highly readable style, for those who wish to avoid algebra and calculus.

Tullock, G. (1965) *The Politics of Bureaucracy*. New York: University Press of America.

This book examines the differences in behaviour between organisations that are subject to price competition and those that are not. Though less famous than Niskanen's work, the book contains perhaps the best account of why public sector bureaucracies are, on average, less efficient than private sector firms in an open market.

Osborne, D. and Gaebler, E. (1992) *Reinventing Government*. Reading, MA: Addison-Wesley.

This has been a highly influential text in promoting less 'hierarchical' forms of public service delivery which draws on elements of both rational choice and cultural institutional analysis.

QUESTIONS FOR DISCUSSION

(1) What are the major factors that distinguish private and public sector bureaucracies?

(2) Can the culture of a bureaucratic agency be changed *without* a change in the economic incentives in the agency concerned?

(3) If bureaucrats are as powerful actors as many political scientists suggest, what is the scope for effective bureaucratic reform?

(4) To what, if any extent, can bureaucrats be considered to behave as a 'class'?

(5) How might technological changes, such as the growth of the Internet, affect the scope of bureaucracy in both the private and public sectors?

Key Words for Chapter 6

budgetary growth / bureaucracy / bureaucratic reform / professional norms / Weber

7 The Courts

David Robertson

CHAPTER OUTLINE

This chapter considers how and why the role of courts, and indeed the judicial process more generally, has become more susceptible to comparative political analysis in recent years. It encompasses a discussion of how this topic has not as yet been central to the three approaches to the 'new institutionalism' which form the basis for this book, and how they can be used effectively. In particular, the chapter will examine the rise of judicial power, the centrality of the rule of law to theorising democracy and how a 'political science' approach can assist our understanding. The chapter concludes with two case studies.

Introduction: The Rapid Rise of Judicial Power

Until quite recently courts and judges have been the missing element in political science. There are still very few genuinely comparative studies of the role of courts in the political process. This is all the more surprising because there is a general consensus amongst those who do study it that there has been a world-wide rise of judicial power. Every single country which has democratised since the 1970s has added a constitutional court to its political institutions. Several of these new courts, particularly the South African Constitutional Court and those in some of the Central and Eastern European region, have been very influential. Indeed one could say that nearly all countries that have had a serious chance to think about their constitutions since 1945 have recognised how important courts can be in politics. So the Canadians, who had always had a Supreme Court, gave it enormous extra power in their new 1982 constitution by adding the *Canadian Charter of Rights and Freedoms* to the constitution, as did the Spanish after Franco and Portugal after Salazar. In 1958 even the draftsmen of the French Fifth Republican constitution added a constitutional review body. Above all, the German constitution builders after the Second World War created one of the most powerful of all constitutional courts, which continues to have enormous international influence. Only in some of the older Western democracies, those which have not had cause to rewrite their constitutions, lack such a body, though even some of them, the UK and New Zealand are the best examples, have strengthened the ability of the judiciary to control legislation to protect human rights.

'Judicial review'

The key phrase in this area of comparative government is 'judicial review'. Normally it means that a court can review a parliamentary statute to see if it is compatible with the constitution. If it is not, the court has the power to invalidate it.

The USA, of course, has had 'judicial review' since its inception, as have the older 'new democracies' like Australia and Canada. If we look briefly at the reason for this, we can begin to work out what the phenomenon of judicial power is all about, see how it might be studied in a comparative manner, and understand why we badly need to be able to do this. What all three of these countries share is that from the beginning they were federal, and also committed to the idea of a 'separation of powers'. Federalism implies that some powers can only be exercised by the national, federal government and others only by the state or provincial governments. (There may also be some powers exercised jointly, which makes the issue even more complex.) The separation of powers means that some things can only be done by one or other of the three classic branches of government: the legislative branch, the executive branch, or the judicial branch. Any set of institutional restrictions like these involve the likelihood that from time to time a political institution will try to exceed its powers. So the federal government might pass a law in an area only the states can deal with, or the executive will try to act like the legislator and create binding rules governing individual behaviour. Whenever this happens there has to be an impartial judge to protect the 'boundary' between institutions.

This is the basic form of judicial review, because the power of guarding these boundaries is nearly always given to the courts. In a sense, any constitution which takes these boundaries seriously has no choice about writing at least some form of judicial review into its constitution. So all American law students early learn the case of *McCulloch* from 1819 which prevented the states from taxing a bank set up by the federal government. The court argued that 'the power to tax is the power to destroy', and thus the federal government had to be immune from state taxes or the power relations in the constitution would be subverted. In *The Engineers Case* in 1920 the Australian High Court had to deal with a similar issue. A good modern example is France. For historical reasons French political culture has always been hostile to the role of judges in politics, and never before 1958 had judicial review existed. But the constitution that came into force in 1958 was also the first democratic constitution to reduce the powers of parliament, and to give a major amount of rule-making authority to the executive. For this reason, and originally only for this reason, the writers of the 1958 constitution abandoned the long tradition of keeping courts out of politics and created a 'court-like' institution, the Constitutional Council, with the power to check that parliamentary laws and executive decrees were only made within the proper areas of authority.

In the USA and Australia nearly all the important court decisions on the constitution in the first decades of their independent political life were about such matters. This is not just a matter of federalism or of the separation of powers – many of the decisions of courts in the new democracies of Central and Eastern Europe are about such structural or 'boundary' issues. For example, the Constitutional Court of the Czech Republic has several times had to intervene to stop the lower house of parliament attempting to reduce the role of the Senate; early decisions of the Polish court were often involved with power struggles between the prime ministers and presidents. Even where the separation of powers is seen as less important and where a country is 'unitary' rather than federal, there will be problems of keeping institutions within the bounds of their constitutional authority. Courts are just not really optional in such situations unless, like the UK, parliament is seen as absolutely supreme. (Even in the UK there is a weaker version of judicial review, known as 'judicial review of administrative action' to keep the executive and local government more tightly controlled by parliamentary power.)

The Rule of Law

The organising concept here is the 'rule of law', which is a crucial element in any theory of democracy. Essentially a system based on the rule of law is one in which individuals as such do not have power over other individuals. Instead broad categories of people are put under legal obligations (or given legal protection) by the passing of generalised laws administered neutrally in ways which are themselves controlled by law. This used to be summed up in the slogan 'the rule of law and not of men'. This simple idea has huge implications for the modern state, and it is because courts are at the centre of the whole process that they cannot avoid being powerful and influential. Why not? One can well ask why simply administering a set of rules makes courts 'powerful' institutions, and many have taken the view that courts are, or certainly should be, passive. No less a figure than Montesquieu, one of the earliest advocates of the separation of powers, thought that judges were nothing more than 'the mouth-piece of the law'. In legal theory this idea, which is still held as an ideal by some, led to a school of analysis referred to as 'slot machine jurisprudence' – you just feed your question intro the court and like a machine it produces the right answer. The first case study, at the end of this chapter, shows exactly how inadequate the slot machine approach is where one is considering the very phrase 'the rule of law'.

Challenging traditional images of the 'rule of law'

There are several reasons why this model of judicial behaviour is false. To start with, in some legal systems known as 'common law' systems the courts actually and overtly do make some law entirely themselves, because parliamentary statutes only cover some areas of life. These are the countries whose legal system derives originally from England, and they include, apart from the USA, most of the old British Commonwealth. (A not dissimilar system applies to the Nordic countries.) In this tradition all law was originally the result of judicial decisions made in specific cases. Under the doctrine of precedent (Americans often refer to the old legal Latin tag *stare decisis* here) other courts faced with the same issues would derive a rule from the earlier case and apply it as a general law. The modern state has taken over whole areas of social life and replaced the old common law rules by statutes; new issues and problems are likely to be covered by statutes even in areas where much common law remains. Nonetheless important areas, especially of laws relating to commercial activity are still largely governed by law which not only *is* judge made, but is *supposed* to be judge made. The more important reason for judicial power, because it applies to all law in all societies, is that laws are never precise enough and broad enough to be totally clear, and this applies as much to the law covering the state itself, constitutional and administrative law, as to any area of statute law. Courts get their power primarily from the need to have an authoritative body to interpret what the statute, constitutional clause, international treaty or even local government bye-law actually means in any given context. In the end, if the court interprets the law, it gets the last say in what the law actually is. Naturally much of this is very automatic, and uncontroversial, though absolutely necessary. But it only takes a few non-automatic cases to give the courts power.

The problem comes when courts seem to be using their interpretive power simply to impose their own policy preferences on society. Again, this does not have to be a dramatic matter of constitutional review. The first effort by a British government to deal with race relations was the Race Relations Act 1965. The English courts however disliked it, and interpreted it far too narrowly, preventing it really getting to grips with the problem, so it had to be replaced by a later act, rewritten to make it impossible for the judges to get round its clear intent. For a while though the courts wielded real power in the area of race relations. The point, of course, is that because it was just a matter of interpreting a statute, the government could get round it – the English courts do not have the power of judicial review. The problem becomes much more intense if a judicial review court interprets the constitution in such a way that a policy becomes illegal, or gives its own interpretation to a preferred policy, justifying this as mandated by the constitution. Constitutions are much harder to change than simple acts of parliament.

Trying to effect constitutional change

This is partly a political matter – the actual mechanism for changing a constitution need not be very difficult, but for a government to start the process of altering a constitution just because it does not like a court ruling involves a lot of political credibility. So for example the French constitution is procedurally easy to change, but it has only twice been changed to get round rulings of the Constitutional council in the nearly 50 years of its existence. (Once by a right-wing government, once by a socialist government, just to show that neither political tradition is happier with the power of courts.) If any reader of this book knows just one famous US constitutional decision it is probably *Brown* v *Board of Education* 1954 because this was the case that ended racially segregated education. But whoever thinks of *Plessey* v *Ferguson,* which was the case before the court in 1896 and which first interpreted the relevant clause of the constitution to allow such racism? How exactly were liberals opposed to racist education policy going to get a constitutional amendment to overcome this ruling? Until the Supreme Court itself changed its mind, more than half a century later, there was no institution in the USA which could stop racists from running schools in this way.

What about our 'rights'?

In fact the examples above involve a different reason judicial review is now so important. The issue in *Brown* v *Board* and in the French cases alluded to was nothing to do with who had the right to pass a certain law. They were about even more fundamental questions – are there some types of law that no part of the political system can pass? This is the business of human rights codes, and it is the world-wide spread of concern for human rights that has had most to do with recent expansion of judicial power. *Plessey* v *Ferguson* allowed racially separated education because of an interpretation of the human rights protection aspect of the US Constitution. The 14th amendment to the constitution, passed after the American Civil War, made it possible for the Constitution's Bill of Rights to be brought to bear on the state governments, preventing them denying their own citizens basic rights. The most important clause in the 14th amendment guaranteed 'equal protection of the laws' – but the Supreme

Court interpreted this in *Plessey*, to mean that 'separate but equal' treatment was acceptable. Thus it was constitutionally permissible to have racially separated schools, at least as long as the state could make a claim that both types of school were equal. All that happened in *Brown* v *Board of Education* was that the court changed its mind and held that 'separate' was inherently 'unequal'. A tiny change, just a matter of a court doing its job and interpreting the meaning of a few words, but a change with enormous consequences for American life. This is what judicial power is all about.

Contradictions

One further point needs to be understood about modern judicial review. Of all the clauses in all the bills and declarations and charters of human rights, one aspect has turned out to be crucial. Central to most modern human rights thinking is a denial of discrimination. It is an easy value to agree with, but it has one major drawback. Virtually all legislation discriminates. It is in the very nature of policy to take from some and give to others, to limit some people's freedom to help another group, to give special protection to one type of person even though this means restricting opportunities for another. Even rights that might not seem to be about discrimination are like this. Consider the following problem, which occurred in both South Africa and the USA at nearly the same time, in nearly identical circumstances (*Garreth Anver Prince* v *The President of the Law Society of the Cape of Good Hope*, 2002; *Dept of Human Resources of Oregon* v *Smith*, 1990). Both constitutions guarantee freedom of religion, and this means freedom to practise your religion, not just to believe what you like. Both countries had drugs laws prohibiting the possession and use of certain drugs often used for recreational purposes. In both countries followers of minority religions argued that it was part of their religious creed to use such a drug in their major ceremonies. As a result, the criminal law involved religious discrimination, which was forbidden by the constitution.

What should be done? How should a constitutional court handle this question? Whatever it does, it exercises power, either to support the state or to defy the state and support sincere religious believers. Anti-discrimination legislation abounds – but so does the need to tell apart 'legitimate' discrimination from forbidden legislation. The state cannot be allowed the last say in this, or there would be no point in having anti-discrimination rules at all. The claimant cannot be allowed the last say, or the state could never impose any policy. The list of discriminations that have been argued about is endless – in Canada, for example, should gay partners have the same right to survivor's pensions as married heterosexuals? The answer matters enormously, not only to the gay partner, but to the state which never has enough money for its welfare schemes. Because discrimination is a matter for the courts, the sheer fact that legislation must discriminate has put judicial power at the very centre of policy formation.

How Do We Study Judicial Power?

This book is explicitly committed to a 'new institutionalist' approach. If it was not, this chapter could not be written, because any non-institutionalist perspective would be hopeless. Nonetheless there remain a host of methodological questions to be answered, and not all perspectives on judicial power are as clearly within the institutionalist perspective as others. We first need briefly to check possible approaches to judicial power against the theoretical perspectives outlined in Chapter 1, rational choice institutionalism, cultural institutionalism and structural institutionalism.

Rules as 'hard' and 'soft' institutions

Very few studies of courts and judges are overtly in any of these schools of thought, in part because they are not often written by political scientists convinced of the utility of such approaches, in part because they are not often overtly comparative. This does not mean that different studies do not tend in one direction or the other. It is a mistake to expect studies, at least those written before the recent upsurge on interest in methodology, to label themselves. Still less does it mean that we cannot outline what each of these approaches might offer future comparative judicial studies. The first question raised in Chapter 1 is about the very definition of institutions. The distinction there between 'hard' and 'soft' institutions is particularly germane, because courts exhibit both types of institutionalism, and it is a question of considerable theoretical interest as to which is the more important. Manifestly the courts themselves, defined by law and perhaps by the constitution itself, are hard institutions. So are the rules for appointment of judges, and many of the procedural and substantive rules by which they practise. At the same time much of the variance between courts may follow from soft institutional norms of how judges, advocates, even litigants ought to behave. It may be more important in the field of judicial power than in some others that some of the defining elements of the institutions lie ambiguously between soft and hard. As an example, consider the 'rule' that a judge ought to disqualify himself from hearing a case if he has any personal interest, or may even be *thought* to have such an interest in the outcome. As this is a rule that defines who can wield the power of the state in certain circumstances it is undeniably both important and institution defining. But in most jurisdictions the way the rule operates is that it is up to the judge himself to decide whether he should recuse himself from a case.

What sort of a rule is it that leaves the person controlled by the rule to decide if it applies? It is a soft institutional norm, clearly. Yet if enough fellow judges decide the judge ought to have recused himself, they may order a rehearing, and that order will have the full force of the state behind it. This is not an imaginary situation. One of the most clearly 'political' cases to come before the English courts in the last 50 years turned exactly on this. In late 1999 General Pinochet, the former Chilean dictator, faced the prospect of being extradited from the UK to Spain to face trial for crimes against humanity (*R v Bow Street Metropolitan Stipendiary Magistrate and others, ex parte Pinochet Ugarte* (2000). His appeal to the Law Lords was originally heard by a five-man bench which included a judge who was not only sympathetic to one of the parties to the case, Amnesty International, but was involved in its organisation, and whose wife worked for it. He did not think this connection important, and did not take himself off the case. Only when counsel for Pinochet discovered the connection and raised a public storm did the Senior Law Lord intervene and order a new hearing. Nothing happened to the judge in question, who is still on the bench. In contrast justices of the US Supreme Court regularly refuse to hear cases where they have even the faintest and long-run involvement. We can see then that the very definition of institution in the context of judicial power requires great care and will forbid us to opt for any simple strong versus weak methodological preference. The rules that define judicial institutions will be of both types, and sometimes will shift from one type to another between countries. The problem is actually theoretically acute, because unlike most political institutions, the courts themselves actually make many of the rules that define them. But also, of course, as many other political institutions are defined partially by positive law, the courts help define other institutions. Again this is no trivial theoretical point.

In Chapter 1 electoral laws were used as an example of 'hard' institutions. Electoral laws, rules about media ownership, even the definition of a political party are all matters that have, in one or more countries, been defined largely by constitutional courts. For example there is a lengthy case law in Germany defining how much financial aid the state may give to political parties, while the Czech constitutional court, to take just one example, has had to decide on what counts as a party when it comes to deciding who can nominate candidates at an election. For over 20 years the attempt by the Socialist Party in France to introduce gender balancing rules into their electoral law was held back by the Constitutional Council.

Which Institutional Perspectives?

However we see the definition of institution, we must ask what sort of institutionalist perspectives work best in studying judicial power. Interestingly this question is not only one for political scientists studying the judiciary. In part it is a question internal to judicial and more general legal self-understanding. This is because one definition of rational choice theory, the 'strong' theory often associated with the Chicago School has a direct equivalent in legal theory. There has for some decades been a very powerful analytic tradition known as the 'Law and Economics' school associated with the University of Chicago. Basically this holds that the purpose of the common law in countries like the USA and UK is precisely to provide optimum rational economic resource distribution in society, thus seeing courts not only as strong-sense rational actors, but as responsible for creating macro-rationality in the society. This school also, unsurprisingly, sees judges as rational choice makers in a strong sense, aiming to maximise their utility. Though what exactly it is that judges seek to maximise when they do this is open to many interpretations. For some it is their core political values, for others their power and influence either individually or for their institution. In one book Posner (1995), who is both a Chicago-based legal theorist of this school and an appellate judge in the US Federal court system, has argued convincingly that judges seek to maximise victories in appeal cases.

Rational choice

Rational choice theories have most typically been used to explain why courts make certain decisions in an attempt to maximise their own power – this approach is particularly common in the accounts of the activities of the European Court of Justice, though those who believe in it would expect it to apply in most other jurisdictional contexts. Writers such as Shapiro also try to make use of another aspect of rational choice theory covered in the first chapter, the idea of the principal–agent relationship in describing courts. Thus writers like Alec Stone Sweet see constitutional courts as constitutional agents, set up to fill in the details of written constitutions and to develop them as their principals would like (Shapiro and Sweet, 2002). The major problem here is working out who the principals are – most commonly they are taken to be the political parties themselves, as descendants of the groups involved in writing the original constitution or amending it over time. A version of principal-agent theory is often used by US scholars to try to account for the nature of constitutional interpretation by the US Supreme Court.

A 'rational plus cultural' approach

One very common and powerful approach to studying courts is a mixture of rational choice and cultural institutionalism, a mixture that Chapter 1 suggests is generally common in comparative government. This goes under various names, the most common probably being the 'attitudinal model', discussed in more detail later. In this sort of research judges are treated as independent political actors seeking to turn their own political preferences into policy via the decisions of their court. Such an approach does combine cultural with rational choice approaches, because it rapidly becomes necessary to study judicial strategy and their methods of reaching coalitions to make their views win.

It is easiest to think of approaches to the study of judicial power as arranged on a spectrum. At one end is the pure legal perspective which sees decisions of courts as entirely determined by legal argument, and denies all sociological or institutional determination. At the other end are those political scientists who see courts as in no way different from any other political institution, making choices from private motives and acting rationally to maximise their power over other institutions. In her study of the Italian Constitutional court, for example, Mary Volcansek (2000) expressly accepts a new institutionalist perspective, citing with approval another scholar's summary that judicial decisions are 'a function of what they prefer to do, tempered by what they think they ought to do, but constrained by that they perceive as feasible to do' (Gibson, 1983). She suggests the two ends of the spectrum are 'the legal model' and the 'extra legal model'. While the first gives primacy to legal considerations, the latter focuses on matters like judicial values and preferences, institutional position and politico-social environment. The two models are abstractions, of course, and the world is always a complex mixture of them.

More important than guesses about a judge's primary motivation is the degree of freedom a judge may exercise. The truth is that judges do differ from all other types of political actors because they rely for any power and influence they have on argument, and argument in a highly constrained and technical form – legal argument. Thus any study of the courts which does not give due attention to the actual legal opinions uttered by courts, and there are far too many such studies, will fail even to explain *what* a court has done, let alone *why* it has done it. It will not accurately describe what has been done, because the political impact of a single decision depends on how the judges really intended it to work, how broadly they intend or expect future courts and administrators to interpret the result, and this can only be known by looking at the reasons they gave (Robertson, 1998).

How courts might affect constitutional reform

Courts cannot make just any decision they like at any point in time; they are deeply constrained by decisions they have taken in other fields, decisions they may wish to take in the future, and how they have argued in the past. Take one familiar example: possibly the most famous decision the US Supreme Court has made since the 1950s was *Roe* v *Wade*, the 1973 decision in which the court legitimised abortion. But *Roe* did not just simply assert that women could have abortions – it set up a complex trimester structure under which a woman's right to abort depended on how far her pregnancy had progressed. Only in the first three months, when the foetus was thought not to be viable, was there an unlimited right to abortion. This however is likely to cause future problems – as the recently retired Justice Sandra Day O'Connor pointed out in one decision narrowly upholding the precedent, '*Roe* is on a collision course with itself' – meaning that as medical science continually reduces the age of viability, the very logic of the decision may collapse. Had the Court in 1973 provided a different justification, the future of abortion as a constitutional right might have been very much safer. Similar points can be made about many such decisions – the arguments the Hungarian court used to abolish the death penalty, for example, severely limited how strong a position they could take, only months later, in their own abortion decision.

This impact can best be seen indeed from another US decision. A year before *Roe* the US Court attempted to abolish the death penalty in America in a case called *Furman* v *Georgia* (1972). There was one way this could easily have been done, had there been a very strong majority on the court against capital punishment. This would have been to apply the 5th Amendment to the constitution, which makes it unconstitutional to impose a 'cruel or unusual punishment'. Plenty of people in America would have agreed that execution was cruel, and judged by international standards in developed counties, very unusual. As it happened the abolitionists only had the slimmest of majorities, at best, of the court. The most that could be agreed on was a ruling that the way the decision to execute or not was made in most death-penalty cases was too random, varied and racially discriminatory to stand. So this, and only this, aspect was ruled to constitute unusual and cruel treatment. The consequence was that the court only achieved a temporary halt in executions, while the individual US states rewrote their laws to get round this specific argument. The moratorium on execution did not even last out the decade, and America has become again the only developed Western country to use the death penalty.

The ruling in *Furman* was on a five to four split, the narrowest of all majorities. So the reasons and arguments in *Furman* are crucial to even knowing what the case did – obviously they are crucial to understanding why it did it. An interesting exercise would be to compare the decision of the South African Constitutional Court on the death penalty in 1994, and to ask how much the ideological differences in the sorts of people who are judges on these two courts is the crucial explanatory variable (*S* v *Makwanyane* 1994). This example also highlights another approach to the power of courts which is certainly cultural, but may not be easily described as institutional. To the extent that courts are political players at times in conflict with other institutions, they require reserves of legitimacy with the mass public. Indeed courts are more in need of such public support because they are less obviously legitimate in a democracy than the parliament and executive – unlike these they are not usually elected. A good example of a genuinely comparative political science study of this aspect was carried out in the late 1990s, and the authors went on later specifically to study the South African court. They chose this court for the second study precisely because it had risked so much in opposing public attitudes with its death penalty decision (Gibson et al., 1998, 2003).

Developing a 'Political Science' Approach

Political science study of courts began with research on the US Supreme Court, and the vast bulk of all that has been written by political scientists remains studies of America. Unfortunately much of this has concentrated on an 'institution thin' approach, often called the 'attitudinal model' where the concentration has been almost entirely on the justices' votes on cases. Their arguments are studied only by those often (unfairly) dismissed as mere 'students of doctrine', in favour of focus on the idea of the judge as only interested in policy, whose votes are to be explained in terms of his political ideology as itself demonstrated by those votes.

This approach characterised the earliest work, where books with titles like *The Judicial Mind* set the course of much later research (Schubert, 1965). More recently, more sophisticated work, largely written on European courts, has been more avowedly institutionalist, though the overall tenor is still to see judges as largely free agents determined to achieve policy ends not legal ends. This is perhaps best characterised by the work of Alec Stone Sweet and those associated with him, for example in his main comparative study, *Governing with Judges* (2000) Stone Sweet's main concern is to describe the courts as rival policy makers to legislatures, indeed to argue that they are best seen as acting as though they were themselves actually 'third chambers' of legislative bodies. Such a view radically minimises the importance of the constraint imposed on judges by their need to conduct legal argument, as well as ignoring crucial differences in the overall institutional position of courts and parliaments, and the vital differences in career experience of judges and elected politicians. Stone Sweet does himself start by acknowledging an important institutional point – the courts we are interested in can be usefully divided into two types. This distinction will be used as a major institutional/structural distinction to organise the next part of this discussion.

Purely Constitutional Courts

There are the purely 'constitutional' courts, for example the constitutional courts of Germany, Italy and Central and Eastern Europe. In contrast to these constitutional courts are courts such as the US and Canadian Supreme Courts and the Australian High Court which, though they deal with constitutional law, are in fact general purpose courts at the apex of their national court hierarchy. Much that is of importance to political science follows from this distinction. (Stone Sweet's work is almost entirely on the first form of court; the bulk of political science studies, being American, are on the second form.) The reason this apparently recondite distinction turns out to be very important when we think about how to explain courts comparatively is impeccably institutionalist, because it goes to the very logic of the institution builders who developed the first type of court.

These courts, the ones which are purely for constitutional matters, are often called 'Kelsen courts'. Hans Kelsen was an Austrian legal thinker who was largely responsible for drafting the 1920 Austrian Constitution, a vital part of which was the first European constitutional court, to which he was appointed, though he was also removed from it in 1930 for political reasons. Kelsen designed the court along lines which have since been copied many times, firstly and most importantly in the design of the Constitutional Court of the Federal German Republic after the Second World War. His court, and those that copy his design, have two related special features. They are not part of the ordinary court system of the country, nor in any judicial hierarchy. Cases are referred to the constitutional court by a variety of routes, but they only ever decide the specific constitutional issues involved, and do not act as general appeal courts. But they are the only courts in the country which can make such constitutional determinations, and they have to be obeyed by all the other courts on these issues.

Second, the judges on the constitutional courts are not career judges from elsewhere in the system simply promoted up to a special level. The actual rules for selecting judges vary enormously across political systems and are themselves an institutional factor which can be important in understanding and explaining the behaviour of courts. What Kelsen courts have in common is the appointment of people mainly from outside the normal judiciary, usually to fixed terms, with the duty of judging the constitutionality of legislation. Because judges in most continental European countries are essentially civil servants, entering the judicial profession straight from law school and moving upwards as in any bureaucratic hierarchy, Kelsen doubted either their capacity or willingness to be genuinely independent, and to have the courage and experience to render wide-ranging decisions against the governments of the day.

There is almost as much variation among Kelsen courts as between them and the alternative model at the detailed level. One could not hope to use a dichotomous variable, measuring simply whether a court was Kelsen or otherwise to explain much, but the very fact that there was a political, almost a 'political science', reason for their design goes to argue for the importance of institutional design in explaining courts. Kelsen's own life story is a case in point. He was removed (unconstitutionally) from his life tenure in the Austrian court in 1930 because of his decisions in which the court quashed decisions of ordinary courts that were ignoring the constitutional right for divorce and remarriage. The judges in the lower courts were unable to stand out against the dominant conservative Catholic culture of Austria at the time – indeed this was only shortly before the country sank into virtual civil war between the right and left. Kelsen lived long enough to be personally involved in the writing of state constitutions for post-war Germany, and was very much an intellectual grandfather of the German court, which has become arguably the most powerful and respected constitutional court in any democracy. A very good indicator of how vital it can be to insulate the judges of constitutional courts from the dominant professional ideology of ordinary judges is shown by the way that all the Central and Eastern European countries, which retook their democratic independence after the Cold War, opted for this design rather than appointing anyone from the existing judiciary – as did post-apartheid South Africa.

Courts as institutions within a broader context

What this example shows is that any research on the political power of courts cannot be purely institutional, certainly not in a narrow sense. Just as important as the structural aspects of the society is the cultural aspect. There are two separate ways in which political and social culture affects the behaviour and power of courts. The first is the relatively narrow question of the cultural orientation of the judges and lawyers. Thus the extent to which judges from different backgrounds are likely to have the instinct or courage to oppose the legislature, the problem Kelsen ran into, is one aspect, and one of the reasons 'Kelsen Courts' are often preferred. So recruitment patterns, affecting what sorts of people get to potentially politically powerful courts, become simultaneously matters of political, or at least social, culture and matters of institutional structure. These two necessarily interweave.

Institutional rules protecting judges from outside influence, perhaps guaranteeing their professional career expectations (or just their pensions) without fear of politicians' disfavour combine with questions about the society's overall view of law to give judicial benches with very different orientations to using their power. It is one aspect of this, the individual judge's private ideology, with which the judicial behaviour studies mentioned before are concerned. Some comparative analysis on this institutional and cultural interaction is provided, for example, in Guarnieri and Pederzoli *The Power of Judges: A Comparative Study of Courts and Democracy* (2002). The reason this type of variable needs to be taken seriously is that courts can have great potential power without ever using it. Most English public lawyers would agree that the English courts could have been much more active than traditionally they have been had the judges themselves actually believed it was appropriate to exercise more influence, to allow their values more of an impact on their decisions.

The broader aspect of political culture, the values and expectations shared by society outside the judiciary are equally important, primarily because of one feature that makes courts unlike other political institutions – they are necessarily not proactive – if cases do not come before them; they are powerless. One need only consider what the power of a parliament would be if it could only pass legislation when asked to by the executive to see how much of an effect this would have, because it is very nearly true in some democracies with powerful executives and strong party discipline. Courts need cases, and this makes them potentially restricted by either institutional or cultural factors which limit the chances of important cases being referred to them. Institutional factors can severely restrict the flow of politically important cases. This was a major concern for those who designed the Central European post-1990 constitutions, so they made as generous as possible the provision for people who felt their rights were affected to get before the constitutional courts.

The model here, as in so much else, was probably Germany where the simple process of 'constitutional complaint' from the beginning made it possible for citizens to approach the court. But cultural factors can very much restrict the flow of cases on which courts can base a politically effective jurisprudence. In part this can be because there is a varying degree of litigation mindedness across societies, in part because courts are not necessarily seen as likely to sympathise with some sectors of society. Again these factors usually interact. The French Constitutional Council was largely unable to act for the first decade of its existence because the rules under which legislation could be referred restricted the right to only four office holders, but also because it was part of the French political culture to keep courts out of politics. Thus it was not until 1970 that an issue of sufficient importance to the French Senate to overcome this disinclination was referred by its president. Even after 1972 when it became much easier to get matters before the council the cultural distrust of courts in politics restricted the case load for some time. It has long been thought that in the UK a historic distrust of courts meant that trade unions never tried litigation strategies common elsewhere, and which could have lead to decisions in their favour.

There is a danger of circularity when taking about cultural constraints on judicial power, which is best seen when one realises that a country's legal rules are themselves a cultural artefact. There is one matter, for example, on which every legal system has to have a rule, and what rule exists is a major constraint on the flow of cases to courts, and therefore on the possibility of political power being exercised by courts. This rule, usually called the rule on 'standing', restricts who may come before a court – must the individual in question be personally affected, for example, or may a citizen who is just generally disapproving of something the state has done take the issue to the court? Restrictive rules on standing, (both the USA and the UK have had quite restrictive rules in the past), make it harder for a court to be politically effective. But are such rules really constraints on judges, or the results of judges themselves having doubts about their right to be politically effective? Without any doubt the core question of whether judges should exercise influence over social values and state policies is itself a question which deeply divides the judiciary in most countries. The very fact that most judicial benches will contain at least a minority of judges who share the objections of elected politicians to judicial power marks courts out as a very different type of political institution.

Other Types of Court

Discussion of types of court started by pointing out that an institutional perspective obviously applied to the study of courts because of the way that one sort of court, the so-called 'Kelsen' courts, were carefully designed results of institutional choice. What is the alternative court structure, and how might it affect the political role of courts? The alternative structure is based on the assumption that there is nothing special about constitutional law – the constitution is simply another matter over which there can be litigation. Thus the ordinary courts may make decisions based on the constitutionality of legislation if the political system accepts that any form of judicial review is applicable at all. I will leave for the moment the question of what happens in countries like the UK, and much of Western Europe, where this assumption is not part of the general understanding of politics. Where courts are entitled to rule on the constitutionality of legislation, but the system does not have a special constitutional court, the final appeal court in the system, for example the USA or Canadian Supreme Courts, becomes the last word on constitutionality, just as it is the final arbiter of any legal issue.

What is crucial to understand is that in these systems constitutional questions can only arise as part of real ongoing litigation – there is no sense of a special right of citizens to have their rights protected directly, and no 'abstract' review of the constitutionality of a statute. In contrast under the Kelsen court system it is usually possible for parliamentarians, or other political institutions, to ask a constitutional court to rule on the acceptability of a new piece of legislation entirely separately from whether anyone has actually yet been harmed by it. (In France, this is the only role for the Constitutional council. Though there have been efforts to give the council other ways of dealing with constitutional questions, they have all been defeated by entrenched political interests.)

Much follows from this distinction between the two basic types of court system, which is of direct relevance to comparative understanding of courts and politics. The question of recruitment and socialisation of judges, already demonstrated to be a potentially crucial interaction of cultural and institutional factors, is perhaps the most important. Typically those who get to the 'top' court in a system are not distinguished judges from lower courts, but generalist judges who have made their careers in ordinary law – and probably as practitioners for a good length of time before becoming judges at all. They will have been selected by the same processes which is used to promote an expert of contract law or trust or whatever, rather than one designed to put politically sensitive constitutional experts into place.

As usual, few generalisations are possible, but it is probably safe to say that those making constitutional decisions in North America, Australia, India and other countries from this legal 'family' are neither like the judges on Kelsen courts, nor like the ordinary judges in countries with Kelsen courts. Systematic differences are likely to follow from this, most probably in the technical nature of decisions, as well as in the greater probability of judicial restraint, an unwillingness to be involved in policy decisions unless such a decision is unavoidable – in truth we have little research on the issue, and much speculation. What is definitely true is that the problem of 'flow of cases' arises more intensely; only where someone can keep his case alive through multiple tiers of appeal will the top court ever have a chance to make a political impact.

One consequence is that judicial politics comes to be constrained by the presence and activities of cause groups who can afford to litigate (technically only on behalf of someone else) to achieve a potential constitutional change. It was the National Association for the Advancement of Coloured People (NAACP) which brought about *Brown* v *Board*, for instance, as a result of years and years of litigating and losing similar cases, and the support of pro- and anti-abortion pressure groups largely determines the flood of cases the US Supreme Court has from which to craft their decisions in 'right to life' cases. It is also probably true that national cultural attitudes to litigation as a natural way to solve problems affect the role of non-Kelsen courts more than in Kelsen jurisdictions. Despite these restrictions such courts, and not only the famously important US Supreme Court, have often been crucial political players. The Australian High Court, for example, early in its history struck down, for all time, central government attempts to nationalise industry. The Canadian Supreme Court in 2005 effectively destroyed the long-term Quebec Provincial policy of banning private medical insurance, regarded as crucial to the working of the state health system.

Role of political culture

Mass political culture comes into play with all courts inevitably, but perhaps especially these non-Kelsen courts, because of the need to gain and maintain political legitimacy. It is generally understood that politically relevant courts take great care to move not too much ahead of public opinion on most issues – there is an old dogma that the US Supreme Court 'follows the election returns'. In practice courts in most systems tend to have higher trust ratings in polls than any other institution in their societies, but courts certainly do not take this legitimacy for granted.

Some analysts have suggested in fact that parliamentary–court relations can best be seen as bargaining games, with the courts being careful to allow legislators ways around their more important blocking decisions. It can in reality be hard to assess the relative power of courts and legislatures in conflict situations, because the rules of political rhetoric tend to require politicians to attack a court whenever it appears to be opposed to them. Whatever the reality a good example was the occasion when the French Constitutional Council struck down an election law which would have imposed a gender quota on party lists.

At the time this was seen by many analysts as an unacceptable imposition of the Council's private values against a democratically elected government. In fact the clause in question was put into the bill by a back-bencher against the preference of the government of the day, which was entirely happy to have it struck out. Years later when the council felt it had to follow this precedent to remove a similar part of a new statute, one the government cared about, the government arranged a constitutional change to override the council. The council made no attempt whatsoever to get round this change, and faithfully changed its doctrine. Was either body, government of council, ever at loggerheads at all on this issue? The example illustrates just how careful one has to be in even reaching a description of court behaviour, as well as how subtle any comparative analysis must be.

Developing innovative roles

A brief consideration must be given to the situation in countries like the UK, where it has never been accepted that courts may carry out judicial review. In such countries, and there are many others, even in Western Europe, parliament is supreme, and courts must apply law, regardless of any bill of rights or other apparent constitutional bar. This by no means suggests that courts are politically irrelevant; judicial review of the constitutional legitimacy of a statute is only one of the weapons in a court's armoury. Much can be achieved, where other factors predispose a judiciary interested in policy influence by lesser means. In particular the general judicial duty to interpret legislation can have a devastating effect on a government's ability to impose its choices though law. Indeed those courts empowered to overturn statutes actually do so quite rarely – much more commonly they simply 'interpret' the act in a way that keeps it consistent with the constitution, whether or not the parliament actually intended any such meaning. That apart, all countries have something equivalent to UK or US 'administrative law', the law governing the executive.

Under a general doctrine usually known by the Latin tag of *ultra vires* courts everywhere can strike down decisions by a member of the executive, whether in local government or a national cabinet minister, unless there is the clearest of justifications for the actions under existing statutes. Everything that applies to comparative study of constitutional review applies, though obviously with modification, to the general political role of courts, and it is a serious mistake to ignore those not officially enshrined as judicial review courts. It is now time to pull together these general observations into a more systematic and schematic form, before engaging in a set of case studies.

Factors Influencing Courts: A Summary Review

Judicial ideology, which includes:

- beliefs about proper judicial role;
- political preferences;
- legal methodological beliefs.

Judicial selection, which includes:

- career judiciary versus other types of appointment;
- who appoints (parliament, the executive, the judiciary itself, election);
- terms of appointment (for life, fixed term, and so on).

Rules on how issues get to court, which include:

- direct reference from other political institutions (abstract review);
- direct citizen complaint;
- referral from other courts;
- legal rules of standing.

Impact of general political culture, which includes:

- public legitimacy of courts;
- attitudes to using litigation for political ends;
- politicians' preparedness to use/tolerate courts.

External factors, which include:

- treaty obligations;
- membership of supranational court systems (European Court of Justice, European Court of Human Rights).

These are only the most obviously important aspects of the study of politics and courts. Any one of these headings and subheadings could be further divided. Every one of them involves major problems of cross-national identification and definition before one can be sure one is comparing like with like. The whole discipline of comparative law within law schools is deeply split on methodological issues, and judges debate furiously whether it is ever safe to compare legal institutions in two or more countries. Comparative political science however is always bedevilled by such problems, and the area of courts and politics is probably not much worse off than others. Care is certainly needed, above all at the linguistic level, because language is so important in any legal debate. We will try to demonstrate both the difficulties and rewards in the following two short case studies.

Case Study One: The Rule of Law – Transition in Central and Eastern Europe

It is almost axiomatic that democracy involves the 'rule of law'. The European Union treated guaranteed operation of the rule of law as one of the prerequisites of joining for new member states in Central and Eastern Europe (CEE). But what does it mean in practice? Is it merely a symbolic value or does the application of the rule of law have real bite on what policies a government and legislature can enforce? And how might political circumstances affect the way a nation or its courts understand the concept? We are fortunate in having an unusually good example of this problem from two CEE countries, Hungary and Poland. Like most countries emerging into democracy in the late 20th century, these countries faced the problem of how to deal with their non-democratic pasts. Specifically should those who had committed crimes in support of the old regimes face punishment? Different countries treated this issue, often called 'lustration' differently, but the legislatures of both of our comparison countries wanted to make at least some people face criminal trials for their past activities.

There was a legal problem however. Most countries have in their criminal law a 'stature of limitations', by which if no action is taken against someone for a fixed period after his alleged crime, he cannot ever be brought to trial. (Murder is about the only crime which has no statute of limitations in most democracies.) These limitations meant that a good number of those suspected of having carried out non-lethal crimes against citizens would not normally be tried. Both legislatures therefore attempted to pass acts which would 'stop the clock' on the statutes of limitations, by ignoring the period between the crime and the fall of the old regime, on the perfectly sensible ground that such people were never in any danger of being tried by those regimes.

This, however, struck many as being equivalent to a breach in a vital element of the rule of law, which is the band on retroactive criminal legislation. It is generally understood – it is part of the European Convention on Human Rights for example – that one cannot be tried for something that was not an offence when one did it. The constitutions of both these countries were clear on the rule of law – it was enshrined at the very beginning of both their constitutions. For Hungary: 'In order to facilitate a peaceful political transition to a state under the rule of law, …'; and for the Czech Republic: 'The Czech Republic is a sovereign, unitary, and democratic state governed by the rule of law, founded on respect for the rights and freedoms of man and of citizens.' Almost identical policy proposals for very similar problems came up as a common commitment to the rule of law. What should a constitutional court do, and what factors were likely to influence them? It will surprise no one that the two courts in question came to diametrically opposed views.

For the Hungarians it was vital to show that the new regime really was very different from the past, and they needed to have completely clean hands. Thus any tinkering with the rule of law, even for essentially just ends, had to be banned. An equally talented bench of eminent constitutional jurists in Prague thought completely differently. In order to demonstrate how utterly different the new system was from the communist regime, it was crucial that the criminals from the past should be open to punishment under the new system. Indeed the Czech bench argued that the true meaning of the rule of law actually required that the statute of limitations did not extend to these people.

There are two general but related explanations for the two courts coming to such different conclusions, both as a result of the nature of their immediate communist past. In Hungary the old regime had in fact been liberalising for some considerable time before the end of the Cold War and collapse of communism. Memories were more distant and less bitter – it was in 1956 that the Hungarians had last felt real violent opposition to reforming movements. In Czechoslovakia the old regime had clung on to the bitter end, and memories of the Russian invasion against reform in 1968 were much more vivid. There was real fear in the latter country that members of the old Communist Party, and especially of the security agencies, would retain influence and damage their new hopes for democracy. The Czech jurists already had experience of constitutional claims trying to limit public disavowal of the past, and were determined to have a clean break. They saw the Czechoslovakian revolution, however 'velvet' it might have been, as a real revolution. They were also very conscious of an earlier ill-fated Czech democratic state which had fallen too easily first to the Nazis and then to the 1948 communist takeover.

In Hungary, in contrast, the court had established from the very beginning that all existing law continued to be valid unless specifically changed, and saw the regime change much more in gradualist and developmental terms rather than revolutionary ones. Furthermore the new Hungarian court wanted a strong doctrine of 'rule of law' to use as a weapon against the government in future cases – they used it, in fact, effectively in many later cases to protect human rights including socio-economic rights like pensions and welfare. The story does not end there however. What the Hungarian court needed was a clear symbolic victory to help them enshrine this useful doctrine. They did not actually need to protect these old regime criminals, and they did need to avoid too intense a clash with the government if possible. Thus they allowed a loophole, which the parliament lost no time in exploiting.

Two years later a new bill was passed by the Parliament that authorised prosecution of such people, despite the statute of limitations, for *international law* crimes, according to an international agreement which the old communist government had actually signed. In this area of international law – largely meant to prevent crimes against humanity – there *is* no statute of limitations. This has been likened to a bargaining process between court and government, which is one of the models political scientists feel happier with. A final moral may be drawn – the Hungarian court was the most active of all the new CEE courts against the government in its first 10 years. One result was that when the terms of appointment ran out for the first bench, every single one of the judges failed to be reappointed. Instead a much more compliant group of judges took over, announcing that there was no longer any need for court radicalism. In contrast the Czech court faced no strong opposition from its government.

Case Study Two: The Problem of Positive Rights

This second case study shows how unpredictable courts can be, and how wary one has to be of technical legal language in describing them, even though I have argued above that it is never safe to ignore the judges' own words. It is also intended to demonstrate a vital difference in general political/legal culture which may be of increasing importance in understanding constitutional politics altogether. Canada is generally an interesting country for students of courts, because until 1982 it did not have a judicially enforceable Bill of Rights. As part of a major constitutional reform in that year the new constitution included the *Canadian Charter of Rights and Freedoms* which immediately changed many aspects of governmental action vis-a-vis citizens. Over the years since then the Supreme Court has enforced many changes to statutes to protect rights as varied as freedom of speech rights, rights to equal treatment for same sex and heterosexual couples, abortion rights, criminal due process rights and religious freedom rights. Though there are critics, both those who feel the court has interfered too much with parliamentary sovereignty and those who think it has not gone far enough, the court has broadly satisfied Canadians, and has suffered no loss of legitimacy.

In one way though the Canadian Supreme Court has actually chosen not to extend its powers where some would have liked it to, and where other nations' courts have. There is a technical distinction in constitutional law usually called the 'vertical versus horizontal effect' question. Despite sounding highly esoteric, it is both simple to understand and potentially vital – indeed a court's position on the issue might well have been added to the list of important variables above. Bills of Rights are usually thought of as existing to protect the citizen against the government. This is 'vertical effect'. Another way of thinking about the issue though is to say that if someone has a right, he or she should have that right protected against any encroachments, no matter whether it is the government or a non-governmental body, or even a single individual, who is threatening it.

Where a constitution is seen as granting protection of rights against non-government actors, it is said to have 'horizontal effect'. One might assume that if a court could manage to wield horizontal effect, it would do so. Certainly those political scientists who think that courts are just like any political actor and seeking always to extend their power and reach should expect this. The German Constitutional Court in one of its earliest important decisions effectively did give itself this power, though cloaked in complicated legal language. Several other courts have faced the question of whether they have, or want to take, such power. It is in itself interesting for our topic to notice that it is largely up to courts, particularly in the early days of a constitution, to decide for themselves many such issues that affect their ultimate power.

Ironically, courts are not always very keen to do so. The first or 'interim' South African constitution after Apartheid had a clause which its constitutional court could have used to give itself powers like those the German court eagerly took. Yet the first cohort of judges was very unwilling to, and refused in a crucial early case to enforce constitutional norms between private actors. (They discussed the German example at great length.) Those who wrote the constitution and who were responsible for developing the interim constitution into a final version were dissatisfied with this lack of eagerness, and wrote a much stronger version of 'horizontal effect' into the second draft. Even now, however, the South African Constitutional Court is unwilling to make much use of this power.

The same issue arose in Canada in the early days of the *Charter* and the Supreme Court resolutely refused to give the charter horizontal effect, thus being self-denying. What these two courts have in common is that they are both staffed by people who have a typical 'common law' training, whose experience is in systems to which extensive constitutional effect in a society is novel and not, professionally, very welcome. The South Africans however are, by any standards, far more radical outside of such narrow technical professional views. (Several of the first bench had been important figures in the anti-Apartheid movements, and all were selected to be sympathetic to those aims.) So when it came to another related issue on which constitutional activism depends, the South African court rapidly became far more interested in wielding power. This is the question about whether or not a court has the power to order a government to actually realise positive social goals. The South African constitution clearly contains a series of 'positive rights', rights to have something like health treatment or adequate housing.

It is important to understand the difference between a traditional or 'negative' right and a positive right. Most rights simply forbid the government to do something that takes away a right. The right to freedom of speech, for example, forbids a government to censor publications; the right to religious freedom forbids a government to restrict which churches may exist, and it may be taken to forbid state help to religious bodies, as in the USA. But a right to housing can be taken to mean the government actually has to deliver some level of housing. It is almost entirely up to courts, if they have any text in the constitution that could be made to justify it, to decide if they are going to enforce positive rights on the government. In a string of cases starting a few years into its post-Apartheid history the South African court has indeed enforced positive rights, ordering the government, for example, to provide anti-HIV treatment when it did not wish to, as well as supporting homeless squatters against the government in the name of the right to housing (*Minister of Health and others* v *Treatment Action Campaign and others* 2002).

Enforcing positive rights, as well as giving, however grudgingly, some horizontal effect to rights, is all part of a specific view of constitutions widely shared in countries with newer constitutions. This idea is that constitutions are not just blueprints for institutional design, but enshrine a society's values, which the courts are there to develop and enforce. So for example the Constitutional Courts in Poland and Hungary have viewed welfare rights as so crucial that they have even struck down parts of their state budgets as unconstitutional because the budgets would mean drastic cuts in such entitlements (Polish Constitutional Tribunal, 1992; Hungarian Constitutional Court, 1995). In all these cases, and there are many others one could cite, it has been a matter of an energetic court imposing its will. A court may not be able to invent such powers out of nothing, but an unwilling court can easily avoid using them.

This therefore is a vital distinction between those courts which do wish to make a constitution into an all pervading mechanism for establishing a value set, and those which wish to use it narrowly to keep government limited in very specific ways. None has ever persuaded the US Supreme Court that a citizen has a right to welfare, and the US law on 'horizontal effect' is extremely limiting. For example where a state welfare agency, through its own negligence, allowed a child in its care to be murdered, the courts held firmly that there was no constitutional duty to protect the child, and refused any compensation to the parents (*DeShaney* v *Winnebago County Dept. of Social Services* 1989). Even the very limited protection the Supreme Court has allowed against private racial discrimination is thought to be constitutionally dubious.

Where is Canada in all this? Until the spring of 2005 no one would have doubted that its Supreme Court was as restrictive as the US equivalent or the UK's House of Lords in terms of enforcing anything like a positive duty. After all, it had very firmly squashed horizontal effect, and had never shown any desire to order the government to do anything it did not want to do. (It would not even forbid the government to repatriate an illegal immigrant who would face the death penalty in his home country, something even an English court might do.) The Canadian Court's radicalism had been almost entirely about discrimination – the government did not have to grant any particular sort of welfare or health benefit, but if it did, it must not discriminate on gender, race or similar grounds. Where it did recognise such discrimination rights, furthermore, it only applied them to the government. For example the court has struck down any attempts to make private employers refrain from age discrimination, though it would not allow a government department to discriminate in such a way.

What happened in 2005 is that the Supreme Court of Canada, out of the blue, struck down a Quebec provincial law banning private health insurance. The law, which has analogues in many of Canada's provinces, is regarded as crucial to the successful running of the state health service. They did so on the grounds that waiting lists for medical treatment were so long than people might die, and would certainly suffer while waiting, because, in the absence of health insurance, they could not afford private health treatment. Thus the law was in breach of the *Charter* guarantee of life. How on earth did the court come to such a surprising decision? Why should a rather conservative and self-restricting court do such a thing? Even the South African Court, despite the HIV case, has always been cautious about cases involving claims for expensive treatment that might damage the state health service. We cannot know the answer to this question, or not yet anyway. It is offered here in part as a warning against overconfidence that one has understood a legal culture, partly to underline the importance of this split between activist-oriented and restrictive courts.

Most of all though, the case is offered here as a fine example of an early point I made – how are we in fact to characterise this decision – what exactly is it an example of – what, in short, did the court do, in political science rather than legal terms? Was it a strong support for a positive rights style position – there is a right to life, and the government must ensure it, at least by removing barriers to alternate forms of health protection? Or is it really a case about protecting property rights? Property rights are not included in the *Charter*, quite intentionally, because they are politically sensitive. Thus the Supreme Court could not rule that the government cannot tell people what they are allowed to spend their money on. But it *can,* apparently, protect someone's right to life in this special sense.

Consider this – are the decisions in *Chaoulli* v *Quebec* (2005) and *Dolphin Delivery* (1986) evidence that the court has shifted from a restrictive and negative rights orientation to an activist and positive rights orientation? *Dolphin Delivery* was the 1986 decision against horizontal effect, *Chaoulli* the 2005 decision on the right to life. But note – the successful defendant in *Dolphin* was the employer, upheld against a trade union that wanted the *Charter* extended to industrial relations conflicts, while one of the successful plaintiffs in *Chaoulli* was a doctor who wanted to be able to practise private medicine. At the same time one might want to note that the minority on the Supreme Court in *Chaoulli*, because it was a bitterly divisive decision, were all from Quebec, and no Quebec judges voted with the majority.

These are the sorts of issues that the comparative study of courts has to handle. The most important thing about *Chaoulli* is what followed – because however conservative the instincts of the majority in the case may have been, future courts will be less free than before to take a purely negative rights orientation to the Canadian constitution. In this way the *Chaoulli* case, and the East European cases demonstrate many of the issues faced by comparative studiers of courts. It is the intermix of institutional and cultural factors combined with problems of identifying the actual meaning of legal decisions that produce the problems, but also guarantee the richness, of such work.

SUMMARY

- This chapter has examined why it is only recently that the courts and judicial processes have come to be included in studies based on comparative political analysis.

- It has discussed the application of new institutionalist theoretical frameworks to assist our understanding of the nature of judicial power.

(Continued)

(Continued)

- We should appreciate the centrality of concepts such as rule of law and practices such as judicial review to the running of democratic political systems.

- We can appreciate that whereas certain countries have dedicated constitutional courts, the functions that they carry out may be dealt with in different ways in those countries which operate according to different institutional frameworks.

- Two case studies, firstly on the importance of the rule of law for democratising countries and secondly on the problem of positive rights, have highlighted how the courts affect the nature of rule-making in democracies.

FURTHER READING

Guarnieri, C. and Pederzoli, P. (2002) *The Power of Judges: A Comparative Study of Courts and Democracy*. Oxford: Oxford University Press.

Gibson, J.L. (1983) 'From simplicity to complexity: the development of theory in the study of judicial behaviour', *Political Behaviour*, 5: 9ff.

Gibson, J.L. and Caldeira, G.A. (2003) 'Defenders of democracy? Legitimacy, popular acceptance, and the South African constitutional court', *Journal of Politics*, 65 (1): 1–30.

Robertson, D. (1998) *Judicial Discretion in the House of Lords*. Oxford: Clarendon Press.

Roosevelt, K. (2006) *The Myth of Judicial Activism: Making Sense of Supreme Court Decisions*. New Haven, CT: Yale University Press.

Shapiro, M. and Stone Sweet, A. (2002) *On Law, Politics and Judicialization*. Oxford: Oxford University Press.

Stone Sweet, Alec (2000) *Governing with Judges: Constitutional Politics in Europe*. Oxford: Oxford University Press.

Tate, C.N. and Vallinder, T. (eds) (1995) *The Global Expansion of Judicial Power*. New York: NYU Press.

Volcansek, M. (2000) *Constitutional Politics in Italy*. London: Macmillan Press.

Cases

Retail, Wholesale and Department Store Union v *Dolphin Delivery Ltd* [1968] 2 SCR 573 (Supreme Court of Canada).

Furman v *Georgia* 408 US 238 (1972) (US Supreme Court)

Retail, Wholesale and Department Store Union v *Dolphin Delivery Ltd* [1986] 2 SCR 573 (Supreme Court of Canada).

DeShaney v *Winnebago County Dept. of Social Services* 489 US 189 (1989) (US Supreme Court).

Employment Div, Dept. of Human Resources of Oregon v *Smith* 494 US 872 (1990) (US Supreme Court).

Decision of 11 February 1992 (K. 14/91) – Pensions Laws Selection of the Polish Constitutional Tribunal's Jurisprudence 1986–1999 (Polish Constitutional Tribunal).

Decision of 30 June 1995 On Social Security Benefits 43/1995 AB (Hungarian Constitutional Court).

S v *Makwanyane and another* CCT3/94 (South African Constitutional Court).

R. v *Bow Street Metropolitan Stipendiary Magistrate and others, ex parte Pinochet Ugarte (No 2)* [2000] 1 AC 119 (House of Lords).

Garreth Anver Prince v *The President of The Law Society of The Cape of Good Hope* 2002 (2) SA 794 (CC).

Minister of Health and others v *Treatment Action Campaign and others* CCT 8/02

Chaoulli v *Quebec (Attorney General)* 2005 SCC 35 (Canadian Supreme Court).

QUESTIONS FOR DISCUSSION

(1) How important is it to study judicial arguments?

(2) Does the system of appointing judges make a difference to how courts behave?

(3) Are judges politically neutral?

(4) Are constitutional courts more like parliaments than they are like ordinary courts?

Key Words for Chapter 7

agency theory / bills of rights / constitutional review / judges / judicial attitudes / Kelsen courts / legal interpretation / rights / separation of powers

8 The Territorial Dimension

Brendan O'Duffy

CHAPTER OUTLINE

This chapter will first define territorial state forms, then develop a classification of federal versus unitary systems that takes into account the distinction between form and function. We will then examine competing explanations from cultural, structural and rational choice institutionalists for the development of federal versus unitary systems, before comparing their performance across a range of political and governance issues.

Introduction

Federalism and federal government are important areas of comparative politics and government for at least three reasons. First, it is the system of government for between one-third and one-half of the world's population, depending on which definition of federation is used, including the most populous democracy (India), the largest (Canada), the dominant states of South America (Brazil and Argentina), sub-Saharan Africa (South Africa) and Europe (Germany), Australia and the current superpower (USA) (Hueglin and Fenna, 2006: 11; Wachendorfer-Schmidt, 2000: 1). According to Stepan, federalism is also 'the form of governance in all stable, multi-national and multi-lingual democracies' (2001: 315).

Second, in addition to formal federations, there is a trend towards decentralisation within unitary states in response to demands for local autonomy by ethnic and ethnonational movements. Unitary states such as Spain, Belgium and the UK have devolved substantial authority to sub-national levels in response to ethnic, national and regional demands for autonomy. By pluralising sovereignty, federal-related forms of power sharing have created incentives for ethno-national separatists in Ireland, Spain, the UK, Indonesia, and India, to moderate or rescind their claims to separate statehood. Federalism and related forms of non-territorial 'power sharing' promote *internal* forms of self-determination that have the potential to reduce the risks associated with state-shattering external self-determination.

Third, these formal and informal federal adjustments attest to the increasing fluidity of relations between state authority and territoriality that has increased as processes of globalisation have challenged the primacy of the nation-state as the dominant locus of political authority and governance. An understanding of the origins and development of federal states is therefore an important guide to the reconfiguration of nation-state sovereignty, both within nation-states and in supra-national organisations such as the European Union. The modern study of comparative federalism focuses on the effects of different forms of inter-governmental relations, especially the form of representation of citizens interests and identity, the organisation of the fisc (taxation and spending) and the organisation of the delivery of governance, whether centralised or decentralised.

Defining Territorial State Forms

The term *federal* is derived from the Latin *foederatus*, itself derived from both *foedus* (treaty) and *fidere* (trust). As a political idea, *federalism* can be defined as the belief in the principle of 'diversity in unity', maintained by constitutional relations between centralised and decentralised institutions of government within a single, territorially bounded state. This notion of a bond or exchange relationship is central to K.C. Wheare's classic definition of the federal principle as a 'method of dividing powers so that the general and regional governments are each, within a sphere, coordinate and independent' (1963: 10).

As a political form, a *federation* or *federal union* has been defined by Daniel Elazar as a form of partnership government founded on the 'distribution of real power among several centres that must negotiate cooperative arrangements with one another in order to achieve common goals' (1984: 2). Arend Lijphart specifies four requirements for a political system to qualify as a federation:

- a written constitution regulating division of powers among territorial units;
- bicameral parliament with one chamber representing national population and the second chamber representing federated units equally (despite territorial size or population);
- participation of federated units in amending federal constitution;
- political decentralisation beyond the administrative (that is, the distribution to sub-national units of some combination of legislative, judicial and executive powers).

As outlined in Figure 8.1 a federal system can be represented schematically as a system in which constitutionally entrenched exchange relations, represented by the vertical lines connecting the central government with the constituent subunits, are institutionalised between the subunits and the central government. Additionally, as the lines connecting the subunits indicate, the horizontal relations between or among subunits are also relevant, especially as the complexity of governance at local, regional and central level has increased (Agranoff, 2007: 268–71).

Lijphart's criteria

Using Lijphart's criteria we can distinguish formal federal systems from three main alternative forms of territorial governance. As Figure 8.1 demonstrates, a *confederation*, unlike a federation, is a treaty-based alliance between or among separate sovereign states, the legal 'personalities' that are the primary unit in the international system. Confederations can be conceived of as entities that are *merely* the sum of their separate constituent parts whereas federations have, in addition to the constituent

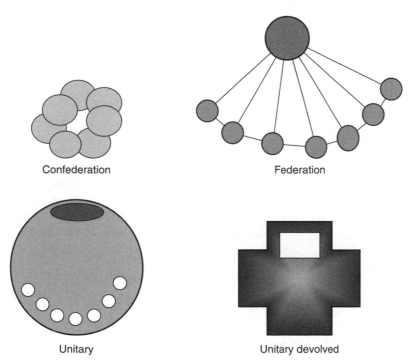

Confederation

Federation

Unitary

Unitary devolved

Figure 8.1   Federal, confederal and unitary forms

states (or provinces), a substantial central government constituting a state that is *more than* the sum of its constituent parts. The European Union, for example, is a confederation because each of its members remains a separate sovereign state within the international system, even though they have individually agreed to devolve some authority to the formal executive in Brussels.

Unlike most federations, each member of the confederation can exit (or secede) without permission from other members. Unlike a federation, the European Union has a weak unicameral (single chamber) legislature – the European Parliament – that represents national populations rather than national or other territorial units. And whereas federations constitutionally entrench *some* legislative, judicial and executive to the subunits, confederations entrench *most* such powers to the constituent sovereign states. The EU, for example, extracts less than 2 per cent of revenues from the member states, compared to between 25 and 50 per cent extracted by comparable wealthy nation-states. The confederal status of the EU has been recently re-enforced by the failure to ratify a constitution (agreed by heads of state in 2004, but rejected in referenda in France and the Netherlands), which gave way to a less ambitious 'reform treaty' (agreed at Lisbon in 2007) which was itself stalled in June 2008, if not defeated, by just over 100,000 Irish voters who rejected the Lisbon Treaty in a national referendum.

We can also distinguish federations from two *unitary* state forms. A simple unitary state is characterised by a national central government, which has unlimited sovereignty over the territory, qualified only by the devolution of some authority to local (usually towns or cities) or perhaps regional tiers of government. In a unitary system, such as that of France or the UK before devolution in 1998, the central government retains legislative, executive and judicial authority at the centre and, through tight controls on budgets, limits the autonomy of sub-state authorities. By contrast, in a devolved unitary system, like that of the UK after 1998, substantial territorial units are granted limited autonomy from the centre that typically go beyond the powers granted to local government in terms of legislative, judicial and executive powers (see Figure 8.1).

In the devolved UK, Scotland has its own Parliament with authority to vary the UK rate of income tax by plus or minus 3 per cent. Wales and Northern Ireland, by contrast, have Legislative Assemblies without tax-varying powers, but with substantial legislative and executive authority over issues such as health, education and welfare. While the UK's devolution reforms represent a substantial shift from unitary *towards* federal-like features, they fail to meet the first three of Lijphart's minimum requirements to qualify as federal. First, there is no written constitution regulating the division of powers, so that on any given day the UK Parliament at Westminster could revoke all authorities devolved to Northern Ireland, Scotland and Wales. Second, the UK does have a bicameral parliament composed of the House of Commons and the House of Lords, but the upper house does *not* represent the devolved entities as in a federal chamber. Finally, there is no requirement for the devolved entities of the UK to participate in amending the constitution. Neither Scotland, Wales nor Northern Ireland would be required to give their assent to a constitutional change such as ratifying the European Reform treaty.

In addition to these four main types of territorial configuration, we should also note a variety of other arrangements that describe the complex reality of modern governance over large or culturally complex terrain. Daniel Elazar's typology of federal political systems also includes configurations such as a league (like the British Commonwealth), which is governed by a secretariat rather than a government and in which members can opt out freely; non-territorial consociation (like Northern Ireland's power-sharing government), which is governed by coalitions representing each of the main cultural, ethnic or national constituents of a divided society; a federacy is a system in which a subunit has substantial autonomy but plays only a minimal role in the governance of the central state, exemplified by Puerto Rico, which is a federacy of the USA or Kashmir in relation to India (Elazar, 1987; quoted in Pagano, 2007). Finally, joint functional authority describes an agency established by two or more sovereign states for cooperative implementation of particular tasks, like the North–South Ministerial Council established between Northern Ireland and the Republic of Ireland to manage cross-border cooperation over aspects of health, education, tourism, fisheries, food safety and so forth. Finally, a condominium is a substantially autonomous polity ruled jointly by two sovereign states, like Andorra which is largely autonomous but ultimately ruled jointly by Spain and France, or as effectively threatened by the British and Irish governments for Northern Ireland if the current consociational system fails.

The diversity of territorial forms of governance in the modern state system is a result and reflection of the complexity of modern governance, especially in the post-Second World War era when the role of the state increased substantially in delivering core welfare provision, on top of the already considerable role in defending borders and projecting power externally to defend strategic interests. Faced with such complexity, comparative political scientists applying 'new institutionalist' analyses go beyond the investigation of formal constitutional forms of territorial governance to consider informal rules, norms and behaviours that affect the performance of governance in federal and non-federal systems. For many comparativists, the distinction between federal and unitary constitutional *forms* is less significant than the distinction between decentralised and centralised *functions* of government (see Castles, 2000; Keman, 2000; Lane and Ersson, 1997).

Keman, for example, compares the organisation of the democratic input or 'rights to decide' and the governmental outputs or 'rights to act'. Rights to decide refer to the 'extent to which citizens and organised interests are fairly represented [e.g. through the electoral system] and can exert influence on the political decision-making of the state' (Keman, 2000: 198, citing Bellamy, 1996). With this criterion we can compare states that have a *unitary* decision-making process, in terms of representation in a 'national' government, with a dominant 'national' legislature, from a *federal* process of 'power sharing', either territorially or based on some other category of communal or functional, representation. In the unitary form, decision-making tends to be majoritarian, in which no territorial or communal level divisions of the polity are recognised. In Stepan's view the unitary form is intended to enable the 'demos' to be represented as unitary whole and therefore legislate and change policy when the majority of citizens vote for such change.

Federal forms, by contrast, divide sovereignty and grant veto rights to territorial, sub-national units in a form of power sharing. In Stepan's (2001) view, federal forms are inherently, and intentionally, 'demos constraining' in that the veto power of minority subunits (such as provinces or states within a federal union) constrains the overall national majority. If, for example, the people of Brazil, voting in a national referendum, decided to establish a national oil fund to invest its newfound off-shore reserves, the federal system could constrain such a democratic decision because, like most federal systems, the federal rules in Brazil grant the territorial chamber – the Senate (*Senado Federal*) veto powers over legislation passed in the popular chamber – the lower house. In Stepan's calculation, the Brazilian federal form is, compared to other federal systems, very demos-constraining because a voting 'win-set' or coalition of states with less than 10 per cent of the national population can block legislation proposed by a clear national majority through the lower house. As we will see below, there is considerable variation among federal systems in terms of the extent to which they constrain the demos from legislating for fundamental policy changes.

Establishing comparative frameworks

Comparativists have attempted to classify distinct models of federation according to the constitutional form of government (presidential, parliamentary, council), the structure of the second legislative chamber (senate, council or nominal), the way power is divided (legislative versus administrative) and the form of intergovernmental relations that have evolved (cooperative versus competitive). Hueglin and Fenna use these criteria to identify three archetypal federal forms (excluding the EU which I have defined as more confederal than federal, see Hueglin and Fenna, 2006: 63–83):

1. The American (US) model considered by many to be the classical model because it was the first to move from confederal to federal by structuring the division of powers constitutionally in a way that balances central, unitary legislative authority with federal, decentralised legislative authority. In explicit contrast to the UK (Westminster) parliamentary system, the American model is characterised by both vertical and horizontal division of powers. Vertical divisions are maintained primarily through constitutional enumeration of powers for the states and the national government, as well as by the

equality of legislative authority given to the territorial chamber (the Senate). While the national legislative chamber (the House of Representatives) is elected to represent national population, the Senate provides equal representation for the states so that California, with a population of over 30 million has equal representation in the Senate as Wyoming, the least populous state with less than 1 million inhabitants.

The US system also divides power horizontally by a formal separation of powers. Executive authority is vested in a directly elected President, while legislative authority is the exclusive competence of the two Houses of Congress (House of Representatives and the Senate). It is believed that the horizontal division of power between the President and Congress reinforces the federal system by concentrating conflict between the national executive and legislature and not between the central branches of government and the states. The maintenance of a dualist system between the centre and the states is also regulated by the federal judiciary's responsibility for interpreting the constitution to decide whether power should evolve to the centre or devolve to the states (Hueglin and Fenna, 2006: 64–5).

2. The Canadian model, in contrast to the American (US) model, combines federation with parliamentary sovereignty and a weak bicameral structure. Whereas the American Federalists were trying to move away from the Westminster model of parliamentary sovereignty, the Canadian federation evolved gradually from the Westminster system and attempted to maintain the integrating role of parliamentary government while regulating the ethno-national conflict between English-speaking provinces and French-speaking Quebec. While the American (US) model was predicated on the principle of maximising individual liberty, the Canadian model struck a balance between individual liberty and ethno-national autonomy of Quebec and French-speakers outside Quebec, as well as non-ethnic regional interests (such as in the western Provinces of Alberta and British Columbia) that have produced a fragmented party system representing regional and ethno-national blocs as well as weak national parties (dominated by Conservatives and Liberals).

By retaining its parliamentary form, the Canadian system produced a weak bicameral system. The upper house (the Senate) does have equal numbers of Senators from each province but the Senate itself has only advisory and review functions and no substantial legislative power. Some believe that the absence of a horizontal division of power at the central level has unintentionally weakened the centre because it has driven the provinces to demand more devolved autonomy since their veto-power at the centre is limited (Hueglin and Fenna, 2006: 68).

Vertical division of power is clearly established in the Canadian constitution to create a legislative federal form. The centre and the Provinces each legislate on matters within their constitutionally defined competence. Though unlike the US system, and consistent with the parliamentary ethos, residual powers evolve upward to the central government rather than devolve as they do to the US states.

3. The German model, in contrast with the American (US) and Canadian forms, is a system of administrative rather than legislative federalism. The central government in Germany has sole legislative authority, while the Länder have sole responsibility for implementing

legislation and policy. The upper house, the *Bundesrat*, is a council chamber rather than a senate as its membership is composed of representatives from the directly elected Länder governments. Constitutionally, the *Bundesrat* has co-equal legislative authority with the national parliament's lower house (*Bundestag*).

The practice of co-decision between the national parliament and the territorial chamber, combined with the Länder's exclusive implementation role, produces a form of *integrated federalism* that differs from the dualist form of the US and Canadian models. German federalism is therefore characterised more by cooperation between the two main levels of government (Hueglin and Fenna, 2006: 71–2).

Despite the formal and functional differences of these three types, in response to national and international demands for greater coordination in the formation and implementation of public policy, they have all developed complex, inter-governmental relations that have led to a high degree of institutionalised cooperation between the two main territorial levels of government. As the next section shows, despite the significant formal differences between the three main types of federation, they converge to a considerable degree in their functions.

Form Versus Function

Despite the important differences in federal forms, Keman's point is that state *form* (unitary versus federal or the sub-types of federation) does not necessarily tell us much about the way government *functions* to deliver the policy made by the demos. The organisation of policy implementation or the 'right to act', which is the right to public regulation (including the right to levy and allocate taxes)' is not necessarily related to the federal or unitary form of government (2000: 198). In *centralised* forms one agency or level of government has 'nation-wide authority to organise and implement public policy', whereas in states with *decentralised* functions, this authority is divided among other territorial bodies or functional bodies. Thus, a formally unitary state such as Sweden can have a unitary system of rights to decide while at the same time having a federal-like degree of decentralisation of rights to act, with strong municipal control over local taxation and policy implementation.

Figure 8.2 reproduces Keman's index of state form and function to reveal four broad types of state within the European and North American systems, plus Australia (students may wish to consider extending this typology to include states beyond Europe and North America). This index measures federal versus unitary form according to the constitutional rules regulating degrees of autonomy between central and sub-national levels, the balance of competences between the legislature and the executive, the formalisation of power-sharing rules between the centre and the sub-national units. To gauge the extent to which governance (the outputs of legislated policy) is centralised or decentralised, the index measures the proportion of tax revenues and public spending of the central government and sub-national levels as proportions of GDP (Keman, 2000: 203–7).

Combining the federal-unitary and centralised-decentralised scales produces a four-fold typology of states (see Figure 8.2):

Type I states, which Keman labels 'Federal-Decentral', are both formally and functionally federal, including Australia, Canada, Germany, Switzerland and the USA.

Type II 'Federal-Central', which include only Italy and Belgium, are formally federal in terms of the formal division of competences between the central and sub-national levels, but function more like unitary states in that fiscal policies and governance outputs are not strongly decentralised.

Type III 'Unitary-Decentral' states include three of the four Scandinavian countries (Denmark, Norway and, at a stretch, Sweden) as well as Austria and Spain. These states are formally unitary but are relatively decentralised in terms of actual governance, consistent with traditions of municipal autonomy in the Scandinavian cases. Austria's high degree of decentralisation is probably a by-product of the same kind of traditions of local autonomy produced by the physical separation of valley communities in mountainous states like Austria and Switzerland. Spain since the mid-1990s should probably be classified higher on

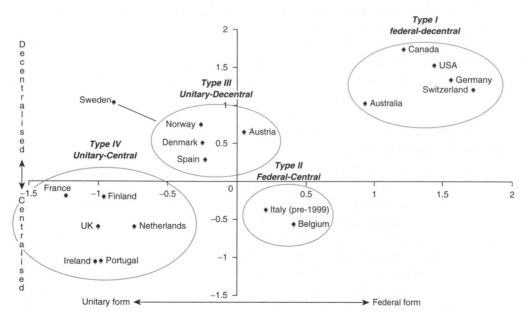

Figure 8.2   Federal/unitary (form) and decentralised/centralised (function)

Source: Keman, H. (2000) 'Federalism and policy performance: a conceptual and empirical enquiry', in U. Wachandorfer-Schmidt (ed.), *Federalism and Political Performance*. London: Routledge.

the decentralisation scale and the federal scale since the decisions of the Constitutional Tribunal taken then have increased fiscal and cultural autonomy for the Basque Country and Catalonia in particular. Norway too has increased its degree of fiscal decentralisation by developing a national deposit account for the profits from the sale of oil resources that is constitutionally beyond the control of current governments.

Type IV 'Unitary-Central' states include Finland, France, Ireland, the Netherlands, Portugal, the UK (prior to devolution in 1998).

Below, we will evaluate the performance of these different state models according to a range of criteria from economic prosperity to more subjective measures of 'quality of life'. We will attempt to evaluate whether and how federal institutions matter in affecting political, economic and social performance compared to non-federal systems. But first it is necessary to explore the evolution of federal ideas since they help us to understand the interests and ideas that led federalists to deviate from the classical liberal theories of the state and propose systems that intentionally pluralised sovereignty through constitutionalism.

The Territorial State and the Federal Idea

Classical liberal theorists of the modern state emphasised the necessity of a unitary conception of state sovereignty to replace the more fluid and anarchic principle of suzerainty which had predominated in the medieval period. Under suzerainty, a monarch would grant substantial autonomy within specific domains to lesser nobles and would expect tributes (in money or kind) and perhaps a commitment to a loose military alliance. English monarchs in the 15th century recognised the autonomy of both Anglo-Irish lords and Gaelic Irish chieftains to rule their own domains within Ireland, in exchange for the payment of tributes. Similarly plural structures of governance characterised the Holy Roman Empire (800–1806).

However, by the middle of the 17th century in Europe, with the modernisation and commercialisation of agriculture, the expansion of mercantile trade and the need for larger standing armies and navies to protect commercial interests and frontiers, monarchic systems began to insist on more regular and uniform systems of taxation and the application of uniform legal systems as the basis of property rights and the enforcement of contracts. The principle of absolute sovereignty was defended by classical liberal theorists such as Hobbes as necessary to prevent the perpetual war that exists in a state of nature in which men, because of their natural equality, are motivated by 'competition', 'diffidence' and 'glory' and will fight unless they are in 'feare of some coercive Power' (Hobbes, [1660] 1996: 120). Subsequent liberal theorists, such as Locke, had less pessimistic views of human nature than Hobbes and advocated less absolutist forms of sovereignty in which the people, rather than a hereditary or

divinely ordained monarch, were supreme. We can observe one of the founding principles of federalism in the thinking of the French philosopher Baron de Montesquieu, who
argued that the supreme value of liberty was best preserved by the *separation of powers*
(executive, judicial and legislative) as codified in a constitution that limited the state's
exercise of sovereign authority.

However, two centuries before, the German Calvinist academic Johan Althusius
(1557–1638) had criticised Bodin's theory of absolute state sovereignty and had
defended the principle of political pluralism of the Holy Roman Empire in which consensual forms of politics prevailed over monarchic absolutism and the autonomy of small
territories (like the Netherlands) was preserved in a nested system of self-governing
consociations. Althusius placed particular emphasis on the 'bottom-up' delegation of
authority, in clear contrast to the top-down model advocated by Bodin and Hobbes in
their justifications of absolutist state sovereignty (Hueglin and Fenna, 2006: 90–6).

The principle of constitutionally entrenched separation of powers was an important
influence on the thinking of the American Federalists, who combined this model of
government with the Althusian principle of territorial divisions of authority and principles of consent that limited the power of the majority by providing minorities (as
states in the union) with veto powers through a bicameral legislature. Federal territorial forms had existed in loose forms among the Greek city-states in the third and fourth
centuries CE and among medieval Italian city-states. Among the earliest stable forms of
*con*federation were the United Provinces of the Netherlands, which came together in
1579 to preserve communal autonomy for different Protestant sects, while resisting
Spanish control and the even older Swiss confederation of three forest cantons –
'Waldstätte' which merged to establish a common legal system for the settlement of
disputes and for mutual defence (Woodard, 1995).

State forms were therefore a compromise between promoting the interests of a
'national' democratic polity while protecting sectoral or factional interests defined by
relations to private property and commerce, or territorially concentrated ethno-
national identities or religious beliefs. For Dicey, 'absolutely essential to the founding
of a federal system is the existence of a very peculiar state of sentiment among the
inhabitants of the countries which it is proposed to unite. They must desire union, and
must not desire unity ... The aim of federalism is to give effect as far as possible to
both these sentiments (1939: 141–3). Similarly, for Stepan, 'in a robust democratic
federal political system, the more citizens feel a sense of allegiance to both of the
democratically legitimated sovereignties, each with its constitutionally guaranteed
scope of action, the more democratically secure the federation' (Stepan, 2001).

Ideally, therefore, citizens within a democratic federation should have *dual* but *complementary* political identities' (Stepan, 2001: 326). Note the similarity in the definition
of mature civic culture, combining citizen activism with deference; and with tension
inherent in liberal-democracy where the freedom of individual or culturally defined

group must be balanced with responsibility for the collective *demoi* or democratic polity (see Chapter 3). In this sense, federalism can be interpreted as a territorial corollary to liberal democracy in its attempt to balance individual liberty with collective prosperity, security and identity. It is precisely the tension between democracy and liberty of citizens that shapes the main debates within the comparative study of federalism. The next section compares different routes to the formation of federations in order to evaluate the structural, rational and cultural forces that shaped federal forms.

Explaining Federal Formation

Structural institutionalist perspectives

Structural institutionalists interpret federalism as a by-product of underlying economic, political and sometimes social forces or structures associated with modern state formation. Strong structuralist interpretations focus on the interests of capitalist classes in developing political structures that would best serve their interests. Bertell Ollman described the US federal project as follows: 'Merchants, bankers, ship-owners, planters, slave traders and slave owners, land speculators, and lawyers, who made their money working for these groups, voiced their interests and fears in clear, uncluttered language; and, after settling a few, relatively minor disagreements, they drew up plans for a form of government they believe would serve these interests most effectively' (Ollman, 2008: 1). These interpretations are consistent with Marxist theories of the state which argued that capitalist development requires sufficient land mass to create economies of scale first for commercial agriculture production and then as a basis for industrial production. Federal forms of government, in this view are merely convenient administrative devices for governing large territories required for mature capitalism.

But why does federalism suit these diverse capitalist interests better than a unitary form of government? Weak structuralist interpretations explain the origins of federal forms according to the relationship between traditional and modernising producer groups. In situations where traditionalists – mainly large landowners involved in commercialised agriculture – were strong, there tended to be sustained resistance to centralisation and unitary forms of government. The UK evolved as a unitary form of government because the modernising, mercantile and commercial interest groups based in the south and east of England were able to overwhelm and then co-opt the traditionalist landed interests of the north and west during the mid-17th-century English Civil War. While the latter supported the royalists in the Civil War, the former supported the victorious parliamentary faction and were able then centralise power without significant opposition from the defeated royalists. By contrast, federal systems tended to emerge in states that developed relatively late in the process of modern state formation, when both traditional and modernising interest groups were too entrenched for either side to win decisively the contest for state power. In both of Britain's North American colonies, late state formation meant that entrenched traditionalists such as the more agrarian, Catholics of Quebec and the agrarian, slave-owning southern colonies were able to resist the centralising attempts by the modernising economic interests of Ontario and New England respectively. A similar conflict of interests forced the modernising Prussian state to federalise rather than centralise power in 1871 after its defeat of Austria and France. In these late-developing states, federalism emerged as a compromise that allowed for centralised power over trade and commerce while allowing traditionalists to maintain local control over some economic, social and cultural matters (Hueglin and Fenna, 2006: 116–17, 125–6).

Rational choice institutionalist perspectives

Rationalist institutionalists tend to accept that structural factors associated with capitalist economies are important elements in explaining the formation of federal states but they emphasise that federal formations are not reducible to particular economic interests or structural forces. Instead, they argue that rational actors form federations to maximise security and individual autonomy. William Riker explains federal formation as a rational response to the specific collective action problem caused by external threats to security (1975: 116). A key argument among the American federalists was informed by the security implications of the Wars of Independence, during which the difficulties of gaining equal tax revenues from the separate colonies was interpreted as a serious threat to future security.

Alexander Hamilton made two related, rationalist arguments in Federalist Paper No. 12. First, he argued that a federal union would, by removing trade barriers and facilitating commerce, make the collection of *indirect* taxes easier. Compared to direct taxes which tend to target landed interests and thereby produce more direct political opposition, indirect taxes, such as sales taxes, are less politically sensitive because they are buried in the costs to consumers. But they also require a customs union to effectively avoid tax-avoiding smuggling. Therefore, Hamilton argued that a federal union would both generate more revenue for collective defence and make such defence physically easier. 'If there be but one [federal] government pervading all the states, there will be ... but one side to guard – the Atlantic coast (No. 12)'. A similar combination of internal fiscal rationalisation and external security characterised the early Dutch and Swiss confederations, and the Canadian and Mexican federations (in response to the threat of US regional hegemony (Lister, 1999).

Challenging Riker's claim to the primacy of security factors, Hueglin argues that it was the *combination* of external threats and the need for economic rationalisation that produced German federation in the late 19th century and a similar combination of economic and security threats that combined to produce federalising policies in the European Community and European Union (2006: 118). The combination of security threats and economic rationale can be seen in the formation of the European Coal and Steel Community, formed in 1951, that had the dual purpose of regulating the price of the core commodities of industrialisation and also as a vehicle for inter-state co-operation that would reintegrate Germany into the post-war western alliance.

While they may disagree on the relative importance of security versus economic rationalisation, rational choice institutionalists tend to emphasise the superiority of federal union in legislating for individuals as opposed to confederal legislation over corporate bodies, that is, states. Federal systems offer more access points to representative democracy by giving citizens the chance to vote for representatives at the local, state/provincial and central legislative and executive offices. The primacy of the federal–individual link in turn promotes individual freedom to source public goods rationally. It maximises choice because it provides citizens with multiple opportunities to 'voice' opinion on provision of public services, at local and state levels, to 'exit' or move freely within a regulated federal territory so that a citizen can be confident that if he or she moves to another state within the federation, the individual can 'shop' for quality education, health, environment from a selection that varies but in which national standards also regulate quality of service. In this scenario, factions, which Madison (Fed. Paper No. 10) sees as the 'price of liberty' do remain, but can be controlled by the diffusion of pluralism; multi-level governance disperses contests for power, localises them rather than leading to corruptions possible in unitary governments.

Cultural institutionalist perspectives

Cultural institutionalists also accept the centrality of relations between modernisers and traditionalists in forming federations, but they tend to have a broader understanding of the interests and identity politics driving federation. For cultural institutionalists, 'traditionalists' are not simply trying to sustain economic privileges but are also driven by cultural factors such as the desire to protect the status of language, religious freedom, ethnicity or a national homeland from the processes of centralisation associated with modernisation. In contrast to the structuralist and rationalist arguments which describe federal formation as a voluntary 'coming together', those new institutionalists that recognise the independent effects of culture identify a separate process of federal formation that Alfred Stepan (2001) has termed 'holding together'. India in 1950, Spain in 1978 and Belgium in 1993 all introduced federal or quasi-federal (Spain) constitutions to hold the state together in direct response to actual or threatened ethno-national separatism. Neither economic structural factors nor desires to preserve individual rationalism were as important as the need to respond to the cultural politics associated with linguistic autonomy and demands for national self-determination.

Assumptions about the cultural prerequisites for stable federal formation are implicit in many and explicit in some of the foundational analyses and advocacies of federation. Consider the remarkable assumption made by John Jay, one of the three contributors to the classical *Federalist Papers,* the series of papers published between October 1787 and August 1788, advocating the transition of the confederation of the 13 founding American colonies into a formal federation. Jay was attempting to convince his readers that the newly independent citizens of these American colonies comprised a *nation* that would make a federal political union natural culturally as well as economically efficient and politically liberal.

> Providence has been pleased to give this one connected country to one united people – a people descended from the same ancestors, speaking the same language, professing the same religion, attached to the same principles of government, very similar in their manners and customs, and who, by their joint counsels, arms, and efforts, fighting side by side throughout a long and bloody war, have nobly established their general liberty and independence. (John Jay, Federalist Paper No. 2.)

In denying recognition to Catholics, African slaves, and indigenous peoples, the white, Anglo-Saxon protestant (WASP) nation of Jay's vision was of course a denial of the same colonists' declaration of independence that had, in the words of Thomas Jefferson, declared that 'all men are created equal'. Nevertheless, it represents one of two main categories of federalism that have been emphasised by comparative scholars applying a cultural institutionalist perspective: the mono-national federation. These federations have what Brendan O'Leary (2001) has described as a dominant *Staatsvolk* or 'state-people', such as the WASP core of the United States, the *Mestizo* core of Mexico, the Anglo-Irish core of Australia or the German core of federal Germany. O'Leary uses comparative data to give empirical support to English constitutional scholar A.V. Dicey's argument (above) concerning the strong degree of cultural homogeneity needed to underpin the 'peculiar state of sentiment among the inhabitants' being united in a federation. Where such sentiment is lacking, O'Leary and others argue that non-territorial institutions such as consociational or power-sharing governance is required to balance ethnic – or civic-national interests and protect particular national and/or ethnic identities.

For comparative acuity, we can further divide the mono-national category into two sub-types: *ethno-national* and *civic-national*. From the discussion of ethno-nationalism in Chapter 3 we can understand the ethno-national type as being dominated by a particular ethno-national group that is either hierarchically ranked in terms of political and civil rights or numerically preponderant and thus politically dominant in democratic systems. Examples of ethno-national federation include Germany and Austria, federations that were predominantly or sufficiently ethnically homogeneous linguistically and in which citizenship has been predominantly based on the principle of *jus sanguinis* or blood lineage. As we shall see, the cultural base of such federations has a significant impact on the functioning and evolution of the federal systems in each of those cases, facilitating a more cooperative and symmetrical form of federation compared to multinational federations described below.

The second sub-type of the mono-national federation is dominated by a civic-nationalist ethos (alternatively described as 'syncretic' or 'Jacobin' after the French Jacobin project to force cultural assimilation on non-French speaking peoples in post-Revolutionary France. In this form, which is more prevalent in 'New World' settler societies such as the Americas and Australia, a dominant ethnic-core used the state to assimilate ('make others similar to the dominant culture') or integrate (make a multicultural society) within a shared civic nation-state where citizenship is based primarily on birth within a territory (*jus soli*).

According to cultural institutionalists, both sub-types have a significant impact on the form, efficacy and stability of the federation that evolves. The dualist or competitive federal forms are only possible in cultural contexts where the interests of the individual citizen are paramount or at least, as in the Canadian case, balanced against communal identities and interests. The 'New World', civic-national federations evolved systems based on the principle of 'divided powers' in which the separate levels of government maintain discrete sovereign authority and separate revenue streams. Legislative competences are set out clearly in the constitution with separate schedules of powers reserved for the central government, the states/provinces and usually with a limited list of *concurrent* powers that require joint deliberation between the central and state/province level. The vertical and horizontal separation of powers is intended to prevent the tyranny of the majority and promote individual liberty.

By contrast, in the German model, which is also sometimes known as the 'European' model, the integration of the Länder and national legislative process and the high degree of cooperation that has developed can only be explained by the national cultural homogeneity that characterises Germany. Substantial deviation of policy on education, language, migration, economic development and the welfare state is seen as unnatural and inefficient whereas national standardisation and the maintenance of a shared national culture and national standards are seen as consistent with Germany's predominantly ethnically homogenous society.

Formation of Multinational Federations

The second main type of federation analysed by comparative scholars is the multinational federation. This type is characterised in principle by a multiplicity of territorially concentrated ethno-nations with aspirations to political autonomy or even independence and may include systems, such as Canada, where more than one nation is recognised as co-founders or co-sovereigns of a federation (Stepan, 2001: 327). Multinational federations include Belgium, Canada, Spain, India, post-Baathist Iraq and post-Apartheid South Africa (on some readings). In each case, at least one of the subunits are dominated by particular ethno-national groups; their autonomous powers are entrenched constitutionally and the upper house of a bicameral parliament is designed to provide ethno-nations with veto power over legislation that threatens their rights and interests as constituent members of the federation.

Comparative analysis of multinational systems observe a strong relationship between the ethnic and national culture and emergence and evolution of federal forms. Jan Erk (2008) has argued, for example, that Belgium's explicitly multinational federal form differs from Germany's mono-national one because Belgium is divided territorially into French-speaking, Flemish-speaking and bilingual Brussels regions and linguistically among French and Dutch and German speakers. These ethno-linguistic differences interacted with structural economic factors as the more industrialised French-speaking region of Wallonia previously dominated the more agricultural economy of Flemish-speaking Flanders. In this context, a formally unitary structure with considerable devolution was effective in balancing the interests and identities of the two main communities. However, from the early 1970s the contraction of the industrial base of Wallonia and the relative prosperity of the service-sector economy of the Flemish region created incentives for a federal compromise to more explicitly allocate authorities to the French – and Flemish-speaking communities.

India's federation had to be substantially reorganised from a mono-national form to a more multinational form (according to ethno-linguistic communities) from the mid-1950s in response to demands that threatened to break up the country. When India was initially formed the anti-colonial movement led by the Congress Party was dominant and was able to impose a strongly centralised form of federalism because the hundreds of minor princely states that had comprised the British Imperial Raj had been weakened vis-a-vis the centre (Congress) and initially in little position to resist the centralising state (Stepan, 2000: 321–2). The first Congress-led national governments after independence in 1948 were able to consolidate the central control by institutionalising a national civil service based on the official languages of Hindi (spoken by nearly half of the population) and English as a lingua franca. Nevertheless, the centralised Indian federalism was almost immediately challenged by non-Hindi ethno-linguistic groups who threatened separatism to force the centre to reconfigure the federal form along ethno-linguistic criteria between the mid-1950s and mid-1960s. A key characteristic of Indian federalism has been the creative balance between the promotion of individual and group rights, over and above the territorial division of authority (Mitra, 2000).

Though not a democracy, two of the founders of the Soviet Union (Lenin and Stalin) believed federation was necessary to manage the huge ethnic and ethno-national diversity of the Union and to speed up the process of modernisation. That a multinational federal form has been adopted by the Russian Federation, which is much more nationally homogeneous than the Soviet Union, further exemplifies the perceived need for state–society congruence along ethnic and national lines. More generally, they believe that where ethno-national groups are concentrated territorially and especially where constitutional claims have been sustained since the early-modern period, that multinational federation is a better alternative than the mono-national French Jacobin or American Republican federal forms (McGarry and O'Leary, 2006: 279–81).

Why Federal Institutions Matter

Rational choice institutionalists explain the origins of federal systems as rational responses to threats and opportunities facing small states, whose leaders agree to co-ordinate to achieve more efficient security and market functions. Riker (1982) empha-sised that individual interests are protected and promoted best when power is divided vertically, between two or more territorial levels and horizontally with the separation of powers of the executive presidency, the bicameral legislature and the independent judiciary to interpret legislation and executive action in accordance with the written constitution. The result is a system that prevents factions, aligned territorially or sectorally, from imposing a 'tyranny of the majority'.

Rational choice institutionalists explain the origins of federal systems as rational responses to threats and opportunities facing small states, whose leaders agree to co-ordinate (for example, Riker), emphasise that individual interests are protected and promoted best when power is divided vertically (separation of powers, e.g. as between presidency, legislature and judiciary in the USA]) but also horizontally (territorially). The result is the prevention of factions, aligned territorially or sectorally, that could threaten 'tyranny of the majority'. 'Multi-cameralism and federalism have enforced localism in parties, and this in turn has forced rulers to persuade rather than to control. The total effect is that policy does not change either rapidly or sharply enough to hurt anyone very badly' (Stepan, 2001). Similarly, Robert Goodin has argued that liberty (of the rational individual) is best preserved by the need for rules requiring super-majorities and near-unanimity (1996: 331–43). Barry Weingast (1995), working within a rational institu-tionalist perspective, argues that federal systems should be understood and compared pri-marily according to their ability to preserve markets, by regulating the economy in terms of fiscal and monetary policy; preventing trade wars through maintaining a common market; and constraining the budgets of both national and sub-national units so that bor-rowing is matched with national wealth and productivity. The fact that municipalities such as Orange County or Vallejo in California can be forced to declare bankruptcy rather than be bailed out by the US government is an example of 'hard sanctions' that rationalists advocate to dissuade local governments from spending beyond their means.

Rationalist institutionalists specify that the chances of politicians and bureaucrats abus-ing their power are greater where fiscal centralisation is higher. By decentralising fiscal control, higher levels of economic growth are likely because leaving fiscal decision-making closer to individual citizens or communities leads to more efficient factor utilisation and lower levels of inflation (Castles, 2000: 178). Against this, others who argue from a comparative public policy approach which rejects the ideology of rationalist individualism, believe that central government control of the fisc maximises government ability to use *Keynesian* policies to regulate the supply and demand of key factors of production, including the money supply (Scharpf, 1991: 212–13). In this view, both efficacy (effective government) and equality (through the distribution of tax receipts, expenditure) requires a high degree of fiscal centralisation and a strong centre able to intervene to correct the imperfections of markets.

So how do federal and unitary states compare in terms of their impact on economic prosperity and governance? Francis Castles studied the economic performance of 21 OECD countries from 1960 to the mid-1990s and found that 'decentralised political and fiscal arrangements are associated with superior long-term economic growth rates' (2000: 187) and lower levels of inflation, though decentralisation had no discernable impact on levels of employment (2000: 189–92). Additionally, fiscal decentralisation was a more important factor in explaining economic growth than the federal or unitary political structure of the state (2000: 192). These comparative findings have significant political and economic implications: in Castles' estimates, if the UK had practiced levels of fiscal decentralisation in line with the OECD average, it would have enjoyed economic growth rates, 27 per cent higher, and post-war inflation, 97 per cent less, than it experienced (2000: 193).

Similarly, Hans Keman, whose index of federalism and decentralisation we used to classify federal and unitary states, found that states with strong federal forms and high degrees of decentralisation did have smaller governments and better performance in terms of inflation and unemployment. Like Castles, Keman argues that fiscal decentralisation does not necessarily relate directly to federal form, so that unitary states seeking to limit the size of their government and achieve fiscal efficiency do not necessarily need to adopt federal constitutional forms.

Other factors such as the left–right complexion of government and the degree to which corporatism (government coordination of wage bargaining between trade unions and the private sector) has been institutionalised are equally important in explaining variations in policy-making and socioeconomic performance (Castles, 2000: 222). Additionally, explicit structural factors like the scale of territory and the level of industrialisation are also relevant. In Keman's comparison of 18 democracies the performance of the larger states, such as Germany and France, was better than the less modernised states of Spain, Portugal and Ireland, but these differences are less to do with federal versus unitary status and more to do with levels of industrialisation and post-Second World War subsidies for rebuilding war-torn economies.

Table 8.1   Satisfaction with democracy in federal and unitary states, 1996–1998[a]

Type I federal-decentral	%	Type II federal-central	%	Type III unitary-decentral	%	Type IV unitary-central	%
Australia	84	Belgium	n/a	Austria	n/a	Finland	n/a
Canada	75	Italy	29	Denmark	n/a	France	67
W. Germany	83			Norway	88	Ireland	81
Switzerland				Spain	63	Netherlands	n/a
USA	84			Sweden	60	Portugal	n/a
	71					UK	71
Average	79		29		70		73

Notes: [a] Percentage responding 'works well'. N/a = data not available for these countries.
Source: Armingeon, K. (2000) 'Swiss federalism in comparative perspective', in U. Wachendorfer-Schmidt (ed.), *Fedralism and Political Performance*. London: Routledge and ECPR.

To summarise, in terms of the rationalist institutionalists' primary concerns with the performance of federal systems in maximising individual autonomy, federal institutions matter, but mainly in the way that they interact with *structural* factors, namely the promotion of liberal capitalist markets, the class basis of governing parties and the lobby weight of dominant economic interests.

But are these relatively narrow 'political-economy' criteria the only important ones in considering the performance of federal systems? What about citizens' perceptions of the performance of democracy? Table 8.1 shows the results of opinion polls for countries classified according to the Keman typology of states introduced above. Overall, there is not a great deal of difference between unitary states and citizens' satisfaction with the way their democratic system works. Unitary Norway and federal Switzerland have high rankings, while the archetypal symmetrical federalism of the USA ranks in the middle of this sample. There is a weak trend suggesting that the purest forms (types I and IV) have higher satisfaction ratings but given the absence of data on type II and the small degree of differences, this cannot be considered a robust finding.

Table 8.2 compares our range of federal and unitary states according to opinions on overall 'quality of life', as measured by opinions on material well-being, health, political freedom, job security, family life, political stability, gender equality and community life. Here again, there is not much difference among the four types, though it is interesting to note that type III (unitary-decentral) states report the highest average of quality of life while they were third out of four on the question of satisfaction with democracy. And type IV (unitary-central) perform poorest, on average, on quality of life measures while they were second highest in terms of perceptions of democracy. Again, this limited sample of wealthy, industrialised, democratic states is too small to reliably conclude whether state form is significantly associated with these broad performance measures, especially without taking into account other factors such as climate, topography, mineral and energy

Table 8.2   Quality of life in federal and unitary states, 2005[a]

Type I federal-decentral	Score (1–10 scale)	Type II federal-central	Score (1–10 scale)	Type III unitary-decentral	Score (1–10 scale)	Type IV unitary-central	Score (1–10 scale)
Australia	7.9	Belgium	7.1	Austria	7.3	Finland	7.6
Canada	7.6	Italy	7.8	Denmark	7.8	France	7.1
W. Germany	7.0			Norway	8.1	Ireland	8.3
Switzerland	8.1			Spain	7.7	Netherlands	7.4
USA	7.6			Sweden	7.9	Portugal	7.3
						UK	6.9
Average	*7.6*		*7.5*		*7.8*		*7.4*

Note: [a] On a scale from 1 to 10.
Source: Economist Intelligence Unit (2005) *The World in 2005*. London: Economist Intelligence Unit.

resources that are likely to affect perceptions of quality of life. Still, the findings taken as a whole do cast some doubt on the stronger claims that federal/unitary and centralised/decentralised state form significantly affect governance and political and economic performance.

In addition to questioning the narrow criteria of federal versus unitary performance, we can also consider the more basic question of state survival. It is one thing to argue that India, for example, will prosper to the extent that it continues its shift towards a fiscal federal model. But a prior question surely is whether India would have continued to exist as a state in the post-independence period if it did not continue to adjust its federal form to meet the 'identity interests' of its diverse population? The same can be asked of federations such as Belgium, Spain, Canada as well as unitary devolved states such as the UK. Comparativists working from a cultural institutionalist perspective argue that cultural factors, not only affect the formation of federal and unitary systems, but that they continue to affect the evolution of representative and governing institutions and the more fundamental regulation of national self-determination.

A strong version of the culturalist perspective is developed by Jan Erk (2008) in his study of the evolution of European and Canadian federations. Erk argued that federal institutions adapt to achieve congruence with the underlying social structure of the state. In mono-national federations such as Austria and Germany, the evolution of the institutions that he studied – education and language policy – was in the direction of centralisation. In Germany, the federal system has evolved into a centralised, cooperative form in which 'there is an overall consensus which associates federal diversity with inefficiency' (2008: 72). The practice of 'federal comity', based on a 'bottom-up' process of concerted action from the Länder, is dominant in the formation of education and a host of other policies, including the practice of co-decision-making and co-representation to the European Union (Börzel, 2001). Hueglin and Fenna go further in suggesting that the contemporary practice of cooperative federalism is a remnant of the Althusian norms of consociation that developed within the confederation of German lands since the beginning of the Holy Roman Empire (2006: 94–6).

By contrast, in multinational federations such as Belgium, Spain, Switzerland and Canada, federal systems have become formally or informally decentralised. In postwar Belgium, for example, two education systems evolved between the French- and Flemish-speaking communities, formalised in 1988 reform legislation and then codified in the 1993 federal constitution (Erk, 2008: 35–6). Similarly, strict separation evolved between Flemish- and French-speaking media ownership and government systems of regulation. In Switzerland, Erk argues that the federal system, as regards education and language policy has 'increasingly become a federation of the two major linguistic communities' (2008: 85). In Canada, while there has been little success in codifying the distinctiveness between French-speaking Quebec and English-speaking provinces of Canada into the constitution, the system has nevertheless come to function in a highly asymmetrical way (2008: 55).

Stepan reinforces the importance of national culture on federal form in his comparison of mono-national and multinational federations where he concluded that all of the mono-national federations (Austria, Germany, Australia, USA, Argentina, Brazil and, questionably, Switzerland) evolved into symmetrical federations while all of the multinational federations (Belgium, Canada, Spain and India) evolved into asymmetrical federations (Stepan, 2001: 327–8).

The distinction between mono-national and multinational states has a direct effect on the performance of one of the key dimensions of federalism: the constraint of the national majority on the liberty of citizens. As we have seen, in mono-national federations the provision of veto powers for the federal units, in the form of separate decision-making powers for the upper house, is alleged to minimise the growth of the central government and maximise the efficiency of markets for private and public goods. But in multinational federations, the ability of the state to create the type of symmetrical institutions required to maintain a minimalist, market-preserving federation is more limited because the demands from ethno-national or ethno-linguistic groups for autonomy are likely to be more variable in their strength and nature. Fiscal decentralisation and the enormously complex systems of intergovernmental relations connecting central and decentral jurisdictions are more difficult to achieve in multinational federations because the relations between the relations between separate national cultures are prone to be competitive rather than complementary, as demonstrated above in Erk's findings with regard to the competitive demands for decentralisation in Belgium, Spain and Canada.

Equally, as Stepan has shown, the federations formed to 'hold together' multinational states have had to strike a balance between federal forms that protect the central interests of the national majority with the decentralising demands of ethno-national minorities. Consider the contrast between mono-national federations such as Brazil and the USA versus the development of multinational federations such as India and Spain. In the former, the federal form is designed to constrain any national majority by a combination of veto powers in the upper legislative house, as well as through the separation of powers among the executive, legislature and the judiciary. In the latter, the demands of ethno-national minorities have forced asymmetrical adjustments towards decentralisation that would have faced considerable obstacles if there were demos-constraining vetoes on constitutional change.

India's federal form, for example, was sufficiently flexible with its weak territorial chamber and strong central executive to reconfigure the federation along ethno-linguistic lines between 1956 and 1966 (Stepan, 2001: 353–4). Spain's quasi-federal constitution was also sufficiently centralised to allow the demos to evolve an asymmetrical form to respond to variable demands of the historic nations (Basque, Catalan and Galician) while maintaining a strong, Castilian-dominated centre. In response to demands for European context, Spain has evolved more German/European style intergovernmental practices to achieve better coordination. Overall, Spain's flexible approach to recognition of ethno-national pluralism has been successful in persuading most Basques and Catalans to see advantages in coordinating their interests with Madrid in the European context rather than risk separation.

While it is too soon to tell if devolution in the UK has similarly reduced the separatist interests of Scottish and Welsh nationalists, it is safe to predict that any process of national self-determination is likely to be constitutional rather than militant and that resulting relations are likely to be characterised by intergovernmentalism and council governance of the type already being developed for Britain's relations with Northern Ireland and the Irish Republic through bodies like the North–South Ministerial Council and the British–Irish Council.

SUMMARY

In this chapter, we have demonstrated that:

- Federations have tended to evolve as alternatives to absolutist, unitary forms of imperial statehood. As such, federations should be understood and analysed as constitutional methods of power-sharing that intentionally pluralise sovereignty.

- The difference between unitary and formally federal states are more of degree rather than of kind. Federal states can develop unitary characteristics

(Continued)

(Continued)

in the form of fiscal centralisation and executive authority while unitary states can develop federal-like fiscal and administrative decentralisation. It is important for any comparative analysis of federalism to bear in mind the distinction between federal form and the degree of functional decentralisation.

- By dividing power, federal systems do have the potential to enhance the liberty of individual citizens. But rational choice institutionalists tend to generalise from 'New World' cases (especially the USA and Australia) and focus on the performance of federal systems in preserving individual liberty through the separation of powers and especially through the economic efficiency promoted by fiscal federalism. Structural factors like the size and resourcefulness of the state, levels of economic development and the left–right character of governments are also significant in explaining the performance of federal versus unitary states.

- The distinction between mono-national and multinational federations is a significant factor that should be taken into account in any comparative analysis of federalism. Multinational federations have to balance the preservation of individual liberty with the recognition of collective identities and interests. As a result, the extent to which they can be judged according to rationalist criteria of efficiency and maximisation of individual choice is limited. Instead, multinational federations should be evaluated and compared on a broader set of criteria including basic political stability of the state, as well as the performance of the federation in protecting collective, ethno-national identities and interests as well as individual interests.

FURTHER READING

Hamilton, A., Madison, J. and Jay, J.(1961) *The Federalist Papers (Hamilton, Madison, Jay)*. New York: Mentor.

The Mentor version is based on the original McLean edition (1788) and has a very helpful Introduction and chapter précis by Professor Clinton Rossiter. Still considered a foundational text of political science and American political theory, The Federalist Papers were published as a defence of the Constitution of the USA and are celebrated for their explanation and defence of a system designed to balance the protection of individual liberty with forms of territorial power sharing and separation of executive, legislative and judicial authorities.

Riker, W. (1975) 'Federalism', in I. Fred Greenstein and W. Nelson Polsby (eds), *Handbook of Political Science*, vol. 5. Reading, MA: Addison-Wesley.

Riker offers the classical rational-choice explanation of the role of federal institutions in maximising individual liberty and choice in political representation and governance.

Burgess, M. (2006) *Comparative Federalism: Theory and Practice*. London: Routledge.

This provides a broad 'new institutionalist' approach to develop a balanced interpretation of the cultural, structural and rationalist factors affecting the development of federal systems.

McGarry, J. and O'Leary, B. (2006) 'Federation as a method of ethnic conflict regulation', in Noel, Sid (ed.), *From Power-Sharing to Democracy: Post-Conflict Institutions in Ethnically Divided Societies*. London: McGill-Queen's University Press: 263–96.

This chapter provides a good defence of federalism and other forms of non-territorial power sharing in cases of multinational states.

Hueglin, T.O. and Fenna, A. (2006) *Comparative Federalism: A Systematic Inquiry*. Peterborough, Ontario: Broadview Press.

A synthetic, 'new institutionalist' introduction to comparative federalism. This book is particularly good at demonstrating the lasting influence of federal theory on contemporary state-building, including substantial treatment of the European Union as a federal/confederal system.

QUESTIONS FOR DISCUSSION

(1) In what ways can federalism be understood as a form of power sharing?

(2) How do the historical origins of federal systems help us understand contemporary forms and functions of those systems?

(3) Why are civic-nations more likely to develop forms of federation that maximise individual liberty rather than collective, ethno-national identity?

(4) Are rational choice and cultural institutionalists really debating the merits of federation or are they actually describing different types of federation? Consider their treatment of mono-national versus multinational federation?

(5) Do federations perform better than unitary states? What particular aspects of federation affect performance?

Key Words for Chapter 8

bicameralism / centralisation / confederation / decentralisation / devolution / ethno-nationalism / federalism / federation / fiscal federalism / power sharing

Part 3

ACTORS

9 Voters, Parties and Participation

Judith Bara

CHAPTER OUTLINE

In this chapter we will consider the main actors who take part in the electoral process, the voters and parties, and what this might tell us about political participation. We will start by focusing on what is the epitomising concept for democracy – representation – and go on to consider how elections are seen as a barometer for political participation, which is itself seen as a measure of whether or not representative democracy is functioning properly. Since parties and voters are so closely related to the practice of elections, we also examine why people vote or do not vote, and if they do, why they vote for certain parties. In the course of all this we discuss how explanatory models can help us understand better why these key political institutions and actors operate in the ways they do.

Introduction

For many people living in representative democracies the only regular occasions in which they deliberately engage in a political act are general elections. Elections are major events involving millions of people who regard them as opportunities to make a comment on whether to retain or change an incumbent government. This may often mean voting for a party which has little to no chance of winning a seat, but people feel the need to cast a vote. Elections are thus central to the process of democratic politics since they symbolise the mechanism which enables us to choose who will act on our behalf, who will, in other words, *represent* us.

What Do We Mean by Representation?

The understanding of the concept of representation has changed considerably throughout the modern era. An early modern meaning of representation is most usually associated with theatrical characterisation in the sense of how one person depicts another. This is an activity which involves interpretation, a certain amount of licence and embodies a good deal of 'personal opinion' on the part of the actor. From the 17th century, representation came to incorporate the idea of a person acting legally 'on behalf of another', a view that reflects Hobbes (1691) *Leviathan*. During the 18th century this developed more overtly political connotations. In parallel with the growth of democratic ideas, representation came increasingly to be associated with the notion representing the wishes of citizens, whether directly or indirectly, through mediators or unmediated (Weale, 1999).

Representation can, according to a Rousseauian, unmediated and direct conception of democracy, be carried out by the citizen body as a whole, in the manner we believe to have been practised in classical Athens. Leaving aside for a moment the argument that Athenian democracy, while it might have been representative of the citizen body, was completely unrepresentative of the majority of inhabitants (since the citizen body was defined very narrowly, omitting women and other categories of resident). Such a model, even if it were constituted inclusively, would in any case be appropriate only for relatively small units of population. This became less and less feasible with the growth of modern society, particularly after the establishment of industrial capitalism, so ideas of indirect democracy, where small groups of people represent the views of the citizen body as a whole came to prevail. Of course there are varying conceptions of how such representation should work, but two of the most notable are the 'microcosmic' and the 'division of labour' interpretations.

'Microcosmic' representation

Early interpretations of the notion of microcosmic representation, especially as applied to national decision-making bodies, are much associated with the period of the American Revolution (1776–1782). It was given credence by President John Adams when he opined that the American Congress should be 'a portrait' of the nation in miniature (McLean, 1996). This suggests that an elected parliament or assembly should represent proportionately the key characteristics of the citizen body. One problem concerning this is how to define these 'key' characteristics. Should we use gender, ethnic identity, class, region, and so forth? And *how* might such factors be incorporated into the elective process? The absence of such assemblies across the world is testimony to the realisation that such fundamental questions are not easy to address or organise in practice, although small vestiges of this method are beginning to be revisited in the shape of deliberative assemblies such as citizen juries (Fishkin, 1993) or Swiss cantonal assemblies (Barber, 1988).

'Division of labour' representation

The division of labour approach argues that there is a division of labour between representatives and those who elect them, with both roles having expected modes of behaviour. Electors vote for representatives to look after their interests, seek redress for their grievances, support appropriate legislation, report back on outcomes and be accountable for their actions. Representatives expect that their electors will continue to support their efforts and continue to vote for them. Thus we have a mediated and indirect system of representation that has provided the basis for most modern democratic parliaments. In modern society, mediation has been effectively monopolised by political parties, and, as we shall see, this has led to disillusion and declining participation in the electoral process in favour of other vehicles for participation such as interest groups, which will be discussed in Chapter 10.

A strong supporter of this modified division of labour approach was Robert Dahl (1960, 1970) who argued that most people are not sufficiently interested in politics to the extent that they want to spend most of their available time engaging in political debate, so they rely on others to do this for them. This does not mean of course that people are politically inactive. Indeed, they may prefer to embrace other institutional forms or indeed non-institutionalised forms of behaviour, for example to participate in mass rallies or protest movements such as the student movement in the USA in the 1960s, which Dahl used as a source of empirical information, or the various anti-war movements that have grown up in many countries in the wake of the American invasion of Iraq in 2003.

Budge (1996) shows how this kind of political activity has come to be a specific feature of contemporary society. Despite all this, however, elections are still seen as both a central feature in the political life of representative democracies and as a measure of our participation. Indeed, if this were not so, why is it that non-representative governments regard elections as important legitimising factors, exemplified by the practice of leaders of military coups, who, having secured control of a country, announce that they will introduce 'free and fair elections' at the earliest opportunity?

The Centrality of Elections and Why We Should Study Them

Why do people vote or not vote in elections? What are the reasons why people vote for different parties? What sort of approaches should we take to explain voting behaviour or electoral outcomes? All of these are fundamental questions of political science.

A commonsensical definition taken from the *Shorter Oxford English Dictionary* states that an election is '[t]his action of choosing for an office … or position; usually by vote … *Specifically, the choice by popular vote of members of a representative assembly*, e.g. the House of Commons' (1983: 636, emphasis added). Thus we can see that an election is almost taken for granted as primarily having to do with choosing members of parliaments. A rather more academic definition by Harrop and Miller is that a competitive election is '[a] formal expression of preferences by the governed which are then aggregated and transformed into a collective decision about who will govern – who should stay in office, who should replace those who have been thrown out' (1987: 2).

Elections are thus important not only for choosing representatives but also enable voters to choose among different sets of policy programmes, which are themselves reflective of different ideological perspectives (Budge et al., 1997, 2001). They also have a much deeper effect on the conduct of politics in the medium term since the outcome of elections determines the complexion of government, what sort of policies it will introduce, how our foreign relations will be affected in terms of likely allies and so forth. Elections as intimated above also confer legitimacy on government and provide it with a mandate to govern. But these are not the only reasons why we should study elections in depth and learn more about their main protagonists, the voters and parties.

Although focusing on the UK, Denver (2007) suggests a wide range of reasons as to why we should study elections. Elections, he contends, are 'fun', 'fascinating', 'provide political education' and 'allow for orderly changes in government' (2007: 3–6). They also 'empower citizens', partly by providing opportunities for participation by large numbers of citizens, possibly so that they can demonstrate loyalty, and of course allow for governments to be held 'accountable'. All of these claims are relative and variable across time, and space and you can decide after reading this book, which, if any, you feel are justified.

Can We Identify Different Types of Election?

As shown in Chapter 2, political analysts love to classify, and elections are events that have led to attempts at classification. Much of this may be linked to efforts to understand political change over time and across countries. How far this activity provides useful tools is a matter of judgement. It may be more worthwhile, given the enormous amount of research undertaken to try to understand and explain why particular election outcomes occur or why people persist in voting for the same parties throughout their lives. This notwithstanding, it is instructive to consider briefly a general example of such a typology.

Harrop and Miller (1987) identify four basic types of election, which are accepted by most analysts, and that show how elections can have deep consequences. The way in which this typology has been derived takes as its starting point V.O. Key's (1955) depiction of a 'critical' election that breaks the existing mould and replaces it with a new one, hence 'realigning' the shape of politics and power relations. By focusing on both patterns and levels of support for parties, Harrop and Miller show that there are in fact several types of election, the outcomes of which bring about different consequences:

- Maintaining (or normal) election: party vote shares change little and alignments existing prior to the election are maintained, such as occurred in (West) Germany in the 1950s and 1960s.
- Converting election: party vote shares are maintained but their underlying support patterns change. An example of this is the situation in Sweden throughout the 1970s and 1980s where party shares of the vote remained quite constant and the Social Democrats remained in power, but their support base shifted significantly from working class to middle class.
- Deviating election: a short-term situation, exemplified by a sharp drop in support for a party that is spread evenly across the electorate. This is what happened in the 1980 Presidential and Congressional elections in the USA where the Republicans, under Ronald Reagan, significantly trounced the Democrats, under Jimmy Carter.
- Realigning or critical election: this breaks the existing mould. Three examples of this have occurred in Britain for example, 1945, which returned Labour with a large majority of seats and votes and altered the basis of policy until 1979, when the Conservatives, with a clear and decisive majority, changed the course of politics until Labour's more recent landslide victory in 1997.

Harrop and Miller also mention two further 'types' (or rather 'derived types') of election – a reinstating election, where the result of a deviating election is reversed and a dealigning election, where traditional patterns begin to break down under conditions of significant volatility, although this is usually not identifiable immediately.

Do Elections Help Us Assess Levels of Political Participation?

Measuring turnout

As stated previously, one central feature of studying elections is to use them as indicators of participation. The key concept here is turnout, defined as '[t]he proportion of the registered electorate who vote in a given election' (McLean, 1996: 504–5). There are those, however, who point out that in the case of the USA, studies indicating low and declining turnout might have been somewhat misleading as they use calculations of turnout which are based on a different premise (Aarts and Wessels, 2005; Blais, 2000). Turnout has traditionally been based essentially on the voting age population (VAP) and this includes residents who are ineligible to vote, such as foreign residents. The situation is further exacerbated by the 'decentralised, voluntary registration procedures' operating in the USA (Aarts and Wessels, 2005: 65), which produce a situation in which registration itself is comparatively low to start with.

Since VAP is also largely dependent upon census material, there may be errors based on the fact that the data may be quite old in a given election year. Precise calculations for small units, especially relevant to countries that have plurality electoral systems, may also be difficult to derive accurately. Thus while the American case may be identified as 'different', it is misleading to include these figures in comparative studies which use the standard measure based on registered voters rather than sub-groups of the resident population as a whole.

The International Institute for Democracy and Electoral Assistance (International IDEA) argues, however, that VAP is a better basis for measuring and comparing turnout globally as it avoids relying too much on registration figures, which may be flawed. Some states, especially those involved in the early stages of a transition to democracy, such as South Africa, might not have used voter registration at all elections, but have relied rather on voters' identity documentation to provide proof of age, status and residence (http://www.idea.int/vt/survey/index.cfm).

International IDEA has produced a global database which provides two sets of turnout figures based on both registered electors and VAP, at least as far as this is possible. The differences can be quite staggering. Taking the case of the first completely free South African parliamentary election in 1999, the figures based on registered electors produced 89.3 per cent whereas those based on VAP yielded 63.9 per cent. For other countries, the difference is actually quite small, such as the case of the first parliamentary election held in the Czech Republic in 1996 after the split of the former Czechoslovakia where the turnout as a proportion of registered electors produced 76.3 per cent and turnout based on VAP yielded 77.6 per cent (http://www.idea.int/vt/survey/index.cfm).

Choosing an appropriate measure

Whichever variant of turnout we decide to use will depend on what we are using the measure for and will also relate to the view of the researcher as to which errors are more dangerous – those associated with the electoral register or those associated with the census. In either case, we need to recognise that we are using a very peculiar tool. Turnout figures, even though reported in good faith and correctly counted, are always inaccurate. First, this is because electoral registers, upon which turnout figures are normally based are always out of date due to deaths or people moving home or emigrating. Second, apart from the few situations where the whole country is regarded as one single constituency, as in Guyana, Israel and The Netherlands, turnout will differ between constituencies or regions because of tradition, culture or electoral history, for example, where a seat or region is seen as the long-term domain of one particular party, turnout is often low.

Turnout as an indicator of participation

Turnout is seen as indicating a high degree of participation in the political system as long as it remains buoyant and indicates that the great majority of voters cast a vote over the majority of elections held. However, turnout today is said to be considerably lower across many established representative democracies than it was half a century ago. Even in countries that have undergone a transition to representative democracy in recent decades, where years of non-competitive politics might lead us to expect higher levels of turnout, the situation shows little difference, whether we calculate it on the basis of the electoral register or VAP. Taking the latter, International IDEA ranked the average turnout for elections held between 1945 and 1998 in 140 countries, although a number of these, such as Kuwait, would not normally be considered as representative democracies. If these countries are removed, we find Italy producing the highest average turnout with an average of 90.2 per cent, which exceeded that of other countries which have compulsory voting, such as Belgium (84.9 per cent) or Australia (84.4 per cent) despite the fact that in Italy penalties are not strongly enforced. From among the newly democratising countries of Central Europe, the Czech Republic (84.8 per cent) and Slovenia (80.6 per cent) appear in the 'top 20' as do South Africa (85.5 per cent) and Portugal (82.4 per cent). Among countries with averages of over 70 per cent were Argentina, which also has weakly enforced compulsory voting (70.6 per cent), Bulgaria (77.5 per cent) and the UK (74.9 per cent), but several long-established Western democracies failed to achieve this level, such as France (67.3 per cent) or the USA (48.3 per cent) (http://www.idea.int/vt/survey/index.cfm).

Are people really participating less?

So does this indicate that people are participating less in politics than they used to? If we regard voting in national elections as an important and effective measure of participation, let alone a civic duty, then this does suggest lower participation. However, we need to take care before arriving at such a conclusion. Measures such as these surveys based on averages, although they may produce interesting results, actually tell us little about whether turnout is declining overall, whether or not it is declining in certain countries but not in others, or whether turnout levels might decline over a certain number of elections and then start rising again. This is important,

Table 9.1   Average turnout in selected established democracies (%)

Country	Average turnout, 1945–2001	Average turnout, 1990–2001
Australia[a]	89.7	95.5
Austria[a]	91.3	83.7
Canada	73.8	65.9
Germany	85.6	79.7
India	59.4	59.1
Italy[a]	89.8	84.5
Norway	81.0	72.3
New Zealand	89.0	85.5
Spain	73.6	74.6
UK	75.2	69.6
USA	55.1	50.6

Notes: Data is based on information from IDEA (http://www.idea.int/vt/index.cfm).
[a]Voting is compulsory in the whole country or part of the country.

not only in terms of assessing levels of political participation but also because there have been numerous assertions by political scientists that turnout levels are falling and have been falling particularly since the early 1990s in Western countries (Dalton and Wattenberg, 2000; Leduc et al., 1996). Arguments about turnout levels, patterns and fluctuations have taken the form of methodological disputes as to the basis upon which turnout is calculated (see above) or why turnout might have fallen (see below). What evidence do we have for declining turnout on such a wide scale in the last decades of the 20th century? Table 9.1 illustrates the general situation on the basis of selected established democracies, defined according to the principle set out by Lijphart (1999) that such countries have enjoyed stable, functioning, competitive democracy for at least 20 years.

Table 9.1 shows that for the majority of these 11 countries, turnout clearly fell, often by quite substantial proportions and only in India did it remain constant. Of the two countries where it did not fall, the rise was quite modest in the case of Spain, which has only experienced competitive elections since 1979. The other case, Australia has compulsory voting, where more effective enforcement of penalties could account for this in part. Austria has compulsory voting in the Tyrol region but turnout has clearly fallen in the country as a whole. It may be that such decline could be temporary, since, as Hague and Harrop (2007: 200) have shown, turnout has begun to rise modestly at general elections in several countries since 2001, such as the UK, the USA and Switzerland.

We have to take care how we interpret these figures. To assert that on the basis of these figures alone, the general phenomenon of declining turnout has been reversed on a global scale would be premature. Again, we need to be especially careful about basing our conclusions on averages, since these may be overly skewed by levels at particular elections. For example, if we look at levels of turnout for elections in the UK between 1990 and 2001, we find that turnout in 1992, at 77.7 per cent, was actually higher than in any election held since February 1974 and that it was the exceptionally low turnout of 59.1 per cent in 2001 that has produced such a low average (http://www.psr.keele.ac.uk/election.htm).

It could thus be the case that the phenomenon of low turnout is cyclical, so that we might get periods of buoyant turnout whereas at others, people seem less than enthusiastic about voting. In any case, turnout at elections for different types of assembly has always been variable. Compared with national elections, turnout at regional or local elections has generally been much lower. The same is true for voting at European Assembly elections by the (now 27) member states. This is arguably because these elections are regarded as being less 'important' in terms of affecting policy, are seen as second order elections and are treated at best as enabling mid-term comments on government performance in the sense that abstention is a form of protest. People are often not prepared to vote for 'opposition' parties but wish to give the government a warning, so they do not vote.

To Vote or Not to Vote?

There are a number of different and often interrelated reasons as to why people decide not to vote as research into many countries suggests. Among the main reasons are modernisation, social change and dissatisfaction with political parties or governments.

Modernisation

Modernisation theories suggest that as a country becomes more effective in terms of economic development, post-industrialism and the growth of the tertiary sector, growth in the level and spread of education, welfare, social and geographic mobility and perhaps especially extension and diversification of the mass media allowing for dissemination of more political information, citizens are more likely to question the point of voting as a way of influencing decision-making as they will become more aware of alternative strategies (Dalton, 2002; Inglehart, 1977). Much of this is also associated with the development of globalisation.

Social change

Major social change over time, affecting in particular class and religious divisions or cleavages, which had been major determinants of political participation and party identification has also loosened the traditional bonds which developed between parties and specific groups of voters. Linked closely to this has been the growth of individualism whereby citizens perceive themselves increasingly as individuals rather than as members of strategic groups, and decide to vote or not on the basis of maximisation of their own, personal cost–benefit analysis. This is closely linked to rational choice theory and derived from the work of Downs (1957). 'Costs' of course could be greater or lesser in different countries and it is arguable that countries which have lower 'costs', for example greater availability of postal voting (such as in certain areas of the UK in recent years) might demonstrate higher levels of turnout, rather than in higher 'cost' countries, for example where it is more difficult to get to the polls in rural areas (South Africa) or indeed where registration is often difficult (as in the USA). Social change is also a powerful factor in emergent democracies, with the development of a new type of economy, formation of new classes and emergence of a new materialist culture (Jasiewicz, 2003).

Dissatisfaction with political parties

Declining turnout is also related to people becoming disillusioned with political parties resulting in a decline in loyalty to a particular party over time, a propensity to 'shop around' and vote for different parties or general alienation from the party process of 'doing politics'. This is known as 'partisan dealignment' and will be discussed in more detail below. Lack of perceived difference between parties is also a factor in deterring voters from participating in elections. There is also an impression that parties have become very remote from their voters, and indeed their members. This perception suggests further that leaders dominate party organisations and use the media to communicate policy intention, in part to show that they are not bound by narrow, partisan interests and can appeal to the 'country' (Curtice and Holmberg, 2005). An extreme example of this is the 'electoral professional party' which suggests that parties, rather than acting as institutions for mass representation simply become electoral servicing machines (Dalton and Wattenberg, 2000; Panebianco, 1988).

Dissatisfaction with government

There is growing evidence that voters feel disenfranchised in the sense that their votes do not matter, or simply that they are unrepresented. This may be because their views on the importance of particular issues are perceived as having been ignored or that government is corrupt. In either case, the outcome is lack of trust and the conclusion that voting is a waste of time. This need not be associated with contempt for democracy or indeed lack of participation in other forms of political and social activity (Norris, 1999). Politicians in many democracies are also seen as sleazy, corrupt and willing to say anything to the electorate in order to maintain office, without actually delivering what they have promised. In some cases they may even enact the opposite policy to what they pledged, such as the case of university tuition fees in the UK, where, despite promising not to charge students 'top-up' fees in their 2001 election manifesto, the Labour Government introduced them during their ensuing term of office.

Institutional factors

Institutional factors, notably the electoral system, can also feed this cynicism. In the case of plurality systems, voters may feel it is pointless voting in 'safe' seats or regions, where specific parties have won with comfortable majorities over many elections. Another problem, especially pertinent to the UK, is that sometimes constituency boundary configurations may favour one party rather than another. In proportional systems, especially those using a preference system, voters may feel aggrieved that 'their' preferred candidates were prevented from gaining seats because of the complicated electoral arithmetic employed. In large multi-member constituencies or in the few instances where the whole country represents one 'constituency', citizens may feel remote from elected representatives.

Who Are the Non-voters?

Abstainers tend to be less partisan and more disillusioned by governments and political parties than voters. They are also more likely to be poor, less well educated, male and young. Those under the age of 24 and the unemployed are even less likely to vote (Franklin, 2004). Members of ethnic minorities are less likely to register and turn out, apart from very specific groups, such as South Asians in the UK (Anwar, 2001). Conversely, citizens who vote regularly tend to be middle-aged, middle to upper middle class, educated and employed. Regular voters also tend to have high levels of 'social capital'; those belonging to a trade union and a religious or other social group will be more likely to vote.

Does low turnout matter?

Does it matter if people do not vote or that turnout is low? If we argue that democracy gives people the choice to vote or not, then the voices of those who choose to vote are the ones which we should take account of. Conversely, if we believe that elections are central to how our democracy works and provide a basis for representation, a turnout level of less than 50 per cent would mean that candidates would be elected on the basis of a very small proportion of the electorate. How representative would those members of parliament be? Low turnout suggests a disengagement from the institutions of democracy, yet there are countries where low turnout, often at a level below 50 per cent, is common. Turnout at Congressional elections in the USA has been consistently low, often below 40 per cent, but most American politicians believe that this is acceptable as those who want to participate do so. In contrast, some commentators argue that low turnout does matter. Commenting on the 59.1 per cent turnout at the general election of 2001 in the UK, Whiteley et al. commented that '… if this is not a crisis of democratic politics in Britain, then it is hard to know what would be' (2001: 222).

How Might Theoretical Models Help Us to Explain Falling Turnout?

Socio-cultural approaches

The idea that certain social or cultural groups do not feel that they benefit by participation in elections for a variety of reasons may help explain low turnout. For example, elections might not figure as part of the traditional culture of certain groups or they may feel alienated by the political system that they see as unsympathetic to their culture. It may also be that they have adopted post material values that regard traditional parties as being unwilling to compromise their materialist ideologies and no others have emerged to attract them. The most likely groups to behave in this way are ethnic or religious minorities, such as citizens of former colonies and their descendants, for example minorities in France or the Netherlands, or original, pre-colonial inhabitants of settler countries, in Australia, New Zealand or the USA.

One significant 'cultural' explanation is that based on the notion of 'cleavage' (or division) first put forward by Lipset and Rokkan (1967). This argues essentially that citizens are primarily members of socio-cultural communities, such as linguistic or religious groups, which have arisen as a result of historical trauma such as the Reformation, and have adopted particular political strategies. Sometimes these communities are linked to specific parties, such as the Flemish and Francophone linguistic-nationalist parties in Belgium or religious parties in many countries, including the Netherlands, India or Israel. If the 'message' of these parties goes unheard, or is compromised in some way, potential supporters may not bother to vote, since alternative parties may be perceived as antipathetic to their interests.

Developments since the 1970s have also resulted in such parties losing supporters who have become more 'secular' or developed interests beyond the scope of their traditional cultural interests. Hence the parties they have traditionally supported no longer offer relevant policy or solutions to their problems.

The party identification approach

This is based on the 'Michigan model' which was pioneered in the late 1950s and early 1960s by political scientists at the University of Michigan. They argued that political and social institutions, especially class and the family, are the paramount influences in determining which party people vote for, and how attachments to these particular parties persist over time. It can also help account for why people may or may not vote. For example, partisan dealignment in which loyalties are loosened as a result of, for example, changes in the underlying class structure, differing generational experiences and so on can lead voters to switch parties or indeed to abstain. Supporters of the partisan identification school have been criticised for being one-dimensional, basing far too much of their hypothesis on American evidence and failing to take account of social and political change, such as the development of new political ideas which lead to the establishment of new parties, for example Green parties.

Rational choice approaches

Rational choice approaches are based essentially on market economic theory, and model a political system on an economy. They assume that voters behave 'rationally' and make informed and conscious choices about their political behaviour. In the case of voting, electors are seen as consumers and the vote rather than money is the medium of exchange. Parties set out their wares and electors determine what their personal needs are in terms of policy, for example, lower taxes or more spent on cycle paths or provision of childcare. They will then examine what the parties are offering. If no party comes close to reflecting the voters' own informed choices, then they will not vote. This is an entirely rational decision. Indeed, it may be irrational to vote, since according to a purist rational interpretation, no party would ever reflect the position of any given individual, so the costs of voting – in terms of time, energy, missing out on alternative activities and so forth would always be too great. This is summed up as the 'paradox of voting'.

So we can see how different models, based on different theoretical approaches, use a variety of criteria to help explain why people vote or not. It may indeed be the case that one or more of these approaches might not offer a satisfactory, comprehensive or universal basis for explanation, and indeed has to be combined with another. After all, these models are conceived at different time periods, often in response to existing models that preceded them. At a certain level they are bound to fail to account for new developments that occur at some time after they have been introduced.

We shall now move on to discuss how theoretically informed models help us to understand the nature of parties and why people vote for them. We will see examples of how specific models may become 'frozen' into a specific time frame and falter as changing political circumstances render them less and less effective.

Political Parties

As with voters, parties are also central features of the electoral process. It is thus important to understand their role and to identify how they might appeal to members and voters. In the remainder of this chapter we will consider a basic definition of what a political party actually is, examine a basis for comparing parties across time and space in terms of the concept of a 'party family' and, finally, identify characteristics of their supporters. This will include a consideration of how the three types of theoretical model introduced in Chapter 1 help us to understand the nature of parties and voters.

What Is a Political Party?

The attempt to understand and define parties is not new. Indeed, Edmund Burke grappled with this as early as 1770, when he suggested that a 'party is a body of men united for promoting by their joint endeavours the national interest upon some particular principle in which they are all agreed' (cited in Ware, 1996: 5).

What does this definition tell us? Well, it actually tells us quite a lot. It tells us that a 'party' is a collective enterprise: that parties are seen as having aims which promote the 'national interest', that is the 'good of the country'. According to how different parties interpret this it is an overriding goal and that efforts are informed by reference to a particular principle, in other words, an ideological position.

Other commentators and scholars since Burke have sought to define parties on the basis of a range of characteristics, opting to concentrate on what they believe to be the most important.

For example we have suggestions that parties are institutions which:

- bring people together so that they can 'exercise power' in the state;
- seek to achieve their aims by legitimate means;
- contest elections in order to monopolise public office;
- endeavour to represent more than narrow interests;
- group together people with similar values, beliefs or interests. (Adapted from Ware, 1996: 2–5)

But, as Ware explains, such interpretations are all flawed. Whilst in no way claiming to cover all eventualities, he paraphrases and updates Burke's definition and suggests that 'a political party is an institution that (1) seeks to influence the state, often by attempting to occupy positions in government, and (2) usually consists of more than a single interest in the society and to some degree attempts to 'aggregate interests' (Ware, 1996: 5). Ware believes that this is a more effective definition than many others in the literature of political science since it incorporates five of the central concerns of political scientists:

- The focus of attention is on the centrality of the state as the object of activity.
- It recognises that many, or at least most, parties see being in government as the best means of being able to exert 'influence'.
- It is not restricted to liberal or representative democracies.
- It is able to distinguish parties from pressure groups.
- It avoids a central focus on the idea that parties must be united by shared principles.

We might also regard parties as fulfilling broader roles traditionally concerned with political education, recruitment and communication. In the 21st century however, much of this has been taken over by the mass media, especially since the inception and growth of the Internet and 24-hour news media. Although parties retain a residual role in providing party-specific information, mainly for members and supporters, this can no longer be seen as a primary function. Recruitment to political office, however, remains an important function that is still largely monopolised by parties, since in most countries it is extremely difficult to win an election at national level as an independent candidate. Aspiring candidates also tend to serve a political apprenticeship before they might be allocated to a seat or sufficiently high position on a party list to ensure election by serving in various capacities within their chosen party and then contesting varying numbers of elections that they will not win. Arguably, certain categories of aspiring candidates in many countries, notably women and those from minority communities, have found it even more difficult to gain a 'winnable' position.

How Should We Compare Political Parties?

So, we have a basic idea of what is meant by the concept of a political party, but how do we compare their policy positions and identify which voters support different parties? There are thousands of parties operating in the contemporary world and some countries have very many parties that operate within the electoral arena, although of course many will never get elected to parliaments. Clearly it is impossible for us to deal with all of these parties, even those which exist only within representative democracies, so we need a viable basis for comparison and explanation, which is both manageable and meaningful.

In the comparative analysis of political parties, especially when we try to compare them across national boundaries, we are often confronted by large numbers of parties that might have similar names but differ considerably in terms of principles or policy. This is especially the case for self-styled 'conservative' parties, since conservatives tend to be guided by the 'traditional reality' of their own country, culture and history and indeed may be difficult to compare. They tend to be grouped together with Christian democratic parties, which often eschew traditional conservatism. It would thus seem appropriate to begin by categorising parties according to factors that can help account for their nature in terms of underlying values, principles and policy. This has been an ongoing concern of political scientists since the 1950s.

Party 'families' as a basis for comparison

Early attempts to categorise parties looked primarily at organisational type which is purported to reflect either cultural or institutional factors, for example, cadre, branch or cell parties (Duverger, 1959). However, this did not allow for adequate identification of broader similarities and differences as there are relatively few types of organisational structure used by parties, and distinction by structure tells us little about party aims, values and so on.

Another popular factor used to distinguish between different types of party, which has proved more durable, has been ideology. One variation of this is the concept of the 'party family'.

Indeed, in their contribution to the *Annual Review of Political Science* for 1998, Mair and Mudde (1998) suggest that the concept of the party family remains an 'attractive and easily grasped metaphor', so much so that it figures prominently as a benchmark for comparative analysis of political parties across a broad section of the literature. Von Beyme (1985), for example, argued that there are nine ideologically informed 'familles spirituelles' (spiritual families), such as liberals, socialists, and so on within which almost all known parties could be grouped. This has been taken up and refined in a number of studies, two of which we will now examine.

Gallagher et al. (1992) have developed a comprehensive study of political parties, first, in relation to Western democracies and, second, extended to encompass the increasing number of countries that were engaged in a process of transition to democracy (Gallagher et al., 2000). They suggest that there are three main characteristics by means of which we might define party families:

- Shared 'genetic' origins – such as formation during a particular period in response to a particular set of circumstances or with the intention of representing similar specific interests, for example agrarian parties or socialist parties.
- Formal links to similar parties across national boundaries – often on ideological grounds, such as party groupings in European parliament, or the Socialist International.
- Shared approaches to policy – although the 'same' policy might mean different things in different contexts.

Following the work of Von Beyme, Gallagher et al. suggest that there are about 10 or so major 'party families' but further condense them into three general groupings in order to allow for ease of comparison. These are identified as:

- Party families of the left – comprising socialists/social democrats, communists, parties of the new left and other variants.
- Party families of the right and centre – comprising Christian democrats, 'secular' conservatives, liberals and parties of the far right.
- Other party families – a varied category which includes agrarians, greens, nationalists, regionalists, ethnic parties and special interest parties.

This classification is somewhat problematic. First, it locks parties into 'left–right' positions which make it difficult for us to look at how they might change over time – for example, the American Democratic Party, in order to attract a broader range of voters, moved significantly to the right in 1992 as did the British Labour Party in 1997 for the same reason. Both have subsequently moved back towards the left. The second group suggests that centre parties are of the right of centre, whereas some may well be of the left of centre. The final general category that brings together a collection of different types of party that do not sit easily together is also unsatisfactory. While the family groupings themselves are very useful for comparative purposes, the three general categories highlight problems in terms of 'forcing' party families within a tight left–right spectrum, which itself may not be without its critics.

The other example of work based on party families has been discussed mainly in terms of a 'left–right' dimension and has drawn heavily on work pioneered by Budge et al. (1987, 2001), originally focusing mainly on OECD countries but later extended to Central, Eastern European and other states (Klingemann et al., 2006). This study analysed party election programmes across the entire post-war period and identified policies, pledges and rhetoric that commonly signifies ideological positions on the 'left' or on the 'right' of the ideological spectrum. In this way parties within families across all countries concerned may be 'measured' in terms of their distance from each other in 'left–right' terms, both within their own party system and comparatively. Movement of party positions can also be traced. These studies are based on a 10-family classification that identifies green, communist, social democratic, liberal, religious (for example Christian democrats), conservative, nationalist, agrarian, ethnic and special interest parties.

Although the left–right spectrum approach is widely recognised and understood, it is also clearly based on what are essentially 'European' interpretations of ideology. While it can be argued that the approach is able to be applied outside Europe, especially to parties in essentially Anglophone countries such as those of North America or Australasia, or indeed countries which have adopted European models for party organisation, such as some former colonies of European imperial powers, it is quite difficult to apply on a global basis. The Peronist Party of Argentina, for example, is extremely difficult to classify according to this approach. So how else might we study political parties within a comparative perspective? One way is to look at parties by reference to their supporters and voters.

Supporters and Voters: Who Votes for Whom and Why?

Two approaches to the study of party support, or as it is more commonly termed voting behaviour, developed in the post-Second World War era. The sociological or socio-cultural approach argued that party support is a function of the fact that people are members of social groups and these group norms and values affect how we interpret what parties have to offer us as members of these collectivities. Indeed, there may even be a specific party, which has formed to represent specific group interests. When we looked at voting and non-voting earlier in this chapter, we encountered the work of Lipset and Rokkan (1967) whose model offers a socio-cultural explanation for the development of parties, party systems and voting behaviour, as well as voter engagement.

The Lipset–Rokkan model

Lipset and Rokkan argue that as a result of three major traumas of modern history, the Reformation, national revolutions and the Industrial Revolution, society became divided along a series of social cleavages or divisions. These represented the most important competing interests pertinent to any given society, which are identifiable on the basis of socio-cultural factors, such as class, religion, language and so on. Following these traumas, new prominent groupings emerged who felt under-represented and wished to be engaged in the decision-making process such as entrepreneurs during the Industrial Revolution. Each major interest develops a political party which seeks to gain support from among members of the particular groupings.

   Of course no single group may be sufficiently powerful to gain control of government in the short term and may have to seek alliances with others. They may even be precluded by the configuration of the political system from even attempting to form a party, such as the working class prior to the extension of the franchise, and would have to form alliances in order to change the system in the first place, for example workers in the 19th century, who were essentially socialist, would form alliances outside parliament with liberals and radicals to campaign for extension of the franchise. The following table shows how the Lipset–Rokkan model explains the emergence of eight different types of party system within different countries, each with different configurations of party.

Table 9.2   Lipset–Rokkan model of party and party system formation

Party system type	Nation building parties	Opposition parties	Example
I	Protestant church + landed interests	Non-conformist dissenters + urban interests	UK: conservatives vs liberals + Celtic fringe
II	Protestant church + urban interests	Non-conformist dissenters + landed interests	Scandinavian countries: Conservatives vs liberals + Christians + Agrarians
III	Protestant-Catholic	Protestant or secular alliance with landed interests + urban interests	Germany: Conservatives vs Liberals with centre
IV	Protestant-Catholic with urban interests	Protestant or secular + landed interests	Holland: Liberals vs Religious
V	Secular + urban interests	Landed or urban interests + Catholics	Spain: Liberals vs Catalans + monarchists
VI	Secular + urban interests	Catholics + landed interests	Italy and France: Liberals/radicals vs Conservatives + Catholics
VII	Catholics + landed interests	Secular + urban	Austria: Catholics vs Liberals + industry interests
VIII	Catholics + urban interests	Landed (possibly + secular)	Belgium: Catholics + Liberals vs Separatists

Source: Adapted with the permission of the Free Press, a Division of Simon & Schuster, Inc., from *Party Systems and Voter Alignments* by Seymour Martin Lipset and Stein Rokkan. Copyright © 1967 by the Free Press. All rights reserved.

The underlying assumption of the model is that, for example, Catholics would tend to vote for Christian democratic parties where these were available, middle-class people would vote for conservative parties, working-class people for socialist or communist parties, often depending on whichever of these their trade union was affiliated to, people in peripheral areas with their own cultural or linguistic traditions would vote for regional or separatist parties, disaffected elements within the majority population might vote for extreme right-wing parties, and so on. Of course, not all Catholics in Italy or Austria, or other countries that have Christian Democratic parties, always vote for Christian democratic parties. For those who might not be members of a party there are also possibilities that they are involved in networks of social and economic organisations, such as trade unions or churches, which have links to parties and provide a channel of voter recruitment.

In the case of the UK, for example, there is the traditional assumption that after the religious settlement, which occurred relatively early, and which had also been reinforced by a peaceful national revolution in 1688 that settled the monarchic succession, a homogeneous society became institutionalised. This meant that the dominant class was drawn from the landed interests in alliance with the established Protestant Church and came to be represented by the Conservative Party. The opposition, composed of urban interests, the emergent bourgeoisie and Protestant dissenters, came to be represented by the Liberal Party. As a result of the Industrial Revolution and the development of a mass electorate, the urban bourgeoisie gained the ascendancy, the landed interests shrank and the two groups joined together, represented by the Conservative Party, while a new opposition, the working class, was represented by the Labour Party. Society was seen as divided only in terms of one social cleavage, that of class with other, less central interests being regarded as less important and could be catered for by smaller parties, for example regional interests in Scotland and Wales. The UK was thus seen as having a stable 'two-party' system.

This model provides a viable explanation of the emergence of modern parties and the party system but is not appropriate as an explanation of current parties or party systems. Indeed, it has arguably failed to provide a complete explanation of parties and party systems since the 1920s. Societies are generally more fragmented now than at the time this model was established in the 1960s, with class no longer seen as central and divisions in terms of region, economic sector, ethnicity and so on, becoming more influential politically. Returning to the example of the UK, the partial resurgence of the Liberal Democrats, the successor party to the Liberals, also undermines the image of a stable two-party system. Devolution has created the existence of different electoral systems and a series of party systems that certainly do not reflect the notion of two-party stability. In recent years political discontent has grown, with a manifest decline in trust of politicians and political institutions, all of which has led people away from the ballot box and towards single-issue politics and direct action.

This does not mean of course that the model is without merit, and the fact that it has been a 'standard' for more than 30 years is testimony to its contribution to the study of parties and party systems. However, its strengths are limited to its suggestions about the formation of parties, why different parties might emerge in different countries and what types of party system might develop, but even here, it is subject to criticism.

Indeed, several criticisms may be levelled against the Lipset–Rokkan model. First, the theoretical basis upon which the approach is based is weak, and its authors have looked only at a small number of cleavage dimensions – emanating from the Reformation, national revolutions and industrialisation. Why not include post-materialism or race? Second, there is an implicit assumption, known as the 'freezing' hypothesis that these social divisions and the party systems that ensued will persist. Third, the ideas upon which the analysis is founded are derived almost wholly from the Western European experience, and how relevant this is to countries outside this area is more debatable.

The partisan identification model

In contrast to Lipset and Rokkan who argued that people come to support political parties by virtue of group membership, party identification models argue that people as individuals develop abiding loyalties to particular parties on the basis of closeness of fit between that party's position on a variety of issues and the individual's own values and attitudes. This may indeed develop into a lifelong relationship between the individual and the party. The model also argues that the most important influence on party choice in the first place is an individual's family, especially parents, but the particular period when the individual becomes politically aware may also be crucial to whether or not they will develop a lifelong relationship with a party. For example, if a voter has a particularly bad experiences during a period of economic hardship, despite the fact that they may become quite wealthy in later years, they may associate the problem with a conservative party and thus consistently vote for a socialist alternative. Social factors are not absent from this model, even if they are played down, and in most cases, class is seen as the most pervasive factor in determining voting behaviour overall.

The Michigan model

The best known example of a model based on party identification is the Michigan model which was developed in the 1950s by Campbell, Converse, Miller and Stokes. They defined party identification as '[t]he individual's affective orientation to an important group object in (their) environment'. In other words, it symbolises 'a general psychological attachment to a political party' (Campbell et al., 1960: 121). This is exemplified by statements such as 'I am a conservative' or 'I am a supporter of the Indian National Congress'. There is no need for supporters to become formal members of the party in question, simply to have positive feelings of attachment to it, and indeed all that is needed to establish the main features of party identification is confirmation of a self-identity with the party, held over an extended period of time.

The Michigan model suggests that voting choices are dependent on three factors – the voter's interpretation of candidates, party policies and party links with groups. Although each of these is important in its own right, their main contribution lies in the fact that they act as 'channels' for shaping party identification and ultimately, voting behaviour. Social factors with the notable exception of the family are underplayed in favour of opinions or reactions to events. So, the main features of the Michigan model are that:

- the majority of voters form an attachment to a political party which is generally 'inherited' from their families;
- this 'party identification' helps the voter to filter political information and know which party to vote for;
- as people maintain their allegiance for longer time periods, the attachment grows stronger. Changes are generally a function of an individual's changing circumstances and are associated with factors such as social mobility or migration;
- people may vote against *their* party at certain times while retaining overall partisanship, for example, the 'Democrats for Nixon' phenomenon in the USA in 1972 or engagement in 'tactical' voting (see Chapter 4) for another party to remove a particularly disliked third party or candidate when *their* party stands no hope of electoral success in a constituency or region.

Like the Lipset–Rokkan model, explanations of voting behaviour based on party identification has come under significant attack in the past two or so decades. For whatever reason, loyalties to parties are breaking down. Less and less people see themselves as strongly identifying with specific parties and people are now much more willing to switch allegiance between parties at consecutive elections. To be fair, the authors of the Michigan model did suggest that party identification was likely to weaken progressively in ensuing generations, but this did not assume the degree of decline that has taken place. What we have here is the phenomenon known as partisan dealignment, and it has rendered voting behaviour more volatile and less predictable.

Partisan dealignment

Harrop and Miller define partisan dealignment as a 'weakening in party loyalties' which they explain as a three stage process. First, '… the decline of class and religious loyalties reduces … the traditional social base of many parties. Secondly, the expansion of education encourages the growth of middle class radicalism and also gives more voters the skills needed to analyse politics in a less partisan fashion. Thirdly, the emergence of television reduces the functional significance of parties as channels of communication and replaces a partisan medium (the press) with [an] … independent news medium' (Harrop and Miller, 1987: 139).

Such developments have rendered traditional explanations of party support less effective, since they have occurred simultaneously with a decline in support for historically dominant parties, such as the Liberal Democratic Party in Japan, an increase in the phenomenon of minority government in many countries, the development of new parties, such as the Greens, or a significant remodelling of other types of parties such as regional parties or parties of the far right.

There are multiple reasons as to why this has occurred, some of which are quite paradoxical. We have seen, for example, the rise of both post-materialism in established democracies and the rise of consumerism in emergent ones. We have lived through the end of the Cold War and seen the pre-eminence of one global super power. Incredibly rapid developments in technology are taking place, especially in terms of communications and biotechnology, alongside a rapidly globalising world economic system with concomitant changes to the nature of class structures. We also see a greater willingness by people to engage in direct action to make political views known – not always of a constitutional nature, as in the various anti-globalisation protests at G8 summit meetings in recent years.

Although not uniform in terms of level or period of decline, partisan dealignment, like falling turnout rates, is manifest at a global level and had clearly become established by the nineties. In some cases, even among the most historically aligned electorates such as the USA or Sweden, there has been a fall of more than 10 per cent, while in many others, such as Japan, the Netherlands and the UK, decline has been between

1 per cent and 10 per cent (Hague and Harrop, 2007: 204; Thomassen, 2005: 256–9). People are now much more willing to desert their long-term party of choice and 'shop around', possibly because of changing political opportunities or because their ties to group norms and values have weakened thus leading them to change political allegiance. This then creates a vicious circle as dealignment, partly brought about by volatility, fuels further volatility as voters shift allegiances from one party to a second and even to a third. Such movement can lead to party system change, as parties decline or split and new parties come onto the scene, a situation that is seen as more likely to occur in a proportional electoral system. But change can also be brought about by reaction to policy initiatives and may reflect a greater willingness to remove governments we do not like. Hence we have a dynamic model (see Figure 9.3).

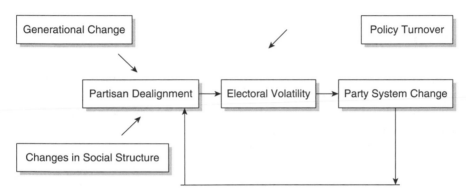

Figure 9.3   Partisan dealignment as a dynamic process
Source: Dr. Martin Harrop and William L. Miller, *Elections and Voters*, published 1987, Basingstoke, Macmillan, reproduced with permission of Palgrave Macmillan.

We must take care not to assume that all voters desert their traditional party, and indeed large numbers of people continue to vote for the same parties from one election to another. There is also a surprising degree of consistency between patterns of voting behaviour in established and new democracies. In both cases voters tend to be concerned with similar socioeconomic issues, mainly reflecting ideologically informed positions such as support for free market economics over support for welfare or vice versa. Post-material issues, such as human rights or climate change, are important for voters in established democracies, whereas in the new democracies of Europe two major dimensions have been observed. Here voters are also primarily driven by the free market–welfare dimension, but are concerned in addition with a modernisation–traditionalism dimension (Jasiewicz, 2003). This reflects a remaining degree of uncertainty in countries that have undergone considerable political and economic upheaval in recent decades.

It is also the case that voters in such countries have demonstrated quite dramatic swings in voting reformist parties out of office and replacing them with governments of a completely different complexion. This is explained by the Dahrendorf (1990) hypothesis, which suggested that in the first decade following regime change, parties in these countries would experience two major swings, initially in the direction of liberalisation and, subsequently in the direction of social democracy. The first is necessary to create conditions conducive to develop a successful market economy – not simply to create distance between parties of the old regime and newly established parties. The second swing is rather more a reaction to the less palatable aspects of capitalism as opposed to nostalgia for full employment or free welfare systems. This is a very different picture from those in some other newly emergent democracies, such as South Africa, where voters have returned the African National Congress since the early 1990s. Issues have also become important generally as informing how people vote, which can tend to undermine the power of both socio-cultural and party identification models.

The rational choice model

The Lipset–Rokkan model was attacked for 'freezing' voter alignments behind parties and failing to allow for change – a sort of cultural determinism – as well as being far too rooted in the European experience. Party identification models have been undermined by the growth in partisan dealignment.

A different type of explanation of party support is offered by rational choice theory. Based essentially on economic models, rational choice explanations assume 'that the voter recognises his own self-interest, evaluates alternative candidates on the basis of which will best serve this self-interest, and casts his vote for the candidate most favourably evaluated' (Enelow and Hinich, 1984, quoted in Harrop and Miller, 1987: 145).

Thus voting is seen as a means rather than as an end in itself, that is it can help to maximise perceived benefits for the individual. The model emphasises voters' political goals and assumes that they collect as much information necessary to make an informed choice. Voters are regarded as sufficiently aware as to discard any thought of voting for a party that would not gain a place in government, and hence not be able to deliver the goods. If they find a party that is likely to 'maximise' their own individual (perceived) benefits if elected to office, they will vote for that party. If none do, then they may think it a waste of time or energy to go out and vote for a party that, at best, would not worsen their current situation. Of course they may go out and deliberately try to stop a party that they perceive would harm them, which would be rationalised as being in their interest. Criteria which voters use may vary. Instead of always acting primarily as consumers they may seek to punish a government for not having carried out promises at a previous election by voting for a different party that might do better for them, which is a form of 'retrospective' voting.

It is of course up to parties to act rationally and position themselves where they believe that their election programmes will appeal to sufficient numbers of voters to enable them to win the election, as parties such as the Democrats during the Clinton era were widely believed to have done. If parties as well as voters act rationally, there should be little room for socio-cultural factors or individual long-term loyalties, since these are regarded as irrational influences on behaviour. It is also arguable that ideological considerations should be discarded if these are not seen to benefit the party or voter. However, in reality we do not experience a situation where complete rationality is possible. It is at best bounded, and socio-cultural factors and individual experiences might indeed act as factors in what is seen by voters as making a rational choice.

Modifying the Models: Short-term Effects

While these three approaches to explaining voting behaviour may be considered as the basis for general models, it is also the case that they may not always provide completely adequate interpretations of the outcomes of individual elections or temporary fluctuations in the basis of party support. Such changes are believed to be associated with short-term 'effects' related to media, party leaders or, especially, the state of the economy. These are not mutually exclusive.

It is especially difficult to disentangle leadership from media effects, especially since television has become instrumental in developing images of party leaders since the 1960s. Indeed, prior to this period party leadership was seen as having little effect. The first real use of television in this regard is believed to have been the US presidential election of 1960, when the 'youthful' democratic candidate, John F. Kennedy, was seen as striking a much more favourable impression than his Republican rival, Richard M. Nixon, as a result of his 'TV image'. The Republican Party paid huge attention to trying to improve Nixon's image, but to little avail (White, 1961). Labour leader Harold Wilson was quick to grasp the importance of creating a favourable 'TV image' during the UK general election campaign of 1964, and realised that in this, he had a great advantage over his Conservative rival, Sir Alec Douglas-Home, who did not. So powerful did the idea of television influencing election outcomes become, that President de Gaulle sought to monopolise airtime as much as possible in France during the run-up to elections in the 1960s. While it is difficult to estimate precisely how much media images might influence election outcomes, the prevailing wisdom until about 1970 was that the media tended to reinforce voter opinion of parties and leaders, rather than change it. Butler and Stokes (1974) averred that a leader's image might have at most a marginal effect on party image. We should take care, however, to view this impression against the backdrop of strong party identification and loyalty. Times have changed.

Harrop and Miller (1987: 221) suggest four reasons to explain why media have become more important since the 1970s:

- Weakening party loyalties render voters more open to receiving information about 'other' parties.
- New issues and events became prominent, for example, energy crises, environmental concerns, failure of welfarism and the end of the Cold War, which gave media an advantage in providing information.
- Ubiquity of television and advances in technology meant that almost all people in representative democracies could be reached with powerful, visual images. Media also built on its image of impartiality and credibility.
- Media, especially television, began to create an agenda for political discussion.

There has also been a move away from monopoly of state regulation of the media to a much freer market with regard to ownership and control of all broadcasting media, as well as huge advances in technology which enables multiple channels through satellite or cable and the ability to view television almost anywhere an individual may be situated (Dyson et al., 1988; Lange and Ward, 2004). Politicians have also sought to harness this to their advantage by creating new sorts of image, projected at appealing to much broader categories of voter. Much of this has been through hiring media consultants and bringing major film personnel on board. Party leaders now look at how their counterparts in other countries achieve success with much greater interest. Indeed, several major consultants, such as Lynton Crosbie from Australia or Stan Greenberg from the USA, have been employed by party leaders in a number of different countries to assist in replicating successes originally achieved with politicians at home, such as John Howard or Bill Clinton, respectively.

Although it is difficult to show just how much the image of a party leader matters it is clear that in an era of partisan dealignment, more potential voters are likely to take account of a variety of party messages and images. Even in the early 1970s, Butler and Stokes (1974) suggested that a leader's image might have a marginal effect on party image, especially in terms of people preferring the leader of a party other than the party they traditionally favoured. The phenomenon of 'Democrats for Nixon' is again an apposite example, but there are innumerable references in opinion polls worldwide where voters believe that leaders of parties other than those they traditionally associate with would make better presidents or prime ministers.

Yet it is not all about leadership image. Policy image is also important and no policy is more crucial than that concerning economic performance. Economic factors, in different ways, are also important to the three general models discussed above. Today, they are probably more important, but, instead of being associated with class or other social or cultural affiliation, they are now mainly interpreted at an individual level (Dalton, 1996, 2002). Politicians are also keen to project their policies as securing economic well-being and those of their rivals as bringing about economic failure. When asked what would secure victory for the Democrats in 1992, Bill Clinton's aide James Carville responded 'It's the economy, stupid!'

One attempt to try and measure the effects of economic and leadership factors has been developed by political scientists at the University of Essex (Sanders, 2003; Sanders et al., 2001). The 'Essex Model' sees economics as the main medium - to long -term influence on how people decide which party to vote for. It argues that there are three underlying influences on the vote: economic expectations (for self and family), tax expectations and immediate political factors. The third element encompasses a broad range of factors, such as leader's image and sense of economic well-being or the impact of a particular disaster, such as the bombing of Atocha station in Madrid just prior to the 2004 Spanish general election. Some of these factors can have a longer effect as we see in relation to the negative perception of the Conservative government's handling of the European Exchange Rate Mechanism crisis in September 1992 extending to their stewardship of the economy in general throughout their term in office to May 1997, despite the fact that the economy had recovered and was actually quite stable. This was a significant factor in facilitating the landslide victory of 'New Labour' in 1997.

Since studies in the mid-1980s (Crewe and Denver, 1985; Dalton et al., 1984) first discussed decline in partisanship on a wide scale, more attention has been paid to the growth of issue voting. With globalisation and greater ease in communication, we now experience not simply transnational political movements, such as Amnesty International or the anti-globalisation movement (see Chapter 10), but the fact that the same issue often figures in elections in different countries. The most obvious of these is the invasion of Iraq in 2003 by an American-led coalition, but increasingly similar campaigns concerning climate change or human rights appear as prominent public concerns in many countries and some are certainly not short-term issues. Existing models may find difficulty in explaining their impact on electoral outcomes and will give way to new approaches in the future.

SUMMARY

- In this chapter we have considered how the concept of representation is activated by the practice of elections and how turnout at elections have been further used to assess levels of political participation.

- As parties are so central to the electoral process in representative democracies we have examined ways of comparing them using ideology and social and cultural factors.

(Continued)

(Continued)

- Given current preoccupations with low electoral turnout we have looked at reasons as to why people choose to vote or not, and if they do vote, why it is that they vote for particular parties.

- We have seen how different models based on theoretical approaches use a variety of criteria and concepts to explain why people vote or not, and if they do why they vote for certain parties rather than others. These models also provide different ways for understanding the nature of political parties within an electoral context.

- We should also appreciate that any one of these approaches alone does not always offer a comprehensive or universal basis for explanation, and indeed needs to be developed further or combined with another.

- This provides a basis for examining other factors, such as the role of issues or leadership effects, for explaining short-term change.

FURTHER READING

Budge, I., Klingemann, H-D., Volkens, A., Bara, J. and Tanenbaum, E. (2001) *Mapping Policy Preferences: Estimates for Parties, Electors and Governments, 1945–98*. Oxford: Oxford University Press.

The introduction and first two chapters of this book provide a detailed explanation of how we might go about examining the dimensions of party competition on a comparative basis using party policy as our basic source of data, and indeed establish a left–right measurement (pp. 21–4).

Franklin, M.N. (2004) *Voter Turnout and The Dynamics of Electoral Competition in Established Democracies Since 1945*. Cambridge: Cambridge University Press.

A thorough, over time investigation of varying turnout across 22 countries based on meticulous empirical analysis, which also represents a good example of engaging in cross-national analysis using a variety of data sources.

Gunther, R., Montero, J.R. and Linz, J.J. (eds) (2002) *Political Parties: Old Concepts, New Challenges*. Oxford: Oxford University Press.

An excellent example of how theory and practice in the study of political parties – and the interface between parties and elections – is carried out using comparative methodology.

Harrop, M. and Miller, W.L. (1987) *Elections and Voters*. Basingstoke: Macmillan.

A useful, if basic, introduction to the dynamics of the electoral process and different theoretical approaches.

Le Duc, L., Niemi, R.G. and Norris, P. (eds) (1996) *Comparing Democracies: Elections and Voting in Global Perspective*. London: Sage.

Le Duc, L., Niemi, R.G. and Norris, P. (eds) (2002) *Comparing Democracies 2: New Challenges in the Study of Elections and Voting*. London: Sage.

These studies have been hailed as landmark texts in the study of elections, electoral and party systems, voting behaviour and turnout. They both provide broad theoretical and comparative understanding of essential aspects of these elements of the political process, and the 2002 volume offers useful, contemporary examples of practice.

Lipset, S. and Rokkan, S. (eds) (1967) *Party Systems and Voter Alignments: Cross-National Perspectives*. New York: The Free Press.

As already suggested in Chapter 4, the introduction to this book is still one of the most widely debated discussions on voting, elections and party systems. Although now over thirty years old, it provides good background material as well as the basis for culturally informed explanation.

Ware, A. (1996) *Political Parties and Party Systems*. Oxford: Oxford University Press.

Another accepted (semi-)classical approach to the analysis of political parties which provides a good basis for comparative treatment of political parties.

Webb, P., Farrell, D. and Holliday, I. (eds) (2002) *Political Parties in Advanced Industrial Democracies*. Oxford: Oxford University Press.

A good contemporary study based on a comparative case study approach to investigating the party legitimacy (linkages between parties and society) as well as the functions parties fulfil and their relative degrees of strength within political systems.

QUESTIONS FOR DISCUSSION

(1)   Is turnout a rational act? Is turnout a reasonable indicator of healthy levels of political participation? What is the best way to measure turnout?

(2)   Why do people vote as they do? Are people more inclined to support an ideology or party positions on issues of importance to them? Why might voters remain loyal to a particular party throughout their lives?

(3)   On what basis should we compare political parties? Is the concept of *party family* a useful aid in this process? What sort of problems might we encounter with this type of approach to understanding political parties in a number of different democracies?

(4)   Why are some types of party more prevalent in some countries rather than others? How do the different institutional models help us to answer this question?

Key Words for Chapter 9

ideology / issues / participation / partisan dealignment / partisan identification / party / party family / representation / turnout / voters

10 Interest Groups

Mark Pennington

CHAPTER OUTLINE

This chapter is concerned with the comparative politics of interest group representation. The first two sections set out some basic definitional issues surrounding the character and form of interest group politics and the manner in which the shape of this political action varies across states. The second and larger part of the chapter looks at the nature of interest representation through the various lenses of the 'new institutionalism'. The focus here is on the competing explanations offered by rational choice, cultural and structural approaches to the questions of why people join or do not join interest groups and the factors that affect the degree of political power exercised by different sorts of groups in different societies.

Introduction

Despite lower rates of turnout in many countries in recent years, participation by way of voting continues, for most people, to be their major source of contact with formal political institutions. A focus on the relatively narrow arena of electoral politics is, however, insufficient to the task of analysing the character of political participation as a whole. This is especially so given that commentators have argued that Western democracies are witnessing a decline in the overall level of political participation via conventional party political and electoral means.

One of the most topical issues in political science in recent years has been an attempt to describe and account for the rise of 'direct action' politics, including the growth of various protest groups or 'new social movements' that have sought to influence political events *outside* of formal institutional channels. The analysis of direct action politics is a relatively new phenomenon, but political scientists have been studying the broader phenomena of civil representation via interest groups for much longer.

Defining interest groups

Interest groups account for a substantial proportion of civil society. The term civil society refers to those actors that lie between the purely 'private' realm of individuals and companies operating in the marketplace and the purely 'state-centred' realm of political parties and government departments. As such, interest groups are organisations that seek to influence government policy, but which do not formally become part of the apparatus of political parties or the state. Within the terms of this very simple definition, however, it is useful to draw a distinction between economic or sectional interest organisations on the one hand and cause-based or attitudinal interest groups on the other.

Economic interest groups/sectional interest groups

To speak of an economic interest group is to speak of a group that is focused on predominantly material or pecuniary interests. People who join such organisations are usually expecting some kind of monetary benefit from their membership or participation. Trades unions and employers associations are typical of economic interest groups – they seek policies that will increase the income or job security of their members.

The term 'sectional' group is often used synonymously with economic interests because such interests are to a large degree 'exclusive'. Exclusivity in this context refers to the fact that the membership tends to be defined by certain objective characteristics which are *unique* to the members of the group concerned. The National Farmers' Union (NFU) in the UK, for example, is a group that campaigns for policies that benefit farmers in the UK and the vast majority of its members share the common characteristic of being employed in the farming or agricultural sector. Similarly, groups such as the National Union of Teachers or the Road Haulage Association are organisations that draw the majority, if not all, of their membership from the ranks of those employed within the particular profession or trade concerned.

Cause groups/attitude groups

It is usually the lack of such a common, objective characteristic, which distinguishes cause or attitude groups from economic or sectional interests. Cause groups are organisations lobbying for a set of values or attitudes rather than the interests of a particular segment of society. Typical examples include pro- and anti-abortion interest groups, environmental movements, animal rights groups and peace campaigners. Historically, most interest group activity has been focused on economic interests, but from the 1960s onwards much has been made of the growth in attitudinal-based campaigning associated with the growth of 'new social movements' and the wider advent of a 'post-materialist' dimension to political activity (Inglehart, 1977, 1990).

Apart from the fact that they tend to be focused on non-material issues, the key distinction between these organisations and economic or sectional groups is that there tends *not* to be some underlying objective characteristic that is common to the target membership. Environmentalist groupings, for example, typically draw their membership from a wide spectrum of society. Anyone may become a member of such a group irrespective of whether they are a teacher, a farmer or a businessman. The membership shares a common subjective idea – that is, of wishing to protect the environment – but the members need not have any objectively shared characteristics. Membership of these groups, therefore, can be considered largely to be a product of *choosing* to support a particular set of values or beliefs.

Interest groups as 'ideal types'

It is important to note that the distinction drawn between economic/sectional interest groups and cause/attitude based groups is an example of what political scientists refer to as 'ideal typical' analysis. An 'ideal type' is the purest possible form of any given phenomena.

- An ideal typical economic interest group is thus one where the membership is decided *solely* by some underlying economic characteristic common to the group members.
- An ideal typical cause group is one where the membership is decided *solely* by ones subjectively choosing to support a particular cause or value system.

In reality, ideal types rarely exist. The NFU, for example, although a seemingly archetypal economic interest group, has in recent years introduced a membership scheme for people who are not active farmers but who hold an interest in 'countryside issues'. Membership, therefore, is no longer linked to the objective occupational characteristic of being a farmer, but to a looser more subjective set of concerns and values. Similarly, some cause or attitude groups may have characteristics that put them closer to the sectional interest category. Women's rights and gay rights organisations, for example, may have sectional characteristics to the extent that their target memberships are made up of people who share the trait of being female or gay, respectively – though membership of such groups may in principle be open to men and heterosexuals who happen to subjectively support the causes concerned.

In the case of minority rights groups based on a particular sexual, racial or religious category, to the extent that delivering the relevant 'rights' may also result in improved economic opportunities for the individuals concerned it may be difficult to separate such organisations from those based on more explicitly material interests. Even in the case of groups, which may appear to represent a more or less 'pure' attitudinal interest, pecuniary motives may also come into play. Environmental interest groups, for example, may draw a large proportion of their membership from people who share an ideological commitment to greater environmental protection, but some anti-development groups may be the product of a 'nimbyist' (not in my backyard) motivation, which may have more to do with maintaining the social exclusivity of a particular neighbourhood or of keeping up property values, than with any notion of 'saving the planet'.

Ideal types may rarely exist in practice, but they are nonetheless useful to political scientists because they facilitate the categorisation of different groups in terms of how closely they accord with the particular ideal. The analyst may compare and differentiate the characteristics of the actual groups observed in order to examine whether they have more or less of the relevant ideal traits. Thus, the NFU may not constitute a pure economic interest group, but it is nonetheless much closer to this notion than an organisation such as Friends of the Earth, which has a more pronounced attitudinal focus to its membership.

Comparing Forms of Interest Representation

Interest group activity in the political system may be seen in large part to reflect the shortcomings of electoral participation as a tool of expression and democratic accountability. Voting in elections is an activity that is relatively infrequent and by its very nature does not allow people to express variations in the structure of their preferences and values. Voters in most electoral contexts do not typically vote on the basis of individual issues but are presented by political parties with a 'take it or leave it' set of policy bundles. One cannot express support via the ballot box for the agricultural policies of one party, the environmental policies of another party and the education policies of a third party, but must instead opt for a representative who will act across the full range of the issue spectrum.

The constraints provided by the mechanisms of electoral choice do not vary significantly between democratic political systems. Systems of proportional representation, for example, while they may allow voters to express a preference for more than one party, cannot allow the expression of preferences on an issue by issue basis. Participation in a range of different interest groups, by contrast, may enable individual political actors to express a more varied set of concerns. The form in which these interests are articulated, however, tends to vary according to the character of the political system, the nature of the issue at hand and the character of the particular interest organisation.

One aspect of interest group lobbying which is relatively *invariant* across liberal democratic states is the focus of activity on the public bureaucracy or civil service. As noted in Chapter 6, the control and implementation of policy in most states rests in the hands of bureaucratic agencies rather than those of directly-elected politicians. While the broad outline of legislation is typically constructed in the legislature and executive, civil servants are actively involved in the drafting of the legislative small print, which determines the contours of policy implementation on the ground. As a consequence, interest groups often seek to influence the legislative process via behind the scenes contacts with senior administrators.

While the bureaucracy tends to be a key point of call for interest groups across all states, the extent to which individual legislators or party political structures are targets of lobbying effort varies in accordance with the character of the party system. Other things being equal, countries with strong party systems such as the UK and Canada tend to witness interest group activity which bypasses individual MPs and focuses instead on senior ministers or members of the cabinet (for example, Landes, 1995). In some cases relations between interest groups and the higher echelons of the decision-making structure are reinforced by formal links between parties and particular interest groupings as with the link between the Labour Party and trades unions in the UK, for example.

In contrast, where party systems and party discipline are notably weaker as in the USA, groups may direct their activities to individual politicians or those points of the political system where the decision-making power of pivotal individuals is greatest. The American congressional system, for example, affords considerable power to issue-based committees, which have the capacity to propose legislation and to modify the proposals emanating from the President. As a consequence, congressional committees are prime targets for lobbyists, well aware of the need of individual legislators, who lack the financial backing from the party machines found in other liberal democracies, to court campaign contributions and other forms of political support in exchange for favourable legislation (for example, Cigler and Loomis, 2002).

With the possible exception of France, most European political systems fall somewhere in between the models exemplified by the UK and the USA. In Germany, for example, where the party system is stronger than in America, but where there is a greater number of parties than in the UK, interest groups tend to divide their time more evenly between efforts to influence individual legislators on parliamentary committees and attempts to pressure the higher reaches of the party structures.

The degree of competition between interest groups in different political systems is a further factor that varies across states. Within this context, many political scientists have focused on the distinction between states characterised by 'pluralist' forms of interest articulation and those where a 'corporatist' pattern is closer to the norm.

Pluralist forms of participation

Pluralist forms of interest group participation refer to those where particular sections of society such as those representing employers, labour interests or 'the environment' tend to be represented by a multiplicity of different organisations, none of which is considered by politicians and civil servants to constitute the definitive 'voice' for the segment of society/issue concerned. In this model, different employers groups compete with one another, different trades unions compete for members with other unions and different environmental organisations compete to reflect public opinion on ecological matters (Dahl, 1993). All of these groups tend simultaneously to press the government for elements of their own particular agenda. While some so-called 'insider' groups may have greater access to the levers of political influence and some may be consulted more frequently than other 'outsider' groups, a key characteristic of pluralist systems is that there is a clear demarcation between interest groups and the government. Typically cited examples of such pluralist systems include the USA, Canada and New Zealand. Other countries exhibiting at least some pluralistic forms of interest representation, meanwhile, include the UK, Japan and France (Lijphart and Crepaz, 1991).

Corporatist forms of participation

In contrast to the pluralist model, in corporatist political systems the organisation of interests is much less competitive with particular societal interests such as those of employers and of workers grouped together into so-called 'peak associations', which represent the vast majority of actors within the sector concerned. In Sweden, for example, almost 90 per cent of the workforce is unionised and the vast majority of these workers are members of a very few 'super-unions', which frequently work in concert (OECD, 1997). The structure of interest organisation in corporatist arrangements tends to be closely intertwined with those of the government itself and in many instances the formulation of legislation is negotiated directly with the relevant associational groupings. Almost by definition in corporatist systems the larger sectional interests in peak associations are 'insider' groups that are consulted directly by branches of the state, as a matter of standard practice. Most of the Scandinavian countries, including Norway, Sweden and Denmark, are considered to fall into the corporatist category, as are Austria, the Netherlands and Germany (Lipjhart and Crepaz, 1991).

The differences between pluralist and corporatist forms of interest representation as sketched above are clearly significant. What is less clear, however, is whether these differences can be attributed to the character of the political systems themselves or whether the existence of corporatist or pluralist structures is a response to the underlying character of the interests that are being expressed in the respective societies. Is, for example, the existence of peak associations a reflection of the fact that historically governments in corporatist societies have been less open or responsive to those sections of the population that have not been organised in such a manner? Or is it that organised interests in such societies have, as a consequence of their lobbying activities, brought a corporatist style of political bargaining into being? These are the sorts of explanatory issues that the 'new institutionalism' has sought to address and which will be considered in due course.

Access and Tactics

One of the key factors that may affect the character of interest representation in both pluralist and corporatist systems is the degree to which groups can gain direct access to politicians and civil servants. Where access to politicians and/or to bureaucrats is relatively constrained, then groups are likely to resort to other political tactics. These may include greater use of media outlets or the option of organising large-scale demonstrations and public protests as the primary source of political pressure. In France, for example, while pluralist access to the higher ranks of government and civil service has increased markedly in recent years, the French state maintains a relatively elitist mode of policy formation, which is somewhat autonomous from direct interest pressure (Stevens, 2003). Consequently, groups have tended to vent their frustrations against policy decisions of which they disapprove via public protest and often violent forms of direct action. As has been witnessed recently, such protests arise from a wide spectrum of French society, including farmers, shopkeepers, students, trades unions, lower-level government employees, and various ethnic and religious-based groupings.

In general, pluralistic political systems tend to witness a wider range of interest group tactics than their more corporatist equivalents. The competition between rival groups in such systems also inclines towards a greater degree of innovation in the form of political communication. In the UK, for example, groups such as Greenpeace have made a name for themselves by staging high-profile media stunts, such as the invasion of corporate and government offices or the destruction of genetically modified crops. These stunts appear to have been motivated, in part at least, by an attempt to attract younger members away from the more conservative environmental groupings, which have opted for a more traditional approach of lobbying politicians and bureaucrats directly (Dalton, 1994; Rootes, 1999). Even in more corporatist structures, however, such innovation is not entirely absent as those groups that do not fall neatly under the umbrella of a peak association or who fall outside of mainstream politics may resort to direct action or other less conventional tactics.

In addition to those characteristics internal to political systems, the specific form of interest group activity may also vary according to the issue concerned and the underlying nature of the group itself. Put in the simplest terms, certain sorts of policy issues do not lend themselves to visible campaigns conducted in the glare of media interest. Negotiations concerning the minutiae of agricultural policy, for example, may well have a substantial effect on the incomes of the farming community, but may be less likely to capture the imagination of the general public. In such cases the relevant interest groups may rely on behind-the-scenes lobbying and negotiations rather than attempt to exert pressure by seeking to influence public opinion at large.

The preferences of the media are also of relevance in this context, for there is evidence to suggest that mainstream media outlets are more likely to cover issues which can be depicted in confrontational terms or where issues can be associated with compelling visual imagery (Chapman et al., 1997). In the case of environmental policy, for example, oil pollution of coastal waters can be presented in terms of a confrontation between the economic interests of the oil industry on the one hand and the demands of conservationists on the other. Similarly, the highly visible nature of the pollution (oil slicks washing up on beaches, combined with dead fish and seabirds) lends itself to photographic coverage on television or in the print media. In contrast, many instances of air pollution are not amenable to analysis in such terms. The source of the pollution may be widely dispersed, resulting from the fragmented impact of many hundred of thousands of car users for example, rather than from a particular 'industry' or company. And, the pollution may be invisible to the naked eye. In such circumstances environmental pressure groups may be more likely to rely on direct lobbying with bureaucrats and politicians, whereas in the case of more visual forms of pollution they may try to influence public opinion via recourse to the media (Rydin and Pennington, 2001).

A further influence on the character of interest group behaviour relates to the nature of the interest itself, and specifically to the kind of resources and political weapons that groups have at their disposal. Other things being equal, cause-based or attitudinal groups are not able to use control of material or economic resources in pursuit of their objectives. This is not to say that such groups lack economic resources, for on the contrary there is often a tendency for attitudinal groups to be drawn from higher income or middle-class strata of society (Ingelhart, 1977). However, because cause groups tend not to be drawn from a clearly defined economic interest or industry, they are not able to organise campaigns involving control of particular economic assets or the delivery of a service.

Economic interest groups, by contrast, are better placed to use their economic functions as a part of a campaigning strategy. Trades unions, for example, may use strike action in an attempt to exert political leverage –and such action may be highly effective where the delivery of key public services is dependent on the cooperation of organised labour. Similarly, employers' organisations may use their ownership of capital assets in particular industries to withdraw services in key areas as did the UK road freight haulage lobby in its protests against high fuel taxes in the year 2000.

The analysis thus far has focused on the manner in which variations in institutional practices between states and the nature of particular policy issues are reflected in the character of interest group politics. Several important questions remain unanswered, however, from this basic comparative account. How and why do variations in the structure of institutions and the character of individual policy issues have the effect on political outcomes that they do? And what factors affect the degree of political power that is exercised by different groups? These are the questions that the 'new institutionalism' in political science has sought to address and it is the insights gleaned from this perspective that the rest of this chapter will consider.

Rational Choice Institutionalism and Interest Group Politics

Much new institutional work on interest groups has been conducted from a broadly rational choice perspective. From this point of view although interest group lobbying involves collective action, in order to appreciate the dynamics of such action attention should be paid to the motivations and incentives facing the individuals that make up the relevant groups. The decision to join a group is like all other decisions, a reasoned choice – it is first and foremost an intentional act where people think through their decisions according to a calculation of benefits over costs. This methodological individualism leads towards scepticism of class-based theories of interest articulation such as those of Marxism. From a rational choice perspective, common interests based on macroeconomic categories are the exception and not the rule. There is, for example, little reason to expect the existence of a unified 'business' or 'capitalist' interest, when the interests of farmers diverge from those of the retail industry; the interests of importers conflict with those of exporters; financial interests clash with manufacturing industry; and even within such categories as 'finance' or 'manufacturing' different subgroups of the relevant sectors, such as banking and property or textiles and computing, may have substantially different interests from each other. Similar divisions may exist within the 'working class' and indeed the interests of many workers may have more in common with those of capitalists in their own industry than with those of workers in other industrial sectors.

Rational choice and the problem of collective action

From a rational choice perspective, even when clearly defined group interests do exist, the motivations of the relevant individuals must always remain the focus of concern. Following Olson (1971), rational choice theorists emphasise that action that is in the common interests of the group may not accord with the interests of the individuals that constitute such groups. Since the results of political lobbying often have the character of a collective good, that is they are provided to the interested parties irrespective of the individual contribution made, they are subject to the free-rider or collective action problem. If individuals can get away with it they will not support an interest group wherever they can acquire the benefits of participating without actually paying the costs of membership. Where such free-riding behaviour is widespread, groups that would benefit from successful lobbying may simply fail to mobilise and as a consequence may be severely lacking in terms of political influence and bargaining power. Power, therefore, is not simply a product of the income or social status of particular interests as is often assumed, but is also dependent on the ability to overcome collective action problems.

At the core of rational choice accounts is the notion that collective action problems strike differentially according to the nature of the interest at hand. Other things being equal, groups that have the largest potential membership, such as taxpayers, consumers and environmental interests will have the greatest difficulty in overcoming free-riding behaviour. In large number situations, the chance that any single individuals' contribution will be decisive to the overall success of the organisation is vanishingly small and the temptation to free-ride is increased. In addition, large numbers make it more difficult for those who are attempting to mobilise collective action to identify and to impose sanctions against free-riders because they are hard to distinguish from members of the general population that do not share the groups' underlying aims.

Olson's analysis

According to Olson, the only way that numerically large interests might be able to overcome such collective action problems is via the provision of material selective/private incentives, such as low-cost health insurance or magazine subscriptions, which individuals can only obtain by joining the group. Alternatively, a group may attain a degree of mobilisation if the gains from collective action for a subset of the potential members are such that they are effectively willing to subsidise the free-riding behaviour of others. Such 'privileged' groups may attain a higher rate of mobilisation than in situations where the potential gains are more evenly distributed between the target members.

According to Olson's model numerically smaller interests face much less severe organisational problems. Producer interests such as businesses and trades unions fall into this category, especially in situations where there are relatively few firms operating in a particular industry and where workers are concentrated in identifiable plants. In such situations the per capita stake of each individual member is likely to be higher relative to the size of the group as a whole and the chance that any single individual will be pivotal to the success of the organisation will also be higher than in larger number situations. Correspondingly, the free-rider problem may be more easily overcome, because those shirking from collective action are more readily distinguished from the population at large and hence are easier targets for the introduction of sanctions and punishments.

The *Logic of Collective Action* model appears to perform relatively well when accounting for the pattern of mobilisation involving sectional economic interests and in particular producer groups. Critics of the rational choice approach, however, point to the large-scale mobilisation of cause-based or attitudinal interests such as anti-war movements, environmental groups and civil rights organisations that has been a growing trend across a variety of different states over the last half century (for example, Green and Shapiro, 1994). At face value such mobilisation is hard to account for in terms of the basic rational actor framework, because most cause or attitude groups are involved in campaigns that might benefit large numbers of people and where the potential membership might cover virtually anyone in the population concerned. From Olson's perspective, therefore, such groups should be disproportionately subject to the free-rider problem.

It is largely as a result of such evidence and criticism that rational choice theorists have increasingly broadened the scope of instrumental rationality to encompass non-material components. According to this approach, higher levels of collective action than might be expected from a focus on material incentives can be explained in terms of the ability of some cause or attitude groups to mobilise a package of *non-material* selective incentives in order to reduce the significance of the free-rider problem (Moe, 1981). Two species of non-material incentives have attracted particular attention.

Non-material benefits

Solidary benefits may include such things as the opportunity to socialise and network with like-minded people (in this case, membership of particular interest groups may act as a signalling mechanism indicating to others 'what sort of person' the participant is) or the desire to avoid social ostracism resulting from the failure to participate in collective endeavour. *Expressive* benefits, in contrast, may include the desire to achieve public approval and status among a particular social reference group from *being seen* to contribute to a fashionable cause (in this case there may be instrumental benefits from adopting a particular political identity), or more straightforwardly, the *entertainment value* of participating in events perceived to be of major historical/political significance. The latter may also encompass Brennan and Lomasky's (1993) view that individuals often derive benefit from the very act of expressing a public preference, much in the way that a football supporter may derive benefits from venting his or her feelings at the ground.

One example of a rational choice approach which draws heavily on the significance of non-material incentives is Chong's (1991) account of the rise of the American civil rights movement. Chong contends that a key factor in the ability of the movement to overcome the collective action problem was the availability of solidary incentives built around local black churches. Churches played a central part in black community life, where individuals were able to develop friendships and social status. In this context, religious congregations were able to transform into civil rights groups by drawing on peoples desire to sustain friendships and other social contacts and could, owing to the familiarity of church attendees with each other, monitor and punish free-riding behaviour via social ostracism.

The initial mobilisation of the civil rights movement was, Chong argues, based on a network of smaller church-based groups but this facilitated a subsequently larger mobilisation of other individuals, outside of the religious network who were seeking to derive expressive benefits. According to Chong, once a group has attained a basic minimum of organisation and may appear to have a chance of political success, then other individuals who wish to derive benefits from being publicly associated with an increasingly fashionable cause (an impression which may be stimulated by media coverage) will then seek to get involved. A 'threshold effect' is operative in which expressive benefits from collective action are triggered once a primary level of mobilisation has been achieved. Chong's theory is falsifiable, because it suggests that attitudinal groups that are unable to access solidary benefits at the local scale will lack the organisation base necessary to trigger the availability of selective incentives – a proposition which can be tested empirically.

While broadening its account to encompass non-material/non-monetary factors, rational choice theory still derives testable hypotheses about the factors that influence collective action. The basic logic of collective action model remains intact, with smaller groups and producer interests expected to be the easiest to mobilise, but with certain larger groups also able to overcome free-rider problems in situations where it is deemed possible to mobilise non-material incentives. What matters is that some political contexts are more likely to lend themselves to the provision of non-material selective incentives than are others. For example, the relative willingness or ability of the media to cover different issues is hypothesised as a key factor in triggering the possibility of access to expressive benefits (Rydin and Pennington, 2001). Within this context changes in technology, which have lowered the costs of mobilising expressive benefits, may have been a key factor facilitating the growth of protest organisations and 'new social movements'.

The spread of technologies, such as the Internet and mobile phones, has enabled groups to circulate information about successful mobilisations with increasing speed. This has, in turn, allowed group leaders to generate still higher levels of participation in social movements from those wishing to publicly associate themselves with what they perceive to be increasingly popular causes. Evidence of cause or attitudinal groups achieving substantial rates of mobilisation in the absence of widespread media coverage would tend to disconfirm the rational choice approach, whereas the persistent failure of such groups to mobilise in such circumstances would tend to confirm it.

Rational choice, interest group power and institutions

A primary implication of Olson's emphasis on the mobilisation advantages of smaller groups is the existence of a structural bias in favour of producer interests such as business associations and trades unions at the expense of consumers and taxpayers. The number of businesses and workers in a particular industry that might benefit from the introduction of a protective tariff or subsidy, for example, is likely to be small in relation to the population as a whole and the gains in terms of higher incomes to individual firms/workers from the introduction of protection might be substantial. The combination of a high per capita stake and the high visibility of the firms in the industry/the concentration of individual workers in specific plants, reduces the extent of the collective action problem as both the incentive to participate and the capacity to monitor and punish free-riding behaviour are enhanced. Consumer interests and taxpayers, by contrast, will each lose only a relatively small proportion of their income as a result of the tariff/subsidy and where hundreds of thousands, if not millions, of individuals are affected it is virtually impossible to discern which sections of the population are genuine free-riders and which sections do not support the groups aims. Even though the combined losses to those individuals who lose from industrial protection may outweigh the combined gains to those who benefit, the former may fail to mobilise owing to the severity of the collective action problem.

Taken on their own the losses from special interest capture in any one policy area may be relatively small, but multiplied across many different issues and policy sectors, Olsonian process point towards persistent inefficiency and special interest exploitation within the basic structures of liberal democracy (Buchanan and Tullock, 1962). As such, Olson's analysis challenges the relatively optimistic picture of democratic choice mechanisms presented by both pluralist political science and more recently by the Chicago School variant of the rational choice paradigm itself. Both of these approaches point towards competition within the political process providing a set of checks and balances against the abuse of power akin to those which hold firms to account within a competitive market.

Pluralists see democratic processes as involving rivalry between a diversity of organisations representing employers, workers and various cause groups, where none can gain systematically at the expense of the rest. Even when they acknowledge inequalities in decision-making influence, pluralists perceive such inequalities to be a reflection of underlying social preferences as represented by the relative strengths of organised groups. Becker (1983), Whittman (1995) and the Chicago School of rational choice present a similar account. In their model, if the burden of taxation or industrial protection becomes excessive for taxpayers and consumers or if there are ways of reducing the costs of transfer programmes to the voting population, then the political process will bring forth interest groups who will push for the relevant alternatives. If such groups are not forthcoming then this is taken to reflect an inadequate level of public demand.

According to Olson and his followers, however, even where political processes *appear* to be pluralistic (as opposed to those which seem more monopolistic or corporatist), appearances are typically deceptive. The competition that pluralists observe is competition between *organised* groups and neglects the possibility that due to individual incentives, some interests may remain *latent* and excluded from effective representation. Failure to mobilise is not necessarily a product of apathy or tacit support for the status quo, but may reflect the overwhelming nature of the collective action problem facing the 'losers' in the political game (Buchanan and Tullock, 1962).

Rational choice institutionalism and the comparative politics of interest groups

When comparing patterns of collective action across different states, institutional rational choice suggests that variations in the extent of group activity are affected by the underlying nature of collective action problems and the manner in which political institutions operate to raise or to lower the costs of mobilisation. At the most basic level, the rational choice analysis suggests that the basic structure of democratic choice mechanisms across states will tend to produce a structural bias in favour of relatively smaller producer groups at the expense of relatively larger consumer or taxpayer interests, but the precise extent of this bias will be dependent on the specific institutional character of the political system concerned.

That the scale of collective action problems is a key variable affecting the pattern of interest group action and the distribution of political power may, from a rational choice perspective, account for some of the most significant variations between the political economies of developed and developing nations. In the former, agricultural interests have tended to be large beneficiaries of government interventions in markets through mechanisms such as the European Union Common Agricultural Policy, whereas in the latter manufacturing and industrial interests based in urban areas have received substantial transfers of income at the expense of rural populations. This differential in the character of public policy between states may be accounted for by the fact that in developed nations agricultural producers constitute a small minority relative to the population of which they are a part, and as a consequence, are easier to mobilise than the large majority of urban consumers who pay the cost of the relevant agricultural policies. In developing nations, by contrast, it is the rural agricultural population that constitutes the majority and is less well placed to overcome the collective action problem than the urban industrial elites who are the primary recipients of government largesse (Bates, 1991).

Within developed nations meanwhile, differences in the extent of collective action on economic issues may be accounted for by variations in the size of the labour market. Comparison of trades union membership rates suggests that in states with relatively small labour markets and a homogenous industrial structure, the proportion of the workforce that is a member of a trades union is substantially higher than in states where the absolute size of the labour market is greater and where the industrial structure is more heterogeneous (Dunleavy, 1991: 27).

Thus, in countries such as Sweden, Norway, Denmark and Austria, all of which have populations of less than 10 million and which are reliant on a relatively narrow industrial base, union membership rates range from between 50–90 per cent. In the USA, the UK and France, by contrast, where populations are much higher and where the industrial structure is more varied, union membership rates are typically less than 30 per cent. From a rational choice perspective, the smaller the size of the labour market the easier it is for interest group entrepreneurs to identify free-riders and to develop a package of sanctions and rewards to encourage people to join. Moreover, the benefits of union membership in smaller economies where there may be relatively fewer alternative sources of employment are correspondingly higher. In larger economies, by contrast, with greater mobility of labour, workers may find it easier to improve their living standards by 'exiting' from a particular industry or locality to seek employment elsewhere.

Variations in market characteristics and corresponding degrees of interest group activity may also account for the differences between corporatist and more pluralistic forms of interest representation. In general, corporatist decision-making forms, where sectoral groupings representing business and labour are grouped together in so-called 'peak associations', tend to be found in smaller states (Sweden, Norway, Denmark and Austria, for example), whereas pluralist processes are found disproportionately in states with larger populations and more diverse economic characteristics (the USA, the UK and France, for example).

While differences in the nature of collective action problems and the way that these vary between countries may account for some cross-country variations in interest group politics, the differential role of states themselves is also seen as a key factor because governments may operate to lower or raise the costs of group mobilisation. Some states, such as Sweden, have fostered interest group and corporatist decision structures by effectively refusing to deal with individuals or subgroups that do not belong to a recognised industrial association or trades union. In this situation, the government effectively creates a selective incentive for individuals to join particular groups, and thus enables them to overcome the collective action problem. The latter phenomenon may account for the existence of corporatist structures in Germany. Although the German economy is diverse and the labour market is very large – conditions which one might expect to increase free-riding – the German state has a long history of encouraging the formation of cartels in both labour markets and in particular industrial sectors, by requiring that groups make representations via recognised labour and business associations.

From a rational choice perspective, an additional ingredient affecting the extent of group mobilisation is the degree of stability within the political system. More stable political conditions may enable groups to build the capacity to organise collectively, relative to those where the rules of political engagement are less fixed. Building on this analysis, Olson accounts for differences in economic growth across the major industrial democracies in the post-war era in terms of the longevity of democratic institutions. According to Olson (1982), in the post-war period, paradoxically it was those states that witnessed the destruction of their institutions following defeat in the war (Germany and Japan), which experienced the most impressive economic growth, relative to the more stable democracies (the UK and the USA). At the core of this thesis is the claim that stable democracies have enabled special-interest coalitions to find ways of overcoming collective action problems and to push for restrictive policies, which benefit them as groups, but restrain the overall level of growth.

Those countries that suffered defeat, conversely, saw many of their special-interest coalitions smashed, and as a consequence have experienced a higher level of economic performance. Olson authored this thesis in the early 1980s, when UK and US growth was sluggish relative to Germany and Japan. The subsequent decline in Japanese and German performance over the last 15 years is, however, consistent with his basic thesis. It suggests that as time has passed since the institutional breakdown brought about by defeat in the war, special-interest coalitions have managed to remobilise and thence to stifle the rate of economic progress. The implications of Olson's thesis are none too optimistic. They suggest that for rapid economic progress to resume, states must be subject to some kind of institutional shock – such as a major war or natural disaster, or an internal economic crisis (such as the 1979 'Winter of Discontent' in the UK) of such a magnitude that the ruling coalition of interests is weakened and is less able to oppose the necessary economic reforms.

Just as political institutions and policies may lower the costs of collective action, so they may also raise the costs of interest group activity and hence intensify the free-rider problem. The existence of laws restricting the right to assemble and to engage in public demonstrations may, for example, raise organisation costs for rational individuals owing to the risks of fines and potential imprisonment. The primary comparative dimension here is between democratic and authoritarian/totalitarian societies. In the latter, the repressive apparatus of the state may constitute an especially severe deterrent to collective action and indeed the state may actually prohibit individual membership in organisations such as trades unions, as did many of the former socialist dictatorships of Eastern Europe. Even in democratic societies, however, governments may act to raise collective action costs, by, for example, breaking up 'closed shop' or union shop arrangements in industry, as the Thatcher administration in the UK did during the 1980s.

Cultural Institutionalism and Interest Group Politics

Whereas rational choice institutionalism focuses on the incentives for individuals to join particular sorts of groups, from the perspective of cultural theory the decision to join a group is not best understood as a rational decision at all. Rather, the interests of individuals and their membership of interest organisations is largely a product of habitual action reflective of prevailing ideas and perceptions widely shared by members of the societies concerned. According to this view, people define their interests in line with meanings, symbols and ritual practices derived from the cultural environment (Wildavsky, 1987). They do not choose to join a group as such, but acquire the values of particular groups from their parents, from their working environment and from their social peers. While culturally acquired symbols provide a shared set of reference points, they are fundamentally contested and help to define which groups are powerful from those which are not (Merelman, 1991; Scott, 1985). Culture is the key variable that determines both the interests that different groups advance and the degree of power that they possess in seeking to pursue such interests.

The focus of cultural theories on values and beliefs does not imply that such theories confine their account to explicitly attitudinal or 'cause-based' groups. On the contrary, both economic-and cause-based organisations can be accounted for in terms of their adherence to common cultural values. In the case of economic interests, cultural theories follow the Weberian view that individuals who share similar economic roles or have a similar income and pattern of consumption, tend to develop a shared set of cultural values and sense of social status, relative to groups performing different economic roles or with differing levels of income (Weber, 1968).

Culture and the basis of interest mobilisation

'Class-based' theories of interest representation form the core of cultural institutional accounts. It is important, however, to distinguish the sense in which the term 'class' is used by cultural theorists from that adopted by structuralists and especially Marxists. First, following Weber, although cultural institutionalism recognises that class relationships *can* involve forms of domination and exploitation, there is no necessary connection between the existence of different economic classes and exploitation. The relationships between social groups need not be zero-sum where the gains of one group come at the direct expense of others. On the contrary, the existence of income differentials between groups may simply reflect the differential contribution of actors to the social product and the manner in which these contributions are valued by markets and other social institutions.

Second, whereas in Marxism the class position of individuals is a product of property relations and ownership characteristics – the proletariat are those who do not own 'means of production', whereas the bourgeoisie are those that do – in cultural theory 'class' is defined in terms of groups possessing similar incomes or occupational characteristics and the attitudes, values and manners that are associated with such traits. Again, following Weber (1968), although it is recognised that ownership/ non-ownership of means of production might give rise to a common identification, cultural theorists maintain that status cleavages are as likely to arise from income or lifestyle differences. It is the size of the income different groups of actors receive from the market and attempts to defend or enhance such incomes that form the core of class-based activity rather than any particular structure of ownership.

Small business owners or investors in companies such as pensioners, who might be classified as 'bourgeois' in a Marxist analysis, for example, may have much lower incomes than people who work in the financial services industry but who would, using a Marxist classification, be described as 'proletarian' owing to the fact that they do not 'own' the enterprise that they work in. Similarly, ownership of consumption goods, such as housing, or access to private education may be a more significant source of the values underlying collective action than ownership of enterprises. Working in this vein, Saunders contends that home ownership is one of the most significant sources of class-based political action in the UK (Saunders, 1990).

In addition, for cultural theory the character of the occupation that one is employed in is also likely to be a key element in the makeup of the relevant identity. People will seek not only to maintain or enlarge their incomes, but will also attempt to defend the status and social perception of the occupational group to which they belong. Seen in this light, there is little reason to believe that people who derive their remuneration from the fashion industry will, for example, develop the same kind of cultural identification than those who work in agriculture or mining, even though the income or ownership characteristics of individuals in these groups may be quite similar. Status cleavages, therefore, may include a range of different factors linked to the nature of the work involved – such as the difference between a predominately urban and a predominantly rural profession or trade.

Values, beliefs and perceptions shared by members of similar income or occupational groups may be related to issues of social class and the economic role of particular groups, but from a cultural perspective such values are not coterminous with economic interests per se. On the contrary, groups may form on the basis of characteristics such as religion, race, ethnicity, regional ethos, or sexual identity. These features may be related to the economic status of the actors concerned in a given society, but equally may represent an entirely different basis to the formation of social cleavages. Writing in this tradition, theorists of 'post-materialism' have argued that in the last half-century many developed nations have witnessed a fundamental shift in the nature of interest group politics, with the role of more explicitly economic cleavages in society declining and being replaced by value-based and attitudinal dimensions. In the USA, for example, much has been made of the significance of the so-called 'culture wars' between 'red' (Republican) and 'blue' (Democrat) states. Interest group politics in this context has often focused on non-economic issues, with conflict between pro- and anti-abortion groups, gay rights groups and evangelical Christians, and those supporting and opposing the right to bear arms. These trends in voting patterns have also been reflected in the campaigning support given to the relevant parties by formal interest groups, with many evangelical organisations such as the Christian Coalition helping to fund and campaign for the Republican Party whereas 'pro-choice' and gay rights organisations have contributed actively to the Democrats.

More generally, the rise of 'new social movements' across the major developed nations has highlighted the significance of values and attitudes as a mobilising force. Initially, such movements in Western politics were associated with a 'leftist' agenda that mobilised in opposition to the Vietnam War, supported civil rights movements such as women's and gay liberation, and raised awareness of environmental issues. Culturally, such groups found common cause by challenging traditional morals based on a particular conception of nationhood, the family and notions of economic progress. More recently, however, similar attitudinal groups have mobilised around the defence of a 'traditionalist' set of values and cultural practices. What might best be described as new social movements 'of the right' concerned about the cultural impact of mass immigration and multiculturalism on national identity, groups seeking to defend traditional rural practices such as fox hunting, and those opposed to sexual liberalism, have become commonplace across the major industrial democracies (Tebble, 2006).

As the above analysis suggests, a cultural institutional perspective points to a complex mosaic of factors that motivate collective action. The precise mix of economic or class-based interests, those based on attitudinal or cause-based motives, and the intersection between the two, will, according to this perspective, vary across countries depending on the way in which different groups and the values they represent are oriented to the political culture at hand. The values and symbols that motivate group solidarity in one society may differ from those that drive a similar cause elsewhere. Consider, for example, the different symbolic attachments of environmental movements in the USA and UK. In the former, the cultural significance of 'the American West' has played a major part in the mobilisation of environmental groups, which have as a consequence focused much of their activity on the symbolic importance of 'wilderness preservation'. In the UK, by contrast, where much of the rural landscape is largely an artifice of agricultural practices, environmental groups have tended to be preoccupied with issues of local amenity and the maintenance of a clear distinction between town and country. Thus, although cultural theories can and do point to the emergence of common cultural trends across societies – such as the rise of new social movements, the emphasis of these theories remains on the way that such trends are moulded by the peculiarities of the culture concerned.

Culture, interest group power and institutions

Just as values and beliefs form the basis of interest mobilisation, so too according to cultural theory do such values and beliefs determine the contours of political power. Most importantly, shared cultural meanings may organise certain issues on to the political agenda and organise others off the political agenda. Institutions such as the state may not respond to interests who fail to express their demands in culturally acceptable terms. The cultural values that prevail in a given society, therefore, help to determine what are considered politically acceptable forms of conduct and the relative status of different interest groups and the policies for which they lobby. Culture may be a determinate factor in deciding which groups are political 'insiders' from those that are 'outsiders'.

For Weberian status analyses, class-based forms of political power tend to reflect the differential earnings of low-, middle- and higher-income groups. Other things being equal, groups whose members exhibit the highest incomes wield the most political clout owing to their greater ability to finance lobbying activities and to gain access to the media. The influence brought about by purchasing power may also be reinforced by the enhanced social status that is often accorded higher-income groups, especially those involved in business. Access to the media is particularly important from a cultural perspective, because it is via such institutions that dominant cultural groups may reproduce their power by ensuring that their own views and interests are depicted as the prevailing cultural norm.

Class defined in terms of income is one factor affecting the capacity of a group to exercise political influence but, according to cultural theory, power may also be conferred on groups owing to their occupational status. Weber emphasised the role that education can play as a source of social power independent of ownership and income. In his discussion of class structure in Chinese society, for example, he contends that the *literati* were one of the most powerful social groups. The source of this power lay not in economic wealth but on the social prestige associated with the achievement of formal qualifications. The cultural respect for educational achievement in Chinese society enabled the literati as a class to legitimise their dominance and to perpetuate a system in which educational attainment was a prerequisite for access to positions of power (Weber, 1968).

In contemporary democratic societies, professional organisations representing groups such as doctors, scientists or architects may benefit from a similar process owing to the social respect for the particular expertise that they hold. In the UK, for example, arguably one of the most successful interest groups is the British Medical Association (BMA); a professional organisation representing the interests of qualified doctors. The BMA is consulted by governments on matters pertaining to developments in the National Health Service almost as a matter of course and has wielded considerable influence in terms of the evolution of healthcare provision.

Cultural institutionalism and the comparative politics of interest groups

What matters from a culturalist standpoint is that variations in social norms and practices are the key explanatory factor which can account for differences in the power structures and the outcomes of interest group politics that we observe across states. While some dimensions of power, such as the tendency for higher income or higher status groups to wield greater influence may be relatively constant, the way in which these tendencies are reflected will vary according to culture. Most cultural analysis would recognise, for example, that groups representing a business interest will be able to wield more power than those drawn from lower-income strata. 'Business', however, is not a unified entity with an identical set of interests so which particular business groups are in positions of power may vary according to the cultural context concerned.

A number of commentators have, for example, contrasted the power of manufacturing business interests in Germany and Japan compared with the relatively lower status of such groupings in the UK. In the latter, the financial services industry appears to have exercised a greater degree of political influence, reflecting a historically embedded tendency to place less value on manufacturing than on finance. It may, therefore, be the particular cultural and attitudinal context within which capitalism has developed that provides the key to understanding which business interests exercise the greatest political power (Hall, 1986).

In addition to income and expertise, groups may find themselves empowered or disempowered in the political process owing to the place that their particular trade, profession or cause holds within the cultural imagination of the society concerned. Thus, agricultural interest groups have exercised influence and have benefited from large-scale subsidy programmes across Europe and in the USA, but the power of the agricultural lobby has been notably more pronounced in some countries than in others. In France, for example, the farming lobby has regularly drawn on a climate of public opinion supportive of its political demands owing to the centrality of the peasant farming sector and traditional farming methods to the common perception of 'what it means to be French'. In the UK and USA, by contrast, while the farming interest is not without political clout, it appears less able to mobilise the same degree of cultural symbolism with which to galvanise sections of the wider community.

Similarly, cross-cultural differences between developed and developing nations might account for the relative weakness of the agricultural interest in the latter. Although constituting a much larger proportion of the population than in industrialised democracies, agricultural interests have tended to be weaker in developing countries and have often been subject to high levels of taxation relative to urban manufacturing industries. Whereas, rational choice theory would explain this phenomenon in terms of the differential effect of collective action problems for the respective interests (see p. 273), from a culturalist perspective the power of urban and industrial elites owes much to the historical and cultural legacy of colonialism found in many developing nations. Urban areas/ports were the centres of European influence and the attitude of indigenous elites developed during the colonial era was that rural areas were culturally and economically 'backward' relative to the more cosmopolitan/European-oriented cities. It is, therefore, the continuation of such an anti-rural bias in the perceptions of governing groups that has disenfranchised rural interests and reinforced the power of urban elites.

Variations in cultural norms may, according to cultural theories, also be the key to explaining the manner in which the political process incorporates interest group demands. Many countries with corporatist forms of participation have a historical tradition which emphasises the importance of social 'solidarity', consensus and a strong sense of national purpose or national 'community'. Seen in this context, the existence of corporatist structures in states such as Germany, Austria and the Scandinavian countries is a reflection of a more communitarian political culture, relative to that found in pluralist societies such as the UK and the USA, which have historically exhibited a more individualist and competitive set of cultural traits.

It is also the case that variations in cultural values may account for differences in the behaviour of interest groups themselves. Consider in this regard the much greater willingness of French citizens to engage in public demonstrations relative to that of citizens in other industrial democracies (39 per cent of the French population claim to have participated in such acts, compared to an average of less than 25 per cent elsewhere, see Almond et al., 2004: 64). From a cultural perspective such acts should be interpreted as part of the French collective imagination in which street protest reflects the continuation of a long-standing tradition of protest, which has its roots in the French Revolution and the storming of the Bastille.

Structural Institutionalism and Interest Group Politics

The dynamics of interest group politics also provide one of the central themes of structural institutionalism. As with cultural theories, participation in collective action is not conceptualised in terms of the cost–benefit analysis emphasised in rational choice accounts. Rather than being defined in terms of relationships to an overarching set of values, however, the interests of individuals as group members are seen to be determined by their relationship to macro-political and economic structures such as capitalism, globalisation and the nation-state. Membership of particular interest categories is determined by an actor's position within the ruling macro-structure and interest group politics is seen in terms of a playing out of the broader power structure. Macro-political structures are in turn seen to reflect a particular stage of economic and technological development and the interests that these stages create.

Structure and the basis of interest mobilisation

Similar to the cultural perspective, a primary basis for interest mobilisation in the structuralist ontology is that of 'class'. Class, however, is defined in a more restrictive sense than in Weberian influenced cultural theory. For neo-Marxists the primary basis of class-based political action is the structural conflict between owners and non-owners of the means of production under capitalism – the bourgeoisie and the proletariat (Braverman, 1974). Interest group politics, therefore, is primarily a battle between 'capital' and 'labour'. Capitalists as a class are, owing to their control of the means of production, able to extract 'surplus value' from the proletariat and it is the battle to control this surplus that is the primary focus of the 'class struggle'.

From a Marxist perspective, the unfolding of the structural laws held to govern particular social systems, such as capitalism, creates the very economic and political conditions within which actors come to recognise their common interests as a 'class'. Marx in particular drew a distinction between a 'class-in-itself' and a 'class-for-itself'. The former refers to the 'objective' position of a group that shares a common structural relationship within a particular mode of production – such as the distinction between owners and non-owners, capitalists and workers. The latter refers to a situation where a group of individuals, who share such an objective characteristic, actually come to realise that their interests are shared and also recognise their common class enemy (Marx and Engels, 1969). In the specific case of capitalism, classical Marxists argued that the logic of the market leads to a concentration of more and more power in the hands of fewer and fewer capitalists on the one hand, and a swelling in the ranks of an increasingly pauperised proletariat on the other. It is in turn these material conditions, which enable the proletariat to acquire a class consciousness and to act as a 'class-for-itself' against an increasingly obvious capitalist enemy (Marx and Engels, 1969).

In light of actual developments in capitalist economies which flatly contradict the predictions of classical Marxism – notably an increasing dispersal of property ownership rather than centralisation and a substantial decrease in the ranks of the manual working class, contemporary Marxists theorists have sought to reformulate the simple dichotomy between the bourgeoisie and the proletariat. The emphasis here has been an attempt to account for the growth and actions of 'intermediate' class groups, which stand 'between' capital and labour (for example, Poulantzas, 1975; Wright, 1985). These include managerial strata in corporations who do not actually own the companies that they work for, various professional groups such as lawyers and media workers, and the self-employed.

In moving towards a more nuanced and complex understanding of class structure, these neo-Marxist theories have shifted closer to a Weberian account. The primary difference between the newer Marxist theories and Weberian theory, however, remains an insistence by Marxists that it is the structural logic of capitalism that drives the nature of class antagonisms and in particular the dichotomy between ownership and non-ownership of the means of production. Seen through this lens, much of the political battle between the bourgeoisie and the proletariat now takes place in an attempt to win over the allegiance of the intermediate strata of society.

In its non-Marxist variants, structural institutionalism examines class dynamics less in terms of ownership patterns and more with regard to the structural position of different economic sectors such as agriculture, manufacturing, capital or labour-intensive industries and export versus importing sectors (Rogowski, 1989). These sectoral interests are examined in terms of how structural changes to the macro-political economy brought about by technological shifts or movements in the terms of trade affect the incomes and relative standing of the respective groups. While this analysis tends to centre on the interests of economic elites such as capitalists and landowners, unlike Marxist-inspired accounts, attention is also focused on the formation of sectoral allegiances *between* classes, where interest group activity centres on the conflict between the shared interests of workers and capitalists in one industrial sector and the shared interests of other workers and other capitalists in rival sectors of the economy. Working in this tradition, Frieden (1991) argues that the primary basis of mobilisation by industrial interests is the degree to which their products are traded or non-traded, whether their markets are domestic or international, and whether their assets are country/site specific or mobile (quoted in Hall, 1997).

In structural institutionalism, both in its Marxist and non-Marxist forms, seemingly non-material or value-based mobilisations are usually interpreted as a by-product of underlying structural processes where some social groups and the values they represent are oppressed or liberated owing to the requirements of the economic system concerned. Marxist analyses of capitalism, for example, maintain that the economic interests of the bourgeoisie require a particular set of social morals, such as support for the nuclear family and a division between household and paid labour. The oppression of groups such as women, gays and ethnic minorities who might challenge aspects of the prevailing moral order is thus necessary in order to sustain the moral conditions required for the continuation of capitalist economic growth. The rise of feminist and various civil rights movements, therefore, is but another dimension of the fundamental conflict between the proletariat and the bourgeoisie. Instead of being conducted on the factory/shop-floor, however, the politics of the new social movements reflects the increasing transfer of the class struggle to the realm of culture and ideas.

Non-Marxist forms of structural theory also reduce the rise of value-based or attitudinal movements to underlying shifts in the parameters of the economic structure. While relying less on theoretical abstractions such as 'capitalism' to drive the explanation, these accounts emphasise the effects wrought by changing technologies or patterns of trade and the manner in which these enhance or constrain the power and status of different social groups. In the case of technological effects, for example, the rise of labour-saving technology in the home and a shift towards light industry and services within the major developed economies is thought to have increased the economic bargaining power of women with respect to their male counterparts and this has in turn facilitated the rise of a more feminist politics.

Structure, institutions and interest group power

If the class position of social actors is the primary mobilising force behind interest groups then, according to structural institutionalism, class is also the primary determinant of the power exercised by social groups. Different actors wield clout according to the functional role that they play within the economic system. Marxist accounts, in particular, maintain that the state apparatus either operates directly in the interests of the ruling class, or allows differential access to its members so that their interests are reflected in whatever policy decisions are made. In the specific instance of developed capitalist societies, the underlying assumption is that the state will act in favour of capital and at the expense of labour. Although there are differences between those theories which maintain that the state is little more than a neutral, functional tool for the administration of capitalist interests, and those that posit a state with autonomous interests but which requires support from capital, the structural privilege granted to capitalist interests is taken by Marxists as a given. Insofar as other groups are granted access to the political process, as for example with the participation of organised labour in corporatist states such as Germany and Sweden, this is interpreted as an attempt to buy off the short-term demands of the proletariat.

For many Marxists, such processes are little more than an institutional façade in which the illusion of effective political participation is presented to the working class while not fundamentally challenging the basis of capitalist diktat. A similar analysis is made in so-called dual-state theories which note a distinction between corporatist decision structures at the national level and more pluralist interest group participation found at the local scale (Wolfe, 1977). According to this thesis, the state varies access to the political system at different levels of decision-making in an attempt to manage potential sources of opposition. Thus, the appearance of interest group pluralism at the local level in which a diversity of economic and cause groups are granted access is an institutional tool with which the national state legitimises decisions that are made according to the imperatives of capitalist rule.

Not all versions of structural theory adopt such a hard-line Marxist analysis. Institutionalist theories which focus more on the structural logic of maintaining the position of the state itself or of the economy, rather than 'capitalism' tend not to ascribe all power to a uniform capitalist class, but instead emphasise the influence of particular groups drawn from both capital and labour. According to this perspective, the interests of state officials in maintaining their own social status require the active cooperation of different sectoral interest groups. While business interests are able to gain influence, owing to their control of the capital necessary for economic growth, the power of labour interests, especially those employed in key industrial sectors, is also significant. Thus, Swenson (1991) explains the rise of corporatist wage-bargaining structures in terms of the need for employers in key export sectors to ally themselves with their workers at the expense of both capital and labour operating in more sheltered sections of the economies concerned.

Whether or not structures of interest representation correspond with a corporatist or a pluralist form will, according to this view, depend on the degree of economic power held by the respective sectors. Corporatist structures are more likely where there is a dominant coalition of interests on which the state is dependent for continued legitimacy, whereas pluralist structures are likely to occur in diverse economies where the state can play off different coalitions of interests. Unlike Marxist accounts, which see both corporatist and pluralist structures as a sham concealing the dominance of capital, this more nuanced perspective recognises that labour and other non-capitalist interests can exercise real bargaining power in relation to both business and the state, depending on the particular macro-structural context concerned.

A related variant of structural institutionalism focuses on the power of different sectoral coalitions and the manner in which the power they wield is affected by structural shifts in the terms of trade and in technology. Rogowski (1989), for example, explains the shift in favour of free trade and away from agricultural protection by the British state in the 19th century in terms of the effects wrought by changes in technology on the power of different social groups. Specifically, as transport costs fell with the development of steam power, both labour and business interests stood to gain from the adoption of a more liberal trading regime and united to secure these reforms at the direct expense of landowners and agricultural interests.

In comparative terms, structural institutionalism focuses on the location of different states and the interests that they respond to in relation to macro-political structures such as the international economy. Marxist perspectives allow relatively little in the way for variations in the structure of interest group power, with most developed capitalist nations exhibiting fundamentally similar processes of domination by capital. Non-Marxist perspectives, by contrast, are more nuanced allowing for considerable variation in terms of the composition of dominant interest coalitions depending on the particular configuration of the economy in question. Which particular business and labour coalitions are in the ascendancy will depend on the manner in which these are affected by shifts in technology and the structure of international trade.

Integrating Theories of Interest Group Politics

Each of the theories considered in this chapter offers some important insights into the nature of interest mobilisation, the determinants of group power and how and why these phenomena vary between states. It is important to recognise, however, that none of these theories can offer an all encompassing account of the processes in hand. While each tradition offers its own variant of 'institutionalist' theory, the most significant contribution that a specifically 'new institutional' approach can offer is one which combines elements from all three theoretical traditions.

The most significant contribution of rational choice theory is its capacity to provide the important 'micro-foundations' that are necessary to understand the factors that drive collective action and the capacity of different groups to exercise power. Both cultural and structural theories with their emphasis on class-based or sectorally based interests fail to provide an account of how these groups are able to organise politically. Classes and sectors are presented as unitary actors that somehow appear on the political stage as pre-formed groups. While such interests can and do organise politically in certain situations, it is equally the case that many class or sectoral interests often fail to act as coherent groups, yet both cultural and structural approaches to interest mobilisation fail to provide any account of why mobilisations occur in some situations but fail to materialise in others. It is here that rational choice theory with its focus on individual incentives can provide an important contribution with its analysis of the differential effect of collective action problems. Factors such as the size of the group and the capacity to offer either material or non-material selective incentives provide the important link between individual action on the one hand and group-based action on the other.

Cultural theories add to our understanding of interest group phenomena by drawing attention to the significance of norms and values as mobilising tools. Groups of people who share similar values, attitudes and traditional practices are more likely to overcome collective action problems than those who do not. Individuals may participate in interest groups and other collective organisations because such action is an integral part of a wider set of behavioural norms, which help them to distinguish their interests from actors who do not belong to a similar identity set. Seen in this light, participation in an interest group may be one of the norms that people follow in order to maintain access to the material and social benefits associated with an identifiable reference group. Much as people may, out of habit, dress in a particular way in order to indicate membership of a particular social group, so they may participate in collective action as a similar badge of cultural identity.

The role of values and identity has tended to be neglected by rational choice theorists, though, as was noted in Chapter 1, such notions may be incorporated with an account that stresses the importance of norm-or rule-following behaviour in conditions of uncertainty and imperfect information. Adherence to traditional rules and practices derived from the cultural environment is a useful 'satisficing' strategy when actors do not possess sufficient information to know what there interests are and how to 'maximise' them.

In the final analysis, however, norms need to be enforced so the cultural emphasis on rule-following behaviour needs to be integrated with a rational choice account that can focus attention on the circumstances in which the cultural norms that facilitate collective action are likely to sustain themselves or to break down. Thus, culturally homogenous societies may be more likely to overcome collective action problems than those where the contours of cultural identity are more fragmented. In the former, free-riders may be more readily identified in 'standing out against the crowd' and may as a consequence prove easier targets for material and social sanctions. In the latter, by contrast, the existence of diverse cultural preferences and reference points may enable 'free-riders' to 'disappear' and prevent the effective enforcement of sanctions.

A similar analysis would predict a higher level of collective action on class lines in societies where the social structure is rigidly fixed compared to those where there is considerable social and geographical mobility. When people are likely to remain in the same class group or locality for all of their lives, then there may be stronger reasons to fear the social sanctions that might be induced to punish free-riding behaviour, but where people are likely to move from one class to another and to exchange one identity set for another, then they are less likely to be constrained by such incentives.

Structural institutionalism is also useful insofar as it draws attention to the way in which macroeconomic changes can have substantial effects on the interests of different groups and their capacity to overcome collective action problems. Changes in technology and in the terms of trade can reduce the costs of organising collective action and at the same time can raise or lower the benefits that can be achieved by different groups from successful political mobilisations. The introduction of new media technologies and macro-phenomena such as globalisation may, for example, stimulate collective action by facilitating the spread of information about successful mobilisations, which may then trigger further mobilisation, owing to the increased availability of the expressive incentives emphasised by rational choice accounts. Similarly, a reduction of transport costs can expose certain sectors of the economy to new forms of competition and this may act as a stimulus to campaigns from sectors seeking to resist competitive forces and from those who might wish to encourage them.

Changes in structural variables such as transport costs may also have significant effects on the cultural integrity of different groups. A lowering of transport costs or technological innovations, such as satellite television, can expose different cultures to one another through trade and the transfer of visual imagery. Such processes may stimulate cross-cultural fluidity that may then exert an effect on the basis of interest mobilisation and the capacity to overcome collective action problems. As noted above, the improved flow of information resulting from global media may stimulate collective action via the increased capacity to learn from successful role models elsewhere and by triggering access to expressive benefits.

Increasing cultural fluidity may however also undermine the strong cultural norms that often facilitate the initial base for collective action at the local/national scale. How, precisely these forces interact will be dependent on the relative strength of the different variables in the particular countries concerned. It should be emphasised, therefore, that the most promising form of structural institutionalism is one that abandons the rigid economic determinism associated with Marxism in its various forms. A genuinely new institutional approach is one that recognises the dynamic interplay between individual incentives, culture and technological change and the manner in which this interplay varies across states.

A similar synthesis of perspectives is required in terms of understanding the determinants of interest group power. Again, the most significant contribution of rational choice theory is to draw attention to the role played by collective action problems. Ownership of property and social status may well be necessary conditions for the exercise of political influence, but without the capacity for individuals who exhibit such characteristics to organise collectively, they are unlikely to constitute an effective political force. Culture and structure, meanwhile, understood in terms of values and technologies, can operate to alleviate or to reinforce the collective action problems faced by different sorts of groups. In a society where there are strong cultural norms that entrench the political power of certain groups then this is likely to tilt the structure of incentives against successful mobilisations from those that are disenfranchised by such norms. Technological shifts, meanwhile, can shift the balance of power between different social groups by raising the status of some groups and lowering that of others, and by altering the structure of costs and benefits associated with successful collective action.

SUMMARY

- This chapter has sought to provide an introduction to the comparative politics of interest groups and to highlight the contribution that a new institutionalist approach can make.

- The great attraction of this perspective is the potential it offers to explain how and why institutions have the effects on political outcomes that they do and the manner in which the interaction of rational choice, culture and structure varies across states.

- However, much more research in a variety of country contexts is required in order to deliver on this potential.

- Considerable work remains to be done to integrate the different strands which make up the 'new institutionalist' paradigm in relation to the study of interest groups.

FURTHER READING

Chong, D. (1991) *Collective Action and the Civil Rights Movement*. Chicago, IL: Chicago University Press.

This is an interesting work, which explores the role of non-material incentives in stimulating collective action in the context of new social movements. The book contains some formal, mathematical analysis but is generally easy to read.

Greenwood, J. and Aspinwall, M. (eds) (1998) *Collective Action and the European Union*. London: Routledge.

This book conducts a comparative analysis of interest group mobilisation in the European Union that tests rational choice and cultural/historical explanations.

Inglehart, R. (1990) *Culture Shift in Advanced Industrial Societies*. Princeton, NJ: Princeton University Press.

In this work, Inglehart explains the rise of 'new social movements' in terms of a shift in culture away from material economic interests to those focused on 'values'.

Olson, M. (1982) *The Rise and Decline of Nations*. New Haven, CT: Yale University Press.

This is a major work in the rational choice tradition. Olson explains problems of relative economic decline in terms of the differential capacity of producer interests to overcome collective action problems.

Poulantzas, N. (1975) *Classes in Contemporary Capitalism*. London: New Left Books.

A classic Marxist account of class relationships in liberal democracies.

QUESTIONS FOR DISCUSSION

(1)   To what extent is the difference between pluralist and corporatist forms of interest representation a reflection of cultural differences between states?

(2)   How can rational choice theory account for the mobilisation of environmental interest groups?

(3)   What role do the media play in the mobilisation of interest groups?

(4)   How useful is the concept of 'class' when accounting for the rise of 'new social movements'?

(5)   Discuss the way in which technological change has affected the political power of the following interest groups: miners, farmers, environmentalists, and religious associations.

Key Words for Chapter 10

attitude groups / cause groups / class / collective action problems / economic interest groups / new social movements / pluralism v corporatism / sectional interest groups / social status

11 Political Leadership
The Long Road to Theory

David S. Bell

CHAPTER OUTLINE

This chapter takes a rather different perspective by focusing directly on individuals rather than institutions and concentrates largely on the 'great men' of recent history. It examines four distinct aspects of the topic: theoretical perspectives; leadership styles and techniques; psychology and leadership; and philosophy and leadership.

Introduction

Leadership is 'one of the most observed and least understood phenomena on earth' and the study of it in the 'political sciences' has increased in recent years (McGregor Burns, 1978: 2; also Edinger, 1964, 1967; Paige, 1965). There are, of course, many biographies of leaders (in a very popular genre) but these almost invariably deal with the spectacular figures of political life, the successes and failures, and rarely with the theory of leadership as such. Although *political* leadership is a relative newcomer as a mainstream preoccupation, there is no doubt as to the pertinence of the topic. Leadership, in contrast, is one of the current interests of the social sciences in general. It has been investigated by psychologists, sociologists and anthropologists as well as by philosophers and historians. Leadership in a wider sense has also been a burgeoning feature of management and business studies for which it is a practical matter (and has consequently spawned a vast range of handbooks of variable quality). Some of these will be of interest to the students of political leadership but politics is a different form of social activity and not reducible to management or business techniques.

There is a long history of research on leadership in the political studies and political theory and it is one of the most ancient preoccupations of political moral philosophy. This branch of the discipline dates back to at least Aristotle and of course includes that handbook for political leaders, Machiavelli's *The Prince,* but it also includes the 19th-century writings of Carlyle, Marx, Engels, Malaparte, as well as the novelist Tolstoy. In the 20th century with the development of more rigorous 'political science', leadership was, while not sidelined, placed on the back burner even though it did produce Max Weber whose notion of 'charisma' (variously interpreted) has been massively influential in the study of leadership. Eminent figures did devote their attention to the topic, but for a time it went against the grain as the preoccupation was to look for statistical regularities and for large-scale mass movements almost to the extent that 'leadership' was written out of the script as a factor in political affairs.

In the 1960s, the attention of academics turned to the study of leadership in a systematic way (Gouldner, 1965). One expression of this interest was Edinger's work and the pioneering edited conspectus *Political Leadership in Industrial Societies* (1967). It was followed by Paige's edited work *Political Leadership* (1972) appositely subtitled 'Readings for an emerging field'. This complemented Paige's (1965) own *The Scientific Study of Political Leadership* and was followed by J.M. Burns' *Leadership* (1978). Paige set out an ambitious programme for leadership investigation but Burns produced a massive omnium gatherum of leadership research throwing light on the relation between leaders and followers as well as containing many fruitful ideas. For Burns, the leader articulates the demands of society, or followers: this is the key political function of leadership and in this perspective the line of sight is very much on the individual as the prime mover and on the way in which leadership moves society in all of its aspects. Burns' sheer scope leaves the reader astounded but the universal pretensions go too far and the moral aspect is not always easy to disentangle from the empirical (curiously, Neustadt goes without mention). Tucker, coming slightly later, moves in a different direction and takes a situational approach to political leadership. Tucker (1981), although less ambitious than Burns, can be seen as overly abstract and general but he places power and interaction at the heart of the theory.

In most work on leadership the emphasis is on contemporary Western societies even though authors sometimes take in the entire world range of political leaders. There are studies of totalitarian, revolutionary, military and authoritarian leaders in non-Western societies but these are discrete topics and the use of violence, guerrilla or military force places them in a different category from Western leaders. In the Cold War totalitarian leadership had received its share of attention as had Nazi and fascist, authoritarian and dictatorial leadership. There are, of course, many forms of violence involved in leadership but those that entirely – or almost – depend on force do not constitute 'political leadership' but a form of power relations. This violent subset constitutes another complexity with its own rules and is, in the main part, non-comparable.

Theoretical Perspectives on Leadership

Political leadership is not, therefore, the property of one particular discipline and is one of the areas of intense interdisciplinary interest (Kellerman, 1984; Jones, 1989; Oppenheimer and Young, 1971). Currently the field is a bit like the beginnings of political science itself as described by Lasswell in which the 'original inhabitants usually migrated from elsewhere in the academic universe' (1963: 36–7). What interests students of politics does not have a constant focus and the progress in each of these fields has moved unevenly and is not confined to leadership in western societies. In reality so many disciplines impinge on the study of political leadership that such inter-disciplinarity is inevitable and at present the political aspects of leadership are a work of synthesis, even though each of the discipline-based investigations is interested in different questions. It is an area of study that raises a number of highly intricate problems and covers several disputed frontiers.

In particular, political leadership research straddles the structure/agency conflict, although most of the findings come down on the side of the importance of the role of the individual in politics. None the less the search for patterns and for regularities sometimes leads to a concentration on the situations and the institutions that promote (if not determine) certain courses of action and hence leadership types (Bendix, 1952; Brewster Smith, 1968; Butterfield, 1963; Byman and Pollack, 2001; Coleman, 1996; Levinson, 1958; Wrong, 1961; Moon, 1995). De Tocqueville remarks at the beginning of his memoirs on the problem of attributing too much scope and influence to individuals or relegating their role to nothing. Those outside organisations tend to see developments in terms of anonymous forces, those within as the outcome of personal decisions. To some extent this is a *faux problème,* as de Tocqueville (1964: 83–4) went on to observe, but it is at the heart of the current debate about political leadership. There has been an understandable reluctance to undertake comparative analysis of a group – political leaders – with so few members and the problem of abstracting one variable (the leader) from a situation has not been easy or universally convincing (Byman and Pollack, 2001). This is a reprise of the dispute between Carlyle who put the emphasis on the role of individuals ('Great Men' or 'Heroes') in making history and the Marxists (and Spencer and others of 'scientific' outlook) who put the explanatory weight on the society (Carlyle, 1993; Spencer, 1969).

Political leadership has been sidelined partially because it is highly particular and the thrust to make the discipline scientific has sought to find what is general and universal and sidelined what might seem to be particular and local. This has led to a gap between the public view of politics, in which leadership is a key factor (sometimes, perhaps, the only factor), and the academic view in which leadership is downgraded to the status of a dependent variable. Counter-intuitive as this may be, there have been many figures in the development of the social sciences in the 20th century who have dismissed leadership as a reflection of other deeper currents in society. Of course, there is an abundance of studies of individuals but the problem for the social sciences is to go beyond an agglomeration of biographical studies. In this the current state of the field divides into the partial theories that look at specific aspects of leadership (some, even more restrictive, that look only at a particular country) and the general theories of leadership that are a study of politics itself and of which Machiavelli's is the best-known example.

On this last point, even the most committed of 'scientific' seekers after social science laws allow some space for individual influence. Marxist writers struggled to find a way of ascribing roles to individuals while maintaining the rigid determinism of the scheme that allowed only for the action of the mass of the class system. Thus Trotsky, writing a history of the Russian Revolution, asks what would have happened if Lenin had not arrived at the Finland Station in April 1917? Trotsky (1965: 343), in an agonised 'counterfactual', is unable to say that the leaderless Bolshevik party would have found the right road and states that without Lenin it might have let slip the revolutionary opportunity for many years.

Isaac Deutscher finds this 'against the intellectual tradition of Marxism' and with Plekhanov dismisses those who think that a 'brick falling from a roof in Zurich could have altered the history of humanity' (1954: 243–5). However, Plekhanov's formulation (1940: 225–6) of this argument is less extreme than Engels' but still leads to the postulate of 'multiple Napoleons'. This is the assertion that if Napoleon had not existed then things would have been unchanged, for somebody exactly like him would have taken his place and the iron laws of society would have determined the same outcome. Leadership is at the parting of the ways between those analyses, on the one hand that look at personal characteristics and those, on the other hand, that look at the environment of institutions and structures or cultures. It is rare for these two perspectives to be combined or brought together in leadership studies generally.

However, the view of leadership as a sequence of 'multiple Napoleons' has never quite taken hold. Carlyle's premise of the 'heroic leader' making history in solitary glory has also been rejected but so too has the idea of leaders as mere corks on the ocean of social life. Moreover, the discussion of leadership has proceeded from other bases by establishing categories and by investigating the properties of different kinds of leadership type. There are, as would be expected, gradations of view in between and many different understandings of the relation of leader to society and to political action. These will be mentioned as they arise below, but it is enough to note that there is no consensus on the issue other than the common assumption that leadership is important and that it is necessary to show when, how and where.

Hence it has been one of the problems of political leadership studies to navigate in between these extremes of biographical individualism and the social science aggregates that allow no autonomy to the political leader. For some theorists a leader's role can be depicted as if they were a billiard player (Jones, 1989). In this analogy political leaders are presented with a position on the table and some can make use of it and others cannot. Leaders of great skill can win impossible looking positions and ordinary leaders cannot. Of, course, great leaders do more than skilfully use set positions, they engineer the situations, but the analogy still holds. There is thus an indeterminacy about the role of political leaders and no outcome is certain, although a range of possibilities might be discerned in most cases (a view of creativity in politics consistent with Riker's [1986]).

Machiavelli remains the starting point for modern studies of leadership as testified by the flow of books and articles on the *The Prince* (Butterfield, 1962; Coyle, 1995; Femia, 2004; Jay, 1987; Ledeen, 1999; Leonard, 1989; Nardin and Mapel, 1992; Neustadt, 1994; Rebhorn, 1988; Viroli, 1998; Wirls, 1994). Despite the frequently voiced objections that the lessons drawn from the brutal world of the Italian Renaissance are no guide to the contemporary world, the deconstruction of *The Prince* (and Machiavelli's other work) is a continuing endeavour because of the centrality of manoeuvre and manipulation to the author. This interest holds not just for students of the political arts but also for management and business for whom *The Prince* has also proved a stimulating workbook that has to be glossed for non-political readers. *The Prince* cannot be neglected in the debate about moral leadership but it is as a technician of power that Machiavelli is incorporated into the 'political sciences'.

Machiavelli's stature as a political thinker remains, of course, very high but *The Prince* remains the pre-eminent handbook for political leadership. Machiavelli is the first 'political scientist' for some and it is this objective and dispassionate account of acquiring and wielding power (combined with a black humour) that has ensured its survival as a *locus classicus* for nearly five centuries. There is no modern Machiavelli but there are works such as Neustadt's (1990) on the American Presidency, which give the reader advice about how the leadership can be made to work in the modern world and how to navigate the political swamp. Neustadt's book explains how Presidents, concentrating on Harry S. Truman, were able to build an assertive presidency but, in its dissection of the essential core to political leadership of persuasion and bargaining, it has lessons for all leaderships.

Max Weber's shadow also falls across the study of leadership and Weber links the social context and the leadership role in a precise way. Weber's theories form a part of a much larger sociological enterprise and his leadership triptych of traditional, legal-rational and charismatic, stemming from the nature of their legitimacy, has been widely discussed in other contexts. 'Charisma' is the main concept used by students of leadership because it is a manageable category that enables many different leaders to be slotted into it and because it is fruitful and suggestive of the scope and weaknesses of this group of leaders (Gerth and Mills, 1947; Spinrad, 1991; Theobald, 1981). Weber's 'traditional' and 'legal-rational' forms of authority are very broad and hence less useful for leadership studies but 'charisma' is Weber's great contribution to the modern vocabulary of leadership study. It attracted wide attention during decolonisation because of the rise of striking personalities (such as Nkrumah, Suharto and others) – something that seemed to demand explanation.

However, Weber's idea, even if inconsistently formulated, places the onus not on the leader but on the perception of followers, the way a leader is seen. When a leader is seen as having more than ordinary talents, as 'heroic' or 'supernatural' then they are 'charismatic' although they may not have the talents ascribed to them. 'Charisma' in this formulation at least is not a personality but a situation in society when the need for creative leadership is acute, usually during a crisis not during normal times.

Weber's theory has been used and criticised and has been subjected to 'conceptual stretch' to the point of distortion (a major problem with any successful concept). It has been unfairly attacked for ignoring the existence of force in leadership (it assumes the use of force but argues that it is insufficient alone) and because it places too much emphasis on the character traits of individuals (when it does the opposite). However, the term has broken free of its Weberian confines and escaped into the wider world so that its boundaries have become impossibly vague. All the same it is a concept that needs definitional precision because it has to be disentangled from other forms of leadership with which – according to Weber – it is always intermingled and no means of doing this is given either by Weber or subsequent Weberians. In addition the accent is on the perceptions of the followers and these are difficult (sometimes impossible) to estimate with the result that the focus switches very easily to the personality of the leader (whether it is larger than life or heroic) and away from Weber's initial focus. These are not impossible difficulties for the users of the notion of 'charismatic' leadership but they make it more difficult to handle than is assumed at first encounter.

Management and business have their own specialities in leadership studies, though they very often conflate management and leadership. These have very often amounted to a checklist of desirable characteristics without much of an indication as to priorities. Leadership is treated as a subset of management and is promoted as a technique or solution to organisational problems but categories of leader have been identified and refined. These have often revolved around the open or 'democratic' styles of leadership and the authoritarian or closed and their comparative effectiveness. Mention must also be made of the anthropological study of leadership and the insights that discipline has brought to western political management. F.G. Bailey has been very influential in this respect through a series of books and articles, as have others such as Sahlins (1993). Bailey (1998) remarks on the rules of interaction and roles, but the relation of leaders and followers and the relative dependence of leaders on the led and the nature of that dependence is crucial and in this view determines the type of leadership.

Leadership Styles and Techniques

Skilful communication and self-presentation are predominant parts of the political leadership. There is, however, a considerable crossover into political analysis from the study of communication with a leavening effect on political studies. As was noted in early studies: 'sharing a language … is the subtlest and most powerful of all tools for controlling the behaviour of these other persons to one's own advantage' (Morris, 1949: 214). There are also serious studies of the techniques of leadership which have uncovered some of the means of leadership dominance in contemporary society and have laid bare the 'language games' that are being played by political leaders (Atkinson, 2004; Bull, 2000; Charlton, 2003; Fairclough, 2000). These include work by Edelman and others on symbolism and representation by political leaders as well as the analysis of images. Edelman has undertaken a substantial body of work from the perspective of the political leader's creation of a political spectacle, how this is done and when. Special consideration must be given to discourse analysis that has analysed the nature of political speeches and how their effects are achieved (or not). Mention must also be made in this subject of the work of Atkinson on direct speech analysis.

With the studies of individual leaders, of which there have been many, the problem of non-additivity is, for the comparativist, a major defect. These were attempts to systematise the many individual and biographical studies that had taken leadership as a focus but which had been, until then, discrete portraits of leaders or of leadership types. Jean Blondel also tackled this problem, from another angle, with a statistical review of leadership in the modern world (in *World Leaders*) and was able, using a mass of material, to make a number of generalisations and to move the study of leadership careers and effects from the anecdotal (Blondel, 1987; Elgie, 1995). The 1980s also saw the emergence of rational choice as a political analysis and, although some writers in this tradition did not see leadership as a subject for investigation, others were keen to relate the actions of leaders to the 'political market' from which they emerged as entrepreneurs.

Robert Tucker (1981) advanced the understanding of leadership with *Politics as Leadership* which presents leadership as a role that requires the depiction of the situation for a group that is then mobilised on that basis. Tucker was complemented by the work of Edelman and Robinson who, while not being specifically related to each other, saw leadership in terms of perception and 'myth' although Edelman lays much more emphasis (excessive, according to Robinson) on symbols and symbolism. In this optic the leader not only gives to a community an understanding of its own structure, possibilities and tasks but is also a political calculator and an instrument. Thompson et al. (1990) used the American Presidency as a test bed for the idea of political cultures and tried to relate the style and scope of different forms of leadership with the setting from which they emerged. This integrated an important section into the study of leadership, though without attaining the sought after comparative framework. However, the classification they deploy is useful and, although some of the classes are very broad, it does distinguish the Communist system's leadership types clearly from those of the West.

There are many studies of the techniques of leadership (mainly from business) but there is a lively discussion about the way western leaders achieve their effects (Atkinson, 1984). This is the core concern of Riker's (1986) influential work on political manipulation that has given a new word to the social sciences (heresthetic) to describe the skilled use of situations to manoeuvre opponents. Riker's is a rational choice approach, but it puts the political creativity of leaders back at the centre of focus and moves away from the idea of the leader as the instrumental utility-maximiser for followers. Leadership, in Riker's perspective, is the calculation (through a rational choice structure) of the winning strategy in any given political situation through the understanding of the desires and priorities of the others involved. This amounts, as Riker makes clear, to a rather bleak set of strategic or tactical experiments and is not concerned with the goals or with 'vision', only with techniques, but it does place the spotlight on a necessary leadership ability (though many would want to add to it the judgement of the goal-directed component).

Atkinson, in a very perceptive book, takes research down the route of speech analysis, asking questions about what makes speeches effective, how messages are put over and how to appear on television, another major area of investigation. Atkinson analyses 'charismatic' speakers and the 'claptraps' or the rhetorical devices that elicit applause from an audience. This art of rhetoric is an old one and was taught in medieval universities for lawyers and those speaking to large crowds (religious as well as political) but has been forgotten and now survives in the collective memory of political culture, although it remains devastatingly effective. There is still something that can be taught (as it has been) for in the age of the electronic media and the sound bite, the addressing of large crowds has become unusual rather than the normal way for getting a political message across. This research seems to indicate that the repertoire is, in fact, rather limited and that the number of devices (pairs, lists, contrasts) is not great and has not been enlarged in the years since rhetoric was taught in universities.

But the study of rhetoric and presentation examines how the structuring and maintenance of authority are accomplished. This is the discourse analysis that is applied, usually, to literary works but which has been extended to the analysis of political power and it is, of course, culture specific (in a way that rhetoric does not seem to be) (Edelman, 1978, 1988; Pondy, 1978; Tulis, 1987). In one view leadership is about making activity meaningful for the people concerned and, by giving the activity meaning in words, the group's politics becomes a social fact accessible to many others and something that can be used.

Leadership and Psychology

With the discussion of the motivations of political leaders the investigation is on thin ground; some of the work on the psychological wellsprings of leadership drives are notoriously bad and some are more or less propaganda. In business and in management this problem of drive may be less of a problem (although it still receives extensive treatment) and it may not be in politics as, after all, the commitment to the public, ideological fire and a determination to succeed are usually considered enough in this domain. However, with top leaders, not just the ordinary local politician, there are some problems that are unresolved and there has been an interesting investigation of motivational psychology in this area (Verba, 1961).

Starting with the 'Master' Harold Lasswell (1963) who, reviewing leadership personalities, identified the dramatising character, the compulsive and the detached personality, many have sought to encapsulate the personal dimension of political leadership. Students of politics have since devoted much attention to the personality aspect of political life but their work has been overshadowed by research in other fields, notably management and psychology, and so far conclusions can only be said to be highly tentative (Barber, 1985; Berrington, 1971; Bronfenbrenner, 1960; Finlayson, 2002; George and George, 1998a, 1998b; Greenstein, 1967, 1975, 1992, 2000a, 2000b; Iremonger, 1970; Lasswell, 1962; Renshon, 1995; Rutherford, 1966; Tucker, 1997). Psychological studies are highly criticised by other researchers and they do tend to ignore other factors than personality and these studies have often departed from political investigation (such as those of Lasswell or Burns), but the concentration has tended to be on the subject of primary interest to those disciplines – less to political life.

However, particularly with the rise of the USA to superpower status, the emotional stability of leaders, despite well-attested intellects, has become a matter of continuing concern: Nixon and Lyndon B. Johnson (LBJ) (to take only two) had flaws of Shakespearean dimensions and some others had emotional undertows that severely impeded their leadership performance. Among the important studies for political analysis are the investigations of the 'authoritarian personality' by T. Adorno and H.J. Eysenck, which have ramifications beyond the study of leadership. Wolfenstein and others have constructed typologies of the personality types in radical leaders but without any follow-up studies (Adorno et al., 1950; Eysenck, 1969; Wolfenstein, 1969).

There has also been the study of UK Prime Ministers by Iremonger, based on the psychological work of Horney and others, that has called attention to traits of character in top leaders that are unexpected if not against the grain. This has been given a sure statistical footing by Berrington but there is not much further that this can be taken beyond noting the interesting correlations. J.D. Barber has developed a two-way classification between active and passive and negative affective and positive affective leaders that throws into relief an unexpected finding that many leaders do not relish their position even when they have no ambition to promote change (Barber, 1972; Greenstein, 1967, 1992; Tucker, 1997). These findings are, perhaps, more American than European and more early 20th century than contemporary (before the professionalisation of politics got underway) but do spotlight a fact that needs explanation.

In political leadership the psychological interest starts from the discovery that many politicians hate or dislike the activity to which they have devoted their working careers. J.D. Barber in a study of American politicians systematised this with a classification of leaders into those who like the top position and those who do not, and those who are dynamic and those who are passive. What emerges from the grid (which is a framework and not an explanation) is that a number of well-known presidents of the USA did not like the job that they did, even if, sometimes, they did very little while in office. One difficulty here is methodological, it is not easy to uncover the real feelings of those involved, and much of the information tends for that reason to be historical and to come from private sources kept secret at the time of the political leader's main career.

This is more than the habitual (although now rare) expression of a modest reluctance to take on the top job and is a very deep distaste for the socialising and meeting and greeting that is a normal – in fact necessary – part of political life. Many politicians do enjoy the task of leadership and they clearly relish the challenges of the top office in the state, but leaders are not always in that happy psychological position. In the cases mentioned by Barber some Presidents, LBJ and Herbert Hoover, may have been unable to cope with the massive problems of the top office (the Vietnam War and the Great Depression, respectively) but the evidence seems to indicate a much more extensive distaste for the leadership than that. Some of these reluctant leaders were, like Hoover, content to let the political world move round the White House but others, like LBJ, determined to make a mark and were formidable workers.

This pursuit of leadership positions, despite the lack of emotional gratification, is why there is some need for psychological explanation and it may be that the search for affection provides the missing element. This in turn is derived from old psychological theory and has been used to suggest that the drive for many leaders is not power but the lack of warmth in early childhood which impels many of them to seek admiration or acclaim in other ways, politics being one (this is not a determinist theory, the same treatment may case people to withdraw). At this point many observers of political leadership have been inclined to step back. It is not possible to get leaders onto the couch, and even if it were, the theory underlying the psychological speculation is dubious. But there are interesting studies of the phenomenon of top leadership. One is by Iremonger who takes a cue from a French psychological speculation on the topic and finds that many UK Prime Ministers up to 1945 were in this category of lacking real affection in childhood (Iremonger, 1970; also Barber, 1985; Lasswell, 1930, 1948; Renshon, 1980, 1996).

Iremonger makes an interesting case for the UK Prime Ministers of the 19th and 20th centuries but the problem is presented with greater force by Berrington in a review of Iremonger's work. Berrington (1971) examines the objectively verifiable facts of bereavement and (despite reservations about Iremonger's figures) finds that the UK Prime Ministers of this era were more likely to have been bereaved than their comparable contemporaries (adjusted for time and class). This leaves out leaders such as of Churchill (whose description of the coldness of his parents is well known), but it is a more robust generalisation about political leadership than is made by Iremonger. Their conclusions are similar: that there is an unusual pattern here at the top that needs explanation. Their analysis is divergent in that Berrington is tentative about the causes whereas Iremonger is more confident of the contemporary psychology. This is an intricate argument but it is set out with a forceful eloquence that makes it an impressive study in its own right. These studies demonstrate a need for the systematic investigation of the psychology of leadership, especially in view of the hypothesis advanced by Iremonger that there are many leaders at the very top who are neurotic, lonely and prone to erratic judgements or that there is no guarantee that the best will choose to run.

One of the other perennial questions of leadership is why so few top positions are held by women – if there is a law in the political sciences then this is a near to one as it is possible to get. Yet this is a difficult problem for the social sciences used, as they are, to finding social reasons for this male performance and the reasons for this divergence has produced an excited debate (Farber and Wilson, 1963; Fausto-Sterling, 1985; Green, 1981; Lewontin, 1984). In this debate the most important work is 'A Theory of Male Dominance' by the anthropologist Steven Goldberg (1993), which has set the standard for investigation and rigorous logic. This controversial book takes the observation that men rule in all societies known to history and anthropology (others, such as the Amazons, are mythical or misinterpreted) and argues that the reasons cannot be reduced to the institutional or cultural or the result of social conditioning. Alongside this book is the study by the philosopher Michael Levin (1987) that draws out some of the implications of the argument for society and for political leadership in particular.

Linked to the problem of motivations is the way in which the leader handles the immediate followers in the 'team' or 'entourage' (rather than the mass which is reached through the media and rallies). Partially this is a matter of organisation, and a leader who cannot bring a team together and get it to work is mismanaging, and getting the best out of aides is a refined skill. Very few politicians work in isolation and most have the essential ability to bring workers together in a functioning team for a common endeavour, although the way that is done varies widely. Machiavelli, in Chapter 22 of *The Prince*, was perceptive about the choice of advisers, and how it redounds to the credit or discredit of the leader, but how the private entourage should be run is a less clear-cut case. This is not a much studied area but has been given some attention – notably in anthropology (Bailey, 1988; Barth, 1959; Elias, 1983; Evans-Pritchard, 1940; Hermann, 1995; Isaacson, 1992; McAlpine, 1992; Rosenmann, 1951; Sahlins, 1963; Stephanopoulos, 1999). There are two opposed models: one of the rational office with clear lines of demarcation and the other with confused and overlapping responsibilities. Both these are used in government and both have their merits and demerits.

Leadership and Philosophy

Political philosophy has its own part in the study of political leadership and is important in the field in a way it is not in other branches of leadership studies, for example in management or business. That is because one of the inescapable areas of discussion of leadership is the moral question. There are, of course, ethical considerations as well as the statistical and more general objective considerations of leadership. These include the problem of how leadership effects are obtained and that is a separate subsection of leadership studies that includes discourse analysis and image analysis as well as the deconstruction of the mannerisms and projection of leadership in the western world. However, for the study of political leadership this is not the general debate on political obedience, rebellion, legitimacy and so on (although these have a bearing on it) but the narrower question of the ethical responsibility of the political leader: being the problem whether the great leader or statesman has a different standard to the ordinary person. This is hardly new and the general lines of debate are those drawn up by the ancient Greeks, but it took on a new lease of life with the move of the USA from the spectator in the international state system to its principal member. There then followed the attempt to define the ethical responsibility of the statesman and much turned on the horrific events of the Second World War – particularly the use of the atomic bomb.

This challenge produced the lucid and logically clarifying work of Arnold Wolfers among which are the articles 'Statesmanship and Moral Choice' (1949) and 'the Pole of Power and the Pole of Indifference' (1951). These articles provide more clarification for a new audience of American leaders than they are original investigations and they take up the ideas propounded first by Weber and by others (such as the utilitarians). However, they have not been equalled in their explanatory force since that time at the beginning of the Cold War. Wolfers takes the view that political leaders are not absolved from the ordinary canons of moral conduct but that the milieu in which they work and the responsibilities which they carry are such as to place them in situations that are far from ordinary. In the contemporary world political leaders will therefore have to take decisions in conditions that are uncertain and that will result in unintended consequences that are debilitating. This does not mean that the leaders are immoral, or that they cannot be judged or that they are different from the rest of the moral universe.

However, the nuclear confrontation of the Cold War and the confrontation by proxy of the superpowers gave the debate a new lease of life. In particular the Vietnam conflict and the conduct of USA leaders in that war reopened questions of what ethical conduct should be in high office. Stuart Hampshire, the philosopher, spoke of the relationship between gentleness and integrity, the virtues of private life and the 'hardness and deceit' required in public affairs. Most people, most leaders, are divided between 'openness and concealment, between innocence and experience' (Hampshire, 1981).

This problem of 'dirty hands' and the situation that a political leader is likely to face between two unpalatable courses of action was first posed by Machiavelli and is reviewed in various forms by many authors (see Coyle, 1995; Femia, 2004; Garver, 1987; Hargrove, 1998; Leonard, 1998; Wirls, 1994). (Machiavelli is, of course, the subject of other extended discourses.) Hampshire examined it in the context of the Vietnam War and the increased destructiveness of the weaponry as well as the nature of the political decisions taken. Hampshire's examination of the tension between justice and other values was not his last word and there are other publications on this dilemma but these elegant investigations have set the standard for subsequent studies of ethics (Booth, 1995; Crick, 1964; Graham, 1995; Kagan, 1989, Lefever, 1972; Nardin, 1992; Nardin and Mapel, 1992; Niebuhr, 1932; Ramsay, 2000; Rost, 1995; Somers and Somers, 2001; Waltzer, 1973, 1994). There has been a recrudescence of this discussion (much of it around the concept of the Just War) in connection with the actions of President Bush and Prime Minister Blair in the Iraq War. This has not changed the overall framework of the debate, that has remained much as it was in the work of Wolfers and Hampshire, although the issues are contemporary (Blix, 2004; Bluth, 2004; Bluth and Hoggart, 2005; Hoggart, 2005; Kampfner, 2004; Sifry and Cerf, 2003; Singer, 2004; Ramsay, 2002). More recently a flurry of activity intended to bring the Iraq War into context has meant another series of debates on this aspect of leadership.

It is from the USA that the more formal examinations of political leadership have emerged. Because of the importance of the American presidential system (and the empirical style of the American academic tradition) this is ahead of much European work in the field. There is a lot of this research that is country specific (see *Presidential Quarterly*, for example) but there is also a good deal that is comparative in nature and transferable across national boundaries even if this transferability is not often the object of the work. European work has been more eminent in the linguistic and discourse analysis than American authors have been but there is a very substantial oeuvre that looks at the symbolism and representational aspects of political leadership and its manipulation of its own political environment. This cross-cultural transfer is always difficult, but within western systems, which are broadly comparable, it can be done.

James MacGregor Burns (1978) was the author of a biographical study of Roosevelt and turned to a more general study of political leadership distinguished, in his view, from power and thus concentrating on the element of mutual exchange in leadership. Burns' very full survey of leadership, which integrates the insights of biography, history, behavioural sciences and politics in a way that has not been replicated, is now over 25 years old, and it has not been updated. By contrast Burns (2003) himself has continued to develop the concepts of leadership from that time and in particular has written about 'transformational leadership' in extended studies. One feature is consistent in Burns' work on political leadership. Burns distinguished between 'transactional leaders' who bargain and exchange favours and 'transforming' leaders who revise the goals and outlooks of societies.

'Transformational' leaders work in times of crisis and change social structures and values but also provide new goals. This is a vigorous form of leadership quite unlike the 'transactional' leader who does not push the limits of the public's understanding and who has no large goals. As 'transformational' leaders the politicians have a high purpose and a very substantial personal sway. This line of investigation has led to a series of studies of the type of leadership that transforms and remoulds. It is certainly the most attractive and exciting form of leadership but it neglects the talents of the ordinary leader in normal times (insofar as any are 'normal') and neglects the ability to keep the ship on an even keel, which, in an uncertain world, is not a common skill. There is a danger in leadership studies generally of concentrating too much on the highly publicised and flamboyant rather than the grey and effective. (As it were Helmut Kohl rather than de Gaulle: 'grey liberation'.) If the leader can make the extraordinary appear commonplace, reassuring a society in times of upheaval, that too is a talent that needs to be explicated in some way by scholars (Macmillan's running down of the British Empire, for example). Times of change may demand a banality of approach rather than the heroic arousal to arms and that may be effective in its own way.

Recently Skowronek's monumental analytical history of the US presidency (*The Politics Presidents Make*, 1999) has provided a substantial support to the students of political leadership by tackling several intricate theoretical problems. Skowronek's work has been much commented on but the interest for the study of political leadership lies in two problems to which the book provides an answer. In the first place Skowronek develops the notion of cycles of presidential power. There are identifiable sequences of authority in the US presidency. These are a product of the coalitions supporting the party and the president as they are put in place, mature and decay. This is critical because the stage in the cycle determines the effectiveness of the individual occupying the office and it has lessons for political leadership, not just for the presidency. This effectiveness is, it has to be underlined, political and not social or economic; that is to say that the politician maintains political support through crisis if the coalition is strong but if it is weak then even the best will find it a struggle to survive.

Skowronek outlines the following sequence of four authority structures: reconstruction, articulation and disjunction, with pre-emption intruding from time to time. In the first place there are the presidents of reconstruction who benefit from a new coalition and who are able to repudiate the past with impunity opening up many possibilities. A president who inherits leadership after a failing coalition (such as Franklin D. Roosevelt and Reagan) can command formidable power based on the repudiation of the past. Unfortunately for political leaders these coalitions are not eternal and at some point adaptations have to be made. This process starts with the 'articulators' who inherit the main thrust of the coalition but who try to follow through the 'political orthodoxy' in new circumstances. Political leaders who come to office in times of 'disjunction' find themselves trapped by a crumbling coalition that will not support any initiatives and which frequently impedes any action. These presidents come to be seen as incompetent although they may, like the examples of Hoover and Carter, be highly talented and insightful individuals, far from the bumblers they are depicted as being at the time. Finally there is the 'wild-card' of the 'pre-emptive' leader who comes to power against the predominant coalition and tries to impose new directions without the backing that the 'reconstructive' leaders have. This is a fraught position and many end up in trouble (and, as pointed out, impeached).

This is a much richer book than can be detailed here and it is tempting to apply the insights (of which there are many) to other western leaderships. Skowronek's ideas of coalition cycles (called 'regime cycles' in the book) is a sweeping attempt to link political possibilities and the accomplishments of leaders and to show how some are confined while others have open paths, but it goes further and suggests what these routes might be finding are patterns across the centuries in the 'politics presidents make'. Skowronek's research opens up many questions and leaves some unanswered. In particular, the theory does not indicate to what extent the coalitions (or 'regimes') are constraining and to what extent the political leaders are free agents and where. It also leaves unexplored the other influences on leadership action like the personal vision of the leaders who are often very clear about what they want to do and how they structure the situations they find themselves in (Riker, 1986). There is, however, a great deal to build on in Skowronek's foundations and this is of substantial importance to comparative political leadership.

Another study that comes from the extensive research into the presidents of the USA, who it reviews in a series of detailed cameos, but which has an explicit comparative perspective, is the model developed by Hargrove (1998) in *The President as Leader*. This is a synthesis of many of the ideas about leadership that have been presented in recent years and it brings them together in a general theory. In this work the idea of the relations of character, circumstance and culture are systematically brought together in a study of what leadership means in a Western (American) society. It looks at how presidents should lead as well as how they do lead but the model is put in the context of leadership studies from the Greeks to the present day. At the heart of the model is the idea suggested by Neustadt of 'teaching reality', which, as it is described in the book, is a genuine concern for the common good of society combined with a skilful understanding of how society will react and how it can be presented to the public. These arts are not common and the model does have a strong moral core (unusual in many studies concerned with the techniques not the ends) that discriminates between the demagogue and the great leader.

SUMMARY

- Having reviewed the theoretical literature concerning the nature of political leadership, this chapter concludes that there are many partial theories and models dealing with aspects of political leadership or with leadership in particular situations but there is no overarching theory capable of providing a thorough understanding of the phenomenon.

- Conversely, there is a general knowledge of the phenomenon shared between many specialists which is derived from both biographical generalisations and direct investigation. Hence there is an understanding derived from particular facts and uniformities, recurrences and wider principles. In particular this relates to styles and techniques of leadership.

- Psychological and philosophical aspects of leadership may be fruitful avenues to explore further in the future.

- This lack of empirical theory (of activities and behaviour rather than of values and ideals) is perhaps one shared with the other social sciences to a greater or lesser degree but the common currency of the field is not strong.

- Theory is also needed to build a body of statements aimed at elucidating the phenomenon of political leadership and rendering it susceptible to comparative analysis.

FURTHER READING

Hargrove, E.C. (1998) *The President as Leader*. Lawrence, KA: Kansas University Press.

This book, although about the US presidency, is a conspectus of leadership theories and raises the main issues in the current debate about political leadership in the west.

Machiavelli, N. (1962) *The Prince*. Harmondsworth: Penguin.

Clearly a tract for Renaissance Italy but the enduring handbook for political leaders of whatever background. Often treated as a crib sheet for gangsters, it has been consulted by many more leaders than dictators and tyrants (Churchill being but one example) and is still used by leaders and analysts to distil messages for the present day.

Berrington, H. (1971) 'The fiery chariot: British prime ministers and the search for love', *British Journal of Political Science*, 4: 345–69.

There is a substantial discussion of the psychology of leadership, much of it superficial, but this article takes previous work and makes some apposite points.

Waltzer, M. (1973) 'Political action: the problem of dirty hands', *Philosophy and Public Affairs*, 2 (2): 160–80.

The dilemmas and intricacies of political leadership are examined in this article that tackles one of the perennial issues of leadership: its moral standing. Can political leadership be exercised morally or does the inevitable conflict of values lead to an essentially amoral outlook at the top?

Skowronek, S. (1999) *The Politics Presidents Make*. Cambridge, MA: Harvard University Press.

Although dealing with the US presidency, this book tries to systematise and categorise the situations leaders find themselves in. It classifies leaders according to the opportunities afforded by the political context in which they work and makes cross-era comparisons of great interest to the student of political leadership.

Burns, J.M. (2003) *Transformational Leadership*. Oxford: Oxford University Press.

J.M. Burns is one of the principal researchers into political leadership. This is an influential book that looks at the nature of dynamic or 'transformational' political leaders. The concept of the 'transformational leader' is important and influential way of looking at political leaders.

QUESTIONS FOR DISCUSSION

(1) What is the role of the individual leader in the political process?

(2) What is the relationship between the leader and the social forces and institutions in any given era and society?

(3) What do the terms 'charisma' and 'transformational leadership' mean in the study of political leadership?

(4) Does the tradition of leadership in the west allow for the 'teaching of reality'?

Key Words for Chapter 11

charisma / comparative leadership / influence / political leadership / power / rhetoric / transformative

Introduction

In summary, we revisit the three theoretically informed approaches to comparative government and politics introduced in Chapter 1 and, with the help of examples drawn from the contributions to the book, we assess whether or not these are useful to our understanding of ways in which modern political institutions and actors operate.

Summary of Development of Comparative Politics

As you will recall, comparative politics first became established in Greece around 350 BCE, and is mainly associated with Aristotle's classification system for types of regime – monarchies, tyrannies, aristocracies, monarchies, democracy and mob rule.

How did he arrive at this system? He basically asked two questions:

How many rule? One person? A few people? Many people?
In whose interests? Their own? Or all citizens?

Much of this type of knowledge became submerged until the Renaissance in the 15th century and especially the Enlightenment in the 18th century. Renewed interest was largely due to the advent of modern theoretical ideas about the state (Hobbes, Locke, Montesquieu) and the growing importance of scientific method (Newton, Darwin).

The fusion of these two schemes of thought occurred in the 19th century, mainly as a result of the influence of philosophy and social enquiry, pioneered by the first modern political sociologists (Marx, Durkheim, Weber, and the elite theorists, Mosca, Pareto and Michels). What was so different about these thinkers?

- Systematic, scientific, logical approaches.
- Explanation guided by theoretical perspectives.
- Related to the 'real world' in that empirical evidence sought to 'prove' theories.

Thus, classifications, reasons for political and social change, the nature of the state and power relations were studied both theoretically and empirically. For the first time, theorists began to look at the 'big picture' and compare and contrast examples across time and space. They also often suggested remedies to problems. However, these were often far from objective. Ideologically charged explanations were employed to legitimise or delegitimise actions by one or other of the protagonists in the Cold War. Indeed, the 20th century might be portrayed as a hundred years of dialogue with Marx.

Even where explanation was not deliberately ideological in orientation, it has tended to be difficult to apply to reality because of the nature of the models used, as is the case with Aristotle's model.

One issue concerns the fact that there is a lack of agreement about how to examine reality, what to examine and what data or information is the 'proper' province of comparative politics. Conversely, such diversity is perhaps what makes the subject really interesting. It is clear that explanatory frameworks based on theoretical-approaches are useful tools in aiding our understanding of the political universe and help us compare and contrast practice in different countries – even if these countries are all agreed to be representative democracies. To be effective such theoretically-based explanatory tools must be able to be used at different levels of activity and be meaningful across time and space. A fruitful place to start looking for such tools is within the tradition of the 'new institutionalism.'

The Three Theoretical Explanations Revisited

Different groups of scholars have adopted specific positions on what they consider to be the 'best' theoretical explanation, thus establishing different schools of thought, or perhaps more realistically, different *lenses* through which the political world can be measured, understood and assessed. Among institutionalists, three of the most useful, as far as comparative analysis is concerned, are the cultural, structural and rational choice approaches. They do not necessarily always explain every single topic fully, and, as we have seen in several contributions to this volume, there are increasing attempts to try and draw on their particular strengths and synthesise these to provide more effective models.

Our main intentions in writing this book were to:

- enhance understanding as to how competing schools of thought see political activity;
- increase appreciation of how these different ways of viewing the world give rise to different types of explanation;
- provide a basis for the critical awareness of strengths and weaknesses of these different approaches.

One of the ways in which we understand better the main similarities and differences between these powerful analytic tools is by looking at the essential properties of the three approaches identified, by, *inter alia,* Lichbach and Zuckerman (1997) as set out in Table A.1.

Rather than focusing on each approach separately, Table A.1 takes three standard elements associated with any theoretical model – ontology, methodology and epistemology – and examines how these differ, how comparisons are made and what shortcomings might be associated with each approach.

Table A.1   Properties of three explanatory approaches

Property	Rational	Cultural	Structural
Ontology *(How do they perceive reality?)*	Rationality; action is deliberate; individual interests.	Rules; norms; shared subjectivity; common values.	Relationships; holism.
Methodology *(Way to undertake investigation)*	Comparative statics; consequences of behaviour, intended or otherwise; path dependency; counterfactuals.	Meaning and significance; culture and identity; norms and values;	Causal analysis; social 'types'; social dynamics.
Comparisons Based on uses offers	Positivism; generalisation; explanation.	Interpretivism; case studies; understanding.	Realism; comparative history; cause/effect.
Shortcomings	Instrumental; mechanical; weak on role of collective actions.	Subjective; teleological.	Deterministic; no place for voluntarism; weak on role individual.

Source: Lichbach, M. and Zuckerman, A. (eds) (1999) *Comparative Politics: Rationality, Culture and Structure.* Cambridge: Cambridge University Press.

Ontology

Ontology relates to the ways in which theoretical perspectives perceive political reality and what basic concepts they use to interpret the world. Thus rational choice theorists would, predictably, use rationality as the basic guiding force for behaviour and focus on explaining why individuals or institutions behave as they do. Thus individuals, for example, would act in a rational manner to maximise their advantage in any given situation and would always behave in the same way when confronted by similar situations. Action is thus deliberate, and decisions whether or not to take action will be governed by perceptions of the utility of expected outcomes for the individual.

Cultural theorists would regard rules or norms of behaviour as the key guiding principle for action. Because members of different groups would subscribe to a common culture, this would form the source for the basic principles guiding behaviour. Structural institutionalists see the world as a whole entity constructed on the basis of a series of relationships between groups or classes. The dominant group or class would have most influence on prescribing forms of action.

Methodology

Methodology is the way in which we go about investigating how political institutions operate across state borders and/or time periods. Rational theorists prefer to use comparative statics. They compare and contrast events or processes as they stand, rather than as series of dynamic developments. They are especially interested in path dependency, an approach developed from behavioural science, which examines consequences of action as a main focus, irrespective of whether or not these were the outcomes actually intended by the actors involved. Another methodology favoured is game theory or other counterfactual type methodology, whereby models are established to predict *what* might happen *if* certain input factors were changed. For example, what might have happened in terms of possible regime change in Iraq *if* the USA government had not invaded in 2003?

Cultural institutionalists employ methodologies that emphasise the meaning and significance afforded to both action and outcome. They utilise concepts that are highly dependent on cultural norms and values – factors that underpin, as they see it, the identity of individuals, groups and institutions, and thus represent the main influences on both means and ends. Structural theorists take a fairly instrumental approach to methodology, favouring the establishment of social types and explanation of social reality as a process of change over time brought about by changing dynamics in the relationships between these types. Hence, they favour causal relationships between events, groups and institutions.

Epistemology

Epistemology relates to how different forms of explanation conceive of the nature of knowledge and specifically how we acquire our knowledge. In a sense this relates to different approaches to a 'science' of knowledge. All three theoretical frameworks have different foci in respect of this, and since we are concerned with comparative analysis here, let us look especially at how these relate to comparison.

Rational choice institutionalists base their approach to knowledge on positivist philosophy, focusing on providing general *explanations* of political behaviour and action. Cultural institutionalists favour interpretivist approaches, pioneered originally by social anthropologists, which seek to bring about *understanding* as opposed to explanation, often on the basis of case studies. Structural approaches argue by contrast that what we have in reality is a series of institutions that are the products of historical events. Hence, institutional forms and behaviour are the *effects* of historical *causation*.

Shortcomings

Throughout this volume we have shown that any one of these approaches in isolation may not always be the most appropriate for enhancing our understanding of political reality or explaining why institutions in any given setting work in the ways that they do. We have also seen that it would often be advantageous for the approaches to combine several of their more powerful features and produce hybrid frameworks based, say, on both cultural and rational elements. It is widely accepted that there have been genuine criticisms levied against each of these approaches and that all have recognizable shortcomings. Table A.1 summarises the most frequent. For example, rational choice approaches are seen as being overly instrumental, mechanical and weak in terms of explaining collective decisions and the outcome of collective action. Conversely, structural approaches are seen as poor in terms of being able to explain individual action, as well as being overly deterministic, so preoccupied as they are with cause and effect. Such approaches are generally criticised for their subjectivity, and hence they are often biased as well as being weak at explaining processes of change.

Applications

Discussion of how we use the approaches and assess their value in explaining the nature of specific institutions and actors in the political arena of representative democracies has been the subject matter of this volume. In conclusion, let us revisit a few of these applications in summary form to act as an illustration of the general properties of the three frameworks.

The nation-state and nationalism

We have seen that there are a number of competing theories that seek to offer explanations of nationalism and the consequent emergence of the modern nation-state and most of them fit quite neatly within our three approaches.

Cultural explanations, exemplified by the views of Anthony D. Smith, argue that states pre-date the modern era as they depend on 'ethno-symbolism' – *re*-inventions of myths, legends, language and so forth. These of course can also be linked to other cultural factors such as religion and language.

Related 'cultural' arguments take a more hybrid approach (such as Adrian Hastings) and argue that the institutional role of religion underpins cultural attachment to a state, for example, Pakistan or Ireland.

There are many *structural* approaches to nationalism and the nation-state, and we have looked at one of the main examples, that of Ernest Gellner, who argued that it was only after the establishment of a modern, industrial system that the nation-state could be realised, based on 'cultural materialism'. Like Benedict Anderson, he supported the idea that it was largely due to the invention of the printing press and the growth of literacy that people could learn about the benefits accruing to them from developing a self-determined, territorial entity. People could see themselves as part of 'imagined communities', sharing values and so on with people they had never met. Even more rooted in the Marxist, structural tradition is Eric Hobsbawm's view that nationalism is part of the class dynamic, as it creates 'invented traditions' which can be harnessed by dominant bourgeois interests.

Rational choice approaches, such as those of Michael Hechter, are probably the least well-supported. These suggest that the development of nationalism is based on the realisation that it provides individuals with 'selective incentives'.

More recently we have heard how, in addition to explaining the establishment of nation-states, these three theoretical models assist our understanding of both the break up of nation states, and also federalism.

Federalism

Cultural interpretations argue that federalism is more effective in terms of providing for stable political systems if the society concerned represents a single or dominant culture, and especially if they can create a myth of representing a 'melting pot', like the USA, where minority interests can be dispersed territorially.

Structural interpretations focus on the idea that federations are efficient in that they can operate economies of scale and are more likely to be successful if they set up effective mechanisms to regulate disputes between different economic interests.

Rational choice explanations argue that federations can act as efficient producers and distributors of public goods and can also, if operated properly, enhance individual initiative and preserve individual liberty. This of course is based on the assumption that there is a lack of internal constraint on individuals, especially in terms of freedom of internal movement and commerce.

Voters and Non-voters

This is an area of the discipline where there is a great deal of research, predicated on one or other of these explanatory paradigms, and which also encompass explanations of why people might turn out to vote or not. Let us revisit the topics of electoral turnout and voting behaviour.

Cultural explanations argue that there may be elements of a group's culture which might mitigate against voting or, more likely, that they do not see any candidates/parties which represent their cultural interests, nor a party so inimical that they have to turn out to vote against it. Such cultural explanations suggest that people vote on the basis of pre-developed attitudes developed on the basis of their interpretation of cultural values and norms. Hence a practising Christian in the Netherlands would vote for the Christian Democrats, if religion superseded other interests like class. If the opposite were the case, they would vote for the Dutch Labour Party.

Structural arguments, from a Marxist-inspired class perspective at least, argue that voting is simply a means of propping up the capitalist class's stranglehold on the state. Other forms of structural institutionalism might argue that the electoral system is inimical to the interests of some individuals, such as some minorities, and thus discourages turn out among those groups.

Moving to those who do turn out, why do they choose the parties they do? *Structural* explanations argue that people vote according to attachment to a deep-seated structural factor such as class.

Rational choice explanations argue that individuals will only vote if they feel that there is something in it for them which maximises their own interests, and if it does not involve extra 'costs'. Theorists argue that individuals vote for parties purely on the basis of their own, often material interests, and if they can argue rationally that there is a party which represents these interests. This is often labelled 'pocketbook' voting as it is usually associated with voter perceptions of which party could maximise their financial interests if elected! This is over-simplistic.

Political executives

Cultural approaches argue that the nature of the executive and its 'rules' of procedure are related to cultural variables such as social cleavage or tradition.

Structural explanations also examine the role of institutions but in terms of the role they play in terms of influencing/undermining freedom of executive action, such as assemblies, bureaucracies, parties. They too tend to concentrate on rules and procedures as foci of attention.

Rational choice theories concentrate on institutional factors – especially negotiating systems in the process of determining policy. How is the role of the executive maximised? Are policy decisions always rational however?

Judicial power

It was argued earlier (Chapter 7) that in considering theoretical frameworks appropriate to the explanation of judicial power, we might commence by positioning the various approaches favoured by political scientists along a spectrum. One end of the spectrum would be occupied by an approach that is purely legal in outlook and views court decisions as based entirely on *legal* argument. Such an approach would deny the validity of sociological or even institutional argument. Hence it could be seen as a purely *legal model*. At the other end we would find an *extra legal model,* which emphasises the idea that courts are simply one set of political institutions among many and thus behave in exactly the same way as a bureaucracy or executive, in terms of making choices which will enhance or maximise their position. Such 'extra legal' models incorporate criteria such as judicial values and socio-political factors in seeking explanations of reality. In reality what we find is a series of interpretations which draw on both these approaches.

Thus, a *rational plus cultural* hybrid approach is arguably the strategy most favoured and adopted by political scientists studying judicial power, although it will be identified under a variety of labels, most commonly the *attitudinal model*. Such frameworks see judges as independent political actors who use their courts to turn their own political preferences into policy. Hence, it is necessary to study judges' strategy and their methods, for example how they seek to build coalitions to make their views succeed. This type of approach thus combines cultural with rational choice approaches.

In studying the role of judges and courts comparatively we need to recognise that they are quite different from other political actors since they rely on highly constrained and technical *legal* argument for their power and influence. Hence it is imperative that due attention is given to the actual legal opinions uttered by courts in any study of the courts. Studies that do not recognise this will fail even to explain *what* a court has done, let alone *why* it has done it. As Robertson demonstrates (1998), the political impact of a single decision depends on how the judges really intended it to work, how broadly they intend or expect future courts and administrators to interpret the result, and this can only be known by looking at the reasons they gave for such a decision.

And Finally

From these summary examples drawn from among our more detailed arguments in the book we can see clearly how the three theoretically informed explanatory approaches to comparative politics upon which we have focused:

- are based on clear and contrasting visions of political reality;
- offer different perspectives on the nature and development of political institutions and behaviour;

- reflect different views of methods and knowledge;
- *may* have shortcomings and cannot *always* provide answers in all circumstances.

   They are not the only models in comparative politics and are not necessarily appropriate to the study of every single aspect of the discipline, as we have seen, for example, in the case of political leadership. Their strength rests in their ability to provide a series of tools to assist us in our quest for explanation, understanding and meaning in the complex world of 21st-century political reality. They equip us with the ability to investigate this world and understand and explain similarities and differences in both the operation of political institutions and the behaviour of political actors across the increasing number of representative democracies that populate our political universe.

References

Aarts, K. and Wessels, B. (2005) 'Electoral turnout', in J. Thomassen (ed.), *The European Voter: A Comparative Study of Modern Democracies*. Oxford: Oxford University Press: 64–83.

Adolphus, J. (1802) *The History of England: From the Accession of King George the Third to the Conclusion of Peace in 1783*, vol. II. London: T. Cadell, Jun. and W. Davies.

Adorno, T. , Frenkel-Brunswick, E. and Levinson, D. (1950) *The Authoritarian Personality*. New York: Harper and Brothers.

Agassi, J. (1960) 'Methodological individualism', *British Journal of Sociology*, 11 (3): 244–70.

Agassi, J. (1975) 'Institutional individualism', *British Journal of Sociology*, 26 (2): 144–55.

Aglietta, M. (1979) *A Theory of Capitalist Regulation*. London: New Left Books.

Agranoff, R. (2007) 'Intergovernmental policy management: cooperative practices in federal systems', in M. Pagano and R. Leonardi (eds), *The Dynamics of Federalism in National and Supranational Political Systems*. Houndmills, Basingstoke: Palgrave.

Almond, G.A. and Powell, G.B. (1966) *Comparative Politics: A Developmental Approach*. Boston, MA: Little, Brown and Company.

Almond, G. and Verba, S. (1963) *The Civic Culture*. Princeton, NJ: Princeton University Press.

Almond, G., Bingham Powell, G., Strom, K. and Dalton, R. (2004) *Comparative Politics Today*. London: Longman/Pearson.

Alter, P. (1994) *Nationalism*. London: Edward Arnold.

Alston, L., Eggertsson, T. and North, D. (1996) *Empirical Studies in Institutional Change*. Cambridge: Cambridge University Press.

Anderson, B. (1983) *Imagined Communities: Reflections on the Origins and Spread of Nationalism*. London: Verso.

Anduiza Perea, E. (2002) 'Individual characteristics, institutional incentives and electoral abstention in Western Europe', *European Journal of Political Research*, 41 (5): 643–73.

Anwar, M. (2001) 'The participation of ethnic minorities in British politics', *Journal of Ethnic and Migration Studies*, 27 (3): 533–49.

Apter, D. (1996) 'Comparative politics, old and new', in R. Goodin and H-D. Klingemann (ed.), *A New Handbook of Political Science*. Oxford: Oxford University Press. pp. 372–97.

Armingeon, K. (2000) 'Swiss federalism in comparative perspective', in U. Wachendorfer-Schmidt (ed.), *Federalism and Political Performance*. London: Routledge and ECPR. pp. 112–29.

Armstrong, J. (1982) *Nations before Nationalism*. Chapel Hill, NC: University of North Carolina Press.

Atkinson, M. (1984) *Our Masters' Voices*. London: Methuen.

Atkinson, M. (2004) *Lend Me Your Ears*. New York: Vermillion (Random House).

Bailey, F.G. (1998) *Humbuggery and Manipulation*. Ithaca, NY and London: Cornell University Press.

Ball, A. and Peters, B.G. (2005) *Modern Politics and Government*, 7th edn. Basingstoke: Palgrave Macmillan.

Barber, B. (1998) 'Participation and Swiss democracy', *Government and Opposition*, 23 (1): 31–50.

Barber, J.D. (1972) *The Presidential Character*. Englewood Cliffs, NJ: Prentice-Hall.

Barber, J.D. (1985) *The Presidential Character*, 2nd edn Englewood Cliffs, NJ: Prentice-Hall.

Barth, F. (1959) *Political Leadership Amongst Swat Pathans*. London: The Athlone Press.

Bartolini, S. (1984) 'Institutional constraints and party competition in the French party system', *West European Politics*, 7: 103–27.

Bates, R. (1991) *Beyond the Miracle of the Market*. Cambridge: Cambridge University Press.

Becker, G. (1985) 'Public policies, pressure groups and dead-weight costs', *Journal of Public Economics*, 28: 329–47.

Bellamy, R. (1996) 'The political form of the constitution: the separation of powers, rights and representative democracy', *Political Studies*, 44, 436-456.

Bendix, R. 'Compliant behaviour and individual personality', *The American Journal of Sociology*, 58: 292–303.

Berrington, H. (1971) 'The fiery chariot: British prime ministers and the search for love', *British Journal of Political Science*, 4: 345–69.

Bingham Powell, G. and Whitten, G. (1993) 'A cross-national analysis of economic voting: taking account of the political context', *American Journal of Political Science*, 37 (2): 391–414.

Blais, A. (1988) 'The classification of electoral systems', *European Journal of Political Research*, 16: 99–110.

Blais, A. (2000) *To Vote or Not to Vote: The Merits and Limits of Rational Choice Theory*. Pittsburg, PA: University of Pittsburg Press.

Blais, A. and Carty, R. (1990) 'Does proportional representation foster voter turnout?', *European Journal of Political Research*, 18 (2): 167–81.

Blalock, H. and Blalock, A. (1970) *Introduction to Social Research*. Englewood Cliffs, NJ: Prentice Hall.

Blix, H. (2004) *Disarming Iraq*. London: Bloomsbury.

Blondel, J. (1980) *World Leaders*. London: Sage.

Blondel, J. (1987) *Political Leadership*. London: Sage.

Blondel, J. (1995) *Comparative Government*, 2nd edn. London: Harvester Wheatsheaf.

Bluth, C. (2004) 'The British road to war', *International Affairs*, 80 (5): 851–72.

Bluth, C. and Hoggart, P. (2005) 'Rejoinders', *Journal of Politics and International Relations*, 7: 588–604.

Bohm-Bawerk, E. von (1959) *Capital and Interest*. South Holland, IL: Libertarian Press.

Boix, C. (1999) 'Selecting the rules of the game: the choice of electoral systems in advanced democracies', *American Political Science Review*, 93 (3): 609–24.

Booth, K. (1995) 'Human wrongs and international relations', *International Affairs*, 71 (1): 103–26.

Börzel, T. (2001) 'Europeanization and territorial institutional change: toward cooperative regionalism', in M. Green Cowles, J. Caporaso and T. Riise (eds), *Transforming Europe: Europeanization and Domestic Change*. Ithaca, NY: Cornell University Press. pp. 144–9.

Bouma, G.D. and Atkinson, G.B.J (1995) *A Handbook for Social Science Research: A Comprehensive and Practical Guide for Students*. Oxford: Oxford University Press.

Bowles, S. and Gintis, H. (1976) *Schooling in Capitalist America*. New York: Basic Books.

Braverman, H. (1974) *Labour and Monopoly Capital*. New York: Monthly Review Press.

Brennan, G. and Lomasky, L. (1993) *Democracy and Decision*. Cambridge: Cambridge University Press.

Brewster Smith, M. (1968) 'A map for the analysis of personality and politics', *Journal of Social Issues*, 24 (3): 15–28.

Bronfenbrenner, U. (1960) 'Personality and politics', *Journal of Social Issues*, 16: 54–63.

Broughton, D. and Donovan, M. (eds) (1999) *Changing Party Systems in Western Europe*. London and New York: Pinter.

Brown, G. (2007) 'Remarks by the Rt. Honourable Gordon Brown MP, Chancellor of the Exchequer, at a seminar on "Britishness" at the Commonwealth Club, London'. Available at: http://www.hm-treasury.

gov.uk/newsroom_and_speeches/speeches/chancellorexchequer/speech_chx_270207.cfm (accessed 1 February 2008).

Brubaker, R. (1996) *Nationalism Reframed: Nationhood and the National Question in the New Europe*. Cambridge: Cambridge University Press.

Bryce, J. (1921) *Modern Democracies*. London: Macmillan.

Buchanan, J. (1991) *Constitutional Economics*. Oxford: Basil Blackwell.

Buchanan, J. and Tullock, G. (1962) *The Calculus of Consent*. Ann Arbor, MI: University of Michigan Press.

Budge, I. (1996) *The New Politics of Direct Democracy*. Oxford: Polity.

Budge, I., Klingemann, H-D., Volkens, A., Bara, J. and Tanenbaum, E. (2001) *Mapping Policy Preferences: Estimates for Parties, Electors and Governments, 1945–1998*. Oxford: Oxford University Press.

Budge, I., Robertson, D. and Hearl, D.J. (eds) (1987) *Ideology, Strategy and Party Change: Spatial Analysis of Post-war Election Programmes in 19 Democracies*. Cambridge: Cambridge University Press.

Bull, P.E. (1988) 'Interruptions in interviews', *Journal of Language and Society*, 7: 35–45.

Burns, J.M. (1978) *Leadership*. New York: Harper and Row.

Burns, J.M. (2003) *Transformational Leadership*. Oxford: Oxford University Press.

Butterfield, H. (1953) 'The role of the individual in history 2', *History*, 139 (9): 1–17.

Butterfield, H. (1962) *The Statecraft of Machiavelli*. London: Collier.

Byman, D.L. and Pollack, K.M. (2001) 'Let us now praise great men', *International Security*, 25 (4): 107–46.

Campbell, A., Converse, P., Miller, W.E. and Stokes, D.E. (1960) *The American Voter*. New York: Wiley.

Carlyle, T. (1993) *On Heroes, Hero-Worship, and the Heroic in History*. Oxford: Oxford University Press.

Castles, F.G. (2000) 'Federalism, fiscal decentralization and economic performance', in U. Wachendorfer-Schmidt (ed.), *Federalism and Political Performance*. London: Routledge. pp. 177–95.

Chapman, G. Fraser, C., Gaber, I. and Kumar, K. (1997) *Environmentalism and the Mass Media*. London: Routledge.

Charlton, P. (2003) *Analysing Political Discourse*. London: Routledge.

Chong, D. (1991) *Collective Action and the Civil Rights Movement*. Chicago, IL: Chicago University Press.

Chong, D. (2002) *Rational Lives: Norms and Values in Politics and Society*. Chicago, IL: University of Chicago Press.

Cigler, C. and Loomis, B. (eds) (2002) *Interest Group Politics*. Washington: Congressional Quarterly Press.

Clarke, H., Stewart, M., Sanders, D. and Whiteley, P. (2004) *Political Choice in Britain*. Oxford: Oxford University Press.

Coleman, J. (1996) *The Individual in Political Theory and Practice*. Oxford: Oxford University Press.

Connor, W. (1994) *Ethnonationalism: The Quest for Understanding*. Princeton, NJ: Princeton University Press.

Cowie, L.W. and Wolfson, R. (1985) *Years of Nationalism: European History 1815–1890*. Oxford: Hodder & Stoughton.

Cox, G. (1997) *Making Votes Count*. Cambridge: Cambridge University Press.

Coyle, M. (1995) *The Prince: New Interdisciplinary Essays*. Manchester: Manchester University Press.

Crewe, I. and Denver, D. (eds) (1985) *Electoral Change in Western Democracies*. Beckenham: Croom Helm.

Crick, B. (1964) *In Defence of Politics*. Harmondsworth: Penguin.

Crick, B. (1973) *Basic Forms of Government: A Sketch and a Model*. London: Macmillan.

Curtice, J. and Holmberg, S. (2005) 'Party leaders and party choice', in J. Thomassen (ed.), *The European Voter: A Comparative Study of Modern Democracies*. Oxford: Oxford University Press. pp. 235–53.

Daguerre, A. (2004) 'Importing workfare: policy transfer of social and labour market policies from the USA to Britain under new labour', *Social Policy and Administration*, 38 (1): 41–56.

Dahl, R.A. (1960) *Who Governs?*. New Haven, CT: Yale University Press.

Dahl, R.A. (1970) *After The Revolution*. New Haven, CT: Yale University Press.

Dahl, R.A. (1993) 'Pluralism', in J. Krieger (ed.), *The Oxford Companion to Politics of the World*. Oxford: Oxford University Press. pp. 704–7.

Dahrendorf, R. (1990) *Reflections of the Revolution in Europe*. New York: Random House.

Dalton, R. (1994) *The Green Rainbow: Environmental Groups in Western Europe*. New Haven, CT: Yale University Press.

Dalton, R.J. (1996) *Citizen Politics: Public Opinion and Political Parties in Advanced Western Democracies*. London: Chatham House.

Dalton, R.J. (2002) *Citizen Politics: Public Opinion and Political Parties in Advanced Industrial Democracies*, 3rd edn. New York: Chatham House.

Dalton, R.J. and Wattenberg, M.P. (2000) *Parties Without Partisans: Political Change in Advanced Industrial Democracies*. Oxford: Oxford University Press.

Dalton, R.J., Flanagan, S. and Beck, P. (1984) *Electoral Change in Advanced Industrial Societies*. Princeton, NJ: Princeton University Press.

Denver, D. (2007) *Elections and Voters in Britain*, 2nd edn. Basingstoke: Palgrave Macmillan.

Denzin, N. (1970) *Sociological Methods: A Sourcebook*. Chicago, IL: Aldine Press.

Denzin, N. (1997) *Interpretative Ethnography: Ethnographic Practices for the Twenty-First Century*. Thousand Oaks, CA: Sage.

de Tocqueville, A. (1964) *Souvenirs*. Paris: Oeuvres Complètes. vol. XII. pp. 83–4.

Deutscher, I. (1954) *The Prophet Outcast*. Oxford: Oxford University Press.

Devine, F. (2002) 'Qualitative methods', in D. Marsh and G. Stoker (eds), *Theory and Methods in Political Science*. Basingstoke: Palgrave Macmillan. pp. 197–215.

Dicey, A.V. (1939) *Introduction to the Study of the Law of the Constitution*, 10th edn. London: Macmillan.

Dolowitz, D., Hulme, R., Nellis, M. and O'Neill, F. (2000) *Policy Transfer and British Social Policy: Learning from the USA?* Buckingham: Open University Press.

Dogan, M. and Kazancigil, A. (ed.) (1994) *Comparing Nations: Concepts, Strategies, Substance*. Oxford and Cambridge, MA: Blackwell.

Douglas, M. (1982) *In the Active Voice*. London: Routledge.

Douglas, M. (1987) *How Institutions Think*. London: Routledge.

Downs, A. (1957) *An Economic Theory of Democracy*. New York: Harper and Row.

Dunleavy, P. (1991) *Democracy, Bureaucracy and Public Choice*. London: Harvester/Wheatsheaf.

Duverger, M. (1951) *Les Partis Politiques*. 1976 reprint, Paris: Armand Colin.

Duverger, M. (1959) *Political Parties*, 2nd edn. London: Methuen.

Duverger, M. (1980) 'A new Political system model: semi-presidential government', *European Journal of Political Research*, 8 (2): 165–87.

Dyson, K., Humphreys, P., Negrine, R. and Simon, J-P. (1988) *Broadcasting and News Media Policies in Western Europe*. London: Routledge.

Economist Intelligence Unit (2005) *The World in 2005*. London: Economist Intelligence Unit.

Edelman, M. (1964) *The Symbolic Uses of Politics*. Urbana, IL: University of Illinois Press.

Edelman, M. (1971) *Politics as Symbolic Action*. Chicago, IL: Markham Publishing Company.

Edelman, M. (1978) *Political Language*. New York, London: Academic Press.

Edelman, M. (1988) *Constructing the Political Spectacle*. Chicago, IL: Chicago University Press.

Edinger, L.J. (1964) 'Political science and political biography', *Journal of Politics*, 26: 423–43.

Edinger, L.J. (ed.) (1967) *Political Leadership in Industrial Societies*. New York: John Wiley.

Elazar, D.J. (1984) *American Federalism: A View from the States*, 3rd edn. New York: Harper & Row.

Elazar, D.J. (1987) *Exploring Federalism*. Tuscaloosa, AL: University of Alabama Press.

Elgie, R. (1995) *Political Leadership in Liberal Democracies*. London: Macmillan.

Elgie, R. (2004) 'Semi-presidentialism: concepts, consequences and contesting explanations', *Political Studies Review*, 2 (3): 314–30.

Elias, N. (1983) *The Court Society*. Oxford: Basil Blackwell.

Eliasoph, N. (2000) *Avoiding Politics*. Cambridge: Cambridge University Press.

Ellis, S.G. (1999) *Ireland in the Age of the Tudors 1447–1603: English Expansion and the End of Gaelic Rule*. London: Longman.

Elster, J. (1985) *Making Sense of Marx*. Cambridge: Cambridge University Press.

Enelow, J. and Hinich, M. (1984) *The Spatial Theory of Voting: An Introduction*. Cambridge: Cambridge University Press.

Erk, J. (2008) *Explaining Federalism: State, Society and Congruence in Austria, Belgium, Canada, Germany and Switzerland*. London: Routledge.

Evans-Prichard, E. (1940) *The Nuers*. Oxford: The Clarendon Press.

Eysenck, H.J. (1969) *The Psychology of Politics*. London: Routledge.

Fairclough, N. (2003) *Analysing Discourse*. London and New York: Routledge.

Fairclough, N. (2000) *New Labour, New Language?* London: Routledge.

Farber, S.M. and Wilson, R.H. (eds) (1963) *The Potential of Women*. New York: McGraw-Hill.

Farrell, D. (2001) *Electoral Systems: A Comparative Introduction*. Basingstoke: Palgrave.

Fausto-Sterling, A. (1985) *Myths of Gender*. New York: Basic Books.

Femia, J.V. (2004) *Machiavelli Revisited*. Cardiff: University of Wales Press.

Fielding, N. (1981) *The National Front*. London: Routledge and Kegan Paul.

Fielding, N. (1993) 'Qualitative interviewing', in N. Gilbert (ed.), *Researching Social Life*. London: Sage. pp. 135–53.

Finer, S.E. (1970) *Comparative Government*. London: Allen Lane.

Finlayson, A. (2002) 'Elements of a Blairite image of leadership', *Parliamentary Affairs*, 55 (3): 586–99.

Fishkin, J. (1993) *Democracy and Deliberation*. New Haven, CT: Yale University Press.

Foucault, M. (1965) *Madness and Civilization*. London: Tavistock.

Foucault, M. (1979) *Discipline and Punish*. New York: Vintage Books.

Foucault, M. (1988) 'The ethic of the care of the self as a practice of freedom', in J. Bernauer and D. Rasmussen (eds), *The Final Foucault*. Cambridge, MA: MIT Press.

Foucault, M. (1991) 'Governmentality', in G. Burchell, C., Gordon and P. Miller (eds), *The Foucault Effect: Essays in Governmentality*. London: Harvester/Wheatsheaf.

Franklin, M. (2004) *Voter Turnout and the Dynamics of Electoral Competition in Established Democracies*. Cambridge: Cambridge University Press.

Gallagher, M., Laver, M. and Mair, P. (1992) *Representative Government in Western Europe*. New York: McGraw Hill.

Gallagher, M., Laver, M. and Mair, P. (2000) *Representative Government in Modern Europe*. New York: McGraw Hill.

Gamson, W.A. (1992) *Talking Politics*. Cambridge: Cambridge University Press.

Garver, E. (1987) *Machiavelli and the History of Prudence*. Madison, WI: University of Wisconsin Press.

George, A.L. (1974) 'Assessing presidential character', *World Politics*, 26 (2): 234–82.

George, A.L. and George, J.L. (1998) *Presidential Personality and Performance*. Boulder, CO: Westview.

Gerth, H.H. and Mills, C.W. (eds) (1947) *From Max Weber*. London: Routledge.

Gellner, E. (1983) *Nations and Nationalism*. Oxford: Blackwell.

Gellner, E. (1996) 'Do nations have navels: reply to Anthony, D. Smith', *Nations and Nationalism*, 2 (3): 366–70.

Gibson, J.L. (1983) 'From simplicity to complexity: the development of theory in the study of judicial behaviour', *Political Behavior*, 5 (1): 7–49.

Gibson, J.L. and Caldeira, G.A. (2003) 'Defenders of democracy? Legitimacy, popular acceptance, and the South African constitutional court', *Journal of Politics*, 65 (1): 1–30.

Gibson, J.L., Caldeira, G.A. and Baird, V.A. (1998) 'On the legitimacy of national high courts', *American Political Science Review*, 92 (2): 343–58.

Giddens, A. (1984) *The Constitution of Society: An Introduction to the Theory of Structuration*. Cambridge: Polity Press.

Goffman, E. (1961) *Asylums*. London: Penguin.

Goldberg, S. (1993) *Why Men Rule*. Chicago: Open Court.

Goldstone, J.A. (1991) *Revolution and Rebellion in the Early Modern World*. Berkeley, CA: University of California Press.

Goodin, R. (1996) 'The defense of deadlock', *American Political Science Review*, 90: 331–43.

Gouldner, A.W. (1965) *Studies in Leadership*. New York: Russel and Russel.

Gramsci, A. (1971) *Selections from Prison Notebooks*. London: Lawrence and Wishart.

Graham, J.W. (1995) 'Leadership, moral development, and citizen behaviour', *Business Ethics Quarterly*, 5 (1): 43–54.

Granovetter, M.S. (1985) 'Economic action and social structure: the problem of embeddedness', *American Journal of Sociology*, 91 (3): 481–510.

Green, D. and Shapiro, I. (1994) *Pathologies of Rational Choice*. New Haven, CT: Yale University Press.

Green, P. (1981) *The Pursuit of Inequality*. Oxford: Robertson.

Greenstein, F.I. (1967) 'The impact of personality on politics', *American Political Science Review*, 61 (3): 629–41.

Greenstein, F.I. (1975) *Personality and Politics*. New York: Norton.

Greenstein, F.I. (1992) 'Can politics and personality be studied systematically?', *Political Psychology*, 13 (1): 105–28.

Greenstein, F.I. (2000a) *The Presidential Difference*. Princeton, NJ: Princeton University Press.

Greenstein, F.I. (2000b) 'The qualities of effective presidents', *Presidential Studies Quarterly*, 30: 178–85.

Guarnieri, C. and Pederzoli, P. (2002) *The Power of Judges: A Comparative Study of Courts and Democracy*. Oxford Socio-Legal Studies: Oxford University Press.

Hague, R. and Harrop, M. *Comparative Politics: An Introduction*, 7th edn. Basingstoke: Palgrave Macmillan.

Hall, P. (1986) *Governing the Economy*. New York: Oxford University Press.

Hall, P. and Taylor, R. (1996) 'Political science and the three institutionalisms', *Political Studies*, 44 (4): 936–57.

Hamilton, A., Madison, J. and Jay, J. ([1778–8] 1961) *The Federalist Papers*. New York: Mentor.

Hampshire, S. (ed.) (1991) *Public and Private Morality*. Cambridge: Cambridge University Press.

Hardin, R. (1995) *One for All: The Logic of Group Conflict*. Princeton, NJ: Princeton University Press.

Hardin, R. (1996) *One for All: The Logic of Group Collective Action*. Princeton, NJ: Princeton University Press.

Hargrove, E.C. (1998) *The President as Leader*. Lawrence, KA: University Press of Kansas.

Harrop, M. and Miller, W. (1987) *Elections and Voters. A Comparative Introduction*. Basingstoke: Macmillan.

Hastings, A. (1997) *The Construction of Nationhood: Ethnicity, Religion and Nationalism*. Cambridge: Cambridge University Press.

Hermann, M.C. (1995) 'Advice and advisers in the Clinton presidency', in S.A. Renshon (ed.), *The Clinton Presidency*. Boulder, CO: Westview.

Hobbes, Thomas ([1660] 1996) *Leviathan*. Cambridge: Cambridge University Press.

Hobsbawm, E. (1990) *Nations and Nationalism since 1780*. Cambridge: Cambridge University Press.

Hobsbawm, E. and Ranger, T. (eds) (1983) *The Invention of Tradition*. Cambridge: Cambridge University Press.

Hoggart, P. (2005) 'Iraq: Blair's mission impossible', *British Journal of Politics and International Relations*, 7 (1): 418–28.

Hood, C. (2000) *The Art of the State*. Oxford: Oxford University Press.

Hopkin, J. (2002) 'Comparative methods', in D. Marsh and G. Stoker (eds), *Theory and Methods in Political Science*. Basingstoke: Palgrave Macmillan. pp. 249–67.

Horowitz, D. (1990) 'Comparing democratic systems', *Journal of Democracy*, 1 (4): 73–9.

Hroch, M. (1995) 'National self-determination from a historical perspective', in S. Periwal (ed.), *Notions of Nationalism*. Budapest: Central European University Press. pp. 65–82.

Hueglin, T.O. and Fenna, A. (2006) *Comparative Federalism: A Systematic Inquiry*. Peterborough, Ontario: Broadview Press.

Hutchinson, J. (2005) *Nations as Zones of Conflict*. London: Sage.

Inglehart, R. (1977) *The Silent Revolution – Changing Values and Political Styles*. Princeton, NJ: Princeton University Press.

Inglehart, R. (1990) *Culture Shift in Advanced Industrial Societies*. Princeton, NJ: Princeton University Press.

International Institute for Democracy and Electoral Assistance (n.d.) 'Survey on voter turnout'. Available at: http://www.idea.int/vt/survey/index.cfm

Iremonger, L. (1970) *The Fiery Chariot*. London: Secker.

Isaacson, W. (1992) *Kissinger*. London: Faber and Faber.

Jasiewicz, J. (2003) 'Elections and voting behaviour', in S. White, J. Batt and P.G. Lewis (eds), *Developments in Central and East European Politics*. Basingstoke: Palgrave Macmillan.

Jay, A. (1987) *Management and Machiavelli*. London: Hutchinson.

Jessop, B. (1990) *State Theory*. Cambridge: Polity Press.

John, P. (2002) 'Quantitative methods', in D. Marsh and G. Stoker (eds), *Theory and Methods in Political Science*. Basingstoke: Palgrave Macmillan. pp. 216–30.

Jones, B.D. (1989) *Leadership and Politics*. Lawrence KA: University Press of Kansas.

Jones, G. (1991) 'West European prime ministers in perspective', *West European Politics*, 14: 163–78.

Judd, C.M., Smith, E.R. and Kidder, L.H. (1991) *Research Methods in Social Relations*, 6th edn. Fort Worth, TX: Harcourt Brace and Company.

Kagan, S. (1989) *The Limits of Morality*. Oxford: Oxford University Press.

Kampfner, J. (2004) *Blair's Wars*. Glencoe, IL: Free Press.

Katz, R. (1997) *Democracy and Elections*. Oxford: Oxford University Press.

Keating, M. (2001) *Plurinational Democracy: Stateless Nations in a Post-Sovereignty Era*. Oxford: Oxford University Press.

Kellerman, B.J. (1984) *Leadership: Multidisciplinary Perspectives*. Englewood Cliffs, NJ: Prentice Hall.

Keman, H. (2000) 'Federalism and policy performance: a conceptual and empirical enquiry', in U. Wachendorfer-Schmidt (ed.), *Federalism and Political Performance*. London: Routledge. pp. 196–227.

Key Jr, V.O. (1955) 'A theory of critical elections', *Journal of Politics*, 17: 3–18.

King, A. (1976) 'Modes of executive-legislative relations: Great Britain, France and West Germany', *Legislative Studies Quarterly*, 1 (1): 11–34.

King, A. (1981) 'How to strengthen legislatures: assuming that we want to', in N.J. Ornstein (ed.), *The Role of the Legislature in Western Democracies*. Washington, DC: American Enterprise Institute. pp. 77–89.

King, G., Keohane, R.O. and Verba, S. (1994) *Designing Social Inquiry: Scientific Inference in Qualitative Research*. Princeton, NJ: Princeton University Press.

Klingemann, H-D., Volkens, A., Bara, J. Budge, I. and McDonald, M.D. (2006) *Mapping Policy Preferences II: Estimates for Parties, Elections and Governments in Eastern Europe, European Union and OECD, 1990–2003*. Oxford: Oxford University Press.

Kornai, J. (1992) *The Socialist System: The Political Economy of Communism*. Princeton, NJ: Princeton University Press.

Kymlicka, W. (2001) *Politics in the Vernacular: Nationalism, Multiculturalism, and Citizenship*. Oxford: Oxford University Press.

Laitin, D. (2007) *Nations, States and Violence*. Oxford: Oxford University Press.

Landes, R. (1995) *The Canadian Polity in Comparative Perspective*. Scarborough, Ontario: Prentice Hall.

Landman, T. (2003) *Issues and Methods in Comparative Politics: An Introduction,* 2nd edn. London: Routledge.

Landman, T. (2008) *Issues and Methods in Comparative Politics: An Introduction*, 3rd edn. London and New York: Routledge.

Lane, J-E. and Ersson, S. (1994) *Comparative Politics: An Introduction and New Approach*. Cambridge: Polity.

Lane, J-E. and Ersson, S. (1999) *The New Institutional Politics*. London: Routledge.

Lane, J-E. and Ersson, S.O. (1997) 'Is federalism superior?', in B. Steunenberg and F. van Vught (eds), *Political Institutions and Public Policy: Perspectives on European Decision Making*. Dordrecht: Kluwer Academic Publishers.

Laver, M. and Schofield, N. (1990) *Multiparty Government: The Politics of Coalition in Europe*. Oxford: Oxford University Press.

Lange, B-P. and Ward, D. (eds) (2004) *The Media and Elections: A Handbook and Comparative Study*. Mahwah, NJ: Lawrence Erlbaum.

Lasswell, H.D. (1930) *Psychopathology and Politics*. Chicago, IL: Chicago University Press.

Lasswell, H. (1948) *Power and Personality*. New York: Norton.

Lasswell, H. (1962) *Power and Personality*. New York: Viking Press.

Lasswell, H. (1963) *The Future of Political Science*. New York: Atherton Press.

Ledeen, M. (1999) *Machiavelli on Modern Leadership*. New York: Truman Talley Books.

LeDuc, L., Niemi, R.G. and Norris, P. (eds) (1996) *Comparing Democracies: Elections and Voting in Global Perspective*. London: Sage.

Lefever, E.W. (1972) *Ethics and World Politics*. Baltimore, MD: Johns Hopkins.

Leonard, J. (1989) 'Public vs. private claims', *Political Theory*, 12 (4): 491–50.

Levin, M. (1987) *Feminism and Freedom*. New Brunswick, NJ: Transaction Books.

Levinson, D.J. (1958) 'The relevance of personality for political participation', *Public Opinion Quarterly*, 22: 3–10.

Lewontin, R.C., Rose, S. and Kanin, L.J. (1984) *Not in Our Genes*. Harmondsworth: Penguin.

Lichbach, M. and Zuckerman, A. (eds) (1999) *Comparative Politics: Rationality, Culture and Structure*. Cambridge: Cambridge University Press.

Lijphart, A. (1971) 'Comparative politics and the comparative model', *American Political Science Review*, 65: 682–93.

Lijphart, A. (1977) *Democracy in Plural Societies: A Comparative Exploration*. New Haven, CT: Yale University Press.

Lijphart, A. (1994) *Electoral Systems and Party Systems: A Study of Twenty-Seven Democracies, 1945–90*. Oxford: Oxford University Press.

Lijphart, A. (1999) *Patterns of Democracy: Government Forms and Performance in Thirty-Six Countries*. New Haven, CT: Yale University Press.

Lijphart, A. and Crepaz, M. (1991) 'Corporatism and consensus democracy in eighteen countries: conceptual and empirical linkages', *British Journal of Political Science*, 21: 235–46.

Linz, J.J. (1990) 'The perils of Presidentialism', *Journal of Democracy*, 1 (1): 51–69.

Linz, J.J. (1994) 'Presidential or parliamentary democracy: does it make a difference?', in J.J. Linz and A. Valenzuela (eds), *The Failure of Presidential Democracy*. Baltimore, MD: Johns Hopkins University Press. pp. 3–87.

Lipset, S. and Rokkan, S. (eds) (1967) *Party Systems and Voter Alignments: Cross-National Perspectives*. New York: The Free Press.

Lister, F.K. (1999) *The Early Security Confederations: From the Ancient Greeks to the United Colonies of New England*. Westport, CT: Greenwood Press.

Lowndes, V. (2002) 'Institutionalism', in D. Marsh and G. Stoker (eds), *Theory and Methods in Political Science*. Basingstoke: Palgrave Macmillan. pp. 90–108.

Lukes, S. (1974) *Power: A Radical View*. Basingstoke: Macmillan.

McAlpine, A. (1992) *The Servant*. London: Faber and Faber.

McGarry, J. and O'Leary, B. (2006) 'Federation as a method of ethnic conflict regulation', in S. Noel (ed.), *From Power-Sharing to Democracy: Post-Conflict Institutions in Ethnically Divided Societies*. London: McGill-Queen's University Press. pp. 263–96.

McLean, I. (1991) 'Forms of representation and systems of voting', in D. Held (ed.), *Political Theory Today*. Cambridge: Polity Press. pp. 172–97.

McLean, I. (1996) *Oxford Concise Dictionary of Politics*. Oxford: Oxford University Press.

Mair, P. and Mudde, C. (1998) 'The party family and its study', *Annual Review of Political Science*, 1: 211–29.

Mainwaring, S. (1993) 'Presidentialism, multipartism and democracy: the difficult combination', *Comparative Political Studies*, 26 (2): 198–228.

Mann, M. (1995) 'A political theory of nationalism and its excesses', in S. Periwal (ed.), *Notions of Nationalism*. Budapest: Central European University Press.

March, J.G. and Olsen, J.P. (1989) *Rediscovering Institutions*. New York: Free Press.

March, J.G. and Olsen, J.P (2006) 'Elaborating the "new institutionalism"', in R.A.W. Rhodes, S. Binder and B. Rockman (eds), *The Oxford Handbook of Political Institutions*. Oxford: Oxford University Press. pp. 3–20.

Marsh, D. and Stoker G (eds) (2002) *Theory and Methods in Political Science*. Basingstoke: Palgrave Macmillan.

Marx, K. (1906) *Capital*. Vol. 1. Chicago, IL: Charles H. Kerr and Co.

Marx, K. and Engels, F. (1969) *Selected Works*. Moscow: Progress Publishers.

May, T. (1997) *Social Research: Issues, Methods and Process*. Buckingham: Open University Press.

Mayhew, D. (1975) *Congress: the Electoral Connection*. Yale, CT: Yale University Press.

Merelman, R. (1991) *Partial Visions: Culture and Politics in Britain, Canada and the United States*. Madison, WI: University of Wisconsin Press.

Merrill, S. and Grofman, B. (1999) *A Unified Theory of Voting: Directional and Proximity Spatial Models*. Cambridge: Cambridge University Press.

Mezey, M. (1979) *Comparative Legislatures*. Durham, NC: Duke University Press.

Milbrath, L. (1965) *Political Participation*. Chicago, IL: Rand McNally.

Miliband, R. (1969) *The State in Capitalist Society*. London: Wiedenfield and Nicolson.

Mitra, S. (2000) 'The nation, state and the federal process in India', in U. Wachendorfer-Schmidt (ed.), *Federalism and Political Performance*. London: Routledge. pp. 40–57.

Moe, T. (1981) 'Towards a broader view of interest groups', *Journal of Politics*, 43: 531–43.

Moon, J. (1995) 'Innovative leadership and political change', *Governance*, 8 (1): 1–25.

Morris, C.W. (1949) *Signs, Language and Behaviour*. Englewood Cliffs, NJ: Prentice Hall.

Nardin, T. (1992) 'International ethics and international law', *Review of International Studies*, 18 (1): 19–30.

Nardin, T. and Mapel, D. (eds) (1992) *Traditions of International Ethics*. Cambridge: Cambridge University Press.

Needham, C. (2007) *The Reform of Public Services Under New Labour: Narratives of Consumerism*. Basingstoke: Palgrave Macmillan.

Neustadt, R.E. (1990) *Presidential Power*. Glencoe, IL: Free Press.

Neustadt, R.E. (1994) 'Virtue and the civil prince', *Presidential Studies Quarterly*, 34 (3): 464–73.

Niebuhr, R. (1932) *Moral Man and Immoral Society*. New York: Scribners.

Niskanen, W. (1995) *Bureaucracy and Public Economics*. Cheltenham: Edward Elgar.

Norris, P. (ed.) (1999) *Critical Citizens: Global Support for Democratic Government*. Oxford: Oxford University Press.

Norris, P. (2004) *Electoral Engineering: Voting Rules and Political Behaviour*. Cambridge: Cambridge University Press.

North, D. and Thomas, R. (1973) *The Rise of the Western World: A New Economic History*. Cambridge: Cambridge University Press.

North, D. (1981) *Structure and Change in Economic History*. New York: W.W. Norton.

North, D. (1990) *Institutions, Institutional Change and Economic Performance*. Cambridge: Cambridge University Press.

Norton, P. (1990a) 'Introduction', in P. Norton (ed.), *Legislatures*. Oxford: Oxford University Press.

Norton, P. (1990b) 'Parliaments: a framework for analysis', in P. Norton (ed.), *Parliaments in Western Europe*. London: Frank Cass.

O'Duffy, B. (2007) *British-Irish Relations and Northern Ireland: From Violent Politics to Conflict Regulation*. Dublin: Irish Academic Press.

O'Leary, B. (2001) 'An iron law of nationalism and federation? A (neo-Diceyian) theory of the necessity of a federal Staatsvolk, and of consociational rescue', *Nations and Nationalism*, 7 (3): 273–96.

Ollman, B. 'Toward a Marxist interpretation of the US constitution'. Available at: http://www.nyu.edu/projects/ollman/docs/usconstitution.php (accessed March 2008).

Olson, D.M. and Mezey, M.L. (1991) 'Parliaments and public policy', in D.M. Olson and M.L. Mezey (eds) *Legislatures in the Policy Process*. Cambridge: Cambridge University Press. pp. 1–21.

Olson, M. (1965) *The Logic of Collective Action*. Cambridge, MA: Harvard University Press.

Olson, M. (1971) *The Logic of Collective Action, revised edn*. Cambridge, MA: Harvard University Press.

Olson, M. (1982) *The Rise and Decline of Nations*. New Haven, CT: Yale University Press.

Olson, M. (2000) *Power and Prosperity*. New York: Basic Books.

Oppenheimer, J. and Young, O.R. (1971) *Political Leadership and Collective Goods*. Princeton, NJ: Princeton University Press.

Osborne, D. and Gaebler, E. (1992) *Reinventing Government*. Reading, MA: Addision-Wesley.

Packenham, R.A. (1970) 'Legislatures and political development', in A. Kornberg and L.D. Musolf (eds), *Legislatures in Developmental Perspective*. Durham, NC: Duke University Press. pp. 521–37.

Padgett, S. (1994) 'Introduction', in S. Padgett (ed.), *Adenauer to Kohl: The Development of the German Chancellorship*. London: Hurst and Co.

Pagano, M. (2007) 'The dynamics of federalism in national and supranational political systems', in M. Pagano and R. Leonardi (eds), *The Dynamics of Federalism in National and Supranational Political Systems*. Basingstoke: Palgrave.

Paige, G.D. (1965) *The Scientific Study of Political Leadership*. New Haven, CT: Yale University Press.

Panebianco, A. (1988) *Political Parties: Organization and Power*. Cambridge: Cambridge University Press.

Pennings, P., Keman, H. and Kleinnijenhuis, J. (1999) *Doing Research in Political Science*. London: Sage.

Peters, B.G. (1996) 'Political institutions, old and new', in R. Goodin and H-D. Klingemann (eds), *A New Handbook of Political Science*. Oxford: Oxford University Press. pp. 205–20.

Peters, B.G. (1998) *Comparative Politics: Theory and Methods*. New York: New York University Press.

Peters, B.G. (2001) *The Politics of Bureaucracy*. London: Routledge.

Plekhanov, G. (1940) *The Role of the Individual in History*. London: Lawrence and Wishart.

Polanyi, K. (1944) *The Great Transformation*. New York: Holt, Reinhart and Winston.

Polsby, N.W. (1975) 'Legislatures', in F.I. Greenstein and N.W. Polsby (eds), *Handbook of Political Science*. Reading, MA: Addison-Wesley.

Pondy, L.R. (1978) 'Leadership is a language game', in M. McCall and M. Lombardo (eds), *Leadership*. Durham, NC: Duke University Press. pp. 87–99.

Posner, R. (1992) *Sex and Reason*. Cambridge, MA: Harvard University Press.

Posner, R. (1995) *Overcoming Law*. Cambridge, MA: Harvard University Press.

Poulantzas, N. (1975) *Classes in Contemporary Capitalism*. London: New Left Books.

Poulantzas, N. (1978) *State, Power, Socialism*. London: New Left Books.

Power, T.J. and Gasiorowski, M.J. (1997) 'Institutional design and democratic consolidation in the third world', *Comparative Political Studies*, 30 (2): 123–55.

Protsyk, O. (2006) 'Intra-executive competition between president and prime minister: patterns of institutional conflict and cooperation under semi-presidentialism', *Political Studies*, 54 (2): 219–44.

Przeworski, A. and Teune, H. (1970) *The Logic of Comparative Social Inquiry*. New Haven, CT: Yale University Press.

Rae, D. (1967) *The Political Consequences of Electoral Laws*. New Haven, CT: Yale University Press.

Ramsay, M. (2000) 'Are Machiavellian tactics still appropriate or defensible in politics?', in P. Harris, A. Lock and P. Rees (eds), *Machiavelli, Marketing and Management*. London: Routledge.

Ramsay, P. (2002) *The Just War*. Lanham, MD: Rowman and Littlefield.

Read, M. and Marsh, D. (2002) 'Combining quantitative and qualitative methods', in D. Marsh and G. Stoker (eds) *Theory and Methods in Political Science*. Basingstoke: Palgrave Macmillan. pp. 231–48.

Rebhorn, W.A. (1988) *Foxes and Lions*. Ithaca, NY: Cornell University Press.

Reeve, A. and Ware, A. (1992) *Electoral Systems: A Comparative and Theoretical Introduction*. London: Routledge.

Renshon, S.A. (ed.) (1995) *The Clinton Presidency*. Boulder, CO: Westview.

Renshon S.A. (1996) *The Psychological Assessment of Presidential Candidates*. New York: New York University Press.

Rhodes, R.A.W. (2006) 'Old institutionalism', in R.A.W. Rhodes, S. Binder and B. Rockman (eds), *The Oxford Handbook of Political Institutions*. Oxford: Oxford University Press. pp. 90–108.

Rhodes, R. and Dunleavy, P. (eds) (1995) *Prime Minister, Cabinet and Core Executive*. London: Macmillan.

Riker, W. (1975) 'Federalism', in I.F. Greenstein and W. Nelson Polsby (eds), *Handbook of Political Science*. Vol. 5. Reading, MA: Addison-Wesley.

Riker, W. (1982) *Liberalism Against Populism: A Confrontation Between the Theory of Democracy and the Theory of Social Choice*. Oxford: Freeman.

Riker, W. (1986) *The Art of Political Manipulation*. New Haven, CT: Yale University Press.

Riker, W. (1986) 'Duverger's law revisited', in B. Grofman and A. Lijphart (eds), *Electoral Laws and their Political Consequences*. New York: Agathon Press. pp. 19–42.

Robertson, D. (1998) *Judicial Discretion in the House of Lords*. Oxford: Clarendon Press.

Rockman, B.A. (1984) 'Legislative-executive relations and legislative oversight', *Legislative Studies Quarterly*, 9 (3): 387–440.

Roeder, P.G. (2005) 'Power dividing as an alternative to ethnic power sharing', in P.G. Roeder and D. Rothchild (eds), *Sustainable Peace: Power and Democracy after Civil Wars*. Ithaca, NY: Cornell University Press. pp. 51–82.

Roeder, P.G. and D. Rothchild (2005) *Sustainable Peace: Power and Democracy After Civil Wars*. Ithaca, NY: Cornell University Press.

Rogowski, R. (1989) *Coalitions and Commerce*. Princeton, NJ: Princeton University Press.

Rokkan, S. (1970) *Citizens, Elections, Parties: Approaches to the Comparative Study of the Process of Development*. Oslo: Universitetsforlaget.

Rootes, C. (ed.) (1999) *Environmental Movements: Local, National and Global*. London: Frank Cass.

Rose, R. (1991) 'Prime ministers in parliamentary democracies', *West European Politics*, 14 (2): 9–24.

Roseneil, S. (1995) *Disarming Patriarchy: Feminism and Political Action at Greenham*. Buckingham: Open University Press.

Rosenman, S.I. (1951) *Working with Roosevelt*. New York: Harper.

Rost, J.C. (1995) 'Leadership: a discussion about ethics', *Business Ethics Quarterly*, 5 (1): 129–42.

Rutherford, B.M. (1966) 'Psychopathology, decision-making, and political involvement', *Journal of Conflict Resolution*, 19: 387–407.

Rydin, Y. and Pennington, M. (2001) 'Discourses of the prisoners dilemma: the role of the local press in environmental policy', *Environmental Politics*, 10 (3): 48–71.

Sahlins, M. (1993) 'Poor man, rich man, big man, chief'', *Comparative Studies in Society and History*, 3: 19–63.

Sanders, D. (2002) 'Behaviouralism', in D. Marsh and G. Stoker (eds), *Theory and Methods in Political Science*. Basingstoke: Palgrave Macmillan. pp. 45–64.

Sanders, D. (2003) 'Party identification, economic perceptions, and voting in British general elections, 1974–97', *Electoral Studies*, 22 (2): 239–63.

Sanders, D. , Clarke, H., Stewart, M. and Whiteley, P. (2001) 'The economy and voting', in P. Norris (ed.), *Britain Votes 2001*. Oxford: Oxford University Press. pp. 225–38.

Sandler, T. (2000) *Economic Concepts for the Social Sciences*. Cambridge: Cambridge University Press.

Sartori, G. (1976) *Parties and Party Systems. A Framework for Analysis, Part 1*. Cambridge: Cambridge University Press.

Sartori, G. (1986) 'The influence of electoral systems: faulty laws or faulty method?', in B. Grofman and A. Liphart (eds), *Electoral Laws and their Political Consequences*. New York: Agathon Press. pp. 43–68.

Saunders, P. (1991) *A Nation of Homeowners*. London: Routledge.

Scharpf, F.W. (1991) *Crisis and Choice in European Social Democracy*. Ithaca, NY and London: Cornell University Press.

Schubert, G.A. (1965) *The Judicial Mind: The Attitudes and Ideologies of Supreme Court Justices, 1946–63*. Evanston, IL: Northwestern University Press.

Scott, J. (1985) *Weapons of the Weak: Everyday Forms of Peasant Resistance*. New Haven, CT: Yale University Press.

Shapiro, M. (1999) 'The European court of justice', in P. Craig and G. De Búrca (eds), *The Evolution of E.U. Law*. Oxford: Oxford University Press. pp. 321–47.

Shapiro, M. and Stone Sweet, A. (2002) *On Law, Politics and Judicialization*. Oxford: Oxford University Press.

Shepsle, K.A. and Bonchek, M.S. (1997) *Analysing Politics: Rationality, Behaviour, and Institutions*. New York: W.W. Norton.

Shorter Oxford English Dictionary (1983) Oxford: Guild Publishing in association with Oxford University Press.

Shugart, M.S. and Carey, J.M. (1992) *Presidents and Assemblies: Constitutional Design and Electoral Dynamics*. Cambridge: Cambridge University Press.

Siaroff, A. (2003) 'Comparative presidencies: The inadequacy of the presidential, semi-presidential and parliamentary distinction', European Journal of Political Research, 42 (3): 287-312.

Sifry, M. and Cerf, C. (eds) (2003) *The Iraq War Reader*. London: Simon & Schuster International.

Simon, H. (1957) *Models of Man*. New York: Wiley.

Singer, P. (2004) *The President of Good and Evil: Taking George W. Bush Seriously*. London: Granta Books.

Sisk, T. and Stefes, C. (2005) 'Power-sharing as an interim step in peace building: lessons from South Africa', in P. Roeder and D. Rothchild (eds), *Sustainable Peace: Power and Democracy After Civil Wars*. Ithaca, NY: Cornell University Press. pp. 293–318.

Skocpol, T. (1979) *States and Social Revolutions: A Comparative Analysis of France, Russia and China*. New York: Cambridge University Press.

Skowronek, S. (1999) *The Politics Presidents Make*. Cambridge, MA: Harvard University Press.

Smith, A.D. (1998) *Nationalism and Modernism: A Critical Survey of Recent Theories of Nations and Nationalism*. London: Routledge.

Smith, M.J. (1998) 'Reconceptualising the British state: theoretical and empirical challenges to central government', *Public Administration*, 76 (1): 45–72.

Somers, C. and Somers, F. (2001) *Vice and Virtue in Everyday Life*. New York: Harcourt.

Spencer, H. (1969) *The Study of Sociology*. Basingstoke: Macmillan.

Spinrad, W. (1991) 'Charisma: a blighted concept and an alternative formula', *Political Studies Quarterly*, 106 (2): 295–311.

Steinmo, S. (2001) 'The new institutionalism', in B. Clark and J. Foweraker (eds), *The Encyclopedia of Democratic Thought*. London: Routledge.

Steinmo, S., Thelen, K. and Longstreth, F. (1992) *Structuring Politics: Historical Institutionalism in Comparative Perspective*. Cambridge: Cambridge University Press.

Stepan, A. (2001) *Arguing Comparative Politics*. Oxford: Oxford University Press.

Stepan, A. and Skach, C. (1993) 'Constitutional frameworks and democratic consolidation: parliamentarism versus presidentialism', *World Politics*, 46 (1): 1–22.

Stevens, A. (2003) *Government and Politics of France*. Basingstoke: Palgrave Macmillan.

Stone Sweet, A. (2000) *Governing with Judges: Constitutional Politics in Europe*. Oxford: Oxford University Press.

Stone Sweet, A. and Smithey, S.I. (2001) 'Governing with judges: constitutional politics in Europe', *International Politics*, 38 (2): 283–9.

Swenson, P. (1991) 'Bringing capital back in or social democracy reconsidered', *World Politics*, 43: 513–34.

Taagepera, R. and Shugart. M. (1989) *Seats and Votes. The Effects and Determinants of Electoral Systems*. New Haven, CT: Yale University Press.

Tanner, J.R. (1966) *English Constitutional Conflicts of the Seventeenth Century, 1603–89*. Cambridge: Cambridge University Press.

Tanzi, V. and Schunecht, L. (2000) *Public Spending in the Twentieth Century: A Global Perspective*. Cambridge: Cambridge University Press.

Taylor, C. (1992) 'The politics of recognition', in C. Taylor and A. Gutmann (ed.), *Multiculturalism and the 'Politics of Recognition'*. Princeton, NJ: Princeton University Press. pp. 25–74.

Tebble, A. (2006) 'Exclusion for democracy', *Political Theory*, 34 (4): 463–7.

Theobald, R. (1981) *Charisma: A Critical Review*. Polytechnic of Central London: Social Science and Business Studies Research Papers No 5.

Thompson, M., Ellis, R. and Wildavsky, A. (1990) *Cultural Theory*. Boulder, CO: Westview.

Trotsky, L. (1965) *The History of the Russian Revolution*. Vol. I, trans. M. Eastman. London: Gollancz.

Tsebelis, G. (1995) 'Decision making in political systems: veto players in presidentialism, parliamentarism, multicameralism and multipartyism', *British Journal of Political Science*, 25 (3): 289–325.

Tsebelis, G. (2002) *Veto Players: How Political Institutions Work*. Princeton, NJ: Princeton University Press.

Tucker, R.C. (1981) *Politics as Leadership*. Columbia, MO: University of Missouri Press.

Tucker, R.C. (1997) 'Personality and political leadership', *Political Science Quarterly*, 92 (3): 283–94.

Tulis, J.K. (1987) *The Rhetorical Presidency*. Princeton, NJ: Princeton University Press.

Tullock, G. (1974) *The Social Dilemma: The Economics of War and Revolutions*. Blacksburg, VA: University Publications.

Tullock, G., Seldon, A. and Brady, G. (2002) *Government: Whose Obedient Servant?* London: Institute of Economic Affairs.

Tully, J. (1995) *Strange Multiplicity: Constitutionalism in an Age of Diversity*. Cambridge: Cambridge University Press.

Van de Walle, N. (2001) *African Economies and the Politics of Permanent Crisis, 1979–99*. Cambridge: Cambridge University Press.

Verba, S. (1961) *Small Groups and Political Behaviour*. Princeton, NJ: Princeton University Press.

Viroli, M. (1998) *Machiavelli*. Oxford: Oxford University Press.

Volcansek, Mary (2000)*Constitutional Politics in Italy*. London: Macmillan Press.

Von Beyme, K. (1985) *Political Parties in Western Democracies*. Aldershot: Gower.

Wachendorfer-Schmidt, U. (ed.) (2000) *Federalism and Political Performance*. London: Routledge.

Waltzer, M. (1973) 'Political action: the problem of dirty hands', *Philosophy and Public Affairs*, 2 (2): 160–80.

Waltzer, M. (1994) *Thick and Thin*. Notre Dame, IN: University of Notre Dame Press.

Ware, A. (1996) *Political Parties*, 2nd edn. Oxford: Oxford University Press.

Weale, A. (1999) *Democracy*. Basingstoke: Palgrave Macmillan.

Weaver, R.K. and Rockman, B.A. (1993) 'When and how do institutions matter?', in R.K. Weaver and B.A. Rockman (eds), *Do Institutions Matter?* Washington, DC: Brookings Institute. pp. 445–61.

Weber, M. ([1922] 1978) *Economy and Society: An Outline of Interpretive Sociology*. Vol 2. Berkeley, CA: University of California Press.

Weber, M. (1968) *Economy and Society*. Berkeley, CA: University of California Press.

Weingast, B. (1995) 'The economic role of political institutions: market-preserving federalism and economic development', *Journal of Law, Economics, and Organization*, 11 (1): 1–31.

Wheare, K.C. (1963) *Federal Government*, 4th edn. London: Oxford University Press.

White, C., Devine, F. and Ritchie, J. (1999) *Voter Volatility: A Qualitative Study of Voting Behaviour at the 1997 General Election*. London: SCPR.

White, T.H. (1961) *The Making of the President 1960*. New York: Athaneum Publishers.

Whiteley, P., Clarke, H., Sanders, D. and Stewart, M. (2001) 'Turnout', in P. Norris (ed.), *Britain Votes 2001*. Oxford: Oxford University Press. pp. 211–24.

Whittman, D.G. (1995) *The Myth of Democratic Failure*. Chicago, IL: University of Chicago Press.

Whittman, D.G. (2004) 'Group selection and methodological individualism: compatible and complementary'. *Advances in Austrian Economics*, 7: 221–49.

Wicksteed, P. (1933) *The Common Sense of Political Economy*. London: Routledge.

Wildavsky, A. (1987) 'Choosing preference by constructing institutions: a cultural theory of preference formation', *American Political Science Review*, 81: 3–21.

Wilensky, H. (1975) *The Welfare State and Equality*. Berkeley, CA: University of California Press.

Williams, M. and May, T. (1996) *Introduction to the Philosophy of Social Research*. London: UCL Press.

Wittman, D. (1995) *The Myth of Democratic Failure*. Chicago, IL: University of Chicago Press.

Wirls, S.H. (1994) 'Machiavelli and Neustadt on virtue and the Civic Prince', *Presidential Studies Quarterly*, 24 (3): 467–73.

Wolfe, A. (1977) *The Limits of Legitimacy*. New York: The Free Press.

Wolfers, A. (1949) 'Statesmanship and moral choice', *World Politics*, 1 (2): 175–95.

Wolfers, A. (1951) 'The pole of power and the pole of indifference', *World Politics*, 4 (1): 39–63.

Wolfenstein, E.V. (1969) *Personality and Politics*. Los Angeles: Dickenson Press.

Woodard, S. (1995) 'The simple guide to the federal idea', *Ventotene, Federalism and Politics*. The Ventotene Papers of the Altiero Spinelli Institute for Federalist Studies: Ventotene.

Wright, E.O. (1985) *Classes*. London: Verso.

Wrong, D.H. (1961) 'The over-socialized concept of man in modern sociology', *American Sociological Review*, 26: 183–93.

Yeager, T. (1999) *Institutions, Transition Economies and Economic Development*. Boulder, CO: Westview.

Index

abortion, 183–4, 277
accountability, 126–7, 137–8
agency problem *see* principal-agent theory
agenda-setting, 128–9, 278
'arena' institutions, 123, 126
assimilation, 81–2
authoritarian rule, 134, 274–5

behavioural approaches to politics, 2–3, 47, 52
bicameral legislatures, 122, 207, 211, 218
bills of rights, 193
bounded rationality, 34
bureaucracy, 145–71, 263
    definition of, 146–9
    reform of, 165, 170
    social attitudes towards, 162, 164
bureaucratic agencies and procedures, 153–6
bureaucratic politics 162–71
bureaucratic power, 155–6, 159, 162–8
bureaucratic rationality, 148–9
business interests, power of, 279–80, 284

cabinet systems, 128, 130, 134
capitalism, 26–7, 32–3, 168–70, 212–13, 230,
    267, 279–84, 314; *see also* print-capitalism
case studies, 57, 60
centralisation or decentralisation of government,
    208–10, 219, 222
charisma, concept of, 295, 297
Chicago School of political economy, 20, 55,
    181, 271–2
choice institutionalism, 13, 16
civil rights movements, 270, 277, 283
class divisions, 275–8, 281–5
classification of political systems and regimes,
    47–51
'cleavages' in society, 240, 246, 248, 277

coalition governments, 104–8, 138, 140
collective goods and collective action, 17–20, 23,
    267–75, 280–1, 285–7
collective responsibility in government, 130
committee cultures, 126–7
common law, 177, 182, 196
comparative political analysis, 13–14, 41–2, 192,
    206, 308–12, 316
    concepts in, 43–5
    development of, 47–53, 308–9
    importance of, 45–7
    of interest groups, 279–80
    measurement in, 45, 56
    methodology of, 41–63, 311
    problems with, 61–3
    theories of, 30–7, 309–12
    variables in, 44–5
condominiums, 205
confederations, 203–4
consociations, 44, 205, 211, 215, 221–2
constitutional change, 178, 183–4, 189, 195–7
constitutional courts, 174–6, 179, 185–8
constitutions, 51, 87–8, 195–7
'contracting out' of public services, 160–1
corporatism, 219, 263–5, 273–4, 280, 283–4
court systems, 174–98
cultural homogeneity, 79–80
cultural institutionalism, 13–14, 21–5, 38, 182,
    214–16, 275–80, 285–6, 309–15
    and bureaucratic politics, 162–7

death penalty, 184, 197
democracy
    indirect, 230
    satisfaction with, 220
    see also liberal democracy
democratisation, 115–16

developing countries, 150, 273, 280
devolution, 201, 204–5, 223
direct action, 259–60, 265
discourse analysis, 59–60, 296–8, 301
discrimination, 179, 197
division of labour, 147, 231

'ecological fallacy', 61
economic growth, 219, 274, 283–4
egalitarian cultures, 162–7
elections
    importance of, 229–32, 239–40
    and levels of political participation, 233–7
    timing of, 134
    typology of, 232–3
electoral systems, 93–116, 136–7, 239
    influences on voting, 111–16
    institutional effects of, 108–9
    measurement of, 96–102
    political effects of, 103–8
    proportionality in, 97–100, 103–7
environmentalism, 261–2, 265–6, 269, 277–8
Essex model of voting behaviour, 255
ethical issues, 301
ethnies, 84–5
ethnocentrism, 47
ethno-nationalism, 70, 80, 201–2,
    215–18, 222–3
ethno-symbolism 84, 86, 88
executive institutions, 121–3, 127–33,
    141, 314
    definition of, 121–2
    relations with legislatures, 131–3
experimental studies, 57–8
expressive benefits, 269–70

federacies 205
federal systems, 139, 159, 175, 201–2,
    205–23, 314
    adaptation of, 221
    and centralisation or decentralisation of
        functions, 208–10, 219
    definition of, 202
    multinational, 216–18, 222–3
    origins and emergence of, 212–16, 218
    performance of, 219–21
    principles of, 210–11
    typology of, 206–8
focus groups, 54
free trade, 284–5
freedom of speech, 196
'free-rider' problem, 17, 19, 268–74, 286

game theory, 135, 311
globalisation, 171, 202, 255, 287
government expenditure, 150–1, 154, 158–61
group processes, 21

habitual actions, 34–5, 275
'hard' institutions, 14–15, 19, 21, 29, 124,
    141, 180–1
historical materialism, 29
human rights, 178–9, 251, 255

'ideal types' in politics, 146–9, 163, 261–2
image, 253–4
imagined communities, 78–9, 86, 313
implementation of programmes and policies,
    129–30, 141, 156
incentives facing individuals, 36–7, 267–9, 272–5,
    285, 313
individualist cultures, 163, 167
'individualistic fallacy', 61
institutional change, 37–8, 159
institutions 1–4
    definitions and nature of, 14–15, 25–6, 180–1
    importance of, 34
    origins of, 19–24, 29, 37
    synthesis between theories of, 30–7
instrumental rationality, 148, 269
interest groups, 259–87
    cause-based, 260–1, 269, 275, 277
    competition between, 263–5
    definition of, 260
    economic and *sectional*, 260, 266, 275
    forms of representation by, 262–5
    as *ideal types*, 261–2
    integrated theory of, 285–7
international law, 194
interval variables, 45
interviews, in-depth, 54

judicial appointments, 186, 189, 192, 195
judicial power, 174–83, 188, 315
judicial review, 175–9, 191

Kelsen courts, 186–90

labour theory of value, 26–7
'law and economics' school, 182–3
leadership, political, 130, 253–4, 290–305, 316
    and philosophy, 301–5
    and psychology, 298–301
    styles and techniques of, 296–8
    theoretical perspectives on, 290–6

leagues between states, 205
left–right spectrum in politics, 245
legislation, drafting of, 263–4
legislatures, 121–7, 131–3, 141
    definition of, 121–2
    diminishing role of, 131–2
    non-legislative influence of, 141
    relations with executive institutions, 131–3
    typology of, 123–7
liberal democracy, 44, 170, 211–12, 262, 271
linguistic communities, 222–3
list systems for elections, 101, 103, 114
lobbying, 265–8, 278
longitudinal studies, 57
lustration, 193

majoritarian political systems, 98–9, 103–4,
    116, 122, 137
mandates, electoral, 129, 134, 137
market failures, 17, 20
Marxist theory 26–33, 37–8, 168–70, 212, 267,
    275–6, 281–7, 293, 313–14
'maximisers', 16–17, 38, 311–13
media influence, 132, 253–4, 266, 278
methodological individualism, 16, 35, 142, 267
Michigan model of party identification,
    241, 249–50
military power, 72, 133, 137, 147
monopoly, 160
multinational federations, 216–18, 222–3

nation-states, 69–73, 81, 169, 202, 312–13
nationalism, 30, 70–7, 80–3, 86–7
    definition of, 70
    theories of, 76–7, 81–3
    see also ethnonationalism
nationality, 73–4
nations, definition of, 70
new institutionalism, 1–4, 13–14, 180, 183, 205,
    265, 267, 285
new public management, 165–6, 170–1
nominal variables, 45
norms, cultural, 286–7, 311

ordinal variables, 45

parliamentary systems, 122, 127–9, 133–41
participant observation, 55
participation, political, 162–3, 233–7, 259
partisanship, 248–55
party systems see political parties
path dependency, 35–7

peak associations, 264–5, 273
performance of political regimes, measurement of,
    45, 56, 96–102, 138
personality in politics, 131
plebiscitary democracy, 132
pluralism, political, 211, 263–5, 271–3, 280, 284
policy transfer, 46–7
political culture, 190–2
political parties, 105–8, 122, 125, 136–9, 238–53
    alternative systems of, 246–7
    comparisons between, 243–6
    definitions of, 242–3
    dissatisfaction with, 238–9
    electoral support for, 246–53
    'families' of, 244–6
    identification with, 241, 249–50
politicians, public attitudes to, 238–9
pollution, 266
'pork barrel' politics, 126
post-materialism, 277
postmodernism, 23, 59
power, theories of, 24–5, 278–9, 283–5;
        see also bureaucratic power; judicial power;
        military power
power sharing, 88–9, 201–2, 206
presidential systems, 121–2, 127–30,
    134–41, 303–5
principal-agent theory, 17–19, 97–8, 182
print-capitalism, 78–9, 85
privatisation, 160–1
professional organisations, 279
proportional representation, 99–100, 103–7, 262
public choice theory, 20

qualitative methods of research, 53–5, 58–60
quality of life, measurement of, 220–1
quantitative methods of research, 56–61

race relations, 177–8
racism, institutional, 166
rational choice theories, 14–24, 30–8, 77, 81–3,
    87–8, 125, 127, 135–6, 142, 148–9,
    156–62, 165–6, 181, 213–14, 218, 238,
    241, 252–3, 267–75, 280–1, 285–7,
    296, 309–15
    strong and weak versions of, 19–20, 33–4,
        37–8, 182
recruitment practices, 166
regime types, 50
religion, 85–6, 247, 313–14
    freedom of, 179, 196
representation, concepts of, 230–1

revolutions, political, 19–20, 28, 71, 194
rhetoric, 297–8
rights
  to decide and to act, 205, 208
  positive and negative, 196–8; see also
    bills of rights; civil rights movements;
    human rights
rule-following behaviour, 34–5, 286
rule of law, 176–7, 193

scientific method in political analysis, 42, 45–7
secular states, 86
selection bias in comparative analysis, 62
self-interest, 16–17, 20, 149, 156, 162, 252
separation of powers, 134, 175, 177, 211, 216
social change, 237–8
socialisation, 125, 136, 189
socialism, 28, 33
socio-cultural differences between voters, 240, 246
'soft' institutions, 15, 19, 21, 29, 124–5, 133,
    138–42, 180
solidarity benefits, 269
sovereignty, 203–6, 210–11
states
  autonomy of, 169
  definition of, 70
  see also nation-states
statutes of limitation, 193–4
structural institutionalism, 13–14, 25–30, 33,
    77–81, 87–8, 212–13, 281–5, 309–14
  and bureaucratic politics, 167–71
structuration analysis, 33
surplus value, 27, 281
suzerainty, 210

swings, electoral, 252
symbolism, cultural, 22, 279–80
systems approach to comparative politics, 49–50

tactical voting, 113
taxation, 218–19
television, 250, 253–4, 266, 297
territorial forms of governance, 204–5
Thatcherism, 29
trades unions, 266, 268, 273, 275
transaction costs, 18
transfer payments, 152–4, 157–8
transferable votes in elections, 102, 112, 114, 122
transformational leadership, 303
transport costs, 287
triangulation, methodological, 58
turnout, electoral, 114–15, 133, 233–40, 314
  declining levels of, 236–40
two-party system, 248

ultra vires doctrine, 191
unitary states, 204–12, 219–21

validity of concepts, 45
value judgements in research, 62–3
'vertical versus horizontal effect' question, 195–7
'veto players', 140–1
veto powers, 222–3
Virginia school of public choice theory, 20
voting, paradox of, 241
voting age population, 234
voting behaviour, 237–9, 314
  influence of electoral systems on, 111–16
voucher schemes, 160